CONTENTS

ABOUT THE AUTHORS

Prof. MC Cant – HoD: Department of Marketing and Retail Management, UNISA

Prof. CH van Heerden – HoD: Marketing, Logistics and Sport Management, Tshwane University of Technology

Prof. M Roberts-Lombard – Head: MCom and PhD programmes, Department of Marketing Management, University of Johannesburg

Prof. P Msweli-Mbanga – Professor of Management SBL, UNISA

M du Toit – Lecturer: Department of Marketing and Retail Management, UNISA

C Erdis – Lecturer: Department of Marketing and Retail Management, UNISA

A Drotsky – Lecturer: Marketing, Logistics and Sport Management, Tshwane University of Technology

Dr T Drotsky – Former HoD: Marketing, Logistics and Sport Management, Tshwane University of Technology

T Petersen – Lecturer: Marketing and Communication Department, CPUT

CH Bothma – Senior Lecturer: Department of Marketing and Retail Management, UNISA

PERSONAL SELLING

JUTA

Personal Selling
First published 2004
Second edition 2011

Juta and Company Ltd
1st Floor, Sunclare Building, 21 Dreyer Street, Claremont, 7708
PO Box 14373, Lansdowne, 7779, Cape Town, South Africa

ISBN 978-0-70218-860-2

Project Manager: Sharon Hendrickse
Editor: Wendy Priilaid
Proofreader: Lee-Ann Ashcroft
Typesetter: ANdtp Services, Cape Town
Indexer: Ethné Clarke
Cover designer: Marius Roux
Printed in South Africa by Academic Press

The authors and the publisher have made every effort to obtain permission for and to acknowledge the use of copyright material. Should any infringement of copyright have occurred, please contact the publisher, and every effort will be made to rectify omissions or errors in the event of a reprint or new edition.

This book has been independently peer-reviewed by academics who are experts in the field.

PREFACE

Personal selling has been part of all our lives for as long as mankind has existed. We are always selling something – be it ourselves, products or ideas. However, some selling approaches work better in some cases than in others.

The emphasis in this book is on personal selling and the personal selling process, and not on sales management per se. The book seeks to explain the role and place of personal selling, the impact it has on the economy, and how it ties in with marketing. In order to clarify issues associated with the selling process, the importance of communication in the selling task is explained and clarified, and a comprehensive discussion on how sales people should manage themselves and their time is included.

Much time is devoted to the selling process and in this respect the key steps in the selling cycle have been identified as the following:

- Step 1: Prospecting – Locating and qualifying prospects and initiating customer relationships
- Step 2: Pre-approach – Obtaining an interview; determining sales call objectives
- Step 3: Approach – Meeting the prospect and beginning a customised sales presentation
- Step 4: Presentation – Making the sales presentation
- Step 5: First trial close – Asking the prospect's opinions during and after the presentation
- Step 6: Objections – Uncovering objections
- Step 7: Meeting objections – Satisfactorily answering objections
- Step 8: Final trial close – Asking the prospect's opinion after overcoming each objection and immediately before the close
- Step 9: Close – Bringing the prospect to the logical conclusion of buying
- Step 10: Follow-up – Serving the customer after the sale

It is made clear in this book that the selling process is an art, and that much time and effort must go into the preparation before the actual sale can take place. Students and practitioners alike will benefit from the practical approach taken in this book, and identify with the case studies and questions in each chapter.

Prominence has been given to the Direct Selling Association (DSA) in this edition as it represents a large number of companies which are involved in this form of marketing. The DSA provides credibility to the profession and ensures that all members adhere to a code of conduct.

This book was written with the needs of university students in mind as well as those from universities of technology and colleges, and from private institutions that conduct in-house training. We trust you will enjoy reading it as much as we have enjoyed writing it.

1

INTRODUCTION TO PERSONAL SELLING

After studying this chapter, you should be able to:

- Comment on the role that personal selling plays in the economy
- Define and explain the term 'personal selling'
- Outline the characteristics of personal selling
- Explain why everyone sells, even you
- Identify the different options available if you want to follow a career in sales
- Summarise the various types of sales jobs and personal selling tasks
- Distinguish between generating new business leads, order getting, order taking, sales support and order delivery as categories of sales jobs
- Describe the job activities of salespeople from a communication perspective, from a marketing perspective, from an evolutionary stage perspective, from a job responsibility perspective, and from the perspective of the vital duties that have to be performed
- Explain that salespeople are: producers of revenue, builders of customer relationships and gatherers of marketplace information
- Explain what it takes to be successful at selling
- Discuss the characteristics of effective and efficient salespeople in terms of communication skills, listening, sales knowledge, trust, self-leadership, the ability to cultivate buyer–seller relationships, honesty, the ability to make a mutually satisfactory sale, customer orientation, competence, dependability and likeability
- Outline, discuss and compare the ten steps in the personal selling cycle, namely:
  - Prospecting – locating and qualifying prospects

↻

- - Pre-approach – obtaining an interview and determining sales call objectives
  - Approach – meeting the prospect and beginning the customised sales presentation
  - Presentation – making the sales presentation
  - First trial close – asking prospects' opinions during and after presentation
  - Objections – uncovering objections
  - Meeting objections – satisfactorily answering objections
  - Final trial close – asking prospects' opinions after overcoming each objection and immediately before the final close
  - Final close – bringing the prospect to the logical conclusion of buying
  - Follow-up – serving the customer after the sale (and continuing the cycle)
- Explain the evolution of customer orientation
- Debate the question of why marketing is important to an organisation
- Illustrate and summarise how the firm's product, price, distribution and promotion efforts are coordinated for maximum sales success
- Explain why an organisation should listen to its customers
- Discuss the role of personal selling in the firm's relationship marketing efforts
- Understand a salesperson's role in consultative selling
- Examine the role of the Direct Selling Association of South Africa

THE LIFE OF A PROFESSIONAL SALESPERSON – THE LOCATION OF PERSONAL SELLING IN THE ENTERPRISE AND THE ROLE OF SELLING IN THE MARKETING MIX

Many examples of personal selling are quoted in the earliest religious scriptures, which makes personal selling one of the oldest professions known to humankind. Since early history, personal selling has helped to improve the standard of living of many households. In fact, bartering and trading between subsistence farmers and artisans shaped early economies.

Currently, thousands of South Africans have chosen a career in sales because of:

- The availability of sales jobs, e.g. in insurance
- The personal freedom sales provides to people working from home
- The challenge of selling products and services, such as Tupperware and Annique cosmetics, in a non-store environment
- The non-financial (job satisfaction) and financial rewards (salary and commission) that can be earned

On the other side of the coin, personal selling has also provided individual buyers with the opportunity to consult with a salesperson and to make a more informed decision when purchasing a product or service.

Early direct sellers – hawkers, peddlers, traders, itinerant merchants and caravans – are part of an ancient tradition that originated in man's basic need to exchange goods and to communicate. Doorbells, catalogues and purchase orders were centuries away from the early direct seller, who relied on his instincts and common sense to make a living through selling.

As he established economic ties with his neighbours, he travelled extensively despite geographical barriers. The development and use of roads and/or water routes for commercial activity were pivotal points in the history of direct selling.

Early man had the option of either contending with geographical barriers like mountains and foothills, or refining the surroundings that hindered trade movements. At the outset, during a period of time called 'prehistoric', trade followed naturally defined routes. Traffic between neighbouring people of eastern Europe, for instance, was hampered by a mosaic of densely and sparsely inhabited areas covered with ridges, foothills and valley floors. These ecological niches were an impediment to commercial exchange between northern and southern Europe.

Early traders developed easily accessible routes to facilitate land travel. Along ruggedly constructed roads trod the early direct seller with his goods. Even before the advent of wheeled traffic, the early direct seller did not hesitate to exchange pottery, stone weapons, tools, agricultural products and raw materials with people from other lands. Barter, the direct exchange of goods for goods, was his principal means of trade. Among the early civilisations, Egypt, Syria, Babylonia and India were actually involved in trade. Ivory and ebony were exchanged for pottery and stone vessels. Indian beads and vases, believed to have originated in remote localities, were found in Babylonia.

In Greece, the caravan trade that connected the Greek world with Asia prospered. Everyday articles, domestic tools, metal kitchenware and ordinary clothes were exchanged. Markets, in their fundamental stages, were meeting places for customers and direct sellers. Frequently, the direct seller used the market as one of his stopping points before continuing his village-to-village journey.

Anatolia, which is present-day Turkey, was an area in which direct sellers, travelling by donkey, sold cloth to people they encountered along the way. The purchase price was generally higher than at trading centres because of the length of the haul and the hazards of the expedition. The early direct seller seized all opportunities to trade his goods when travelling. Fairs connected with religious feasts brought him to the armies stationed in the fields. Swarms of salesmen procured for the troops all the goods they needed.

The direct sellers' activities were influenced, certainly, by the cultures from which they emerged. As early as 2000 BC, the Code of Hammurabi, a monument of

Babylonian law, protected the general welfare and integrity of the Babylonian direct seller, who was then referred to as the 'peddler'. The code stated that 'the peddler shall swear the oath of God' if any enemy caused him trouble in his travels. It also said that the merchant who sells the goods must be aptly compensated. Trade by land, though hindered by poor roads, continued to grow after the birth of Christ.

In the 5th century AD, Athens was involved in a great deal of direct selling. Many producers who sold directly to the consumer without the intervention of a middleman continued to sell their goods in this fashion, despite the growing urban population which spawned a new class of retailers. The direct seller of the 5th century either sold his wares about the street or exhibited them for sale on stalls and in shops. Others travelled from place to place, following armies on the march. They visited great festivals and fairs as well, and sold from village to village.

The 10th century marked the beginning of worldwide economic expansion. As commercial opportunities grew, so did the opportunities for the direct seller. He was the native merchant in western Europe, for example during the Middle Ages, and he played an important role in bringing about the perpetuation of trade during the Commercial Revolution of the 10th to 13th centuries. He witnessed great progress in road building at this time. In France, the direct seller contributed to the growth of trade by bringing 'novelties' from the large cities to small villages. Many of the more prosperous French towns were graced with the opportunity to buy woollen and silk belts, bonnets, brass rings, thimbles and writing tablets from the direct seller.

The travelling merchant was cited in mythology as a notable direct seller. Ulysses, the mythical hero, once posed as a merchant. The little tale, repeated by many ancient authors in many different forms, makes reference to Ulysses as a travelling merchant. He antedates the American peddler by almost 3 000 years. At a palace, Ulysses offered ornaments for sale that he had placed on his arm. The king's daughters were 'engrossed with the contents of the merchant's pack'.

In the 17th century, *The Winter's Tale* by William Shakespeare was inspired by a girl peddling flowers. This flower girl was reminiscent of the direct seller of the Middle Ages who walked tirelessly through the village streets displaying his goods.

In early America, for instance, the renowned Yankee peddler walked to his customers while those of grander stature rode on horseback. The prosperous sellers rode in wagons or carriages.

As immigrants began to filter into early American territories in the 18th and 19th centuries, many became direct sellers. Like their predecessors, these direct sellers began their treks on trails marked by nature. Good roads developed slowly on the frontiers of early America. Early Indian trails evolved into major roads and eventually turnpikes. As the roadways expanded, the Yankee peddler's influence on trade was reinforced.

Yankee notions consisted of items like pins, needles, hooks, scissors, combs, small hardware and perfume. The Yankee peddler carried his goods in oblong tin trunks slung on his back by a harness or a leather strap. Sometimes he used large wagons. He travelled by land primarily until rivers and lakes became connected by canals. Then direct selling in early America branched out to the frontiers of the West and the Canadian territory in the north. The Yankee peddlers, as did the Phoenicians, preferred to trade via water routes.

Nearly every culture shares a heritage of direct selling. The direct seller of tropical Africa walked the streets of cities and towns crying out his wares. Some cycled from village to village. 'Colporteurs' of France sold flowers directly to their customers and used purchase orders as early as the 14th century. The Chinese direct seller sold, bought, exchanged, mended, entertained and catered to the personal wants of man in almost every conceivable way.

European gypsies, after emigrating to America, practised their native trade of direct selling in their new land. They brought the direct selling tradition from England, Scotland, Ireland, Germany and Hungary to colonial America and took to tinkering, peddling and horse dealing.

The selling tradition continued to thrive through the end of the 19th century and into the 1900s. The advent of the home party in the 1950s added a new dimension to direct selling as customers gathered at the home of hostesses to see product demonstrations and socialise with friends. Direct selling offered opportunities for many who had previously run into barriers because of age, education or sex. The growth of the industry allowed many to become successful where no opportunity has existed before.

Today, at the beginning of the 21st century, the customer still benefits from a personal and convenient way of purchasing products. The Internet has become an important element of direct selling – essentially giving each direct seller a worldwide customer base. Direct sellers have been empowered by use of the Internet and find direct selling to be a rewarding way of improving their quality of life, reaching specific earnings objectives, facilitating social contact and selling products they love.

THE IMPACT OF THE SELLING PROFESSION ON THE ECONOMY

Salespeople are critical to the successful growth of any nation's economy. In the absence of salespeople, it would make no difference if nothing were produced, for who would there be to sell it? Goods would pile up in warehouses and massive unemployment would follow. In their endeavours to restructure their economies from centrally planned to market-based in the previous century, eastern European countries had to learn the importance of selling. In a market-based economy, personal selling plays a crucial social role in terms of providing time, place and possession utility (the right products at the right time in the right quantity);

increasing total demand for goods and services; fighting inflation by lowering prices; and increasing innovation through better business practices (an example would-be salespeople convincing manufacturers to use cutting-edge and cost-saving technology in production processes) and more effective household consumption (an example would be salespeople convincing households to use energy-saving light bulbs).

Yet few professions are more misunderstood and mistrusted than selling. Many people stereotype the average salesperson as a smooth talker who is adept at manipulating people into buying things they do not need, or as the sort of person that cannot be trusted or believed. This image of the average hard-working salesperson is false. He or she is in fact industrious, knowledgeable, motivated and dedicated; has integrity; and is vital to the sale of products and services to the value of billions of rand in the economy.[1]

Spotlight On The Global Industry[ii]

International statistics from the World Federation of Direct Selling Associations (WFDSA) compiled from statistics received from its affiliated 62 national direct selling associations (DSAs) worldwide reflect global retail sales of US$115 billion through the activities of 65 million sales people (direct sellers).

The WFDSA-affiliated national DSAs are located in the following countries: Argentina, Australia, Austria, Belgium, Brazil, Canada, Chile, Colombia, Costa Rica, Croatia, Czech Republic, Denmark, Dominican Republic, Ecuador, El Salvador, Estonia, Finland, France, Germany, Guatemala, Honduras, Hong Kong, Hungary, India, Indonesia, Ireland, Israel, Italy, Japan, Korea, Latvia, Lithuania, Malaysia, Mexico, Netherlands, New Zealand, Norway, Panama, Peru, Philippines, Poland, Portugal, Romania, Russia, Singapore, Slovenia, South Africa, Spain, Sweden, Switzerland, Taiwan, Thailand, Turkey, Ukraine, United Kingdom, United States, Uruguay and Venezuela.

Direct selling companies are seeing growth in recruiting and retention rates in Q1 2009 with statistics reporting that *600 000 new distributors (direct sellers)* are joining the industry across the globe *each week*. Global trends show that the industry is attracting more full-time sales people, more men and couples, and more retirees as distributors. Trends also indicate that there has been greater industry self-regulation, greater government regulation, more press coverage and a greater use of technology and the Internet.

In South Africa, over one million direct sellers were involved in the industry with annual sales increasing to R5.75 billion in 2008 (annual reported figures July 2009). The industry currently provides full-time employment for over 4 000 people in South Africa. The first DSA was founded in the US in 1910 – celebrating its 100 years of existence this year. The first Direct Selling Education Foundation (DSEF) was established in the US in 1976, and the WFDSA was founded in 1978.

DEFINE AND EXPLAIN THE TERM 'PERSONAL SELLING'

People often think that 'personal selling' and 'marketing' mean the same thing. Personal selling is in fact one of many marketing communication activities. Other examples of such activities are advertising, sales promotion, direct marketing, publicity and sponsorship. These activities are also referred to as promotion elements.[2] When they are integrated for the purpose of communicating about an organisation's activities and its products and services, they are referred to as the integrated marketing communication mix.[3]

Personal selling can be defined as the process of person-to-person communication between a salesperson and a prospective customer in which the former learns about the latter's needs, and seeks to satisfy those needs by offering the prospective customer the opportunity to buy something of value, such as a good or a service.[4]

This definition refers to the idea that a customer should be satisfied. No one buys a product or service for itself, but only for the satisfaction it provides. The role of the salesperson is to communicate those satisfactions, and persuade the customer of the advantages of possessing that product.[5] Selling is therefore a human medium and the best marketing communication tool for building a relationship to the mutual long-term benefit of both parties.[6] It must be noted that the interpersonal communication may take place face to face, over the telephone or even through interactive computer links. Personal selling is therefore regarded as person-to-person dialogue between a customer and a salesperson, therefore salespeople have to remind, inform or persuade (or all three) as they discover customer needs, build relationships, communicate benefits and show buyers how problems can be solved.[7]

What is direct selling?[iii]

Direct selling is a form of personal selling that is the sale of a consumer product or service, person to person, away from a fixed retail location, marketed through independent sales representatives who are sometimes also referred to as consultants, distributors or other titles. *Direct sellers are not employees of the company*. They are independent contractors who market and sell the products or services of a company *in return for a commission* on those sales.

Orders are usually placed in person or via the consultant's Web page. Sometimes the phone is used to place orders or reorders, but only about 12% of sales take place this way. Home shopping parties are the most widely recognised sales method, where friends, family or acquaintances get together for a few hours to learn about or sample a range of products or services. However, the majority (about 70%) of the direct selling industry's sales actually occur using a one-to-one approach where one seller may present the products or services to a single consumer.

Just about any product or service can be purchased through direct selling somewhere in the world. Many people think of cosmetics, wellness products and home décor as products that are often sold through direct sales, but add to that countless other product categories including kitchen products, jewellery, clothing, organic gardening supplies, spa products, scrapbooking supplies, rubber stamps and much, much more.

Direct selling should not be confused with other types of sales that take place away from a fixed retail location such as magazine sales, home repair services, telemarketing, wholesaling, real estate sales, or 'work-from-home' businesses such as envelope stuffing or product assembly.

THE CHARACTERISTICS OF PERSONAL SELLING[8]

Personal selling has a few important characteristics: it is flexible, it builds relationships, it allows for more efficient communication, it is a form of dyadic communication, it can be expensive and sometimes it may involve unethical practices.

Personal selling is flexible

The sales presentation can be adapted to situations or clients. The salesperson can answer and overcome objections, focus on points of customer interest and elicit immediate feedback.

Personal selling builds relationships

The term 'relationship management' refers to managing the account relationship and ensuring that buyers receive the appropriate services.

Personal selling allows for a more efficient communicative interchange

Personal selling allows for a more efficient communicative interchange between a salesperson and a customer, while most other promotional activities, such as advertising, rely on one-way communication, which does not guarantee that the customer will understand or receive the communication message.

Personal selling enhances the understanding of the marketing message when a product has to be explained or demonstrated to the buyer, particularly in industrial marketing and the marketing of services. It is recognised, however, that personal selling is a relatively expensive means of communication.[9] It is important to remember that customers prefer a sales presentation that is adapted to their needs, not a canned approach that is simply memorised.

Personal selling is a form of dyadic communication[10]

'Dyadic communication' means direct or one-on-one communication between two people. This offers the salesperson an advantage over other forms of marketing communication media, for a number of reasons:

- *Tailoring of the message.* While other media, particularly mass media, have a large audience to address, personal selling allows the sender to specifically tailor the message to the receiver. This means that the message can be adjusted to attract and maintain attention, and more appropriately address the needs and concerns of the receiver.
- *Lack of distraction.* Another advantage of this form of communication is that in a one-to-one situation there are (ideally) no distractions. For example, in a selling situation the salesperson will have the attention of the potential buyer, with few or no interruptions, distracting noises or activities, etc. This allows the receiver to concentrate fully on the exchange, reducing or eliminating 'noise'.
- *Direct feedback.* In this form of communication, the sender can directly gauge the feedback from the receiver. If the receiver appears bored and/or uninterested, the sender can change the message. If the receiver does show interest, the sender can continue along the path taken. Direct feedback will allow the sender to know how well the message is being communicated, when to ask for the sale, etc.

Personal selling is expensive

This is because it involves one-on-one communication, and recruiting, training, paying and supporting salespeople are expensive tasks. Being more expensive is not necessarily a disadvantage. While it is much more costly than other media on a per-contact basis, personal selling may warrant the expense.[11] While other media may make potential customers aware of or interested in the product or service, the personal salesperson closes the deal – i.e. he or she gets the sale. In situations in which the product or service is expensive (e.g. furniture or cars in the consumer market, or major contracts in the business-to-business market), the cost of the contact is easily offset by the value and profit of the sale. The seller could also cross-sell more effectively than is possible if other media are used. While other media may make alternatives available, the salesperson can make specific recommendations, offer suggestions and provide information on the benefits of the other offerings. Salespersons may assist buyers by making them aware of products or services that will benefit them which they otherwise would never have known about.

Consider a business-to-business example: A salesperson, John, is attempting to make a sale of computer equipment to a small business. The total sale might involve 20 to 30 computers – a sizeable sale, which would yield a significant profit. The buyer, Jean, has specific needs that require straight answers.

Not being very technical, Jean does not understand the technical jargon. John helps Jean diagnose her needs, assists her in understanding the jargon, and meets her needs. After the sale has been made, John, as an efficient salesperson, will also recommend other equipment that would benefit the client – laptops for the salespeople, scanners and additional printers. As the client requires more equipment, she calls the salesperson back to place additional orders. No other medium will allow for such an exchange to take place. The value of the sale by far exceeds the costs.

ETHICAL ISSUES

There are a number of ethical issues that must be addressed in personal selling. The first one that comes to mind is the manipulation of potential customers. You may know someone who has encountered salespeople that are pushy, make unrealistic claims about the product and give improbable guarantees, and just will not take 'no' for an answer. These people give the sales profession a bad name. Likewise, some salespeople give out gifts, money or favours in exchange for purchases. In some cases, this practice is equivalent to bribery, and can be illegal. Inaccurate expense accounts and call reports are also areas where some sales representatives practise manipulation.

Question

One of the advantages of personal selling is the ability to communicate dyadically. Explain what the term 'dyadic communication' means. Why does this give personal selling an advantage over other media?

EVERYONE SELLS, EVEN YOU

Everybody sells because each of us develops communication techniques for trying to get our way in life. We are involved in selling when we want someone to do something and we use personal persuasion skills to persuade someone to act. For example, if you want to get a date, ask for a pay increase, negotiate with your lecturer for examination tips, or apply for a job, you are selling.[12]

In fact, our ability to communicate effectively is a key to success in life, and not only in a career in personal selling. The skills and knowledge gained from a sales course can be used in any type of business and in any career, such as engineering, law, health care, journalism, advertising, accounting and sport. Any business that wants to successfully tender for a contract and attract investments or the best employees has to use sales skills.

A CAREER IN SALES

One often hears or reads: 'Salespeople are born, not made'. This statement has a lot of appeal because of its simplicity. While some people are more 'outgoing' than others or more intrigued by the challenge involved in sales work, the statement is false because of the following considerations. There are many kinds of sales jobs. Some call for 'aggressive' behaviour, others for friendly chats, and others for little more than checking out orders.

There is no born salesperson that fits all of the roles, and there are roles enough for just about any type of person. Most salespeople would admit, if pressed, that they do not just go out and dazzle the customers. They train, prepare, study customers and their needs, study the products for sale, and rehearse their presentations. Companies spend a lot of money on sales training programmes, many of which deal specifically with particular selling situations: 'What do I say if the customer asks such-and-such a question?' These firms and their salespeople would not invest the money and effort if these programmes could be avoided by simply hiring 'born salespeople'.[13]

The salesperson[iv]

They show certain variety of goods to you, try to explain the features of the products, demonstrate the functioning of the items if required, inform you about any price concessions available, persuade you to buy the product and also in some cases promise to bring you certain items of your choice in future. So not only do they inform and explain to you about the product but they also persuade you to buy those items and want you to buy from them in future also. On the other hand, you also gather more information about the product, and see and handle it personally in order to judge it better.

The person who sells goods to you in this way is called a 'salesperson' and the technique of selling is known as 'personal selling' or 'salesmanship'. Thus, personal selling refers to the presentation of goods before the potential buyers and persuading them to purchase it. It involves face-to-face interaction and physical verification of the goods to be purchased. The objective is not only just to sell the product to a person but also to make him or her a permanent customer.

You can also find personal selling in some shops where salesmen are employed by the shopkeeper to use this technique. For example, you can find such salesmen in jewellery stores, consumer goods stores, etc. In case of some services, we also find personal selling used in shops. For example, we find people going to the same barbershop to have their hair cut and get a massage from a specific barber. This shows that in case of personal selling the seller usually come to know about the tastes and preferences of the customer and thus attracts him to buy the goods or services.

Is a sales career right for you?[14]

Some questions to ask yourself

- What is my personal selling record like? What was it like at school? What was it like during my studies?
- What are my future goals in terms of a career?
- Would I like to be independent? Do I have an interest in people? How much freedom do I want in a job?
- Do I want to take responsibility for my own future?
- Do I like travelling? How much travel is acceptable?
- Do I have the personality characteristics for the job?
- Am I willing to transfer to another city – away from family? Am I willing to transfer to another province?

Once you have answered these questions, you should

- Determine the industries (e.g. medical or retail), the types of products and services (insurance, timeshare, pharmaceuticals), and the specific companies (Sanlam, SA Breweries) in which you have an interest.
- Talk to people currently or formerly involved in sales.

Once you have decided whether you have the motivation and the interest to make sales your career, you should identify examples of entry-level sales jobs and find more information on them. The following examples may be helpful:

- *Consumer products*, e.g. selling to retailers, discounters, chain stores, etc. (Pick n Pay, Metro Cash & Carry, and Clicks)
- *Missionary selling*, e.g. selling to doctors, pharmacies such as Pharmavalu, hospitals such as the Netcare Group
- *Intermediate selling*, e.g. offering free desk copy textbooks (Juta Publishing) to university academics who make decisions about prescribing books and then advising bookstores such as Juta to order the book and keep inventory on the shelves
- *Industrial trade selling*, e.g. selling industrial products, parts and tools to resellers such as Builders' Warehouse and Buchels
- *Business-to-business selling*
  - Selling a product to businesses that they will use in their manufacturing or in their operations, e.g. Becker car radios to BMW for fitment into all 3-series BMWs at the Rosslyn plant (the radios will not be for sale to individuals)
  - Selling computers, IT systems and electronics to universities and technikons, small businesses and large companies such as Telkom and Iscor

- Selling office equipment such as photocopiers and printers to businesses, e.g. BizHub, Canon, Nashua and Samsung
- *Selling services to businesses*, e.g. telecommunications (Telkom's PABX systems)
- *Cleaning services*, e.g. Office Care (many companies have outsourced such services)
- *Maintenance and repair*, e.g. The Repairman (many companies have outsourced such services)
- *Selling recruitment*, e.g. The Job Placement Company
- *Selling advertising space*, e.g. in newspapers and magazines, or advertising time on radio or television to retailers, businesses and not-for-profit organisations
- *Selling hospitality*, e.g. convention and conference space, and hotel rooms to businesses and groups (Holiday Inn, the Durban Convention Centre, Gallagher Estate)
- *Selling to consumers*, e.g. insurance (Sanlam, Old Mutual, OUTsurance) or investments (Allan Gray)

Sales careers can also be classified in terms of the following:

Types of sales jobs
- *Selling in retail.* A retail salesperson sells goods or services to consumers for their personal, non-business use. Three common types of retail sellers are the *in-store salesperson* (interacting with walk-in customers); the *direct seller* who sells face-to-face away from a fixed store location such as Tupperware, Annique, Table Charm and *Genovese*; and the *telephone salesperson* (selling from a distance, i.e. telesales).
- *Selling for a wholesaler.* Wholesalers buy products from manufacturers and other wholesalers and sell to other organisations. A *wholesaler salesperson* sells products to parties for resale; for use in producing other goods or services; and for operating an organisation. Firms engaged in wholesaling are called wholesaling intermediaries. They vary greatly in the products they sell, the markets to which they sell and their methods of operation.
- *Selling in business markets.* An *account representative* calls on a large number of already established customers; a *detail salesperson* concentrates on promotional activities and introducing new products rather than directly soliciting orders; a *sales engineer* sells products that call for technical know-how; a *non-technical industrial products salesperson* sells tangible products to industrial buyers; a *service salesperson* sells intangible products such as financial, advertising or computer repair services; and an *order getter* gets new and repeat business using creative sales strategy and a well-executed sales presentation and has two selling challenges, namely that he or she must often create discontent with what the prospect already has before beginning to sell constructively and also, he or she often has to overcome the most powerful and obstinate resistance.

> ### Question
> ....
> Which type of sales career would you prefer and why?

Irrespective of the type of sales job or sales representative, personal selling is extremely important as it helps to increase sales. It is often claimed that it is the only marketing action that brings money into the business, but there are other features as well which make it important. Let us discuss the importance of personal selling from the point of view of manufacturers as well as consumers.[v]

From the manufacturer's point of view
- It creates demand for products both new as well as existing ones.
- It creates new customers and thus helps in expanding the market for the product.
- It leads to product improvement. While selling personally the seller gets acquainted with the choice and demands of customers and makes suggestions accordingly to the manufacturer.

From the customer's point of view
- Personal selling provides an opportunity to the consumers to know about new products introduced in the market, thus it informs and educates the consumers about new products.
- It is because of personal selling that customers come to know about the use of new products on the market. The sellers demonstrate the product for the prospective buyers and explain the use and utility of them.
- Personal selling also guides customers in selecting goods best suited to their requirements and tastes as it involves face-to-face communication.
- Personal selling gives an opportunity to the customers to put forward their complaints and difficulties in using the product and get the solution immediately.

VARIOUS TYPES OF SALES JOBS AND PERSONAL SELLING TASKS
Sales managers must decide which skills go with which selling jobs, so it is useful to distinguish between a number of types of sales job and selling task categories. These are: generating new business leads, order getting, missionary sales, order taking, order delivery and sales support.

Generating new business leads
Salespeople are primarily responsible for obtaining information, such as contact details, about prospective customers by inviting them to attend promotions, or by intercepting them

at events. The salesperson can prospect, approach and establish customer relationships at trade shows or other industry activities, such as event promotions, that offer exposure to new customers. After the initial contact the prospective customers will be contacted to set up an appointment with a salesperson. Once the customer has become an established account, he or she may be turned over to sales support personnel for an ongoing relationship with the organisation.[15]

Order getting

Order getting is developing business by seeking out potential customers at their homes or workplace, providing them with necessary information, and persuading them to purchase. It also requires that salespeople determine and analyse customer needs in order to solve problems. Sellers interpret product features in terms of benefits and persuade buyers to purchase the right quality and volume. Pioneers focus on generating new business, while account managers maintain ongoing relationships with existing customers. Order getting might also be referred to as 'creative selling'[16] – salespersons must assess the sales situation, determine the needs to be met, present the capabilities for satisfying these needs, and get an order.

Order taking

Order taking is simply completing transactions after customers have already decided to buy. The role of the order taker is more casual, often requiring only the writing down or delivery of the order. When changes are required, there may be a limited need for creative selling. Order takers write up orders and assure good order processing. Cold canvassing through telemarketing and door-to-door campaigns are used to initiate orders. Suggestive selling is offering an additional item or service to be purchased with the order: 'Would you like something to drink with your Big Mac?' Outside, or field, salespeople may also be order takers, simply restocking predictable orders for routinely purchased items such as Colgate toothpaste.

Sales support

Sales support salespeople are primarily responsible for maintaining existing customers. This means ensuring continuous customer satisfaction by being responsive to customers' needs and resolving customer concerns promptly and satisfactorily. Further, these salespeople must be proactive in providing customers with relevant information and identifying areas of opportunity so that a positive relationship will be maintained. Sales support functions include, but are not limited to, technical support, missionary sales and detailers (in the pharmaceutical industry).[17]

A form of supportive sales is 'missionary sales' – where the missionary representative will introduce new products, new promotions or new programmes. Sometimes, there may be additional account responsibilities. The missionary builds goodwill by providing information and by 'checking in' with customers. Cross-functional sales teams involve others such as technical specialists in engineering or logistics, or master salespeople. Account service representatives serve the field team from the corporate headquarters by answering questions about delivery, installations or other problems.

Order delivery
Order delivery involves getting products to the customers after the deal has been closed and the order has been processed. Often outside agents such as couriers and drop-shippers are used.

Integrating the Internet into the various types of sales jobs and personal selling tasks[18]
The following examples explain how a personal salesperson can use the Internet:
- *Order getting.* To fulfil the requirements of creative selling, it is necessary to conduct a situation analysis, determine needs to be met, prospect and get the order. The wealth of information on the Internet can assist with this. The Net can be used to identify potential prospects. It is an excellent place to find or source information, and it is a cost-effective way of communicating with potential customers to convert them into prospects.
- *Order taking.* The Net has become a cost-effective tool for order placing. Imagine a straight rebuy situation where stocks need only to be replenished. This hardly requires a sales visit. By having a website, the provider makes it very easy for clients to make purchases – either first-time or rebuys. This makes it convenient for the customers, saving them time, and also for the salesperson, who can be using his or her time more effectively.
- *Missionary sales reps.* The missionary sales rep is an information provider. He or she introduces new products, programmes, promotions, etc. Much of this may require personal calls, but once a strong relationship has been established with the client, much can be done over the Internet and the telephone (particularly when they are used together). Secondly, the missionary sales rep can prospect, and can provide potential clients with information without being intrusive. Qualified prospects can then receive a follow-up visit to close the sale.

To summarise: The Internet provides a wealth of information, the opportunity to communicate and the ability to prospect at a fraction of the cost of personal sales. In the industrial market this may be even more pronounced as the RFPs (requests for proposals) can be posted, saving both parties significant time and money.

THE JOB ACTIVITIES OF SALESPEOPLE

The job activities of salespeople can be defined from different perspectives, namely from a communication perspective, from a marketing perspective, from an evolutionary stage perspective, from a job responsibility perspective and from the perspective of vital duties that need to be performed.

From a communication perspective[19]

Salespeople are often the client's window on the company. They serve four distinct communication functions, namely information gathering, information providing, order fulfilment and relationship building.

Gathering information

Sales representatives serve as the eyes and ears of the company, gathering information on consumer needs and behaviour as they research the marketplace and monitor the competition.

Good salespeople impart a lot of information to prospects in an articulate and persuasive manner. Personal selling involves all three parts of the IMC triangle ('say > do > confirm'). What the representative does creates the relationship between the company and customer.

Fulfilling orders

The salesperson is tasked with 'closing' – securing an agreement (the sale) with a client. This is something that only a one-on-one meeting can bring about well.

The salespeople must ensure that there is complete follow-up after the sale, and that goods and services are delivered correctly ('do' and 'confirm').

This is the point where cross-functional management between the sales department and the production department gets coordinated, and good internal communication between these departments assures good external relationships with customers who expect the order to be fulfilled as the sales agreement specified.

From a marketing perspective[20]

Building relationships

The salesperson should be the ultimate relationship marketer. Customers want to buy from people they like. Salespeople build relationships by paying attention to three simple things:

- *Keeping commitments.* Salespeople must ensure that products and services are delivered on time and correctly. This task is made more difficult if they must deal with the effects of puffery and over-promises in advertising.
- *Servicing their accounts.* Keeping communication lines open and supporting clients with services is paramount.

- *Solving problems.* Uncovering customers' problems can lead to successful relationships and successful advertisements.

Three major roles salespeople play in the overall marketing effort are: as revenue producers, as customer relationship builders, and as marketplace information gatherers.

Salespeople are revenue producers

They are the front line of the organisation and responsible for making sales. They are the direct link between the organisation and the customer and, along with management, shoulder the responsibility of bringing in revenue.

Salespeople are customer relationship builders

They are responsible for obtaining, satisfying and maintaining profitable customer relationships. In this capacity they must continuously balance the needs of the customer with those of the organisation so that the relationship is kept in harmony. This means being customer oriented and ensuring that the expectations of the customer are met or exceeded.

Finally, they are marketplace information gatherers

They are the organisation's principal source of competitive information and customer feedback. Integrated into their day-to-day activities is the task of gathering information. This means keeping their eyes and ears open and tuned to competitive information, customer feedback and industry trends. Because of their proximity to the market, salespeople are the best source of market information.

From an evolutionary stage perspective[21]

The personal selling area is constantly evolving. Five distinct stages of personal selling can be identified:

1. *The provider stage.* Sales activities are limited to accepting orders for the available product offerings.
2. *The persuader stage.* An attempt is made to persuade the market to buy the supplier's offerings.
3. *The prospector stage.* Buyers with a need and with the resources and authority to purchase the product are sought out.
4. *The problem-solver stage.* The seller aids the buyer to identify problems and translate them into needs, presenting a selection from the seller's offering, and helping to satisfy those needs.
5. *The procreator stage.* Selling defines the buyer's problems, and the solutions through active buyer–seller collaboration by creating a new market or by modifying existing offerings to solve the buyer's problems.

From a job responsibility perspective[22]

The following are regarded as the job responsibilities of the sales force:

- *Locating prospective customers.* Searching for and qualifying prospective customers
- *Determining customers' needs and wants.* Collecting more information on the prospect and determining what needs or wants exist
- *Recommending a means of satisfying customers' needs and wants.* Recommending a possible solution to the problems and needs of the potential customer, and maybe also identifying alternative solutions that might work
- *Demonstrating the capabilities of the firm.* Showing the prospect that the firm represented is the best choice
- *Closing the sale.* Getting the commitment of the prospect, i.e. getting the sale
- *Follow-up and servicing the account.* Including all activities involved after the sale has been made, for example providing additional services, making sure the customer is satisfied and cross-selling.

From the perspective that vital duties need to be performed[23]

- *Dispensing information to customers.* Without relevant information, consumers are likely to make poor buying decisions.
- *Acting as a source of information to management.* Marketing success depends on satisfying customer needs. Marketing must be informed if present products and services are unable to meet customer needs. Customer complaints or dissatisfaction may lead to new product development or product modification.
- *Providing service.* The salesperson's job does not end with the sale, because between orders the salesperson must act as advisor, trainer and consultant.
- *Contacting new buyers.* It is critical for business growth and cash flow that the sales force continuously identifies possible new users, since reorders come at intermittent intervals.
- *Coordinating the sales effort.* An account manager may supervise all sales force activities when the number and range of products sold to a particular company increase and the company's internal needs expand. An example is when a big customer such as Telkom requires that a supplier assign a particular sales manager just to service all Telkom's needs and to coordinate all activities such as client–customer relationships, client–customer communication, order procedures, maintenance and service back-up.

Success in selling – what does it take?

- Love of selling. Belief in the products being sold. Enthusiasm about the products
- Willingness to work hard, work smart, then work some more. Working long hours
- Need to achieve. Accepting challenges enthusiastically. A need to succeed

↻
- An optimistic outlook. A belief in oneself. A positive mental attitude
- Knowledge. Keeping up to date with all the aspects of the company (advertising campaigns, new products, etc.). Being aware of new selling techniques
- Being ruthless about time. Following the Pareto principle (20% of sales calls generate 80% success rate). Carefully planning each day
- Asking questions and then listening to discover customer needs. Always listening well
- Serving the customer. Gaining the customer's confidence. Respect for customers, leading to mutual respect. Treating customers fairly. Honestly liking them
- Being physically and mentally prepared. Exercise elevates your mind by increasing energy. Get into an exercise programme. Learn about the dietary and physical aspects of your body

Question

Nine success characteristics are described in the above box:
1. Love of job
2. Willingness to work hard
3. Need to achieve success
4. Optimistic outlook
5. Knowledge of job
6. Careful use of selling time
7. Ability to listen to customers
8. Customer service
9. Being physically and mentally prepared for life and the job

Why do you think they are important for achieving success as a salesperson?

THE CHARACTERISTICS OF EFFECTIVE AND EFFICIENT SALESPEOPLE[24]

Effective salespeople are good communicators who strive to provide high-quality service to customers. On the road to a successful career path, salespeople develop a range of skills through study, experience and practice whereby they enhance their ability to think strategically, relate to other people, and understand the technical aspects of their business and their products and services. In the future, successful salespeople will need to be well informed about the diverse needs of corporate decision makers, be able to ethically develop long-term customer partnerships, and to use technology such as the Internet.[25]

The characteristics of an effective salesperson include communication skills, sales knowledge, trust, self-leadership,[26] the ability to cultivate buyer–seller relationships,[27] and the ability to make a mutually satisfactory sale.[28] The nature of these attributes varies depending on the sales context. This is discussed below.

Communication skills

Successful communication is based on whether the salesperson understands the needs of the prospective customer with whom he or she is interacting. Effective communication can build up the customer's trust and confidence. Communication, in a sales context, is the act of transmitting verbal and non-verbal information and understanding between seller and buyer.[29]

Verbal communication involves the transmission of words either in face-to-face communication, over the telephone or through written messages. Success in verbal communication depends on the ability to maintain interest and to control the conversation. Salespeople should be cautious not to provide an information overload in their sales presentations. They should speak clearly and slowly to enable the customer to absorb the sales message. The selling task in South Africa is very challenging, as more and more people of various language groups become involved in commercial life. When communicating across cultures, salespeople should maintain an attitude of empathy and sensitivity. Messages should be phrased in a more elaborate way to prevent misunderstanding.

A salesperson's delivery of words affects the way in which the customer will understand and evaluate his or her presentation. Poor voice and speech habits make it difficult for customers to understand the salesperson's message. Voice characteristics include rate of speech, loudness, pitch, quality and articulation. Culture can have an effect on how loudly we speak. Research indicates that white South Africans talk in much softer tones than black South Africans when in public places. Feedback can be used to ensure that the listener has received the message as intended.

Non-verbal communication includes forms of expression such as body language, space and appearance, which communicate thoughts and emotions without using words. People communicate non-verbally in different ways. One way is the physical space between the buyer and the seller. A salesperson should not enter the buyer's personal space and make the prospect uncomfortable.

Research has indicated that most white people in South Africa need a spatial zone of about 1.2 metres, while most black South Africans need only about 40 centimetres. The handshake is another important form of non-verbal communication and is usually among the first messages received by the prospective buyer. A handshake should be firm (without being painful) and be delivered while smiling and maintaining eye contact. Cultural differences can be seen in the duration and strength of the handshake. Most black people in South Africa are comfortable with, and enjoy, shaking hands. Black South Africans often use three-point handshakes, which start with the conventional handshake movement, then go on to slant the hand slightly upwards to gently take hold of the other person's thumb, and finally returning to the conventional position. Black people also tend to hold the handshake for longer.[30]

General appearance, including age, gender, height, weight and physical characteristics, is another medium of non-verbal communication. A salesperson's hairstyle, clothing and body language are the first things a buyer notices and they will create trust or distrust. If a salesperson overdresses, the clothing may distract from the sales presentation. A salesperson has to remember that body language also sends a message to the prospect. This is also true of the prospect, and the salesperson can pay attention to facial expressions and arm, hand or leg positions as signals of acceptance, disagreement or rejection from the prospect. A salesperson ought to be able to recognise non-verbal signals, correctly interpret body language and respond non-verbally or verbally to a buyer's non-verbal communication signals.

Many differences in opinion exist on the requirements of a successful communication approach in personal selling, but the following should be kept in mind to ensure that the customer and salesperson communicate on the same wavelength:[31]

Table 1.1 *The communication interaction between salesperson and customer*

The customer	The salesperson
The customer must convey his or her needs to the salesperson	The salesperson must have good listening skills
The customer must feel that the salesperson is believable and trustworthy	The salesperson must conduct him- or herself in a professional manner
The customer must be given the opportunity to voice his or her objections, doubts and fears, and have them accepted by the salesperson	The salesperson must provide opportunity for feedback
The customer must feel that he or she has made a decision freely without being pushed or manipulated	The salesperson should not use unethical sales practices to coerce the customer into the buying decision

Listening

Many salespeople unwittingly believe that their job is to talk rather than to listen. Effective listening is the single most important part of communication and is an essential part of selling. Listening has been defined *as the process of receiving, attending to and assigning meaning to aural and visual stimuli.*[32]

Successful salespeople know that they have to listen to prospective customers' wants and needs and be prepared to react to buying signals. Good listening will help to avoid a breakdown in communication by allowing the seller to understand the prospective customer's objectives. Cultural differences regarding when to talk and when to remain silent are common. In some cultures, silence signals respect and trust, while in others it is seen as a lack of confidence. If we are to listen effectively, it is important to understand what members of another culture think about the nature of the conversation. Because culture influences our use of language, it also influences the way we listen to and interpret language.[33] Salespeople can increase their ability to listen by using the LEAN strategy. LEAN stands for Listen, Evaluate, Ask strategic customer-focused questions and Never interrupt the customer.[34] Effective listening is a skill that can be learned through training and experience. It allows the salesperson to work 'smarter' while also achieving higher performance goals.

Sales knowledge

Salespeople have to be knowledgeable to be effective in their jobs. Knowledge and expertise will help the salesperson to increase his or her self-confidence, to increase the buyer's confidence in the salesperson, and to build relationships. Successful salespeople should have a sound knowledge of their organisation, the industry, the market, their customers, their products and services, and their competitors. Knowledge enables the salesperson to satisfy customer needs and practise adaptive selling. If salespeople become a reliable source of information to prospective buyers, they win the buyers' respect and trust. Product knowledge may include technical details such as performance data, physical size and characteristics; how the product operates; specific features, advantages and benefits of the product; and how well the product is selling in the marketplace. Knowledge of the organisation includes information about its history, policies, procedures, distribution systems, promotional activities, pricing strategies and technology. Salespeople also need to know about their competitors' products as well as their own, since they are frequently asked to compare them. Comparisons of competitors' products for a customer's decision are critical, especially when the features and benefits of a salesperson's product are superior to those of the competitors. Salespeople have to display knowledge generally exceeding that of their customers, not only in terms of the products and services they are selling, but also in terms of the full scope of the customer's financial and business operations.

There are many sources of information for salespeople, such as annual reports, policy manuals, product data sheets, price lists, promotional brochures, marketing research reports, sales records, customer databases, sales supervisors, sales managers, department staff and human resources staff.

Trust

One of the most basic attributes needed to build relationships with customers is trust. The better the salesperson's knowledge, the easier it is to build trust and gain the confidence of the buyer. Trust has been defined as 'the situation where the buyer believes that he or she can rely on what the salesperson says or promises to do in a situation where the buyer is dependent upon the salesperson's honesty and reliability'. Trust is created when salespeople are customer oriented, honest, dependable, competent and likeable. Dependability centres on the predictability of the salesperson's actions. One way is to demonstrate an ability to handle confidential information. Buyers and salespeople in a relationship need to understand what is driving each other's business, their roles in the relationship, each organisation's strategies, and any problems that arise during the course of the relationship. Customer knowledge can facilitate communication and build trust. To build trust, salespeople need to be consistent in meeting the commitments they make to customers. They also need to demonstrate their concern for the well-being of customers.

Self-leadership

Self-leadership is concerned with how well the salesperson's selling activities are aligned with his or her goals. This happens when the salesperson establishes priorities in the form of objectives before expending valuable time and resources. Salespeople often operate without close supervision, and organise their own time and set priorities for their activities. Self-leadership translates into a process of first deciding what is to be accomplished and then putting into motion the proper plan designed to achieve those objectives. The process of self-leadership consists of five steps. First, goals and objectives have to be set that properly reflect what is important and what is to be accomplished. This is followed by an analysis of the territory and a classification of accounts. Next, the salesperson has to design and implement the strategic plans to achieve the objectives through proper allocation of resources and effort. The fourth stage maximises the effectiveness of allocated resources by using technology and automation to expand resource capabilities. Finally, assessments are made to evaluate performance and goal attainment and to assess possible changes in plans and strategies. Salespeople should be the first to be notified of problems encountered by customers. They need to be able to solve problems in ways that are acceptable to the customer and to their own employers.

The ability to cultivate buyer–seller relationships

There are five main attributes that a salesperson should possess for the effective cultivation of buyer–seller relationships. They are honesty, customer orientation, competence, dependability and likeability.

Honesty

Honesty refers to the 'up-frontness' of the salesperson; in other words telling it like it is. It is the foundation of trust building. If the customer cannot trust what the salesperson is saying, a trust-based relationship will not develop.

Customer orientation

Customer orientation refers to the degree to which the salesperson attaches priority to the buyer's interests and needs. Salespeople must be able to understand the customer's business from the customer's perspective. By demonstrating their interest in the customer's success, salespeople are better able to establish a trust base.

Competence

Competence refers to the ability of the salesperson to meet established buyer expectations. This means having the knowledge and means to provide the customer with value.

Dependability

Dependability refers to the ability of the salesperson to consistently meet the buyer's expectations. The salesperson must do as promised to the customer. Dependability means more than being reliable, it means being competent all the time.

Likeability

Finally, likeability refers to the degree to which the buyer enjoys the salesperson's approach. Inherent in this attribute is the salesperson's ability to adjust his or her behaviour so that favourable interpersonal interaction can occur with a wide range of buyer personality types.

The ability to make a mutually satisfactory sale

The following elements make a sale satisfactory to both customer and salesperson:

- *A mutually beneficial agreement.* The salesperson provides the customer with products of at least equal value to the money the customer will pay in exchange.
- *Trust and respect.* If a sale is appropriate to the customer's needs and ability to pay, the sale will lead to satisfaction. If not, the customer will experience a feeling of being 'ripped off'. A salesperson should not sell to those who cannot afford the product or those who will not get value from the offering. Good sales practices will be to the benefit of the salesperson – repeat business is generated when the customer feels that the salesperson has offered the best deal in terms of value for money.
- *An interdependent relationship.* A good sale is the beginning of a long-term relationship in which customer and salesperson serve each other's needs. The customer wants value for money and the salesperson wants repeat business. Each sale should increase the customer's loyalty, and eventually a salesperson will build a core of steady repeat customers or clients.

- *A real or perceived benefit or service that fills a customer need.* If there is no need or limited need for what the salesperson is selling, repeat business may not materialise. Successful salespeople identify unsatisfied needs in the marketplace and then 'fit' their product or service to satisfy that need. Beware – mediocre products are killed more quickly when people become aware that such products do not satisfy their needs.

THE SELLING CYCLE

The selling cycle (as, for example, applicable to direct sellers) is a logical, sequential series of actions that can greatly increase the chances of making a sale, bearing in mind that the ultimate aim is to address customer needs and build long-term relationships that generate repeat sales. A retail salesperson who engages with walk-in customers at retailers such as Dion Wired would not follow such a cycle but they still need skills as discussed in the section *Characteristics of effective and efficient salespeople.* They also need skills in handling objections, closing sales and serving the customer after the sale.

Many textbooks refer to the personal selling process and there is not real consensus about the number of steps or phases. In this textbook the process is regarded as a cycle consisting of ten steps. These steps are:[35]

Step 1: Prospecting – Locating and qualifying prospects and initiating customer relationships

Prospecting is a process of identifying likely customers from creative sources such as prior customers, trade associations, government publications and observation. Qualifying is a process of evaluating a prospect's potential by asking key questions about the prospect's need for the product, and the ability and authority to buy.

Step 2: Pre-approach – Obtaining an interview; determining sales call objectives

The pre-approach involves making an initial contact and establishing rapport with the prospect. Success in the approach is the basis for effective communication by letter, phone or personal visits. The goal is to make a good impression and to solidify the prospect's willingness to listen to the sales presentation. Information is gathered that will aid the planning of the presentation.

Step 3: Approach – Meeting the prospect and beginning a customised sales presentation

The approach involves further uncovering of needs; relating product benefits to needs; and using demonstration, dramatisation, visuals and proof statements.

Step 4: Presentation – Making the sales presentation

The sales presentation is the attempt to persuasively communicate benefits and to explain appropriate courses of action to the potential buyer. After focusing the prospect's attention, statements, models or the product itself are commonly used to develop interest and desire. Note that these steps are not always verbal: body language is involved.

Step 5: First trial close – Asking prospect's opinions during and after presentation

If the sale is not immediately made, ask for and handle objections.

Step 6: Objections – Uncovering objections

The step in the creative selling cycle where the salesperson responds to questions or reservations expressed by the prospect is termed 'handling objections'. Objections tell the salesperson what points need to be more strongly stressed. Questions and objections may also show how close the prospect is to making a decision.

Objection handling is the way in which salespeople tackle obstacles put in their way by clients. Some objections may prove too difficult to handle, and sometimes the client may just take a dislike to you (a.k.a. the hidden objection). Here are some approaches for overcoming objections:

- Firstly, try to anticipate them before they arise.
- The 'Yes, but' technique allows you to accept the objection and then to divert it. For example, a client may say that they do not like a particular colour, to which the salesperson counters: 'Yes, but X is also available in many other colours. '
- Ask 'why' the client feels the way that they do.
- 'Restate' the objection and put it back into the client's lap. For example, the client may say: 'I don't like the taste of X', to which the salesperson responds: 'You don't like the taste of X', generating the response 'Since I do not like garlic' from the client. The salesperson could suggest that X is no longer made with garlic to meet the client's needs. The sales person could also tactfully and respectfully contradict the client.

Step 7: Meet objections – Satisfactorily answering objections

Plan for and anticipate objections, handle them as they arise, stay positive, listen to the customer and understand the basis of the objections.

Step 8: Final trial close – Asking the prospect's opinion after overcoming each objection and immediately before the close

During this step, techniques are used by salespeople to elicit a signal from the customer, which may indicate how close he or she is to (or how far away from) making a buying commitment.

Step 9: Close – Bringing the prospect to the logical conclusion of buying

Closing is the attempt to obtain commitment to buy. Closing signals are signs that reveal that the prospect is ready to buy or that the prospect is questioning the value. Four closing techniques are identified as: narrowing the alternatives to a choice of two; the direct, straightforward approach; the standing-room-only ploy; and the summative approach.

Step 10: Follow-up – Serving the customer after the sale

The final step is to contact the buyer, after the sale is made, to make sure that everything has been handled properly. Obtaining an order is the beginning of an organisation's relationship with a customer. Satisfied customers give positive word-of-mouth recommendations and ensure repeat sales.

Before a sales presentation is attempted, some important preparations need to be made. This involves initial prospecting (step 1) and then the subsequent planning (step 2) of the sales presentation. Steps 3 to 9 comprise the eventual sales presentation and step 10 involves the important, and often neglected, follow-up phase of the selling cycle to ensure customer satisfaction. To ensure a long-lasting buyer–seller relationship, sales personnel should follow up on orders to guarantee that they are delivered in proper condition on schedule and that after-sales services are provided. Building customer loyalty and generating repeat business creates a cycle that regenerates itself every time that a customer and a salesperson engage with each other.

The 'most important' step?

One might be tempted to wonder which one of the steps is the most important. One approach would be to ask: 'Which can be left out?'. The answer, of course, would be: 'None'. No subsequent steps can succeed without preparation; no objections can be handled unless the customer is found. Since we are dealing with a logical, step-by-step process, *all* steps are important.

Many sales training courses focus on sales presentation techniques and methods of 'talking' a customer into a close. Neglecting the first and last steps in the personal selling cycle, which are not glamorous at face value, will cause the best possible sales presentation to fail.

The first step in the selling cycle is to initiate customer relationships. The three primary activities in initiating customer relationships are prospecting, pre-call planning and approaching the customer. Prospecting is the process of searching for and identifying qualified potential buyers. Often an organisation will have established criteria that customers must meet before they can be designated as qualified. Typically, these criteria revolve around ability to purchase (do not sell to those households which really cannot afford the product!), potential volume, and so forth.

Pre-call planning is the process of developing the action plan for the sales call. This step includes gathering relevant information about the customer, setting sales call objectives, and selecting an appropriate presentation style. Effective pre-call planning is a critical first step for successful sales calls. Approaching the customer involves arranging the sales call, usually by making an appointment, and extends into the first sales call when introductions are made and the salesperson attempts to develop the basis for further sales activity.

It is often argued that 'the close' (step 9) is the most important step. It may not happen that a sale is made to every potential customer on every call, but the purpose of a sales call is to make sales. Thus, the close is to experienced salespeople arguably 'the most important step' in that it is the sale that drives the whole process and on which the organisation rests.[36]

The following must be repeated from step 10: 'Obtaining an order is the beginning of an organisation's relationship with a customer. Satisfied customers give positive word-of-mouth recommendations and ensure repeat sales. To ensure a long-lasting buyer–seller relationship, sales personnel should follow up on orders to guarantee that they are delivered in proper condition on schedule and that post-sale services are performed'. Therefore the last step should not be neglected.

The entire selling cycle, which indicates a strong customer orientation in selling, will be discussed in more detail in later chapters.

WHY IS MARKETING IMPORTANT TO AN ORGANISATION?

In the introduction to this chapter it was implied that many people associate marketing with selling, yet the act of selling is only one part of a firm's overall marketing communication activities. The task of providing products that satisfy consumers' wants forms the basis of the South African marketing system. Marketing is an exchange process between buyers and sellers, the purpose of which is to satisfy the buyers' needs and wants through the purchase of the sellers' products.[37]

Marketers, in a nutshell, have the following basic objectives:

- Maximise the sales of existing products in existing markets
- Develop and sell new products
- Develop new markets for existing or new products
- Provide the quality of service necessary to satisfy customers with their transaction and for doing business with their organisation.

The first three objectives specify that the main role of marketing in an organisation is to generate revenue.

The following statement is important: the money generated by marketing is managed by the financial people and used by the production people in creating products and services. What this implies is that marketing activities are important because they generate sales to enable the firm to stay in business.[38]

Another important objective is that marketing has to provide quality customer service. Marketing provides more to the marketplace than just needed products and services. It helps generate sales by providing the quality of service customers expect.

Excellent service creates loyal customers who continuously buy more and who influence others to also buy. Sales maximisation is therefore achieved.[39]

COORDINATING THE FIRM'S MARKETING MIX EFFORTS FOR MAXIMUM SALES SUCCESS

A marketing mix is the overall marketing offer that appeals to a target market. The traditional view is that the marketing mix consists of decisions in four basic areas, while the services marketing mix or extended marketing mix spans seven decision-making areas.

The sales and marketing relationship[vi]

Marketing and sales are very different, but have the same goal. Marketing improves the selling environment and plays a very important role in sales. If the marketing department generates a potential customers list, it can be beneficial for sales. The marketing department's goal is to increase the number of interactions between potential customers and the company, which includes the sales team using promotional techniques such as advertising, sales promotion, publicity and public relations, creating new sales channels, or creating new products (new product development), among other things. It also includes bringing the potential customer to the company's website for more information, or to contact the company for more information, or interact with the company via social media such as Twitter, Facebook, a blog, etc.

The relatively new field of sales process engineering views 'sales' as the output of a larger system, not just that of one department. The larger system includes many functional areas within an organisation. From this perspective, sales and marketing (among others, such as customer service) are labels for a number of processes whose inputs and outputs supply one another to varying degrees. Considered in this way, to improve the 'output' (namely sales) the broader sales process needs to be studied and improved as would any system, since the component functional areas interact and are interdependent.

In most large corporations, the marketing department is structured in a similar fashion to the sales department and the managers of these teams must coordinate efforts in order to drive profits and business success. For example, an 'inbound' focused campaign seeks to drive more customers 'through the door' giving the sales department a better chance of selling their product to the consumer. A good marketing programme would address any potential downsides as well.

The sales department's goal would be to improve the interaction between the customer and the sales facility or mechanism (e.g. website) and/or salesperson.

Sales management would break down the selling process and then increase the effectiveness of the discrete processes as well as the interaction between processes.

For example, in many out-bound sales environments, the typical process is out-bound calling, the sales pitch, handling objections, opportunity identification and the close. Each step of the process has sales-related issues, skills and training needs, as well as marketing solutions to improve each discrete step and the whole process.

One further common complication of marketing involves the inability to measure results for a great deal of marketing initiatives. In essence, many marketing and advertising executives often lose sight of the objective of sales/revenue/profit, as they focus on establishing a creative/innovative programme without concern for the top or bottom lines. Such is a fundamental pitfall of marketing for marketing's sake.

Many companies find it challenging to get marketing and sales on the same page. Both departments are different in nature, but handle very similar concepts and have to work together for sales to be successful. Building a good relationship between the two that encourages communication can be the key to success, even in a down economy.

The traditional marketing mix

The traditional marketing mix for tangible products consists of four variables: product, price, place (distribution) and promotion – the so-called Four Ps. The *product* variable encompasses the development of a product, service, or idea to exchange, physical attributes, benefits and prospective need satisfaction. *Pricing* involves the marketing manager, who establishes each product's price as well as overall pricing policies such as discounts and what to charge for the exchange between customer and company. Getting the product to the right *place* at the right time in the right format is the *place* (distribution) variable and also focuses on how to get the product, service or idea to the target market to complete the exchange between customer and company. The *promotion* or marketing communication variable spans how to communicate with the target market about the possible exchange, and increases demand by communicating information to potential customers via personal selling, advertising, publicity and sales promotion.[40]

Personal selling as a marketing communication variable

Personal selling offers several advantages over other forms of marketing communication. First, personal contact enhances the level of customer satisfaction and brings the human element into selling. This creates an opportunity for relationship building between the organisation and the customer.

Second, personal selling has the advantage that the salesperson can provide instant feedback on questions, supply detailed explanations and transmit complex information.

The salesperson can also demonstrate the product or use visual aids. Lastly, the communication can be directed at qualified prospects, making a sale more the communication that can be directed at qualified prospects, thus improving the possibility of a sale. The primary disadvantage of personal selling is that a salesperson can communicate with only a small number of potential customers at a time, making it more costly per person reached than the other communication elements.[41]

Firms must carefully consider the role of the sales force in their promotional programme or promotional aspect of the marketing mix. A firm has to decide if a sales force is a viable direct-marketing tool; and if so, which types of selling activities optimally promote its products. The different levels of relationship marketing (transaction selling, relationship selling and partnering) allow salespeople to create customer loyalty. In this manner, they can keep today's customers while generating new customers for tomorrow.[42]

Personal selling must be integrated into the promotional mix to achieve success. Personal selling efforts should support, and be supported by, other promotional mix elements:[43]

■ *Combining personal selling and advertising*. A complementary relationship should exist in which advertising is used to support personal selling efforts, and vice versa.
■ *Combining personal selling and public relations*. Personal salespersons must often perform public relations activities. For example, public appearances, speaking engagements, etc. are all beneficial to the organisation, and can be carried out by the sales staff. In return, public relations sponsored by the firm supports the image of the salesperson.

When is personal selling most effective when compared to other media?

Personal selling will be most effective when the product is complex, has non-obvious benefits, requires persuasive selling efforts or is characterised by high price and profit margins (or any combination of these). In these cases, non-personal media may not be sufficient to convey the information necessary, or may not be persuasive enough to close the sale.

Personal selling may also be more effective in business-to-business situations in which the product or service requires detailed explanations, demonstrations or consultative selling activities, or some combination of these. In many situations, the salesperson is relied upon to make the best decision for the company.

Product examples that may fit some of these criteria include computers or other high-tech products (complexity, demonstrations, consultative selling); insurance (persuasion and information transmittal required); automobiles (persuasion and demonstration as well as high profit) and products such as home-bottled water (persuasion) or water-softening systems (non-obvious benefits).

One way that marketers have found of reducing the costs of personal selling is by supporting this function with direct marketing. Letters or phone calls may be designed to solicit leads, screen potential customers, close sales or as a follow-up to the salesperson's efforts. The net result is a more effective and cost-conscious programme. There has been a rapid growth in the use of the telemarketing–sales combination.

Combining personal selling and sales promotions is effective as sales promotions targeted at resellers benefit the sales force as well. Likewise, many sales promotions (such as contests, motivational programmes, etc.) are targeted directly at the sales staff.

The extended marketing mix

The services marketing mix is an extension of the traditional marketing mix and three additional decision-making areas have been added, namely people, process and physical evidence. The *P for product* is also modified because a service product has certain unique intangible features. Apart from its intangibility, it differs in other ways from a physical and tangible product.

These differences create distinct challenges for the personal selling approach for services. Services are heterogeneous in quality and offering, they are inseparable from the service provider, and they are perishable.

The *P for people* relates to the skills, abilities and attitude of individuals who offer or provide the service. Because of the simultaneity of production and consumption in services, the firm's personnel occupy a key position in influencing customer perceptions of the service product's quality. The *P for physical evidence* consists of the physical manifestation of the service and also relates to the environment in which the service is delivered and any tangible goods that facilitate the performance and communication of the service. Lastly, the *P for processes* relates to the procedures, mechanisms and flow of activities by which a service is acquired[44] and also includes operating and service-providing features and processes.

THE EVOLUTION OF A CUSTOMER ORIENTATION

The current customer-oriented approach to business strategy was preceded by a number of other marketing phases over the years.

Initially, *production-oriented* businesses assumed that people would buy whatever was efficiently produced. This concept gradually evolved into a *sales-oriented* approach in which firms generally depended on effective sales approaches to stimulate consumer demand for a product. Today's philosophy is marketing oriented; it is the phase where the *marketing concept* focuses on a firm's desire to increase sales while anticipating and satisfying consumer needs.

Progressive businesses today are much more consumer oriented than firms were in the past. The marketing concept is a business philosophy that states that the customer's want satisfaction is the economic and social justification for a firm's existence. Consequently, all company activities should be devoted to determining customer needs and then satisfying them, while still making a profit.[45]

The marketing concept therefore has three fundamental principles:[46]

- All company planning and operations should be customer focused.
- The goal of the firm should be profitable sales volume and not just volume for the sake of volume alone.
- All activities in the firm should be coordinated to support the entire marketing and sales effort.

Reflect on the implications of the new Consumer Protection Act on selling practices.

WHY SHOULD AN ORGANISATION LISTEN TO ITS CUSTOMERS?[47]

What you have read thus far in this chapter has hopefully made you aware that customer orientation is of the utmost of importance in generating sales, which in turn should be managed to such an extent that the business can grow and prosper. It is therefore a pity that although businesses are aware that their customers are important, they are too busy or tend to neglect to listen to them. Many businesses take their customers for granted but fail to notice that they are losing profitable and loyal customers to their competitors who are serving them better – this is the so-called 'leaky bucket' effect.

Customer churn involves spending more on other forms of marketing communication, such as advertising, to attract new customers to replace those that have been lost. Finding new customers is much more expensive than keeping current ones – 'customer service pays, it does not cost money'. It is argued that firms understand the cost of acquiring new customers, but they do not understand the cost of losing them. The cost can be enormous if calculated over the lifetime of a business, which will in any case be shortened if customers are 'chased away' by aggressive salespeople who deliver poor service quality.

What is a customer?[48]

- A customer is the most important person in this office – in person, over the telephone or by mail.
- A customer is not dependent on us – we are dependent on him or her.
- A customer is not an interruption of our work – he or she is the purpose of our work.
- We are not doing a customer a favour by serving him or her – he or she is doing us a favour by giving us the opportunity to do so.
- A customer is not someone to argue with – nobody wins an argument with a customer.
- A customer is a person who brings us his or her needs – it is our job to satisfy them.

(Based on a poster displayed at the LL Bean Company.)

> ## Lost a customer? Don't blame price, blame yourself
>
> Customers often say: 'Your price was too high' when salespeople ask why they bought from a competitor. This is often just a smokescreen. Customers often feel we take them for granted.
>
> - The only time we show interest in them is when we want an order.
> - We spend too much time on prospects.
> - We do a poor job communicating with them.
> - We are interested only in big accounts.
> - We pay less attention to them once we have made the sale.
> - Often customers do not leave because of someone else's lower price – they leave because we do a poor job of taking care of them.
> - Customers will tolerate many things, including less-than-perfect service. What they are unable to accept is being neglected.
> - It is easier to keep a customer than to find a new one.
> - Service after the sale pays in the long run.

THE ROLE OF PERSONAL SELLING IN THE FIRM'S RELATIONSHIP MARKETING EFFORTS[49]

Relationship marketing emphasises creating customers for tomorrow and has as its basis strategies for creating customer loyalty. Organisations use combinations of products, prices, distribution, promotions and service to achieve this goal (the Four Ps or the Seven Ps).

Four basic guidelines can be followed to define the sales force's role in relationship marketing:

1. How much selling effort is needed to gain customers and keep them loyal?
2. Is the sales force the best marketing tool compared to advertising and other sales promotion methods such as competitions and sampling, in terms of cost and results such as acquiring new customers and generating repeat sales?
3. What type of sales activities will be necessary, for example frequency of sales calls and technical advice?
4. Can the firm's sales force create a relatively strong sustainable advantage or differentiation compared to that of competitors?

Based on the idea that important customers need continuous attention, three levels of relationship marketing are subsequently identified:

- *Transaction selling.* The customer buys something and is never contacted again – sales satisfaction and future customer needs stay unknown or unmeasured, and the seller has no idea what its current level of customer loyalty is, nor can sales efficiency be determined.

- *Relationship selling.* Contact the customer after purchase to determine satisfaction and future needs. Salespeople are no longer regarded as individuals who manipulate people into buying unwanted or unsought goods to earn huge commissions or to reach high sales targets. Salespeople strive to be consultants, problem solvers and partners for customers.[50] (Figure 1.1 illustrates the four main elements in the customer relationship process used by salespeople to build relationships).
- *Partnering.* The seller works to continually improve the customer's business in terms of operations, sales and profits.[51]

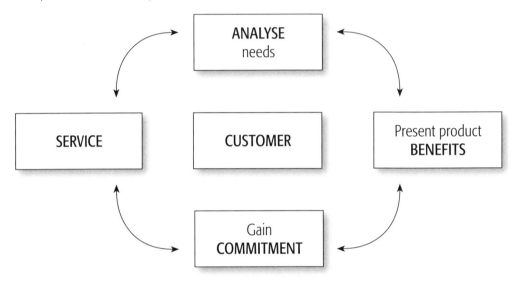

Figure 1.1 *Main elements in the customer relationship process*[52]

In relationship marketing, the seller and the buyer become partners who work together to solve problems. This results in a major benefit to the seller in that he or she can be completely honest with the client, will feel welcome in the client's office, and will feel better about him- or herself overall. In addition, the focus of attention for the seller is to become more informed and knowledgeable about the business as a whole, and specifically about the client, rather than trying to determine ways to 'sell'. The client also benefits. As noted, the salesperson is now a welcome sight – not someone trying to push something onto the buyer but as a partner. The client can let down his or her guard, knowing that the seller can be trusted and that they are working together. Two minds are now working to solve the problem at hand. In addition, the seller can bring new information to the table in regard to how his or her other customers are solving their problems, new products being offered, special promotions, etc.[53]

In a relationship marketing context the sales force's objectives can be summarised as:
- Generating demand for goods and services
- Influencing profits by making sales efforts more cost efficient and more customer service oriented

- Satisfying customers to such an extent that they buy again, again and again, and getting their referrals to other prospects
- Coordinating a high level of service quality from the various groups within the seller's organisation

---

Question
....

Describe how a customer and a salesperson would benefit from relationship marketing.

What does it take to be successful at building relationships with customers?

Anybody can become a successful salesperson through training and by properly developing and applying skills and abilities that benefit customers. A salesperson should believe in the product or service being sold, must be willing to work hard, must have the desire to succeed, and must maintain a positive outlook toward both selling and him- or herself. In addition, a successful salesperson should be knowledgeable, be able to plan, and use selling time wisely.

A SALESPERSON'S ROLE WHEN PRACTISING CONSULTATIVE SELLING

A new approach to personal selling – that of consultative selling – requires the salesperson to take on the role of a team leader, business consultant and long-term ally. By performing these three roles, the salesperson can reduce the relationship gap so that the customer is satisfied with doing business with the seller.[54]

From a consultative perspective, a professional salesperson will offer the following services:
- Create new customers.
- Sell more to present customers.
- Build long-term relationships with customers.
- Provide solutions to customers' problems.
- Provide additional service to customers.
- Help customers resell products to their customers.
- Help customers use products after purchase.
- Build goodwill with customers.
- Provide the company with market information.

CONCLUSION

Thousands of people have selected personal selling as a career because of the availability of jobs, the challenge it brings, the opportunities for success, personal freedom and the potential for both non-financial and financial rewards. A successful career in selling depends on training, the application of knowledge, the development of skills, a willingness to work hard, a desire to succeed, having a positive outlook and managing time effectively.

DISCUSSION QUESTIONS

1. Discuss the role of personal selling in the economy.

2. For each of the following, say whether you would expect the salesperson to be an order taker or an order getter:
    - Selling DStv subscriptions to homeowners
    - Selling industrial power tools to purchasing agents in the building industry
    - Selling blocks of season tickets to businesses that entertain customers at major soccer matches
    - Selling paper product supplies to office supply stores

3. 'Salespeople are born, not made.' Do you agree? Why or why not?

4. What are the steps in the selling cycle? Which is the most important step?

5. Why do many tertiary students want to avoid a career in personal selling?

6. How important are personal appearance and proper dress in personal selling?

7. Many salespeople take clients to restaurants for lunch. What should a young salesperson be told about entertaining at lunch?

8. A sales manager tells the sales team that he is under a lot of pressure to increase sales for the quarter, which ends in a week. Afterwards, a salesperson calls a prospect who has recently mentioned that she is almost ready to place an order for a competitor's product and arranges to take her to dinner at an expensive restaurant. At dinner, after ordering the best of everything, the salesperson says a number of negative things about the way the competitor does business. Some of these statements are not completely accurate. The salesperson normally would not be misleading but really wants to make a quick sale to help the sales manager out. Has the salesperson done the right thing?

9. Salespeople must be able to cultivate the trust of their customers. What attributes should salespeople have in order to do so?

10. What may happen to a company if customers are dissatisfied with its products or with the level of service offered by the salespeople?

11. Describe the five stages involved in the evolution of selling. Explain the salesperson's role at each stage.

12. Read the section on the DSA and discuss why the direct selling profession needs an industry body.

13. Distinguish between direct marketing; distance selling (telemarketing, direct mail and direct response); direct selling; affiliate marketing; and relationship selling.

FURTHER READING[vii]

THE DIRECT SELLING ASSOCIATION OF SOUTH AFRICA

Welcome to the Direct Selling Association (DSA) of South Africa

The **Direct Selling Association** (DSA) is a national trade association founded in 1972 representing 40 direct selling companies that manufacture and distribute goods and services through direct sellers* directly to consumers in a face to face manner away from a fixed retail location.

* *Throughout the DSA web site we refer to direct sellers, but also referred to as distributors, consultants, managers, sales agents, independent business operators and other various names, and all are independent contractors.*

The term 'direct selling' encompasses companies involved in classical direct selling, multilevel marketing, network marketing and referral marketing. (Refer Direct Selling Explained.)

DSA purpose

We are a self-regulating association of direct selling companies that promotes and protects the interests of its members, distributors and consumers.

DSA vision

We are the leading ambassadors of the direct selling industry and proactively champion the interests of member companies who passionately create an enabling environment in which lives are positively changed in our country.

The DSA is the direct selling industry's voice and works together with national and provincial government (both at administrative and trade level) to ensure fair and equitable regulation of the marketplace and works together with the Consumer Affairs Committee in response to industry self-regulation and consumer protection activities.

The DSA also provides a forum for its **members** and **supplier members** to develop and expand their businesses and to network with industry colleagues, and the opportunity to keep up-to-date with global industry trends and events.

The **World Federation of Direct Selling Associations** (WFDSA) and its national DSAs have always understood the necessity for ethical conduct in the marketplace and as such the WFDSA has developed a World Codes of Conduct for Direct Selling which all national DSAs have approved and implemented in their national codes. The DSA in South Africa has taken this code and worked in close co-operation with the Consumer Affairs Committee to establish a local industry **Code of Conduct** (Code of Ethics). All direct selling companies agree to be bound by the code as a condition of membership. All direct sellers are bound by the code when representing a DSA member company.

The DSA strives to ensure that all persons involved in the industry observe the highest standards of integrity and ethics in their trading activities. The relationship between the direct seller and the consumer has to be of the highest order, and the correct representation of goods, services and business opportunities is imperative. Also, good relationships between the direct seller and the direct selling company are equally important and essential to industry growth. Both consumer and distributor guidelines are covered in the **Code of Conduct** (Code of Ethics).

DSA Code of Ethics (abridged version)

- Direct sellers shall truthfully and clearly identify themselves, their company, and nature of their products to the prospective consumer.
- Direct sellers shall offer consumers accurate and complete product explanations and demonstrations.
- Direct sellers shall not use misleading, deceptive or unfair sales practices.
- Companies shall establish, publicise and implement complaint-handling procedures to ensure prompt resolution of all complaints.
- Direct sellers shall explain the terms of guarantee to the consumer at the time of sale.
- Promotional literature, advertisements and mailings shall not contain deceptive or misleading information.
- Companies shall provide adequate training to enable direct sellers to operate ethically.
- Companies shall adhere to strict qualities of control in product manufacture.
- There shall be no pyramid selling, and no involvement in **illegitimate pyramid schemes.**
- Companies and direct sellers shall not use comparisons that are misleading. Points of comparison shall be based on facts that can be substantiated.
- This code requires a level of ethical behaviour from companies and direct sellers.

(Download the full Code of Ethics from http://www.dsasa.co.za)

Direct selling explained by the Direct Selling Association

Direct selling encompasses classical direct selling, multilevel marketing (MLM), network marketing and referral marketing. Direct selling is a dynamic, vibrant, rapidly expanding channel of distribution that has proven to be a highly successful and effective method of compensating direct sellers (independent contractors) for the marketing and distribution of products and services directly to consumers.

Collective statistics from 62 national DSAs worldwide report sales of US$115 billion generated though 65 million direct sellers (independent contractors).

In South Africa, over one million direct sellers were involved in the industry with annual sales increasing to R6.34 billion in 2009 (annual reported figures July 2010). The industry currently provides full-time employment for over 3 600 people in South Africa.

Direct selling provides important benefits to individuals who desire an opportunity to earn an income and build a business of their own; to consumers who enjoy an alternative to shopping centres, department stores or the like; and to the consumer products market.

It offers an alternative to traditional employment for those who desire a flexible income earning opportunity to supplement their household income, or whose responsibilities or circumstances do not allow for regular part-time or full-time employment. In many cases, direct selling opportunities develop into a fulfilling career for those who achieve success and choose to pursue their independent direct selling business on a full-time basis. Direct selling allows individuals to become proactive and positive about their lives instead of waiting for the economy to improve, the next salary increase or hoping for circumstances to change.

The cost for an individual (direct seller) to start a direct selling business-within-a-business (with a DSA member company) is typically very low. Usually, a modestly priced sales kit is all that is required for one to get started, and there is little or no required inventory or other cash commitments to begin. This stands in sharp contrast to franchise and other business investment opportunities, which may require substantial expenditures and expose the investor to a significant risk of loss.

It also brings the advantage of benefiting from an existing business strategy. Individuals enjoy all the benefits of being in business for themselves whilst at the same time benefiting from administrative and marketing support, top quality products, and on-going product, business and life skills training – all provided by the direct selling company.

The products sold globally by direct sellers are as diverse as the people themselves and include: cosmetics and skin care products; home care and personal care items; household specialties; household cleaning products; food and nutrition products; toys, books and educational products; financial products, and jewellery and fashion accessories; just to mention a few.

Consumers benefit from direct selling because of the convenience and service it provides, including personal demonstration and explanation of products, home delivery, and generous satisfaction guarantees. Moreover, direct selling provides a channel of distribution for companies with innovative or distinctive products not readily available in traditional retail stores, or who cannot afford to compete with the enormous advertising and promotion costs associated with gaining space on retail shelves. Direct selling enhances the retail distribution infrastructure of the economy, and serves consumers with a convenient source of quality products.

Direct selling should not be confused with terms such as direct marketing or distance selling such as telemarketing, direct mail and direct response. Although direct selling organisations occasionally use some direct marketing or distance selling techniques and technology to enhance their businesses, the primary difference between the two methods of marketing is the face-to-face or personal presentation that is always an aspect of the direct selling relationship.

No restrictions

Anyone can become involved in direct selling. Thousands of men and women across all age groups have achieved success beyond their dreams. From teenager to beyond 'official' retirement, people can enjoy the benefits of financial reward and personal development. And as the direct selling company provides the training to get going, no previous experience or stipulated education levels are required.

Systems of direct selling

The direct selling industry encompasses classical direct selling, multilevel marketing (MLM), network marketing and referral marketing. These are **selling systems** which offer a variety of compensation plans (financial reward) and administrative systems, individual to each company. The main difference between a multilevel marketing company and a network marketing company is the structure and benefits of the COMPENSATION PLAN.

Classical direct selling

Direct sellers sell products directly to a wide customer base and earn financial rebates or volume discounts on all products sold. Depending on the product range, it is often that products are required on a regular basis bringing repeat sales and further income. New customers are sought to add to a growing client base. The emphasis in classical direct selling is for the direct seller to sell products to a wide base of **their own** customers, thereby earning rebates on all products **they** sell.

Multilevel and network marketing

These terms refer to a marketing system in which individual direct sellers recruit, train and develop a team of product users. These new direct sellers also recruit, train and develop their own team of product users, who also recruit, train and develop their own team, etc.

Although there can be variations between companies, the basic concept is that any individuals sales performance can be multiplied by using the efforts of others. The multi-level/network marketer creates a 'network' of people who work directly for themselves and indirectly for the person who introduced them into the network i.e. 'A' contacts 'B' who contacts 'C' who contacts 'D', and so on. This lineage of people is (typically) called a 'downline'. Financial reward is gained through rebates paid on the individual's product sales, and rebates paid on his or her downline product sales.

More and more classical direct selling companies now use elements of multilevel/network marketing as they recognise its potential for exponential growth. Over half of the direct selling companies worldwide, and almost all new direct selling companies, use multilevel/network marketing as a means to promote their business.

However, the success of any business depends upon how well individuals 'duplicate' their efforts – all direct sellers, whatever level, should personally be using the products and should receive and give regular training regarding products, business skills and life skills.

The emphasis in multilevel and network marketing is for the direct seller to be a **product user**, to **sell products to a small base of their own customers**, and **to recruit, train and develop many other product users who will also sell products** to a small base of their own customers and recruit, train and develop other product users, etc.

Referral marketing

This term refers to a marketing system in which individual direct sellers refer other direct sellers to a network marketing or multilevel organisation for the purpose of selling or providing products and services. Such referrals usually take place down to four or six levels with all referring direct sellers earning a referral income for the products or services introduced to the marketing organisation.

Person-to-person selling and party-plan/group presentations are **selling methods** used within classical direct sales, multilevel and network marketing and referral marketing.

Person-to-person selling

This is a method of direct selling where direct sellers sell services and products directly to people on a one-to-one basis in the home, office or workplace, away from a retail outlet. The business opportunity is also often presented during this meeting.

Party-plan or group presentations

This is a method of direct selling during which sales are made to individuals who are part of a group. The direct seller invites a 'hostess' to hold a 'party/group presentation' for eight to ten prospective customers, usually at a home, but it can also be at an office or workplace. The objective of the presentation is to sell products and to present the business opportunity, but it's also about people having fun and shopping in a relaxed environment. Products are attractively displayed and enable consumers to look, feel, touch, smell and taste the products (depending on the product being demonstrated!).

Because it is a group meeting, the direct seller needs to make just one sales presentation to secure many product orders. Party-plan/group presentation selling is efficient as it achieves the maximum results in the minimum amount of time. It also utilises group dynamics to start sales. The hostess is rewarded with a gift for the collective sales made at the party, the value being according to the total value of sales. In addition, customers are invited to host their own 'party/group presentation' for their friends and associates – leading to additional new customers and further sales.

(Some copy is referenced from the WFDSA website: http://www.wfdsa.org)

DSA membership

The DSA in South Africa currently has a membership of 40 direct selling companies. As a condition of membership, all DSA member companies have to adhere to the industry **Code of Conduct** (Code of Ethics). It is also compulsory for members to complete an annual industry survey questionnaire that provides updated industry statistics, published in July each year. There are three categories of membership for the DSA: **probationary membership, full membership** and **supplier membership.**

Probationary membership – companies applying for DSA membership have to be operating as a direct selling company with a fixed physical address in South Africa, and registered as a business in South Africa. DSA membership application forms are available from the DSA secretariat: Jean McKenzie jeanemck@jcci.co.za. Once the form and a non-refundable application fee of R250 have been received, the form is sent to the DSA membership director for evaluation and follow-up. Evaluation includes a visit to the company offices and a detailed look at all printed documentation to ensure that the company complies with the DSA **Code of Conduct** (Code of Ethics). If it's noted that changes need to be made in order to comply with the code, the application for membership will only proceed once an undertaking has been given by the applying company to make these changes.

When the membership director is satisfied that the applying company is compliant with the code, a motion will be proposed at the next general DSA meeting (five meetings per year) that the application be accepted. A representative of the applying company must be present at this meeting to field questions from DSA members. If those DSA members present agree to the proposal for acceptance as a probationary member, the company begins its 12-month probationary period. This 12-month probationary period enables the DSA to assess the company's compliance to the code, and gives time to the company to ensure that all required changes, if any, have been made.

Full membership – After a 12-month probationary period has been satisfactorily completed, during which time the company must have attended at least three DSA meetings, the company is proposed for full membership of the DSA. Should there be no objection from existing members, the company is awarded full membership.

Supplier membership – The category **DSA Supplier Membership** caters for companies who provide products and/or services to the direct selling industry in South Africa. The supplier member company has to be nominated by a full member company, for whom it has worked for a consecutive 12 months, and must align with the DSA Supplier Member Ethical Standards and abide by the Supplier Members' Ethical Responsibilities Code.

DSA member companies – FULL MEMBERS (as at 1 April 2010)

AFRICA DIRECT (TABLE CHARM)
Head Office: Johannesburg
Depots: Cape Town, East London and Johannesburg
System: Network marketing and direct selling
Products: Tableware, home textiles

AIM AFRICA INC.
Contact: Information
Tel: 011 675 0477
Fax: 011 675 0427
Website: www.aimafrica.co.za
System: Multi-Level Marketing
Products: Complementary Health Food Supplements

AMC COOKWARE
Contact: Information
Tel: 086 111 1262
Fax: 021 797 5092
Email: info@amcsa.co.za
Website: www.amcsa.com
System: Direct Selling
Products: Cookware, Cutlery

AMWAY SOUTH AFRICA
Contact: The Manager External Affairs - Makhaya Manie

Tel: +27 21 405 1700
(Direct: +27 21 405 1736)
Fax: +27 21 405 1736
Email:
makhaya_manie@amway.com
System: Direct selling and network marketing
Products: Beauty, Health and Wellness, Home

ANNIQUE SKINCARE PRODUCTS
Contact: Marketing
Tel: 012 345 9800
Fax: 012 345 9853
Email: renette@annique.com
Website: www.annique.com
System: MLM
Products: Internationally Award winning Rooibos Skin Care Products, Health Products, Cleaning Products

AVON JUSTINE
Contact: Information
Tel: 011 245 7000
Email: queries@avon.com
Website: www.avonjustine.co.za
System: Direct Selling
Products: Cosmetics, Personal Care

AVROY SHLAIN COSMETICS

Contact: Customer Service
Tel: 0860 114 182
Fax: 011 266 8115
Website: www.avroyshlain.co.za
System: Direct Selling and Network Marketing
Products: Skincare, Fragrance, Bodycare, Suncare, Colour and Vitamin Supplements

BALLTRON

Contact: Client Relationship Centre
Tel: 0861 11 22 33
Fax: 021 521 8990
Website: www.balltron.com

BOUTLE BUHLE (TRASTWARE)

Contact: Information
Tel: 011 832 2155
Fax: 011 455 3170
System: Direct Selling
Products: Glassware, Crockery, Cookware

CANYON ORGANICS

Contact: Mike Phillips
Tel: 011 886 2932
Email: mikep@canyon.co.za
Website: www.canyon.co.za
System: MLM
Products: Health Food Supplements, Personal Care, Cleaning Products

CASH COMMUNITY CARD

Contact: Louis Gerber
Tel: 0861 70 70 70
Fax: 086 669 1109
Email: louis@iug.co.za

IFA/CLIENTELE LIFE

Tel: 011 320 3000
Fax: 011 884 9056
Website: www.clientelelife.com

System: Network Marketing, Telesales, Direct Mail
Products: Life Insurance Plans

FOREVER LIVING PRODUCTS

Contact: Information
Tel: 021 761 6001
Email: operations@flpsafrica.co.za
Products: Aloe Vera Products

GENOVESE

Contact: Mr. Fabrizio Genovese
Tel: 011 337 1858/9
Fax: 011 337 4711
Email: info@finehometextiles.co.za
Website: www.genovese.co.za
System: Direct Selling
Products: Home Textiles, Home Wares

GNLD INTERNATIONAL

Contact: Distributor Relations
Tel: +27 (0) 11 409 3000
Toll Free: 0800 600 790 (South Africa only)
Fax: +27 (0) 11 409 3820
Email: mail@gnld.co.za
Website: www.gnld.co.za
System: Network Marketing
Products: Nutrition, Herbals, Home Care, Skin Care, Personal Care

HERBALIFE INTERNATIONAL SOUTH AFRICA

Contact: Imtiaz Ebrahim
Tel: 011 554 1000
Fax: 086 631 2589
Email: imtiaze@herbalife.com
Website: www.herbalife.com/za
System: MLM Network Marketing
Products: Weight Management, nutritional supplements, personal care, skin care, cosmetics

HONEY FASHION ACCESSORIES
Tel: 010 207 3600
Website: www.honeyaccessories.com
System: Direct Selling
Products: Costume Jewellery and other Fashion Accessories

HOUSE OF HEALTH
Contact: Gordon Wilson
Tel: 087 310 4641

ICI MARKETING (A division of StratEquity Pty Ltd)
Contact: Information
Tel: 0861 511 015
Fax: 012 643 7450
Email: info@ici.co.za
Website: www.ici.co.za
System: Network Marketing
Products: Wealth Creator Subscription Plan

JEAN GUTHRIE BEAUTY CARE
Contact: Jean Guthrie
Tel: 011 880 8581
Fax: 011 447 8810
Website: www.jeanguthrie.com
System: Direct Selling
Products: Skin Care, Cosmetics, Fragrances, Personal Care, Home Care

KMI – THE SPRAY VITAMIN COMPANY
Contact: Information
Tel: 011 740 5465
Fax: 011 740 4352
Website: www.kmihome.com
System: MLM/Network Marketing
Products: 30 different Vitamins and Herbal Oral Sprays

MIGLIO DESIGNER JEWELLERY
Contact: Lesley Grimbeek, Group Sales
Tel: 0861 30 40 50
Fax: 021 854 9600
Website: www.miglio.co.za
System: Classical Direct Selling
Products: Jewellery

MISSING LINK EDUCATION
Contact: Aliya Mohammed
Tel: 011 648 5815
Fax: 011 648 7631
Email: info@mle.co.za
Website: www.mle.co.za
System: Direct Selling
Products: Educational Products

NUTRI-STAHL COOKWARE
Contact: Mike Le Seur
Tel: 021 931 9211
Fax: 021 932 6030
Email: mike@nutristahlcookware.co.za
System: Direct Selling
Products: Stainless Steel Waterless Cookware

PRES LES
Contact: Les Ruhrmund
Tel: 0860 773 753
Email: les@presles.co.za
Website: www.presles.co.za
System: Direct Selling
Products: Bedroom Textiles, Dinnerware and Induction Cookware

SH'ZEN
Contact: Information
Tel: 021 704 2940
Fax: 021 704 2941
Email: Ingrid@shzen.co.za
Website: www.shzen.com
System: Direct Selling
Products: Skin Care, Cosmetics, Make-up

SPORTRON INTERNATIONAL

Contact: Eleanor Scott
Tel: 011 317 8300
Fax: 011 317 8400
Email: Eleanor@sportron.co.za
Website: www.sportron.co.za
System: Network Marketing
Products: Nutritional/Health Products, Skin Care and Household Products

STEMTECH AFRICA

Contact: Debra Pretorius, General Manager
Leigh-Ann Schenkl, Marketing Manager
Tel: 011 803 3633
Fax: 011 803 2419
Email: dpretorius@stemtechmail.com
lschenkl@stemtechhealth.com
Website: www.stemtechhealth.com
System: Direct Selling, MLM
Products: Stem Cell Enhancer. Other products include StemFlo, StemPets & StemEquine

STOCK MARKET COLLEGE

Contact: Hardus van Pletson (082 908 33320) or Lee Mienie (083 556 5731)
Tel: +27 (011) 315 1000
Fax: +27 (011) 315 1005
Email: hardus@stockmarketcollege.co.za
lee@stockmarketcollege.co.za
Website: www.stockmarketcollege.co.za
System: Direct Selling and MLM
Products: Stock market education and charting software

SUNRIDER SA

Contact: Information
Tel: 011 315 1338
Fax: 011 315 1315
Email: info@sunrider.co.za
Website: www.sunrider.com
System: Network Marketing

Products: Herbal Beverages, Foods, Concentrates and Dietary Supplements

SWISSGARDE

Contact: Debbie Botha
Tel: 011 256 8000
Fax: 011 256 8079
Email: debbie.botha@swissgarde.com
Website: www.swissgarde.com
System: Network Marketing
Products: Healthcare, Skin Care, Fragrances

TABLE CHARM

Contact: Richard Clarke
Tel: 011 226 1600
System: Network Marketing and Direct Selling
Products: Tableware, Home Textiles

THE UNLIMITED

Contact: Information
Tel: +27 (0) 31 716 9600
Fax: +27 (0) 31 716 9791
E-Mail:
icorbishley@theunlimitedworld.co.za;
msclanders@theunlimitedworld.co.za;
cmaree@theunlimitedworld.co.za
Website:
http://www.theunlimitedworld.co.za/
System: Direct Selling
Products: Annuity Based Insurance and Lifestyle Products

TIANSHI SA (TIENS)

Contact: Information
Tel: 011 787 5452
Fax: 011 787 8310
Email: yusuf@tiens.co.za
Website: www.tiens.com
System: Network Marketing
Products: Healthcare-Chinese Traditional

TUPPERWARE SOUTHERN AFRICA
Contact: Charlene Tregoning
Tel: 011 367 8500
Fax: 011 367 8501
Email: SAFCustomerCare@Tupperware.com
Website: www.tupperware.co.za
System: Direct Selling - Independent Contractors
Products: Tupperware and related products

20TH CENTURY DISTRIBUTORS
Contact: Information
Tel: 011 493 3710
Fax: 011 493 2702
Email: 20thcentury@lantic.net
System: Direct Selling
Products: Cookware and Crockery

VANDA COSMETICS
Contact: Phidias Chrysochou
Tel: 011 422 3710
Fax: 011 422 3750
Email: phidias@vanda.co.za
Website: www.vanda.co.za
System: Direct Selling
Products: Cosmetics and Fragrances

VOX TELECOM
Contact: Janet Benest
Tel: 087 805 0000
Fax: 011 388 4686

WATKINS VALEUR
Contact: Information
Tel: 021 532 2640
Fax: 021 532 2660
Email: csilber@valeur.co.za
Website: www.watkinsvaleur.co.za
System: Direct Selling
Products: Beauty and Fragrance, Skin Care, Homeopathic and Household Products

WORLD BOOKS
Contact: Information
Tel: 011 781 0919
Fax: 011 789 4790
Email: worldbooks@worldbooks.co.za
System: Direct Selling
Products: Educational Reference Books

PROBATIONARY MEMBERS
Companies that have applied for DSA membership and are currently serving their initial one year of probationary membership: CHANNEL 4 LIFE and MY BIZ

NOTES

1. Marks, R. 1994. *Personal Selling: An Interactive Approach*. (Fifth edition). Boston: Allyn & Bacon Inc., p. 2.

2. Zikmund, W.G. & d'Amico, M. 2002. *Marketing*. (Sixth edition). Cincinnati: South-Western College Publishing, p. 13.

3. Belch, G.E. & Belch, M.A. 2001. *Advertising and Promotion*. (Fifth edition). Boston: McGraw-Hill Irwin, p. 10. Also read Belch, G.E. & Belch, M.A. 2009. *Advertising and Promotion: An Integrated Marketing Communications Perspective*. (Eighth edition). Boston: McGraw-Hill Irwin.

4. Adapted from Futrell, C.M. 2000. *ABC's of Relationship Selling*. (Sixth edition). Boston: Irwin McGraw-Hill, p. 1; and Abratt, R., Connett, B.I. & Blem, N. 2000. *Sales Management*. (Second edition). Cape Town: Heinemann, p. 7. Also see Futrell, C.M. 2004. *Fundamentals of Selling*. Boston: Irwin McGraw-Hill; and Futrell, C.M. 2008. *ABC's of Relationship Selling Through Service*. (Tenth edition). Boston: Irwin McGraw-Hill/Irwin.

5. Rogers, L. 1988. *Retail Selling*. London: Kogan Page, p. 10.

6. Arens, W.F. 2002. *Contemporary Advertising*. (Eighth edition). Boston: McGraw-Hill. Also read Arens, W.F. 2009. *Advertising Management Contemporary Advertising*. (Twelfth edition). McGraw-Hill.

7. Zikmund, W.G. & d'Amico, M. 2001. *Marketing: Creating and Keeping Customers in an e-Commerce World*. Cincinnati: South-Western College Publishing, p. 522.

8. Drawn from Hammann, P. 1979. Personal selling. *European Journal of Marketing*, 13(6): 141–176; and Zikmund & d'Amico, 2001. op. cit., pp. 523–525.

9. Hammann, op. cit., pp. 141–176; and Zikmund & d'Amico, op. cit., p. 522.

10. Belch & Belch. 2001. op. cit., p. 615. Belch & Belch, 2009.

11. Ibid., p. 619.

12. Futrell, C.M. 1999. *Fundamentals of Selling*. (Sixth edition). Boston: Irwin McGraw-Hill, p. 4.

13. Drawn from Zikmund & d'Amico. 2001. op. cit., Instructor's CD-ROM.

14. Adapted from Futrell, 2001, op. cit., p. 15. Futrell, 2008.

15. Adapted from Bearden, W.O., Ingram, T.N. & Lafarge, R.W. 2001. *Marketing: Principles and Perspectives*. (Third edition). Boston: McGraw-Hill, p. 443.

16. Belch & Belch, op. cit., p. 620. Belch & Belch, 2009.

17. Bearden et al., op. cit., p. 443. Belch & Belch, 2009.

18. Belch & Belch, op. cit., p. 629. Belch & Belch, 2009.

19. This section draws from Arens, op. cit., pp. 294–295.

20. Bearden et al., op. cit., p. 445.

21. Belch & Belch, op. cit., pp. 617–618. Belch & Belch, 2009.

22. Ibid., pp. 620–621.

23. Marks, op. cit., pp. 12–16.

24. This section draws from Du Plessis, F., Bothma, N., Jordaan, Y. & Van Heerden, N. 2003. *Integrated Marketing Communication*. Cape Town: New Africa Books, pp. 164–169. Also read Du Plessis, F., Van Heerden, N. & Cook, G. 2010. *Integrated Marketing Communication*. (Third edition). Pretoria: Van Schaik. Also read *Selling – Building Partnerships* by Weitz, B.A., Castleberry, S.B. & Tanner, J.F. 2007. Boston, MA: McGraw-Hill Irwin.

25. Futrell, op. cit., pp. 188–189. Futrell, 2008.

26. Bearden et al., op. cit., p. 448; and Futrell, op. cit., p. 105.

27. Bearden et al., op. cit., p. 453.

28. Smith, R.D. & Dick, G. 1984. *Getting Sales*. UK: Kogan Page, p. 11.

29. Blem, N. 1997. *Achieve Excellence in Selling: The South African Approach*. Cape Town: Oxford University Press Southern Africa, p. 47. Also read Blem, N. 2008. *Achieving Excellence in Selling – A South African Approach*. (Third edition).

30. Du Plooy-Cilliers, F. & Olivier, M. 2001. *Let's Talk about Interpersonal Communication*. Sandton: Heinemann, p. 121.

31. Adapted from Zaiss, C.D. & Gordon, T. 1993. *Sales Effectiveness Training*. New York: Dutton Books, p. 7.

32. Wolvin, A.D. & Coakley, C.G. 1996. *Listening*. (Fifth edition). Dubuque, IA: Brown & Benchmark, p. 69.

33. Du Plooy-Cilliers & Olivier, op. cit., p. 206.

34. Hill, J.B. 2001. Listen with a LEAN strategy to increase your sales: Strategies for strategic customer-focused listening. *The American Salesman*, 46(11): 27–29.

35. Futrell, op. cit., 1999, p. 33; Futrell, op. cit., 2000, p. 29; Futrell, 2004; Futrell, 2008.

36. Drawn from Zikmund & d'Amico, op. cit., instructional CD-ROM.

37. Zikmund, op. cit., pp. 16–18.

38. Futrell, op. cit., 1999, p. 45. Futrell, 2008.

39. Ibid.

40. Bearden et al., op. cit., pp. 10–11.

41. Churchill, G.A, Ford, N.M., Johnston, M.W. & Tanner, J.F. 2000. *Sales Force Management*. (Sixth edition). Boston: McGraw-Hill, p. 37, as quoted by Jordaan, Y. in Du Plessis et al., op. cit., p. 153.

42. Futrell, op. cit., 1999, p. 52. Futrell, 2008.

43. Belch & Belch, op. cit., p. 614. Belch & Belch, 2009.

44. Jobber, D. 1995. *Principles and Practice of Marketing*. London: McGraw-Hill, pp. 679–680. Also read: Jobber, D. & Lancaster, G. 2009. *Selling and Sales Management*. (Eighth edition). FT Prentice Hall.

45. Futrell, op. cit., 1999, p. 43. Futrell, 2008.

46. Ibid.

47. This section draws heavily from Futrell, op. cit., 1999, p. 50.

48. Adapted from Manning, G.L. & Reece, B.L. 1987. *Selling Today*. (Third edition). Boston: Allyn & Bacon Inc., p. 7.

49. This section draws heavily from Futrell, op. cit., 1999, pp. 50–55.

50. Ibid., p. 57.

51. Ibid., p. 57.

52. Futrell, op. cit., 1999, p. 24. Futrell, 2008.

53. Belch & Belch, op. cit., p. 618. Belch, & Belch, 2009.

54. Futrell, op. cit., 1999, p. 59.

i http://www. directselling411. com/about-direct-selling/history-of-direct-selling/ (accessed on 4 April 2010).

ii For further insight and information go to: http://www.wfdsa.org. Further resource about direct selling www.directselling411.com (accessed on 4 April 2010).

iii http://www.directselling411.com/about-direct-selling/ (accessed on 4 April 2010).

iv http://hubpages.com/hub/personal-selling/ (accessed on 2 April 2010).

v http://www.nos.org/Secbuscour/22.pdf/ (accessed on 2 April 2010).

vi Sales vs Marketing – The Battle of the Words?.ezinearticles.com Available from: http://www. business-opportunities-internetonline.com/blog/2009/01/19/sales-vs-marketing-the-battle-of-the-words/

vii For more information visit http://www.dsasa.co.za

2

THE CUSTOMER AND THE BUYING PROCESS

LEARNING OUTCOMES

After studying this chapter, you should be able to:

- Explain what is meant by a selling process or sequence
- Explain the different steps in Maslow's hierarchy of motives
- Describe the factors that influence the customer's buying decision
- Explain why buying is a choice decision

INTRODUCTION

In order for a salesperson to be able to sell, it is important that he or she knows what customers or clients want. People and companies buy products in order to satisfy a need, to obtain a solution to a problem or to meet a set objective. This implies that in order to sell, the salesperson must determine the needs of customers and then match the features and benefits of the product or service to these needs. In the process the salesperson must also convince customers that these benefits and features meet their needs, and in order to do so the salesperson must know how customers make their decisions when purchasing a product or service. Customers' reasons and motives for buying products and services will be explored in this chapter, as will their needs, the factors that influence their buying decision, and how buying is a choice decision

ESTABLISHING THE NEEDS OF CUSTOMERS

It is not possible to just walk in and sell to customers before first establishing their needs and then seeing how the product or service fits their needs. This means that salespeople must know the features and benefits of their product and then sell the benefits (not features) to prospective customers. It must be remembered that the features of a product refer to the actual product (e.g. what it is made of, the price of the product, the range of colours, and so on). Examples of the benefits and advantages of using a product (if, for example, it is a car) are that it has a five-year maintenance plan and a mobile road assistance plan, and a log management system for fleet-car owners. These benefits are usually what customers are looking for – and what they use to compare competing products.

It is therefore important that salespeople establish what customers are looking for before attempting to sell. Customers buying a car for their daughter, for example, would first looking for a vehicle that is reliable, safe, economical, compact and inexpensive to maintain. They do not only look at price or colour, as those are offered by all. The salesperson in this case should rather focus on what benefits the customer is looking for that are more important than only price or colour.

Order of selling

It may be advisable for the salesperson to have some sort of format or process to follow when selling to customers. A standard one would be to start off with the features of the product, for example that it has a standard warranty, has been serviced as per the manufacturer's requirements and is accident free, and so forth. It can then be pointed out that the main advantages are the fact that along all major routes in the country free roadside assistance is available, and that there are countrywide spares and service centres. Lastly, the benefits of the particular vehicle can be pointed out. These may, for example, be that it is light on fuel, economical to maintain, reliable, safe (e.g. it has four airbags), and that it also has a flat tyre indicator, making it an ideal choice for a student or as a first car for a young person. The process followed, of course, will depend on the customer and will need to be adapted as the situation warrants. Prospective customers must be given the opportunity to ask questions or query any benefit they are unsure of. This is the stage where the salesperson must be on the lookout for any signals that the customer is ready to buy, and go for a trial close.

A trial close is a selling technique that can be used in a sales presentation to check the attitude of the prospective customer towards the offering. This implies that the salesperson must be tuned in to the signals from the buyer in order to go for the close. A buyer's signal can be negative or positive. In other words, it can be anything that a potential buyer says or does that indicates mental ownership or rejection. The whole process of closing is discussed later in the book and will not be discussed here. It is sufficient to say that the trial close helps the salesperson spot the moment when the buyer is ready for the close. Depending on the product or service, the readiness to buy can be immediate or even take years. It is generally accepted that the higher the value of the product or service and the longer the time frame of the contract is, the more complex the buying decision will be and the longer it will take to make.

To have a process in the selling situation streamlines the presentation but it must be remembered that it is the salesperson's task to be able to adapt to changing scenarios and situations, as well as knowing when to keep quiet.

Consumer motivation

A generally accepted approach to understanding consumer motives is to use Maslow's hierarchy of needs model.[1] The basic principle of this theory lies in the fact that people progress to the next level as soon as one level of needs is satisfied. Needs are ranked from the most basic at the bottom of the hierarchy to the top where the highest order of needs is fulfilled. Maslow suggests that as a particular need is satisfied, it loses its potency as a motivator and other unfulfilled needs gain in potency.

The following classification shows the lowest order of motives at the bottom proceeding to the highest at the top:

Figure 2.1 *Maslow's hierarchy of needs*

There are numerous other theories, but we see Maslow's theory as most relevant for our purposes. The different levels are very helpful to salespeople in the planning of their selling effort. It must be noted that few selling actions focus on the lowest level of basic motives. These refer to the need for food and water, for example, and no advertisement or sales pitch will solely focus on the need to quench thirst or satisfy hunger. There will rather be a connection to some other motive, such as love or affection. Take, for example, a person buying a Police watch. The main motivator might be to be part of a group – to seek affiliation with them – and not actually to read the time.

Maslow's theory also suggests a number of needs that may motivate customers to buy. Take the marketers of golf clubs, for example. They meet the needs of the market in terms of affiliation by using the likes of Tiger Woods and Ernie Els in their advertising as supporters of their products. Vodacom's association with rugby and soccer is another example of this type of association. In South Africa with its high crime levels, companies marketing burglar alarms, security gates and other such products link their products to the market's need for safety. Many use fear as their motivator to address the needs of the market. Companies such as ABI, which markets Coca-Cola, use social needs and affection as the basis for marketing, as is evident from the advertisements they use. For special days such as Valentine's Day and Mother's Day the needs of love and care are exploited by businesses in their marketing actions.

It is important to understand that most needs of customers fall in the categories as indicated by Maslow, but that does not mean that one level has to be completely satisfied before the next is approached. One of the more difficult needs to target is the higher order needs of self-actualisation. These refer to the needs of a love for culture and the finer things in life. Bell's Whisky has run a campaign of an art collector who goes to isolated, and faraway places looking for rare art and in this way associate their product with these needs of customers.

Types of motives

Motives that tie in with the values and norms of society are usually more apparent in the behaviour of people than those which do not. When asking a person, for example, why they drive a Mercedes-Benz, the answer might be that it is because it is safe and well designed, and offers more protection in the event of an accident. There may, however, be the other reasons which the buyer does not voice. These might be that it shows status, puts the buyer in a higher social class and is indicative of the buyer's financial worth.

The motives which are usually mentioned in such a case are referred to as *manifest* motives.[2] The ones that the buyer may be reluctant to admit to or unaware of are known as latent motives. Both latent and manifest motives may influence a purchase, or maybe only manifest motives will operate. Figure 2.2 illustrates how the two types of motives may influence a purchase.

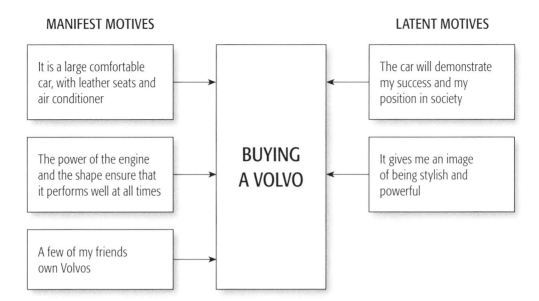

MANIFEST MOTIVES

It is a large comfortable car, with leather seats and air conditioner

The power of the engine and the shape ensure that it performs well at all times

A few of my friends own Volvos

BUYING A VOLVO

LATENT MOTIVES

The car will demonstrate my success and my position in society

It gives me an image of being stylish and powerful

Figure 2.2 *Latent and manifest motives in a buying situation*

FACTORS THAT INFLUENCE THE BUYING DECISION

It stands to reason that the more expensive a product, the more complex the decision-making process will be. If the amount to be spent on a product is high (say R15 000), more thought will be given to the purchase decision than in the case of a R150 product. When buying a new fridge, TV or car, much more time will be spent on consulting a number of resources for information, which means more time and effort. Buying everyday or low-value items will usually be done with little effort and can be seen as routine decision making. As is indicated later, routine decision making is applied when consumers purchase low-involvement products, such as petrol, bread and milk.

A consumer's buying behaviour is usually influenced by social factors, family, demographics, psychographics and personality factors, as well as culture. Each of these factors is discussed briefly below.

Social/cultural factors

Social and cultural factors impact on the behaviour of all people and need to be understood by marketers in order to capitalise on them. The social forces that impact on the behaviour of consumers include family, social class, demographics, psychographic characteristics, personality and cultural groups. Each of these factors is discussed in turn.

Family

The family probably plays the single most important role in an individual's early attitude formation and in determining the consumer's lifelong buying behaviour.[3] Most families pass through a sequence of stages, which are defined by a combination of factors such as age and marital status, as well as parenthood.

Table 2.1 *Stages in the family life cycle*[4]

Stage in the family life cycle	Buying behaviour
Single stage: young singles	Purchase of car and furniture, rent, fashionable clothing, vacations and leisure pursuits.
Newly married couples: young without children	Highest purchase rate (dual income), highest average purchase of durable goods, particularly furniture and other expensive items.
Full nest I: young married couples with children below the age of 16 years	Home maintenance items, baby goods, vitamins, toys, and furnishings for the children.
Full nest II: older married couples with children above the age of 16 years living with them	Replacement of old furniture, consumption patterns are heavily influenced by the children, purchase of food and cleaning supplies in larger-sized packages, paying for the children's extramural activities.
Empty nest: older, married couples, whose children no longer live with them and who may either be still in the labour force or retired	Buying luxury items, spending on vacations, travel and recreation.
Solitary survivors: older, single people, who may either be in the labour force or retired	May sell their home and purchase/rent smaller property, spend more on health-oriented products, spend on vacation and recreation.

The stages as outlined above do not necessarily follow the same pattern in real life, but are an important guide to marketers. The fact that many parents work far from home means, for example, that the family unit may be different from the norm and may consist of only older children looking after the smaller children, or grandparents or uncles and aunts forming the nucleus of the family. The consumption pattern of such families will therefore be different from the traditional family structures as depicted in the table above.

Family consumption decisions involve at least five definable roles that can be assumed by the husband, the wife and/or the children. These include the role of gatekeeper, influencer, decider, buyer and user, as illustrated in Table 2.2.

Table 2.2 *Family role behaviour*

Role	Consumption decision
Gatekeeper	Initiator of family thinking about buying a product and the gathering of information to aid the decision.
Influencer	Decides the criteria that should be used in purchases, and which products/brands most likely fit those evaluative criteria.
Decider	The person with the financial authority to choose how the family money will be spent and which products and brands will be chosen.
Buyer	Acts as a purchasing agent by visiting the store, writing the cheque and bringing the product home.
User	The person who uses the product.

The roles as indicated above are not set, and can and will differ depending on the product being bought. The type of car to be bought may be primarily the decision of the husband in a household, but this will be influenced by the mother and the number and age of the children. The types of food consumed in a house will probably be strongly influenced by the children, as would the type of toothpaste used, even though the mother is the purchaser of the products. Children tend to have a greater influence in purchase decisions involving products for their own use, whereas their influence is more limited on more expensive, higher-risk products. Marketers are aware that children exert direct influence over parental spending when they request specific products and brands. The children's market has captured the attention of marketers worldwide because of the enormous influence they also exert over spending power in a growing number of product categories such as clothing and footwear.[5]

The family purchase decision-making process can be complex, but answering the following questions helps identify the purchaser–consumer relationship:

1. Who is making the purchase?
2. Who are the principal characters in the decision-making process?
3. Who are the users of the purchased product/service?

Traditionally, the primary responsibility of the man in the house was to earn the money while one of the woman's roles was to do most of the purchasing of the products for the house. These roles have, however, over the years changed as more and more woman are holding senior positions, and more and more are working and generating their own income.

This fact, namely that more females now occupy top positions at work, implies many return home from work late, which impacts on the consumption patterns of couples. TV dinners have become more popular, and time- and energy-saving appliances (such as slow cookers, for example) are more popular as a result of these changes. More people are living together instead of getting married, which means that households have two incomes, so there is more opportunity for travel, a higher probability of owning two cars, and firmer preferences for style, colour and product design.

Social class

Social class may be defined as relatively permanent homogeneous divisions in a society in which individuals or families sharing similar values, lifestyles, interests and behaviour can be categorised. Social class is directly related to a large proportion of consumer decision making, including product and brand usage patterns, the frequency of shopping trips, interpersonal consumer relationships and innovative behaviour. Class is determined by factors such as occupation, wealth, income, education, power, prestige and class consciousness.

The general trend is that people in the lower classes will aspire to form part of the higher classes. They look up to these classes, and buy the products and services associated with them. Buying, for example, food only from Woolworths by somebody in a 'lower' class may be a way of associating with those in a 'higher' class, as is buying only Amstel or imported beer. Many people have the mistaken belief that money, for example, places them in a higher social class. This is a fallacy (we have all heard the saying that 'money cannot buy class'). Factors such as education, culture, and so forth also play a role in this regard.

Buyer demographics, psychographics and personality

The concepts of demographics, psychographics and personality each describe a different approach to identifying individual differences in consumer behaviour. Individual difference variables describe how one person varies from another in his or her distinctive patterns of behaviour. Demographics is defined as the size, structure and distribution of a population. Demographic variables include age, gender, income, religion, marital status, nationality, education, family size, occupation and population group. Information in this regard is freely available through Statistics South Africa, and is gathered via the census. Demographic characteristics help to predict everything from which products will be in demand, to what school enrolments will be in the future, to which crimes can be expected to be on the increase in ten years' time.[6]

It is important to know
■ How the population make up is changing
■ How people are spending their financial resources

- What products or services they prefer
- How people choose their friends
- How people support social programmes

These characteristics are then used to determine how consumers will behave. They can also be used to guide new product development, product repositioning, brand extension, distribution strategies, or media and creative appeals in communication programmes when marketers do not have primary research. Demographic characteristics of consumers have two important uses in the segmentation process. Firstly, they can be used either singly or in combination to describe various subcultures whose members share certain values, needs, rituals and behaviours. They essentially help to identify cultures and subcultures that salespeople can target with their sales strategy.

Example 1:   By using a combination of education, occupation and income, a measure of social class can be developed.

Example 2:   By using a combination of age, marital status and number of children, a measure of the stage in the family life cycle can be obtained.

Secondly, demographics can be used to describe consumers who are classified into segments via other means.

Consumer analysts use demographic trends to predict changes in demand for and consumption of certain products and services by monitoring which population groups will be growing in the future. However, it is not enough to just study the demographics of consumers alone. This is because people in similar situations buy many of the same products as do others in the same age, geographic or income category, yet this is not always the case.[7] People act differently because of basic traits and social–psychological makeup that reflects their personality, personal values and lifestyle.

The assessment of lifestyle through psychographic analysis represents a second approach to identifying individual differences among consumers. Through psychographic analysis, consumer researchers describe segments of consumers in terms of how they live, work and play. Lifestyle is a summary construct defined as patterns in which people live and spend time and money, reflecting their activities, interests and opinions as well as demographic variables discussed above. Simply defined, lifestyle is 'how one lives'.[8] It has been used to describe three different levels of aggregation of people:

- An individual
- A small group of interacting people
- A larger group of people (a market segment)

Lifestyles have a tendency to change rapidly; therefore researchers have to keep their research methods and marketing strategies current. Marketers measure lifestyles by psychographic analysis. The term *psychographics* refers to the idea of describing the psychological makeup of consumers. Psychographic studies are used to develop an in-depth understanding of market segments and sometimes to define them. For example, single men between the ages of 24 and 32 who actively participate in outdoor sports and care about nutrition. Psychographic studies usually include questions to assess a target market's lifestyle, its personality characteristics and its demographic characteristics.

People's personalities can also affect buying behaviour by influencing the types of products that fulfil their particular needs.[9] One of the best ways to examine personality is to consider a buyer's self-concept.[10] Internal or personal evaluation may influence a buyer's attitude towards the product desired or not desired. People essentially have a need to behave consistently with their self-concept, and this perception of themselves forms their personality. It is important to note that people have more than one self-concept. Table 2.3 illustrates the various types of self-concept.

Table 2.3 *Types of self-concept*

Types of self-concept	Description
Actual self	How a person actually perceives themselves.
Ideal self	How a person would like to perceive themselves.
Social self	How a person thinks others perceive them.
Ideal social self	How a person would like others to perceive them.
Expected self	How a person would like to act.
Situational self	A person's self-image in a particular situation.
Extended self	The impact of possession on self-image.
Possible self	What a person would like to become, could become, or is afraid of becoming.
Connected self	The extent that a person defines themselves in terms of their connection with other groups or individuals.

A relationship may be found between the self-image of a person and of certain products that he or she buys. Products for which this finding has been proven to be true include cars, health products, cleaning products, grooming products, leisure products, clothing, food, cigarettes, home appliances, magazines and furnishings.[11] Products that are most likely to be viewed as symbols that communicate one's self-concept to others have three characteristics:

- *Visibility* – their purchase, consumption, and disposition to others is clearly visible.
- *Variability* – some consumers must be able to have the resources (time or money) to own the product, whereas others must have neither the time nor the money to do so. Essentially the product must be a symbol.
- *Personalisability* – the product must have a distinct stereotypical image of the average user.

It is important to note the fact that it is rather difficult to find a direct relationship between a set of personality variables and assorted consumer behaviours such as purchases, media choice, product choice and social influence. This is because personality is one of the variables in the consumer decision-making process that is difficult to use in selling. People with common personalities can represent wide variations in demographic variables, and mass media are primarily segmented on a demographic basis.[12]

Culture

Culture is defined sociologically as the values, beliefs, norms and practices, and material objects that together form a people's way of life.[13] One classic definition is that culture is a set of socially acquired behaviour patterns transmitted symbolically through language and other means to the members of a particular society.[14] Essentially culture is:

- A way of life that is learned and not necessarily in our genes. It is transmitted from generation to generation, influencing future members of the society.
- Adaptation and changes as a society faces new problems and opportunities – a means of satisfying needs. By providing norms or rules of behaviour, a culture gives orderliness to society. People need to know what is expected of them, what is right and wrong, and what they should do in various situations.
- Reflective of certain factors such as ethnicity, race, religion, and national or regional identity. When the factors within a society change, so does the culture.
- Both abstract and material in nature – which allows the description, evaluation and differentiation of cultures. Abstract elements include values, attitudes, ideas, personality types, religion and politics. Material components include books, tools, buildings and specific products, such as a pair of Levi jeans.

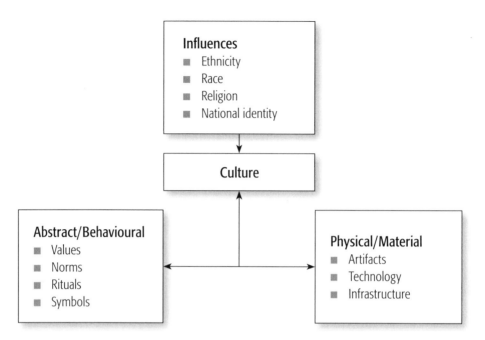

Figure 2.3 *Influences on culture*

Some of the more important characteristics influenced by culture are the following:
■ Communication and language
■ Dress and appearance
■ Food and eating habits
■ Time and time consciousness
■ Relationships (family, organisations, government)
■ Values and norms
■ Beliefs and attitudes
■ Mental processes and learning
■ Work habits and practices

The use of culture as a segmentation tool is of critical importance to marketers, not only in South Africa but worldwide. Many businesses have lost huge contracts due to a lack of understanding of the cultures of the people they do business with. In South Africa there are many cultures and culture groups who are very sensitive and easily offended.

Two important elements of culture are values and norms.[15] *Norms* are the rules of behaviour held by a majority or at least a consensus of a group about how individuals should behave. *Values* are those shared broadly across groups of people; however, values may vary among people in the same culture.

Culture has a profound effect on why people buy and consume products or services. It affects the specific products people buy as well as the structure of consumption, individual decision making and communication in a society. Culture affects how consumers are likely to search for information. In some cultures, word of mouth and advice from a family member about a product or brand choice are more important than information found in advertising.

Situational influences on buyer behaviour

Consumer situations consist of the temporary environmental factors that form the context within which a consumer activity occurs. Consumer situations are relatively short term and have relatively less impact in comparison to social factors such as culture and personality. There are five types of consumer situations, and these include:[16]

- *Physical surroundings.* The concrete physical and spatial aspects of the environment encompassing a consumer activity
- *Social surroundings.* The effects of other people on a consumer in a consumer activity
- *Time.* The effects of the presence or absence of time on consumer activities
- *Task definition.* The reasons that occasion the need for consumers to buy or consume a product or a service
- *Antecedent states.* The temporary physiological states and moods that a consumer brings to a consumption situation

There are categories of products that may be defined by the situations in which they are used. For example, wristwatches are positioned based on usage situations. One can find formal watches, sport watches, everyday watches and speciality watches (e.g. for diving). Groups of people can then be identified with an unmet situational need, such as the desire to have a watch with a timing function for sprinting. A product that meets this need in this case would be a watch with a stopwatch capacity. The company can then create promotional material that positions the product to its situational use.

BUYING IS A CHOICE DECISION

Consumers generally have a number of options or choices when wanting to buy something. They may, however, consider only one or a few and not all options. Buying the weekly or monthly groceries does not mean that a person will consider all the options in the neighbourhood or town from whom to buy, but rather two or three options based maybe on the type of product, location and prices based on previous experience.

Evaluating alternatives

Figure 2.4 illustrates the pre-purchase evaluation process which is the manner in which choice alternatives are evaluated.

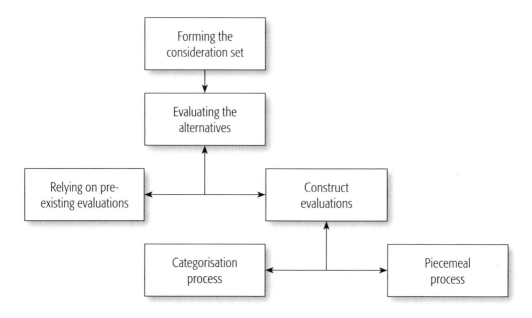

Figure 2.4 *The pre-purchase evaluation process*

Those alternatives considered during the decision-making process compose what is known as the consideration or evoked set.[17] The alternatives to be considered by consumers are only a portion of the total number of alternatives available to them. How any alternatives will be included depends solely on the consumer. If consumers are, for example, very loyal to a particular brand of washing powder such as Omo, they will only have this brand in their consideration set. On the other hand, consumers buying their first microwave or refrigerator may experience difficulties in deciding which in a range of alternatives to choose. In such a situation the alternatives may be developed in several ways. Friends' opinions, parents' advice, advertisements on TV and in media, or colleagues at work may all be taken into consideration. Consumers who are less informed or knowledgeable about the product will generally be more susceptible to external influences such as store atmosphere in their creation of a consideration set. The more knowledge consumers have, the better is the chance that their memory and experience will play an important role in selecting alternatives. In this case, the consideration set would depend on the consumer's recall of choice alternatives from memory, for example which brand of refrigerator or microwave they had or used in the past that performed well. In other situations consumers will, for example, be led by their recognition of a particular brand or packaging on the shelves of the store. The washing powders on the shelves are many and diverse, but the consumer may recognise a particular one and select it.

Consumers must also decide how the considered alternatives will be evaluated. There are basically two options:[18]

■ Either rely on pre-existing product evaluations stored in memory
■ Or develop new evaluations based on information acquired through internal and external search

A very powerful evaluation criterion is the evaluation of a particular product based on experiences with it in the past. The consumer will have a pre-existing evaluation of the product, which will impact either positively or negatively. In other instances the experiences of a friend or acquaintance may be used as evaluation criteria, which may be the deciding factor in the decision as to whether to buy or not.

A second method in evaluating alternatives is the developing of new evaluation alternatives. It is not just the new consumer who will choose to develop new evaluations. Experienced consumers possessing pre-existing evaluations may elect not to use these evaluations if considerable time has elapsed since their last purchase and they may question whether they are still adequately informed.

The basic processes by which consumers can develop evaluations are:

■ *The categorisation process.* In this case the evaluation of a choice alternative depends on the particular category to which the alternative is assigned. Imagine a scenario where a salesperson is trying to sell Reebok running shoes to an athlete, who may evaluate the shoes based on his or her liking of the Reebok brand. Typically, the categorisation process is associated with some degree of liking or disliking.[19]
■ *The piecemeal process.* This essentially involves constructing an evaluation of choice alternatives using bits and pieces. First the consumer must determine the particular criteria or product dimension to be used in evaluating choice alternatives. These can range from safety, reliability, price, taste, brand name, country of origin, and warranty or guarantee. The feelings that come from owning the product may also be considered. These include prestige, excitement or status. The consumer then has to consider the strengths or weaknesses of each considered alternative along the particular criteria that are important in making the choice. The consumer might consider the price or the desired feeling evoked from using the product. The final step in the piecemeal process involves using one's judgement about the performance of the considered alternatives to form the overall evaluation of each alternative's acceptability.

The consumer choice process

The evaluation of alternatives is crucial, and as soon as this process has been completed the next step is to make a choice between, for example, a Defy or Kelvinator refrigerator, or the Omo or Surf washing powder. How consumers go about making choices is strongly influenced by the type of decision process in which they are engaged. The choice process differs if consumers use a high-involvement as compared to a low-involvement approach. Similarly, if the consumer is using an experiential approach the choice process is altered.

High-involvement choice

High involvement is what it says – a high level of involvement from the purchaser due to the type of product (e.g. a software program to be used in all operations of a business), its price (e.g. a car or house) or even the volume involved (e.g. buying the stock for a multibillion rand clothing company). Under the conditions of high involvement, consumers analyse each alternative in a broad evaluative fashion so that high ratings on one attribute may compensate for low ratings on the other.[20] In such a process all the information on the attributes of a brand are combined into an overall judgement of the preference for the brand. Such an evaluation is made for each of the brand alternatives. The brand that has the highest overall preference is chosen. For example, a car might be rated poorly on acceleration; however, because it is rated highly on other attributes such as style and interior, the brand could still be chosen.

Low-involvement choice

In these conditions, high ratings on some attributes may not compensate for low ratings on others. The consumer is essentially viewed as comparing alternative attributes one at a time. One attribute is chosen and all alternatives are compared to it. The person then moves on to the next attribute and does the same thing. The process then continues in a hierarchical manner. When consumers are in low-involvement situations, they are unwilling to engage in a large amount of the information-processing effort required in high-involvement choice decisions.

Experiential choice process

In this situation, choice is viewed as resulting from consumers considering their feeling about alternatives, thus little emphasis is placed on the development of beliefs about attributes.[21] As a result, the purchase is made with little cognitive control, and seems to happen in an automatic way. The different types of consumer choice that can be categorised as being experiential processes include the following:[22]

- Situations may occur where consumers base their choice on their overall emotional response to an alternative rather than examining attributes of beliefs. For example, consumers who express brand loyalty also reveal highly positive affect toward the brand, thus when making a purchase they do not go through an extended or even limited decision process. Rather, they simply refer to their feelings when making a choice.
- Brand awareness may also influence consumer choice through a process where consumers base their choice on their overall emotional response to an alternative.

- Impulse purchases occur where a buying action is taken without a problem being previously recognised, or a buying intention is formed prior to entering the store. An impulse buy is accompanied by a sudden urge to buy something immediately.
- Variety seeking purchases occur where consumers spontaneously buy a new brand of product even though they continue to express satisfaction with the previously purchased brand. This is often an attempt by the consumer to reduce boredom.

SUMMARY

The art of selling has undergone many profound changes over the years and this is increasing as the global marketplace becomes smaller and smaller. To sell today the needs of the market must be considered and aligned to the advantages and benefits of the product or service. It is the responsibility of the salesperson to have some sort of selling process in place to present products to prospective customers in a manner that flows naturally from their features, advantages and benefits.

A useful way to understand consumer motives is to use Maslow's hierarchy of needs model. Maslow explains the nature of human needs by ranking then in a hierarchy from the lower-level needs such as physiological and safety needs to higher-level needs such as self-actualisation.

A consumer's buying behaviour is influence by social factors, family, demographics, psychographics and personality factors, as well as culture. Social factors are those external forces that constitute an individual's environment which play an important role in consumption behaviour. The family probably plays the single most important role in an individual's early attitude formation and in determining the consumer's lifelong buying behaviour. Family consumption decisions involve at least five definable roles that can be assumed by husband, wife and/or children. These include the roles of gatekeeper, influencer, decider, buyer and user.

Social class may be defined as relatively permanent homogeneous divisions into a society in which individuals or families sharing similar values, lifestyles, interests and behaviour can be categorised. Social class is directly related to a large proportion of consumer decision making, including product and brand usage patterns, the frequency of shopping trips, interpersonal consumer relationships and innovative behaviour. Class is determined by factors such as occupation, wealth, income, education, power, prestige and class consciousness.

The concepts of psychographics, demographics and personality each describe a different approach to identifying individual differences in consumer behaviour. Individual difference variables describe how people differ from one another in their distinctive patterns of behaviour. Demographics are defined as the size, structure and distribution of a population. Demographic variables include age, gender, income, religion, marital status, nationality, education, family size, occupation and population group. Psychographics, on the other hand, describe segments of consumers in terms of how they live, work and play.

People's personalities, particularly their self-concept, influence their attitude towards the product desired or not desired. People essentially have a need to behave consistently with their self-concept and this perception of themselves forms their personality. People are also influenced by their culture, i.e. the values, beliefs, norms and practices that form their way of life.

Situational influences on consumer behaviour include physical surrounding, social surroundings, time, task definition and antecedent states. These are temporal environmental factors that form the context within which a consumer activity occurs.

DISCUSSION QUESTIONS

1. Discuss Maslow's hierarchy of needs and how salespeople use this theory to fulfil the needs of their customers.

2. Describe how you would use a sell sequence or process to sell a swimming pool to an identified homeowner.

3. Outline the latent and manifest motives in buying an exclusive ladies' perfume such as Estee Lauder's *Beautiful*.

4. Discuss a specific purchase decision of a low-involvement product and a high-involvement product that you have bought in the past month or so.

NOTES

1. Maslow, A.H. 1954. *Motivation and Personality.* New York: Harper & Row.

2. Mower, J.V. & Minor, M.S. 2001. *Consumer Behaviour: A Framework.* Upper Saddle River: Prentice Hall.

3. Foxall, G.R. 1980. *Consumer Behaviour: A Practical Guide.* Biddles Ltd.

4. Murphy, P.E. & Staples, W. 1979. A modernized family life cycle. *Journal of Consumer Research,* 6: 12–22.

5. Gregan-Paxton J. & Roedder, J. 1995. Are young children adaptive decision makers? A study of age differences in information search behaviour. *Journal of Consumer Research,* 21(4): 567–580.

6. Foot, D.K. 1996. *Boom, Dust and Echo.* Toronto: MacFarlane, Walter & Ross, p. 2.

7. Engel, J.F., Blackwell, D.R. & Miniard, P. W. 1986. *Consumer Behavior.* (Fifth edition). CBS Publishing.

8. Anderson, W.T. & Golden, L. 1984. Lifestyle and psychographics: A critical review and recommendation. *Advances in Consumer Research,* 11: 405–411.

9. Futrell, C. 1988. *Fundamentals of Selling.* (Second edition). Irwin Inc., pp. 85–87.

10. Futrell, op. cit.

11. Belk, R., Bahn, K.D. & Mayer, R.N. 1982. Developmental recognition of consumption symbolism. *Journal of Consumer Research,* 9: 4–17.

12. Blackwell, R.D., Miniard, P.W. & Engel, J.F. 2001. *Consumer Behaviour.* (Ninth edition). Fort Worth: Harcourt College Publishers.

13. Mufune, P. 2003. African culture and managerial behaviour: Clarifying the connections. *South African Journal of Business Management,* 34(3): 25.

14. Wallendorf, M. & Reilly, M. 1983. Distinguishing culture of origin from culture of residence. *Advances in Consumer Research,* 10: 699–701.

15. Blackwell, R.D., Miniard, P.W. & Engel, J.F. 2001. *Consumer Behaviour* (Ninth edition). Fort Worth: Harcourt College Publishers.

16. Belk, R. 1975. Situational variables and consumer behaviour. *Journal of Consumer Research,* 2: 157–163.

17. Wildt, A.R. 1992. Consideration set measurement. *Journal of the Academy of Marketing Science,* 235–243.

18. Blackwell, R.D., Miniard, P.W. & Engel, J. F. 2001. *Consumer Behaviour* (Ninth edition). Fort Worth: Harcourt College Publishers.

19. Mervis, C.B. 1985. Categorization of natural objects. *Annual Review of Psychology,* 32: 89–115.

20. Wright, P. 1976. Consumer strategies: Simplifying versus optimizing. *Journal of Marketing Research,* 11: 71–82.

21. Weinberg, P. & Gottwald, W. 1982. Impulsive buying as a result of emotions. *Journal of Business Research,* 21: 43–87.

22. Mower, J. C. & Minor, M. S. 2001. *Consumer Behaviour: A Framework.* Upper Saddle River: Prentice Hall.

3

COMMUNICATION

LEARNING OUTCOMES

After studying this chapter, you should be able to:
- Understand the sales communication process
- Understand verbal communication and its elements
- Explain key words and listening
- Use non-verbal communication
- Recognise non-verbal signals and what they mean
- Recognise barriers to communication
- Use written communication in selling
- Explain the ways in which customers' interest and values can be determined

INTRODUCTION

The ability to communicate effectively in the new market economy is an essential component of personal selling. We are living in the information era, and organisations that are capable of satisfying the need for information become market leaders. One way of giving information to customers is through personal selling. In selling, communication is the exchange of ideas or information verbally or non-verbally between the customer and the salesperson. The aim of communication in personal selling is to inform the customers and persuade them to purchase a product or service. Personal selling takes place directly with the customer through face-to-face communication, therefore it can be seen as a two-way transaction between the salesperson and the customer. Figure 3.1 is a graphic representation or model of how communication works. The model has a number of elements, namely the salesperson, who is seen as the sender of a message; a medium, which can be a telephone, a letter, e-mail or direct face-to-face communication;

the consumer, who receives the message; and noise, which is anything that may disturb or influence the communication process. In Figure 3.1 the seven elements of the process of communication are shown. The influence of noise on the process will be discussed, since it does not always come from outside sources – noise is anything that leads to the breakdown of the communication process.

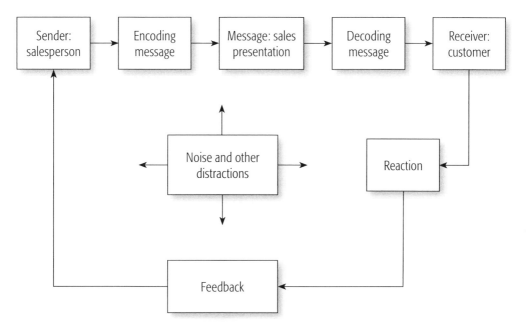

Figure 3.1 *Communication model*

Sales communication consists of two separate elements which are interdependent and contribute equally to the success of the communication process. The first of these is verbal communication, which includes listening, telephone conversation, public speaking and any other form of oral discussion. The second is non-verbal communication, which includes things like body language, dress and anything that is written. The communication of the sales message can be influenced by barriers, either verbal or non-verbal, that may be created or exist between the salesperson and customer. One of the reasons for communication barriers is that in South Africa we are in the unique situation of having 11 official languages and a variety of different cultures that have different ways of communicating, verbally and especially non-verbally. To be a professional salesperson requires studying the different methods of communicating and being able to build rapport with the customer in order to improve customer relationships.

VERBAL COMMUNICATION
It is sometimes said that 55% of communication is non-verbal, 38% is conveyed through

tone of voice and only 7% through the words that are spoken.[1] However, these figures have been shown to be taken out of context – it has been proved that verbal communication plays a far bigger role in communication.[2]

The specific words that are used can also have an effect on the outcome of a selling presentation. Remember, it is the salesperson's responsibility to adapt to the customer's way of verbally communicating, and not the other way round. Therefore the salesperson should adopt every aspect of the customer's way of communicating, even the way they use their voice, in order to build rapport with the customer. The focus of the presentation should not just be on talking but also on listening and asking questions to keep the customer involved in the discussion, in order to determine the customer's real needs and wants.

Words

A good vocabulary and understanding of words is an asset to any salesperson that wants to be seen as a professional. The use of vulgar language and slang in a sales call is a definite no, and will create a bad impression of the salesperson and the organisation that he or she represents. Salespeople should evaluate the words they use and see how they can be improved in order to persuade and inform the customer to the best of their ability.

Key words have been identified as being more persuasive in communication. The 15 key words that every salesperson must make part of his or her vocabulary are:[3]

- *Discover.* This generates interest, evokes a feeling of opportunity and suggests a better life.
- *Good.* This evokes stability and security.
- *Money.* Few people feel that they have enough and everyone wants more.
- *Easy.* This indicates simplicity and the ability to do things more easily.
- *Guaranteed.* This means that the customer does not have to risk anything.
- *Health.* If the product enhances or aids financial, emotional or physical health, it is a good extra selling point.
- *Love.* This is one of people's most basic needs.
- *New.* If it is new, it must be better.
- *Proven.* Customers want something that is reliable and that they can trust.
- *Results.* When spending money or time, people want to know that they will get results.
- *Safe.* We all want a product that is safe to use.
- *Save.* For customers and companies, it is better to save than to spend.
- *Own.* Talk about owning rather than buying. 'Own' implies possession, rather than spending.

- *Free.* This word is one of the best attention getters.
- *Best.* This word is an indication that your product has been tried and tested.

Salespeople should study all these words and make sure that they become part of their vocabulary.

Tone, pattern, pitch

One way to build rapport with a customer is to mirror the tone, pattern and pitch of the customer's voice. The way that one's voice is used can determine the differences between failure and success, not only in sales but also in life. Through voice patterns, salespeople can indicate to the customer whether they are relaxed, stressed or confident. In cases where salespeople are stressed, they will talk more rapidly and the pitch of the voice will be higher than normal. To correct this, salespeople should focus on their breathing while speaking to customers. In sales a voice that is too high pitched will not be taken seriously, and the salesperson should correct all deviations from what is to be expected in normal speech. Most voice problems can fixed with exercise. It is advisable for salespeople to record a sales call in order to monitor the pattern, pitch and tone of their voice and identify any problems.

Listening

Everybody wants to be with someone who makes them feel special. This is as true in selling as it is in other areas of life. The best way to make someone feel special is to listen to them intensely – this is an indication that you care. Listening also builds rapport with customers and makes them feel that the salesperson has their best interests at heart. Every salesperson can become an effective listener by wanting to learn about his or her customers and the needs that they have; every salesperson can develop good listening skills by practising. Listening can be divided into three levels:[4] firstly, *marginal or passive listening*, which is the lowest level. At this level, the salesperson does not really pay attention and is easily distracted. Secondly, *evaluative listening*: at this level, the salesperson listens to what the customer says but does not make an effort to understand the information. Lastly, *active listening*: this is the level for which all salespeople should strive in sales. In active listening the listener evaluates the information being communicated, participates, and elicits a response from the customer. The basic rule is to stop talking and to start listening. To improve active listening there are certain key activities that the salesperson can carry out:

- Value the customer by listening and evaluating information from the viewpoint of the customer.
- Listen to what the customer says and try to get to the full story.
- Encourage the speaker to continue by keeping quiet.

- Avoid the tendency to think about what you are going to say when the customer has finished talking. Focus fully on the customer.
- Take notes, but be careful not to take extensive notes while you listen, as it could appear that you are not interested in what the customer is saying.
- Listen to what is not said. Try to hear the truth and what the customer is implying. If the customer uses words like 'unsure' and 'I don't know', it is a sign of uncertainty.
- Focus on the customer's body language. It might indicate what the customer is really thinking.
- Clarify information by repeating the customer's comments to make sure he or she knows that you are paying attention.
- Ask follow-up questions to make sure you understand what the customer has said.
- Do not let your attention be caught by outside distractions, for example a phone call or a personal assistant coming into the office. Stay calm and guide the customer back to the discussion.
- Indicate to the customer that you are listening by nodding your head or giving verbal indications like 'yes', 'uh huh' and 'I see'.

Listening is one of the elements of verbal communication most often neglected by salespeople. Effective listening, like any other communication skill, can be learned. Salespeople must focus on listening – this will help them to solve the customer's problems and increase sales.

Questions

As imperative as listening is, asking effective questions to determine the customer's needs and wants is just as important. The salesperson can dominate the sales presentation or can choose to maintain and guide the discussion by asking effective questions. Since selling has moved from transactional to relationship selling, the focus of the sales call has changed from just selling a product to determining and satisfying the needs of the customer. To establish the requirements of the customer, the salesperson has to ask questions. The use of questions also involves the customer in the presentation and indicates that the salesperson is paying attention. Different types of questions have been developed to get the customer involved, questions that elicit information or get the customer to think. To elicit more information from the customer, the salesperson can use open-ended questions. In such a case the salesperson will use words like *when, why, how, where, tell*, etc. On the other hand, closed questions can be used to try to limit the customer's responses to specific answers. This type of question will be used when exact answers are needed. A third kind of question is the double-bind question. This kind of question gives the customer only two choices when he or she answers it. It is very effective to use the double-bind question in the closing stages of the sales call, since it limits the customer's choices. An example of this is when you ask the customer: 'Would you like the red shoes or the white ones?', thus limiting the choices and forcing the customer to make a decision. Questions can be an effective way to get customers to interact with you during the sales presentation or to elicit information. They are also a key to determining and overcoming objections.

The telephone is another method in which a salesperson can communicate verbally with a prospect. Telephone guidelines and etiquette will be discussed in greater detail in Chapter 6.

NON-VERBAL COMMUNICATION

The way that one moves and uses one's body makes up a large part of one's communication. Good salespeople are capable of picking up non-verbal signals and interpreting them and then determining the customer's thoughts by using listening to guide verbal communication. The first time salespeople meet a customer they must make sure that their non-verbal communication to the customer is positive by carefully choosing the clothes they wear and monitoring the way they use their own body language. The customer will form an impression from the salesperson's external communication even before he or she has been introduced or has started with the presentation. The salesperson should keep in mind that impressions tend to be formed quickly and automatically. The impressions are based on external non-verbal characteristics and they could be incorrect.

Eye movements

Salespeople have only started realising the important role that eye movement plays in the last two decades. Through the study field of neurolinguistic programming (NLP), salespeople have become aware that eye movements can be used to determine what kind of customer they are dealing with, which is a guide to knowing what type of verbal and non-verbal language to use in order to influence the customer. People can be classified into three categories according to how they evaluate information, namely *seeing* (creating pictures in one's mind), *hearing* (auditory or the making of sound) and *feeling* (kinaesthetic). The salesperson can adapt his or her presentation to the way the customer evaluates information.[5]

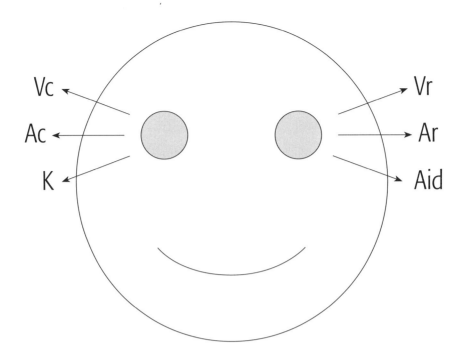

Visual constructed (Vc):	Used to create visual images
Visual remembered (Vr):	Used to access visual images
Auditory constructed (Ac):	Used to imagine new sounds
Auditory remembered (Ar):	Used to access memories of sound
Auditory internal dialogue (Aid):	'That little voice in your head'
Kinaesthetic (K):	Used to access feelings that include emotion, senses and body awareness

Figure 3.2 *Visual eye-accessing cues*

By asking questions and watching the customer's eye movements the salesperson will be able to determine the customer's information-accessing preference.[6] Accessing is the method that someone uses to evaluate information. It is important to note that it might seem that your customer's eyes move in all directions, but the majority will have one dominant method of evaluating information. Certain words and actions have been identified to assist the salesperson in dealing with each of the different type of customers.

When dealing with visually oriented customers, show and demonstrate the product and how it works. Use words like *see, view, look, picture, watch, show, clear* and *bright* in the sales call. With auditorily oriented customers, talk about the product and give the customer as much information as possible. Use words like *tell, hear, talk, ask, sounds, quiet, bang* and *speak*. With kinaesthetically orientated customers, allow them to touch and play around with the product. Also talk more slowly to the kinaesthetic types, since they process information more slowly. Use words like *touch, feel, take, hit, pressure, grab, reach* and *hold*. It is said that the eyes are the windows of the soul. In the case of selling they are the windows to your customer's thinking. Salespeople must make sure that they determine the type of customers they are dealing with to improve sales and build a long-term relationship with them.

Body language

The ability to evaluate the body language of customers has become an integral part of personal selling. Eight different categories of body language have been identified in the sales situation. These are only guidelines for evaluating or determining the customer's attitudes or emotions. Once the salesperson has determined the customer's attitude, the sales presentation can be adapted to the customer.

The eight categories are:[7]

1. *Dominance, superiority, power.* This type of client wants to be in control, and will immediately show the salesperson this through his or her actions. There are certain signals that will indicate this type of customer: a large desk; a chair higher than the visitor's chair; fingertips touching; hands at the back of the neck; exaggerated leaning over the desk; piercing eye contact; standing when others are seated; and a handshake with the palm downward. The salesperson should not allow the customer to intimidate him or her and should also not start a power struggle with the customer. Mimicking customers' movements allows them to think that they are in control all the time.

2. *Submission, apprehension, nervousness.* A customer who falls into this category will use the following types of signals: fidgeting; fingers clasped; head down; hand to face; minimum eye contact; shifting from side to side; briefcase guarding body; constant blinking; and twitching. Such customers are usually unsure about the decisions that they make, therefore the salesperson must keep on assuring them that they are making the right one.

3. *Disagreement, anger, scepticism.* Signals that such customers show are: reddening of the skin; making a fist; a negative shake of the head; finger pointing; squinting eyes; crossed arms; frowning; and turning the body away from the salesperson. The salesperson should always look out for this situation, which means that something has been said or done that has made the customer unhappy. The salesperson should not react aggressively or confront the customer but rather stay calm and determine what the objection is.

4. *Boredom, disinterest.* The following types of signals will be used by the customer: shuffling papers; lack of eye contact; looking at the door, watch or window; playing with something on the desk; and staring blankly. Make sure that the client's interest

is always maintained and watch out for signs of boredom. If you notice the signs, do something to get the customer's attention. Ask questions, do a demonstration or use promotional material to get the customer involved. Remember that a presentation that works with one customer may not be effective with all clients.

5. *Suspicion, secretiveness, dishonesty.* This is one of the most important body language elements, since the salesperson needs to find out exactly what the customer is unhappy about. The customer will not always indicate verbally why he or she does not want to buy a product and by looking at the customer's body language you will be able to determine if he or she is not telling the truth about a specific subject in your presentation. The following body movements can indicate that a customer is being dishonest or lying: touching the nose, pulling the ear or covering the mouth while speaking; avoiding eye contact; gesturing incongruously; moving the body away; crossing the arms and legs; or squinting. Make sure that you are congruent in the information that you give to the customer. Remember that body language works both ways.

6. *Uncertainty, indecision, stalling.* Often salespeople will overload the customer with information. This can lead to indecision and uncertainty. Body signals that indicate this must be noticed since they could mean that the customer has some sort of objection or is not clear about the information presented. Look for the following signals: pacing back and forth; tilting the head; biting the lip; scratching the head; shifting the eyes from right to left; a look of concentration and concern; head down; and tongue in the side of the mouth. If you notice these signals, give the client time to think and formulate a response.

7. *Evaluation.* When doing the presentation the salesperson wants to ensure that the client is interested in what is said and is listening to the sales message. Signals that the customer is evaluating information or the message are: hands gripping chin; head tilted slightly; nodding (the most important signal); stroking the chin; raising the eyebrows; making good eye contact; and turning an ear towards the speaker.

8. *Confidence, honesty, cooperation.* This is the body language that all salespeople want to see when doing the sales presentation because it shows that the customer is happy with what he or she is seeing and hearing. The customer will give the following signals: open hands; sitting up in the chair; making good eye contact; making movements with hands and arms; moving the body back and forth; blinking slightly; and smiling.

The eight physical categories are an indication of how the customer can react to the sales presentation. The salesperson should keep in mind that these categories are just guidelines. For example, if the customer's arms are folded it is not always an indication that he or she is closed to new ideas or what the salesperson is saying. It could be that the client is feeling cold, so all external factors should be taken into account when evaluating a customer's body language.

Handshake

The shaking of hands is a simple action done by people on a regular basis and is the standard way of greeting people in the business world. One could go as far as to say that the handshake is the first communication with the customer. As such, the first evaluation that will be made of the salesperson will be done so on the basis of the handshake. The message given by the handshake will be determined by five factors: eye contact, degree of firmness, depth of interlock, length, and degree of dryness of the hand. In South Africa, we have a unique situation in that two groups dominate our culture, namely Western and African, and they have different methods of non-verbal communication and ways of shaking hands. The differences that will be given between Western and African culture are not set in stone, since the two cultures have influenced each other, but rather they are guidelines. The salesperson should evaluate the situation and decide on appropriate action when meeting a customer for the first time. Western handshakes are short, lasting no more than three seconds, and consist of only one movement with a firm grip. Eye contact is kept during the handshake as an indication of honesty. African handshakes are the opposite of Western handshakes. In African culture the handshake lasts much longer, the grip is soft and, as a sign of respect, no eye contact is made. In most cases it consists of more than one movement. There are two handshakes that should never be used in sales. Do not do the double handshake (using both hands) and also do not place one hand on the customer's elbow. Handshakes between people of different cultures have led to a lot of distrust and misperceptions, so the salesperson should make sure that he or she adapts to the customer's preferred way of greeting.

Spatial distance

Stand up and let your shoulder touch the shoulder of the person standing next to you. Now without moving backwards or away, turn to face the person. Notice how it feels.

Humans have certain set zones that determine how close they allow another person to get to them. These zones are determined by the social interaction with the person. This is called spatial distance. Four different spatial zones have been identified, as shown in Figure 3.3. Each of these will be discussed, together with their consequences for the salesperson.

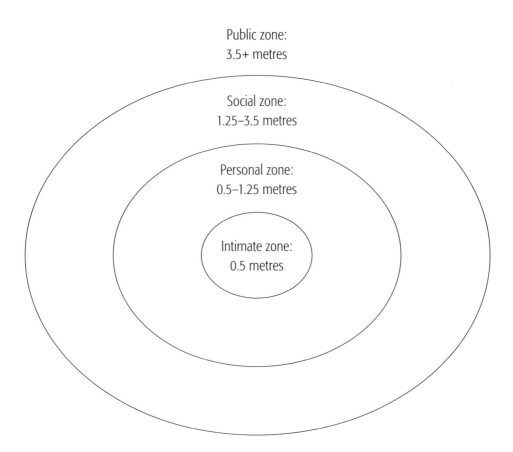

Figure 3.3 *Spatial distance*

1. The intimate zone is any area up to half a metre from the customer or closer. This zone is reserved for intimate friends and family only. Salespeople must make sure that they stay out of this zone, since any movement into this area can be seen as aggression, or can make the customer feel uncomfortable.
2. The personal zone is the area 0.5 to 1.25 metres from the customer. A person will allow close friends and associates in the personal zone. This zone can still create a feeling of distress for the customer, so the salesperson should stay clear of it if possible.
3. The social zone is the preferred area in which the salesperson must do the sales presentation. This is the area 1.25 to 3.5 metres from the customer. This zone is usually on the opposite side of the customer's desk and plays a role when the salesperson is dealing with the customer for the first time.
4. The public zone is for the general public and group settings where presentations are made. The salesperson will use this zone when dealing with more than one customer in the sales presentation.

The salesperson must keep these zones in mind when making the sales presentation. There are things that the salesperson can do to prevent customers feeling that their personal space is invaded. When sitting at the customer's desk, the preferred place is to one side of the desk, since this is a non-conflict setting and it breaks down the barriers that the desk may create. The preferred place of seating is next to the customer – this is where cooperation occurs. However, sitting next to the customer can be dangerous, since the customer's personal space can easily be invaded. Figure 3.4 shows the different seating positions that the salesperson can use.

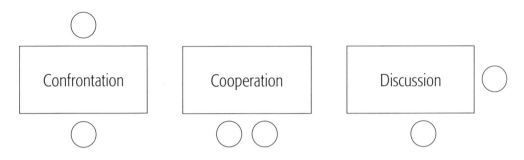

Figure 3.4 *Seating in sales calls*

When showing the customer information on any promotional material, never use your hand to point out something. Rather use a neutral object like a pen to indicate something to the customer.

The salesperson will have to make sure to obey the unwritten rules when it comes to spatial distance and how they are seated in the sales presentation.

Dress

The first evaluation that the customer will make of the salesperson is the way that he or she is dressed. Professional salespeople will always make sure that they are well groomed and taken care of physically. Dressing more formally will not just have an influence on customers but also salespeople, who will feel more confident if they are dressed appropriately. There are different things that men and women should focus on in their appearance.

Salespeople must always make sure that they adapt their hairstyles to their customers' expectations and what the organisation that they work for prescribes and expects. Saleswomen must preferably have a simple, businesslike shoulder-length hairstyle. A man's hair should not extend below the back of the neck. Facial hair in the case of men is a definite *no* and should be avoided at all costs. Of the top 100 salespeople in the United States, for example, not one has facial hair. If the salesperson does decide to grow any facial hair, he must first get the opinion of his friends and family about whether the look is professional. Shoes should always be clean since that is one of the first things people look at when they meet a person for the first time.

Women have to maintain their image by not dressing too suggestively or wearing too much makeup or jewellery. It is also important for women to have a briefcase rather than a handbag. Men should only wear necessary jewellery such as a wedding ring and watch. Earrings are a definite no for male salespeople, and women should not wear earrings that are too big. Remember the golden rule: dress according to the customer's expectations.

Selling in the global market[8]

More and more organisations are starting to do business in the global market as, due to the ever-changing economy, they have to sell internationally to survive. Here is some advice in dealing with customers in other countries.

- *Arab countries:* Do not use your left hand when shaking hands or receiving any gifts or products since the left hand is used to touch toilet paper. Handshakes are long and are more limp than in Western countries.
- *China:* It is disrespectful to talk business on the first meeting or to refuse a cup of tea – always drink the tea even if you do not want it. Colour plays an important role in Chinese culture. It is preferable to use black and white printed materials. Deals will be closed in a social setting, and more people will be involved than in a Western selling situation. Focus will be on the long-term relationship between buyer and seller. It is also essential to get to know the businessperson's family.
- *European countries:* In France, meetings should not be planned before 10 a.m. Give gifts that are made locally. Stay away from wine as a gift. In Germany, meetings are stiff and inflexible. Never call somebody by their first name unless invited to do so, and do not arrange meetings at breakfast time.
- *Central and South America:* Handshakes are lighter and longer than in the West. Time is not very important, so do not make too many appointments in a day. There will be a great deal of negotiating before a deal will be accepted.
- *Japan:* Shake hands and bow slightly towards customers. Gifts from well-known stores are preferred, and the higher the position the person holds, the better the gift should be. Never cross your legs and show the soles of your feet – this is seen as insulting.
- *Vietnam:* Never touch people and only shake hands when they extend their hand. If the person bows, also bow.
- *Asian countries:* Do not stare into somebody's eyes, as this is seen as discourteous, and in the Middle East do not ask how your customer's family is, since this is seen as too personal.

When selling in foreign countries, try to find out about the culture of the country and what behaviour is acceptable before doing any business.

WRITTEN COMMUNICATIONS

A part of non-verbal and verbal communication is any written material that the salesperson sends to the customer to get his or her message across. In the communication model the message can be any form of communication. This section will look at all the different elements of written communication.

Written communication is a way for the salesperson to introduce the product or service to the customer and it can be used as an introduction to the sales presentation. The salesperson must always remember that any written material that is sent to the customer represents the salesperson and the organisation that he or she works for. All written communication must keep general guidelines in mind. Firstly, the material represents the salesperson's organisation, therefore it must be written according to the regulations of that organisation. For example, such regulations may cover things from the way the letter is written to the colour of paper used. Secondly, make sure that the customer will not see the communication as junk mail. Prevent this by putting the customer's name on the material. Thirdly, keep the communication to the point and indicate exactly what you want or what you are informing the customer about. Fourthly and most importantly, make sure that the information in the written communication is correct, and ensure that spelling and grammar are correct. Lastly, if possible, follow up on any written communication to make sure that the customer has received the correct message. The written word is a quick and easy way to communicate with the customer. It saves the salesperson time and money.

In the following section, the elements of written communication will be looked at.

Sales letter

There are a lot of different kinds of letters. One type used in countless industries is the assumptive letter, which is based on the assumption that people reading the letter will think the salesperson is personally writing to them. The assumptive letter can basically target a group of people who have a predisposition toward something, in this case a service or product. The salesperson must make sure when mailing the letter to people that they have been showing buying interest and have a predisposition to buy something in the organisation's general line.

The sales letter can be a good communication tool and, as seen in the example below, it is short and to the point so as to keep the customer's attention. Also focus on the wording that is used and experiment with different kinds of wording in your sales letters.

Postcards

Using postcards as part of your written sales communication tool is very effective. There are several reasons for this.[9] Firstly, the postcard is already open and the customer cannot help but read it. Secondly, it creates the feeling of a personal note from someone you know, and lastly, the customer can evaluate it quickly. It is important to note that your postcards should tell the customer where they can get more information about the organisation or how they can contact you.

Example of a sales letter

It will start with an assumptive statement:

Dear [Prospect]

I know you've been contemplating [considering/reviewing/evaluating/thinking about*] buying a [such and such] or replacing [such and such] and moving up to a more advantageous position in your business or professional life.

I share the awareness of what a positive impact [what a difference/how much of an improvement/savings/enrichment*] doing that can mean to you. That's why I'm writing this letter.

I've made arrangements for you to [check out/try out/preview/acquire/purchase/sample/audition/experience*] that in either your home or office without risk or obligation. Why am I doing this? One simple reason:

In my opinion, you can't possibly know [the benefits/experience/exhilaration/enrichment/security/peace of mind/productivity*] you can bring to your life through [............ *] unless you experience it.

I don't think you should have to decide anything until you first experience for yourself how meaningful or beneficial [............ *] will be, so I want you to let me take the risk for a change. That's right!

Everybody else says: 'Buy from me. Give us your money', etc. I'm saying, do the opposite. Let me allow you to [experience, evaluate, check out, preview*] the product before you buy!

[*choose whatever you consider to be appropriate]

Email

Email is one of the most difficult written communications to use effectively. Every day most businesspeople people receive a large number of email messages, and therefore the message that the salesperson wants to convey must be clear, and the salesperson has to make sure that the customer reads the email. Do not waste the customer's time by sending unnecessary information. Only send what is required and, once again, keep it as short as possible. As in the case of any written material, edit the email to make sure that all the information is correct. Email communication and etiquette will be discussed in greater detail in Chapter 15.

Proposal

Proposals, just like sales letters, are used to propose a product or service to a client. Unlike a sales letter, a proposal is written for one specific customer, and the salesperson must gather all possible information on the customer before writing it. The information must be used to draw up a proposal that will indicate how the product or service will be of benefit to the client. In many cases the proposal will lead to a sales presentation by the salesperson, therefore it should be done professionally.

BARRIERS TO COMMUNICATION

Communication barriers influence both verbal and non-verbal communication, and the salesperson must eliminate all possible influences that can cause the communication process to break down. There are a multitude of reasons why communication can be unsuccessful with customers. Take note of the following when communicating with customers:

- When meeting customers for the first time, resist using first names, as this can be seen as disrespectful.
- Keep the customer's culture in mind and do not say or do anything that could be offensive to the customer.
- Do not talk about politics or religion.
- Do not make any distasteful jokes. Rather do not tell any jokes unless you know the customer really well.
- During the sales presentation, speak clearly and do not use too much technical jargon. If possible, use plain language that the customer will understand.
- If you have a cellphone, make sure that it is turned off during the sales presentation. Nothing can make the customer lose interest as quickly as a salesperson's cellphone ringing.
- Make sure that you are dressed according to the customer's expectations.
- Be careful about your personal hygiene.
- Determine the customer's values and present in accordance with them.

The above should be kept in mind during every step in the sales process. To overcome barriers in communication, salespeople need to determine their customer's main interest and values. Through using observations and questions salespeople can establish what is important to their customers. If they can do this successfully they will increase their chances of selling their products and services dramatically. To do this salespeople must ask questions and observe the following in their customers' surroundings:[10]

- How do they fill their space? (What is in their office – photos of family, degrees, achievement awards, etc. ?)

- How do they spend their time? (Do they work most of the time, go away on holiday with family, study, etc. ?)
- On what do they spend their energy?
- On what do they spend money?
- Where are they the most organised?
- What are they most disciplined in?
- What do they think about most of the time?
- What do they talk about most of the time?
- What inspires them the most?
- What do they set goals for?

How can salespeople use the information on a customer's' values that they gather with the above questions? What you focus on discussing in your sales presentation will be different for customers who have photos of family compared to those who have degrees and achievements all over their office. If you are dealing with customers with photos of family in their office, you might point out, if appropriate, that with your product they will save time and be with their family more. In the case where there are achievement awards you can indicate that your product will provide them with an edge in the workplace that will most probably lead to faster promotion opportunities. As seen with the examples given, by knowing their customers' interest salespeople can adapt their presentation, which will lead to greater success in selling.

Remember the three golden rules to successful communication:
1. Become genuinely interested in people.
2. Be a good listener.
3. Talk in terms of the other person's interest.

SUMMARY

The communication model gives us a clear indication of how the communication process works, from the salesperson (sender) who conveys the message (verbally and non-verbally) to the consumer (receiver) and noise (any outside distortions) that influence the effectiveness of the communication process.

When verbally communicating, salespeople must apply all available techniques to make sure that their message is heard and understood by the customer. By avoiding talking all the time, keeping quiet and listening to customers, salespeople will be able to gather all the information necessary for a successful sales call. If they listen effectively, they will be able to ask questions that will indicate that they are interested in their customers, which will build rapport with them.

Non-verbal communication can give a multitude of signs to the salesperson and can be used to evaluate people. By studying how customers use body language, salespeople will be able to understand them better and therefore sell more effectively. In the last two decades especially, there has been study of eye movement.

Understanding eye movement is an important part of evaluating customers. By becoming aware of your customer-accessing cues you will be able to adapt the sales presentation to the customer's preference, be it seeing, feeling or hearing.

Although a lot of focus in selling is placed on other elements like the selling process, prospecting and time management, if you are unable to communicate with your customers effectively, all these elements are useless. Personal selling is personal face-to-face communication, and the salesperson who is capable of persuading and informing the customer best will be the most successful at the end of the day.

CASE STUDIES

1. One of your co-workers is going on an international sales trip to introduce a newly developed microprocessor that your organisation is selling. The salesperson plans to visit about six different countries. This is the first time that the person will be selling internationally. You have been on international sales trips in the past and have dealt with several different cultures. The salesperson asks your advice on the key elements to look at when selling in other countries, so as not to offend any cultural group.
    - Make a list of the key things that the salesperson should look at in any culture.

2. Your organisation is planning to put a new watch on the market. Since you are responsible for the whole of the Gauteng region, and it will be impossible to visit all the jewellery stores in this area, you decide to use sales letters as your main method of informing possible prospects about the new watch.
    - Create a sales letter that you will send to possible prospects.

3. You have just finished your studies in Durban and have been appointed as the new sales representative of a well-known canned food organisation in KwaZulu-Natal. The majority of your customers are situated in rural areas and you sell to a wide range of outlets, from spaza shops to the well-known bigger supermarket groups. Selling in rural areas is a new experience for you since you grew up in a big city and are not used to the cultural differences and ways of doing things in rural areas. In your studies you have learnt how to sell and you apply all that you have learnt in your theoretical studies and your experiential training in Durban. However, it does not seem to help – you have lost customers that had been buying the product for several years. You hear from other salespeople that the customers see you as disrespectful although you feel that you treat

everyone with respect. Sales have dropped by about 60% and your manager calls you in to ask what is wrong and why sales have declined. You think about what could have gone wrong, and realise that your main problem is that your communication seem to be ineffective.

- What, in your opinion, is the main reason for the failure in communication? (Remember that in rural areas people tend to be more conservative.)
- What will you do to fix the problem?

4. Since 2002 Susan has been selling industrial supplies to businesses and has been doing quite well. In the last year she outsold all the other salespeople in the organisation, but last week she visited a new prospect for the first time and the sales call did not go as planned. She found the prospect intimidating. The customer gave her a choice of where she wanted to do her presentation. She decided to do it at the prospect's desk so as not to inconvenience him. The prospect's chair was set higher than hers and his desk was quite big. After the sales presentation she felt that it had not gone well at all and there was a feeling of conflict between her and the customer.

- What would you advise Susan with regard to the seating arrangements and spatial distance? How could she have overcome these problems?
- What signals can Susan look at to determine whether there is a conflict situation?
- What can Susan do about her method of communication in order to rectify any conflict or disagreement?

SELF-ASSESSMENT QUESTIONS

1. Evaluate the communication process.

2. Develop effective verbal communication strategies.

3. Compose a sales letter.

4. Judge the body language of any person that you know.

5. Identify your own personal preferred accessing cues.

6. Compile sentences that will improve your verbal communication.

DISCUSSION QUESTIONS

1. Sketch the communication model and indicate why it is important in personal selling.

2. What influence can culture have on the communication process?

3. What barriers can get in the way of communicating with your customer verbally? What can the salesperson do to overcome barriers in verbal communication?

4. When you entered the office of a new customer, the customer was seated with arms crossed and glared at you. The glare was maintained even when you started your presentation.

   - What assumption can you make based on this body posture?

   - How can you get the customer involved in the sales presentation?

5. You are a salesperson selling motor vehicles that are new to the market. Create key sentences that can be used in your sales presentation to demonstrate the effectiveness of the new vehicle.

6. You are on a sales call and while you are busy with the presentation the customer's phone rings and the personal assistant comes into the office to give the customer some documents. You realise that you have lost the customer's attention. How can you get the customer involved again and solve the problem?

7. What type of questions will you use in the following selling situations?

   - Getting to the end of a sales call (you are selling cellular phones).

   - You want a clear indication of how many shoes a retailer wants to order.

   - You are not sure how the customer deals with the reselling of the product.

8. A co-worker is using the telephone to make appointments with customers, but is unsuccessful in doing so. She comes to you for advice on what to do. What will you advise her about planning telephone calls?

9. You are selling a printer that is new on the market. The printer can print full-colour pictures and is faster that the current competitive products on the market.

   - How will you use accessing cues to determine what type of customer you are dealing with?

   - After you have determined the type of customer, how will you use your body language, words and product to demonstrate the product? Give examples for each type of customer.

10. You are visiting a new customer. When you enter the customer's office you see that there are two big chairs next to each other. How will you do your presentation? Will you move the chairs?

NOTES

1. Marks, R.B. 1997. *Personal Selling: A Relationship Approach.* (Sixth edition). New Jersey: Simon & Schuster.

2. Hall, M.L. & Johnson, C.E. 2000. Blasting away the old NLP myth about non-verbal dominance. Available at: http://neurosemantics. com/Articles/non-verbal_Communication.htm (accessed on 21 July 2003).

3. Johnson, K.L. 1993. *Selling with NLP.* London: Nicholas Brealey.

4. Futrell, C.M. 2002. *Fundamentals of Selling.* (Seventh edition). Boston: McGraw-Hill.

5. Walluca, M. 2003. Calibration and eye accessing cues. Available at: http://www.manifesto.com/ neurorotoys, calibrate.php3

6. Anon. 2000. Neurolinguistic programming. Available at: http://www.salesrepwinner_net.com/ leisure/lfads02.html

7. Gschwandtner, G. & Garnett, P. 1985. *Nonverbal Selling Power.* New Jersey: Prentice Hall.

8. Anon. 2003. Marketing communication and personal selling. Available at: http://www.swcillege. com/marketing/lamb/essentials_3e/features_archives/ch.doc

9. Leduc, B. 2003. Postcards as a sales tool. *Journal of Marketing*, 9. 3: 41.

10. Demartini, J.F. 2006. *The Heart of Love.* Carlsbad: Hay House Inc.

FURTHER READING

Burgoon, J.K., Buller, D.B. & Woodall, W.G. 1996. *Non-verbal Communication.* (Second edition). New York: McGraw-Hill.

Buskirk, R.H. & Buskirk, B.D. 1992. *Selling: Principles and Practice.* (Thirteenth edition). New York: McGraw-Hill.

Cooper, S. 1997. *Selling: Principles, Practice and Management.* London: Pitman.

Coppett, J.I. & Staples, W.A. 1994. *Professional Selling.* Cincinnati: South-Western.

Dwyer, J. 1993. *The Business Communication Handbook.* (Third edition). New York: Prentice Hall.

Faria, A.J. & Johnson, H.W. 1993. *Creative Selling.* (Fifth edition). Cincinnati: South-Western.

Green, C.L. 2003. *Selling.* Melbourne: South-Western.

Henderson, B. 1991. *Profit from Successful Selling.* Cape Town: Juta.

Hogan, K. & Horton, W. 2002. *Selling Yourself to Others.* Louisiana: Pelican.

Ingram, T.N., LaForge, R.W., Avila, R.A., Schwepker, C.H. & Williams, M.R. *Professional Selling.* Fort Worth: Harcourt College Publishers.

Jobber, D. 1997. *Selling and Sales Strategy.* Musselburg: Butterworth-Heinemann.

Jude, B. 1998. *Body Language the South African Way.* Goodwood: Zebra.

Manning, G.L. & Reece, B.L. 2001. *Selling Today*. (Eighth edition). New Jersey: Prentice Hall.

Mondy, R.W., Premeaux, S.R. & Young, J.R. 1998. *Personal Selling: Function, Theory and Practice*. (Second edition). Houston: Dame Publications.

Quigg, B. & Wisner, B. 1998. *Selling the Right Way*. New Jersey: Prentice Hall.

Rix, P., Buss, J. & Herford, G. 1999. *Selling: A Consultative Approach*. (Second edition). Sydney: McGraw-Hill.

Weitz, B.A., Castleberry, S.B. & Tanner, J.F. 2000. *Selling Building Partnerships*. (Fourth edition). Boston: McGraw-Hill Higher Education.

4

SALES KNOWLEDGE

LEARNING OUTCOMES

After studying this chapter, you should be able to:

- Discuss the reasons why a salesperson needs to have sales knowledge
- Identify the main things that the salesperson needs to know about
- Demonstrate how the salesperson can apply this knowledge in a sales call
- Discuss the sources where sales knowledge can be obtained
- Explain why technology is important

INTRODUCTION

Accuracy builds credibility
Jim Rohn

In the last few decades, sales have changed from the mass production and selling of products to the current sales strategies of forming long-term relationships with customers by customising products and services to suit them. The only way that a business can do this is to make sure that its sales force gives the correct information to the correct people at the right time. Training sales staff and making them knowledgeable can improve the quality of service that they deliver to customers. Having a well-trained sales force will not only be beneficial for the organisation but also for the salesperson, since knowledge means power, and power will lead to confidence in the selling situation. If customers realise that the salesperson knows the product, this will build trust since they will know that the salesperson will be able to advise them on the best solution to their problems or needs.

The responsibility for gaining sales knowledge is not only the organisation's but also that of the salesperson. Selling is a professional career and, as professionals, salespeople have a responsibility to themselves, their organisations and their customers to be the best they can be at what they do. Sales knowledge can be gained from a multitude of different sources, which will be discussed in this chapter. Salespeople should also acquire specific information on the organisation that they are working for, the product that they are selling, the customers, discounts, prices, their industry and competitors. They will also have to keep a database of customers so as to know exactly what they require. The advance in various technologies and the development of new computer software has improved the methods of keeping records on customers. The new developments in selling mean that in future salespeople will have to be trained and retrained in the specifics of their job. All the knowledge that they acquire can then be used in the sales of their products to make sure that they have the best solution for the customers.

Qualities of a salesperson engaged in personal selling[i]

It is very difficult to list the qualities of people engaged in personal selling as these will vary from time to time and from situation to situation. They also depend on the customers' demand and the nature of the product. Again, a salesperson may be effective in one situation but may fail in another, so in real life certain qualities may be suitable for one particular line of product and irrelevant in another. However, there are certain common qualities which all salespeople should possess in order to become successful. These are listed below:

- *Physical quality.* Salespeople should have a good appearance and an impressive personality.
- *Health.* They should also have sound health.
- *Mental quality.* Good salespeople should possess certain mental qualities like imagination, initiative, self-confidence, sharp memory, alertness, etc. They should be able to understand the needs and preferences of customers.
- *Integrity of character.* They should posses the qualities of honesty and integrity, as they need to be able to gain the confidence of their customers. They should be able to understand customers' needs and guide them on how to satisfy them. Employers too should have faith in their salespeople, who should be loyal both to their employer and to their customers.
- *Knowledge of the product and the company.* Salespeople should have full knowledge of the product and the company they are representing. They should be able to explain each and every aspect of the product, i.e. its qualities, how to use it, what precautions to take, etc. They should be able to explain the business and service record of the company, and have knowledge of products of rival companies so that they can convey the superiority of their own products.
- *Good behaviour.* If salespeople are not cooperative and courteous, they will not win the confidence of their customers, and their manner should not change

if the customer does not actually buy the product. Salespeople should not feel irritated if customers ask a lot of questions, even if they are irrelevant.

■ *Ability to persuade.* Salespeople should be good conversationalists so that they can engage the person they are dealing with in conversation. They should have the ability to sway their customers and create the desire in their mind to posses the product.

THE SALES KNOWLEDGE PROCESS

In obtaining sales knowledge it is not always clear what a salesperson will need. With the growth of specialisation it is increasingly the case that the information that is required will be specific to one industry or to just one customer. The sales knowledge process requires the salesperson to determine what knowledge is needed. The knowledge process has seven stages:[1]

1. *It has to be determined what knowledge is necessary.* The amount and type of knowledge that the salesperson requires will be determined by the organisation, the type of customer, the price, the industry and a multitude of other factors. To help determine what knowledge is needed, the goals of the organisation and the salesperson have to be evaluated. If salespeople know what the goals are for themselves and their organisation, it will be easier for them to seek out specific information.

2. *Determine the knowledge available.* The salesperson will have to determine what information about the organisation is available internally and externally. Internal information can be obtained through manuals and records, and external data from outside sources like journals and customers, and any other outside data available about the organisation.

3. *Identifying the knowledge gap.* The knowledge gap is the difference between the available knowledge and what the customer requires from the salesperson. The salesperson should take note of the knowledge gap so as to gather only the information that is required.

4. *The development of sales knowledge.* If knowledge is not available, the salesperson must undertake to gather primary information. Doing research can develop knowledge, and asking customers about different aspects of the product will give an indication of what is required. The Internet and electronic communication have improved the methods of gathering data and putting together useful information from it. The salesperson can also acquire sales knowledge by asking the organisation to do market research on the industry or on customers.

5. *The sharing of knowledge.* The sharing of knowledge is important in sales. By talking to other sales representatives in the organisation, the salesperson will acquire useful knowledge, and this in turn will help in the transfer of information between the different people involved in the sales process. Salespeople must also approach different departments

such as the research and development department and the production department, and any other personnel in the organisation who would be able to help them obtain more information about the product.

6. *Knowledge utilisation.* It is not good enough for the salesperson just to gather the information – it must be applied. The knowledge gathered must become part of the competitive selling points in the solving of customers' problems. This can provide the salesperson with a competitive advantage in the marketplace.

7. *Evaluation of the sales knowledge.* The quality and usefulness of the knowledge should be looked at on a regular basis. Evaluation can occur in various ways: firstly, by checking whether the customer is still satisfied; secondly, by doing research on whether the knowledge gained has been used in the selling situation; and lastly, by benchmarking the knowledge against other organisations and salespeople. The sales knowledge process will help the salesperson determine what information is needed, if it is still useful and if it is up to date.

SOURCES OF INFORMATION

Sales knowledge is available from a variety of different sources, each of which will supply a diverse amount of useful information. The information may come from formal sources such as organisation records and product tests, or from informal sources such as customers, newspapers or industry magazines. Good salespeople will keep track of all these sources to make sure that they keep in touch with what is going on. To be excellent in sales, it is not good enough to use just one source.

Sales training

The training of new personnel has to be the first step in any organisation. Salespeople will have to receive all the knowledge necessary for becoming successful at selling from the organisation they work for. They should not only attend and receive sales training when they start working for an organisation, but also on a continuous basis throughout their careers. Sales training must include information like what their function will be in the organisation, the history of the organisation, what the current financial situation of the organisation is, staff benefits and future plans. Since salespeople are in a unique job situation they will need specialised training. This will include things such as the organisation's policies and procedure in selling products, giving credit and discounts, and ordering products. In the current selling environment salespeople also must have basic computer skills such as how to work with spreadsheets and word-processing documents. Many organisations have computerised ordering systems and software programs that salespeople will have to learn to utilise. Sales training must be given on a regular basis. Salespeople must keep up with all the changes that take place in the organisation, especially regarding what is going on in product development and of any new products that the organisation is selling or marketing. The organisation will also have to give salespeople all information on advertising campaigns if they are likely to have an influence on the sales of the product.

Written material about products

Salespeople must study all written material about the product and must keep track of all of it in order to keep up to date. Such material can be in the form of manuals provided by the organisation or industry journals. Product manuals are one of the most useful things to study since these contain all the product specifications and uses, and can be used to identify the features, advantages and benefits of the product. Other written material such as industry journals can be used in the sales presentation as proof of the quality or effectiveness of the products.

Talking to people

Knowledge can be gained from a lot of different people in and outside the organisation. Inside the organisation the salesperson can consult with other salespeople, the production managers and the development team. The advantage of talking to these different people is that the salesperson will get first-hand knowledge of the product and how it is developed. Talking to other salespeople will give the salesperson the opportunity to determine what does and what does not work in the sales situation. One of the vital sources of information or knowledge of the product is from the customers. By asking customers specific information about the product, such as their likes and dislikes about it, the salesperson will get all the information needed to sell more effectively to other customers.

Knowing the organisation

The salesperson is the link between the customer and the organisation, and therefore must know exactly what is happening internally since this will influence the customer directly or indirectly. To be effective at the job the salesperson needs the following information:

- *Organisational procedures and policy.* Each organisation has it own way of doing business. Some of the policies the salesperson will have to deal with include credit policies, delivery policies and order-taking methods. Organisations have different methods of giving credit, which include things such as the period of credit, payment and the amount that can be given on credit. Salespeople have to know about the organisation's pricing methods, discounts that can be given to customers and the type of discounts. They must also be able to inform customers about the delivery of the product and how it will take place, and make sure that the correct documentation is filled in, e.g. delivery notices or invoices.
- *Organisation.* As stated before, the salesperson must have basic knowledge on the following aspects of the organisation: management structure, history, financial standing,

size and position in the industry. The salesperson has to be able to tell customers where the organisation comes from and where it is heading. If the salesperson can talk about the organisation's achievements and growth, this will improve the chances of customers buying from the organisation, and help them evaluate not only the product but also the reliability of the organisation.

- *Production of the product.* In the current selling environment the production process is vital. Customers are· demanding more and more customised products and services. It is therefore important for the salesperson to know each step in the production process. With this information the salesperson will be able to tell the customer two things: firstly, exactly how the product is made, and secondly, whether it can be modified according to the customer's requirements.
- *Service facilities.* The delivery or availability of service facilities has become a part of the added value of sales in many organisations. The salesperson must know what services are available to the customer after the product has been purchased. Customers might want to know if the organisation has an after-sales service department or if after-sales training is available to their employees. The salesperson should also be able to tell customers how the after-sales service works and how they can make use of it.
- *Promotional programmes.* Personal selling falls within the promotional activities of the organisation, but the salesperson must be aware of all the other promotional activities inside the organisation in order to be able to use them effectively in the sale of the product. (This will be looked at under communication knowledge). Organisational knowledge will give the salesperson the necessary background to inform, make choices and deliver service of the highest standard to the customer.

KNOW THE CUSTOMER

To obtain information on customers is one of the most difficult things for a salesperson to do. It important for salespeople to ascertain who makes the buying decisions in an organisation, and this is why they must set up a profile of the customer. The salesperson should have or collect the following information on the customer:

- *Contact details of the customer.* This includes things such as physical address, telephone numbers and email address. Salespeople who deal with more than one customer per day must make sure that they have all the correct details of all their clients.
- *Type of customer.* Salespeople have to determine what their customers are going to use the product for. Will they use it to produce a new product, or are they going to resell it to another customer? The salesperson has to determine this in order to make sure that the right product is sold to the customer.
- *Reselling of product.* Salespeople should find out who constitutes their customers' market in order to find solutions for them more readily.

- *Amount that the customer buys.* The salesperson should ask the following questions: How much of the product does the customer need? How frequently and in what amounts and sizes does the customer buy? This information will help the salesperson determine how much time to spend on a customer's account and what type of deal to structure.
- *Organisation policies and procedures.* The customer's credit rating should be looked at by the salesperson to make sure that the necessary funds are available to purchase the product or service. The salesperson has to evaluate the structure of the customer's organisation in order to find out who the buyers and decision makers are. Customers' organisational policies may differ in the purchasing of products, and the salesperson must keep within the requirements.
- *The customer's past and future.* Records should be kept on the customer's organisation to show how it has reacted at various times: this will give a clear indication of how the organisation will behave when making a buying decision, and will extend the service given to the customer. The salesperson must also keep track of what the customer will do in the future in order to determine the customer's possible actions.

In dealing with individual customers, the salesperson should keep detailed records on personal information. To improve relations and build rapport with the customer, the salesperson must obtain the following information on every customer: name, address and telephone numbers, family status, important dates, education, hobbies, recreational interests, likes and dislikes. Although not all this information will be used, it is useful as a background when dealing with a customer.

Customer information can be gathered in different ways by the salesperson. The salesperson should observe, listen and ask questions. By looking around and by reading the magazines and journals that deal with a possible market one can find information on the customer. Information can also be obtained by networking with other salespeople who have sold to the customer and by the use of technology such as databases or the Internet.

In Chapter 6 (prospecting), more methods of obtaining customers will be discussed. These methods also can help in gathering information.

KNOW YOUR PRODUCT

To be able to sell your product successfully you must have confidence in what you are saying to the customer about your product. The only way to build confidence is to have knowledge about your product or service. The level of knowledge that salespeople will need to have is determined by the complexity of the product being sold. They should know everything possible about the product in order to answer any questions that the customers might have about it.

As a salesperson, you should firstly know the features, advantages and benefits of the product. This is important so that you can differentiate your product from that of competitors. Evidence about the features and benefits of the product can be given in the following ways:[2]

- *Expertise.* You should refer to the opinion of an expert on the product, or you can qualify yourself as an expert by attending courses.
- *Numerical data.* If you have numerical data, you can use it to prove the effectiveness of your product. Just make sure that you keep up to date with the newest developments.
- *Test.* If possible, test your product to find out how it works for you.
- *Guarantee.* If a guarantee is given, it could be an indication of quality. Make sure that you go through the guarantee in detail with the customer.
- *Case histories.* By indicating to your customers how other organisations have used the product, you can show how it can be useful to them. In a lot of cases the customer will be able to relate to what has happened to the other organisations.
- *Testimonials.* In many cases you will have proof from other customers that have used the product. The customer then will be able to contact them to find out of the product really works that well.

Secondly, you should know the performance data of the product and how it operates. If you are in a sales situation and the customer wants a demonstration, you must be able to do it. You should also know all about the accessories that might be sold with the product.

Thirdly, you should know about the physical characteristics and size of the product. Basic information on the product such as the available colours and different sizes it comes in is important to know.

Lastly, you must know how the product is selling in the marketplace. This is essential for resellers such as retailers and wholesalers. Such customers want to know if they will be able to sell the product to their customers.

COMMUNICATION MIX

As stated earlier, personal selling is part of the organisation's communication process. The salesperson should be conscious of the other methods of promoting that the organisation is using since this can have an influence on the sales of the product. In many cases, personal selling and the other elements in the communication mix are combined to improve the efforts of selling the product. In many situations, advertising or sales promotion is used to create a demand for a product, which makes it easier for the salesperson to sell it to retailers and wholesalers. The integrated communication mix has seven elements:[3]

1. *Advertising* refers to any paid-for, non-personal communication about a product or service.
2. *Direct marketing* occurs when the organisation communicates directly with the customer to get a response.
3. *The Internet* is used for direct interactive communication with the customer.
4. *Sales promotion* is marketing activities that provide extra incentives to the sales force, the distributors or the consumer, its aim being to stimulate immediate response.

5. *Publicity* is non-personal information about the organisation, although the organisation will probably spend money on it and it is carried out by an identifiable sponsor.
6. *Public relations* is aimed at changing customer attitude, and garnering understanding and acceptance from the public.
7. *Personal selling* is face-to-face selling to inform or persuade the customer to purchase the product or service.

Salespeople must have knowledge of all the different communication elements, as this can help improve sales. If customers have any enquiries about information they have gathered from another communication mix element, the salesperson must be able to comment on it. The organisation may ask salespeople to focus on selling one specific product if it is running a big advertising campaign. One element the salesperson must be especially knowledgeable on is sales promotions. To increase retail or wholesale sales the salesperson can make use of point-of-purchase material such as banners or premiums where the consumer is given an article as an incentive to buy. The salesperson must also make sure that all products get good shelf space. This should be at eye level since this is the best position for display. Knowing a fact like this will give the salesperson the edge when selling.

KNOW YOUR PRICE AND DISCOUNT

Price is the value or the worth of a product that the consumer is willing to exchange money for. Salespeople can use various methods to set the price for a product or service. In many cases they will have the freedom to do so if the organisation does not stipulate one, as long as they stay within a certain mark-up on the product. Organisations and industries differ in their distribution channels, promotional allowances, return on investments, retail or wholesale set-up, etc. that must be dealt with, therefore salespeople should establish as quickly as possible how the mark-up policy works in their company. (As there are many differences in industries and organisations, mark-up will not be discussed in this textbook.)

Sales discounts are also given by organisations to tempt customers to buy the product. These are usually developed by the organisation and then given to the salesperson to use in sales calls. Salespeople should familiarise themselves with the organisation's discounts and credit policies in order to gain a competitive advantage in the market. The following types of discounts can be used by the organisation:[4]

- *Cash discounts.* The consumer receives a deduction in the price if the product is paid for in cash, or if payment occurs within a certain time, usually 30 days.
- *Quantity discount.* This is a price reduction for consumers who buy large volumes. If consumers buy a certain amount they get a discount.
- *Functional discounts.* These are given to channel members in return for certain services, such as selling or storing the products.

- *Seasonal discounts.* These are given at certain times of the year when the demand for a product or service is not high.
- *Allowances.* If customers turn in an old product for a new one, they get an amount of money back.

The different discounts can be used by the salesperson to improve sales and maintain customer satisfaction.

KNOW YOUR COMPETITORS

If salespeople know the strengths and weaknesses of the competitor's products, it will be easier to position their products in the market. It is the responsibility of the salespeople to acquire all the necessary information on competitors in order to deal with any enquiries from customers about their products in comparison to those of their competitors. There are guidelines that can be used in dealing with competitors in the sales presentation:[5]

- Never refer to or talk about the competition in your sales presentation. This will only place focus on your competitors.
- Do not discuss the competition unless you have accurate details. If you comment on the competition and you make an incorrect claim, it can harm your credibility.
- Steer clear of criticising the competition. If you get emotional the customer might become suspicious of your reactions.

The salesperson must keep up with the changes in competitors' products and services. Information on competitors can be gathered by reading trade journals, evaluating promotional activities or using technology like the Internet.

KNOW THE ECONOMY AND INDUSTRY

To become knowledgeable about an industry or the economy is easy. It will demand time and incentive from the salesperson to gather and evaluate all available material. Knowledge about the newest trends can lead to the identification of prospects and improve the satisfaction of current customers. Salespeople can get information from reading trade journals or magazines, or by talking to experts from a specific industry. They can get news from television, radio and the daily newspapers. If salespeople keep track of the newest developments in these areas it will indicate to their customers that they are a professional who keeps track of what is going on. Salespeople must schedule a few hours every day to read material that is not directly related to their specific industry in order to get a broader view of what is currently happening.

KNOWLEDGE OF TECHNOLOGY

Part of the training of salespeople must include the newest technology available on the market. To stay ahead in today's competitive marketplace those that deliver the fastest and best-quality service will be the most successful. They must learn how to use personal computers, laptops, the Internet, cellphones and email. New technology has improved different aspects of sales: the way that salespeople manage themselves and their time, and the way they stay in contact with the organisation and customers. Owing to the increase in customers' demand for time and personalised attention, technology has become an integral part of the salesperson's life.

Salespeople should have some knowledge of certain aspects of the new technology that is available. There are a large number of programs on the market that show salespeople how to manage their time and their contact with customers, most of which have step-by-step guidelines for users. The salesperson should also know at least one word-processing program and one spreadsheet program. There is a multitude of such programs available, and there are many training courses and books available on the different products on the market.

KNOWLEDGE OF SELF

Sales is one of the most performance-driven jobs in the marketplace. Sales are the lifeblood of any organisation, so it is important for salespeople to be at the top of their job. To stay ahead and perform at optimal levels, salespeople should acquire knowledge about the way they motivate, educate and improve themselves. There are seven principles of self-knowledge that salespeople should look at. If they apply the principles not only will it improve their career, but they will also be able to help customers more effectively.

The seven principles are as follows:

1. *For your sales knowledge to improve, you need to improve.* Knowledge will not acquire you; you need to acquire it. You will have to make sure that you grow in your job. You will have to constantly stay on track to acquire sales knowledge. It is advisable not just to take courses presented by the organisation that you work for, but also other non-organisational courses to improve your overall knowledge.

2. *It does not matter what your past sales experience is; all that matters is your future sales.* Salespeople tend to become discouraged, especially if they move from one organisation or industry to another. It can also happen that the salesperson has had a few sales that were not successful. You must never let past sales influence your future sales: you should focus on the future.

3. *There is no failure, only feedback.* One of the best places to gain sales knowledge is in unsuccessful sales calls. Salespeople should not blame themselves if the sales call is not successful, but rather study the call and see where there is room for improvement and what should be learned to make sure that they do not make the same mistakes again.

4. *You are only as free as your options.* Have you limited yourself to the knowledge that your company provides or are you creating more options? Salespeople make the mistake of focusing only on the manuals and training that they receive from the organisation they work for. Good salespeople will also acquire knowledge from other sources to make

sure of getting a broader view of the product that they are selling and how it fits into the marketplace. Self-development must be a priority. As stated at the beginning of this chapter, salespeople that have knowledge will be confident, and confidence will lead to trust between them and the consumer.

5. *In every 'unsuccessful' sale there is a greater or equal benefit.* You will receive the benefit of knowing what still needs to be learned if you fail in a sale.

6. *You can learn anything you need to learn to get what you want.* The best proof that something can be done is that someone else has done it before you. People's tendency to say that they are not knowledgeable enough to succeed in sales is not true. In any industry there are salespersons that have succeeded before and it is also possible for you. Sales knowledge is available in books, or you can ask other salespeople who also sell in your industry for advice.

7. *Your mind creates the limits to your sales.* If you do what successful salespeople do, you will enjoy the same results. If you don't, you won't. If there is one place where you must build self-knowledge, it is in running your own mind. If you are not in control of your thinking it means that you will allow your outside environment to run it for you. Therefore you must ask the following question: *What would my sales be like if my mind was full of courage, determination, flexibility and confidence?*

Self-knowledge is often neglected by salespeople. They believe there is no time for self-development or self-improvement, but nothing is further from the truth, since if they know themselves and their capabilities they will do well in sales.

REMEMBERING WHAT YOU KNOW

Would you buy a product from someone who remembers the details of the product or from a salesperson who first has to look the details up in a manual or brochure? A salesperson who is knowledgeable about all aspects of the product will be more trustworthy and look more professional. Table 4.1 gives an indication of how much information is lost by the salesperson after a sales training course. Think of the amount of money that the organisation will lose because of information that is not remembered.[6] Salespeople must develop methods to remember what they have learnt.

Table 4.1 *Spitzer experiment*

After	Percentage remembered	Money lost from every "training rand"[7]
1 day	54%	46c
7 days	35%	65c
14 days	21%	79c
21 days	19%	81c
28 days	18%	82c

For example, you should keep a record of all articles about your product so that you can refer to them in the future. One way of remembering is to make the information more memorable by using a technique and studying it. One method that can be used is the SEAHORSE technique.[8] This is an acronym for 'senses, exaggeration, action, humour, order, rehearse, specify and enjoy':

- *Senses* are the first important thing that you must use to remember information. To make boring information more interesting you must be fully involved in the learning process.
- *Exaggeration* of the product's functions will make it easy to remember what the functions are.
- *Action.* You should try to imagine how the product works, or that you are in a sales situation demonstrating it to the client.
- *Humour.* Do not take the learning process too seriously. This will make you tense, and limit your ability to take in information.
- *Order* your information so as not to mix up different ideas or concepts. In many cases you will have to sell products that are closely related. Keep your facts in order and do not mix them up.
- *Rehearse* the different ways that you can demonstrate the product and how you will use the information in your sales presentation.
- *Specify* the advantages, features and benefits of your product. If you only remember the main points of these three aspects, it will already limit the amount of information that you need to remember.
- *Enjoy* the process of gaining sales knowledge and know that what you have learnt will enable you to become a better salesperson.

In today's age of more and more information it is not easy to keep track of everything. Thanks to advancements in technology, it is becoming easier for salespeople to keep track of information, but it is still a confidence builder if they do not have to rely on too much technology to remember facts in a sales presentation.

SUMMARY

Sales knowledge is not just the information that the salesperson gathers, but also the skills that are obtained in day-to-day dealings in the sales environment. To make sure that all the information that is needed is acquired, it is necessary to go through the seven stages of the sales knowledge process: determining what knowledge is necessary, finding out what knowledge is available, identifying the knowledge gap, developing knowledge, sharing knowledge, using knowledge and evaluating the knowledge.

Sources of information should be readily available to the salesperson from talking to people inside the organisation and to people outside it, such as customers. Training is something that must be taken seriously in the acquisition of knowledge since training will give the salesperson all the skills needed to do the sales job. Professional salespeople will also keep records of all the written material on their industry and product to know what the newest developments are. By keeping records on customers, the salesperson will know the customers and what they need.

Information on how the customer buys and who makes the buying decision in an organisation can help a salesperson develop a selling strategy that is especially designed for a customer.

All the aspects of the product's function, performance and warranties should be closely studied by the salesperson so as to make sure that the right information is conveyed to the customer. Sales are part of the communication mix, and different elements of this mix will influence each other. Pricing and discounts that can be given will make a difference in convincing the customer to purchase one's product.

In the market, there will be competition. The successful salesperson will be the one who knows how the competitors think and work. Self-development and knowledge of oneself will build confidence. Being able to recall information easily and knowing what to expect from yourself will make you a better salesperson.

CASE STUDY 1

You have been employed by a big pharmaceutical organisation in the last two weeks. Although you have been in sales all your life, this is the first time you will be selling pharmaceutical products. You used to sell home appliances and you were expected to know all the different brands and models that were available on the market. On the day you started your new job, the organisation gave you all the material and manuals you needed on the products and a day-long training course on the organisation's history, and current and future plans. You studied all the manuals and made your first appointment to see a pharmacist to demonstrate the products you were selling. The sales call did not go as planned. The customer asked you questions on specific interactions between certain medications. None of the journals or manuals had any of this information.

- What are you going to do to solve this problem now and in the future?
- Where specifically will you look for sales knowledge?
- The organisation that you are working for sends you a questionnaire on how it can improve training. What will your answer be?

CASE STUDY 2

John has been working in the production industry, selling drill bits to medium- sized and large organisations. He has been the top sales representative in his organisation for five years in a row. He feels that he is not just good at knowing his products but that he also has a well-balanced knowledge of all the other elements that may influence his market and customers. This is why he also reads an engineering magazine that is not related to his field of production. He is approached by his organisation to develop a training plan for five new sales representatives. The background to John's organisation is as follows: it has been in business for 20 years, selling 70 different types of products ranging from drill bits to oil used in the production of foodstuffs. The organisation prides itself on the fact that it has salespeople that know about everything that is going on in the organisation and that they deliver good service.

- How should John do the training?
- What will he focus on in the training of the new sales staff?
- How can he help the sales representatives remember the information better?
- John knows that to be a good salesperson one must not just have knowledge about the product and organisation, but also about oneself. What advice can John give his trainees about self-knowledge and why it is important?

SELF-ASSESSMENT QUESTIONS

1. Why is sales knowledge important for salespersons?

2. Evaluate what you know about different industries.

3. How can you use the SEAHORSE principle in your educational growth?

4. Evaluate your own skills with regard to self-knowledge.

5. Talk to someone in your own field and find out what extra knowledge you can gain.

6. What can you do to improve your sales knowledge?

DISCUSSION QUESTIONS

1. You are on a sales call. The customer gives you a list of everything he requires of the product that he might buy from your organisation. When you read through the requirements you realise that your competitor's product is exactly what the customer is looking for. If you can get this sale it will mean that you will receive a large bonus at the end of the month. What would you do in a situation like this?

2. The organisation which Susan is working for sells its products at R190 each to its consumers. The organisation takes a 35% mark-up on the product, of which Susan receives 10%. How much money will Susan make out of the transaction?

3. List the top five types of knowledge you should have for each of the following organisations:
    - A clothing organisation
    - A pharmaceutical organisation
    - An organisation in the motor vehicle industry

4. Choose any industry. Find a magazine or advertisement that deals with this industry and evaluate it. What information can you obtain from this source (numerical data, test results, guarantees, etc.)? Write down this information and show how you will use it in a sales presentation.

5. Why is advertising important for selling?

6. What will be the best communication elements to use in sales?

7. How can you really acquire sales knowledge and how will you remember all the information?

8. What type of discount is each of the following?
    - The customer receives a money discount for buying more than 100 lawnmowers at a time.
    - The customer has paid back the money owed within 30 days and receives a 5% discount.

9. You are selling clothes for a clothing manufacturer. The manager wants to determine what information he needs to gather to improve your knowledge. What sources would you advise him to get?

10. John has been in sales for the last 20 years and a lot has changed. Although he is well informed about the various products, his sales have been declining. John does not believe in new technology and says that paper works just as well as computers.
    - How will you persuade John to use technology?
    - What technology will be important for John to start using and how can he acquire knowledge of the various technologies?

NOTES

1. Beijers, R.P. 2000. Knowledge management in small and medium-sized companies. *Journal of Knowledge Management*, 4(2):162–179.
2. Green, C.L. 2003. *Selling.* Melbourne: Mason South-Western.
3. Belch, G.E. & Belch, M.A. 2001. *Advertising and Promotion.* (Fifth edition). Boston: McGraw-Hill.
4. Kotler, P. 1997. *Marketing Management.* (Ninth edition). New Jersey: Prentice Hall.

5. Manning, G.L. & Reece, B.L. 2001. *Selling Today.* (Eighth edition). New Jersey: Prentice Hall.

6. Pauk, W. 2000. How to build a strong memory. Available at: http://www.cecs.csulb.edu/rallison/pdf/How_to_Build_a_Strong_Memory.pdf

7. Horsley, K. 2010. *Presentation: Enhance Your Brain for a Change.* Pretoria: KJ Horsley.

8. Horsley, K. 2003. *Introduction to Memory Technologies.* Pretoria: KJ Horsley.

i   http://www.nos.org/Secbuscour/22.pdf (accessed on 2 April 2010).

FURTHER READING

Burgoon, J.K., Buller, D.B. & Woodall, W.G. 1996. *Non-verbal Communication.* (Second edition). New York: McGraw-Hill.

Buskirk, R.H. & Buskirk, B.D. 1992. *Selling: Principles and Practice.* (Thirteenth edition). New York: McGraw-Hill.

Cooper, S. 1997. *Selling: Principles, Practice and Management.* London: Pitman.

Coppett, J.I. & Staples, W.A. 1994. *Professional Selling.* Cincinnati: South-Western.

Dwyer, J. 1993. *The Business Communication Handbook.* (Third edition). New York: Prentice Hall.

Faria, A.J. & Johnson, H.W. 1993. *Creative Selling.* (Fifth edition). Cincinnati: South-Western.

Green, C.L. 2003. *Selling.* Melbourne: Mason South-Western.

Henderson, B. 1991. *Profit from Successful Selling.* Cape Town: Juta.

Hogan, K. & Horton, W. 2002. *Selling Yourself to Others.* Louisiana: Pelican.

Ingram, T.N., LaForge, R.W., Avila, R.A., Schwepker, C.H. & Williams, M.R. *Professional Selling.* Fort Worth: Harcourt College Publishers.

Jobber, D. 1997. *Selling and Sales Strategy.* Musselburg: Butterworth-Heinemann.

Jude, B. 1998. *Body Language the South African Way.* Goodwood: Zebra.

Manning, G.L. & Reece, B.L. 2001. *Selling Today.* (Eighth edition). New Jersey: Prentice Hall.

Mondy, R.W., Premeax, S.R. & Young, J.R. 1998. *Personal Selling: Function, Theory and Practice.* (Second edition). Houston: Dame Publications.

Quigg, B. & Wisner, B. 1998. *Selling the Right Way.* New Jersey: Prentice Hall.

Rix, P., Buss, J. & Herford, G. 1999. *Selling: A Consultative Approach.* (Second edition). Sydney: McGraw-Hill.

Weitz, B.A., Castleberry, S.B. & Tanner, J.F. 2000. *Selling Building Partnerships.* (Fourth edition). Boston: McGraw-Hill Higher Education.

5

MANAGING YOURSELF AND YOUR TIME

SPECIFIC OBJECTIVES TO BE ACHIEVED

This chapter introduces you to self-management, which is a four-dimensional process that consists of time management, territory management, record management and stress management.

LEARNING OUTCOMES

After studying this chapter, you should be able to:

- Explain why self-management is important
- Explain the importance of goals
- Apply the guidelines to set effective goals
- Distinguish between performance goals, activity goals and conversion goals
- Demonstrate the five dimensions of time management
- Explain the five activities that require analysis in time management
- Explain the methods used to save time
- Demonstrate territory design by making a classification of customers, doing a break-even analysis, and routing visit plans
- Identify the reasons for stress
- Discuss stress management

INTRODUCTION

Selling is a 24-hour job. This does not imply that sales representatives spend 24 hours a day working but that they are constantly aware of their job and they must be open to opportunities that may assist them to do it. To achieve top performance requires that sales representatives must be able to manage themselves.[1] The fact that salespeople work independently of supervision most of the time makes self-management an important aspect of their life, and they must plan their personal life in such a way that it integrates with the selling job, which requires organisation.[2]

Time is a valuable resource because, like gold, it is in limited supply. Once lost, it cannot be reclaimed, and it is this that makes self-management so important. To be a successful salesperson the sales representative must make every hour count. Salespeople, by the nature of their job, are managers too. In building partnerships with their clients they must manage themselves (their career) and their territory, schedule their time, keep their own records, practise self-discipline, analyse their own performances, and know how to manage stress.

The development of information technology, especially the accessibility of computers, means that the organisation's activities are now linked up through the intranet and the Internet, and employees have to manage themselves. Information technology enables employees to do their job from any place as long as they have access to a computer and a cellphone.[3] Sales representatives are in a unique position when it comes to self-management, especially time management, because they function independently and have no fixed structure, unlike those who work in an office. They have to create this structure for themselves and therefore their attitude towards their work and themselves is very important when it comes to self-management.

Sales force automation (SFA) is one of many reasons why self-management has become important. Technology is transforming the very nature of how we do business.[4] By means of the cellphone, the customer can reach the salesperson at any time and at any place. The salesperson of today has to deal with 'virtual time' due to the use of such electronic communication technology. 'Virtual time' is time that is created by the technology; it is real for practical purposes but cannot be quantified. The salesperson must be able to manage this 'time-consuming' situation.

In this chapter, self-management in selling will be discussed as a process that includes time management, territory management, records management and stress management. Self-management involves the setting of objectives, the utilisation of resources, namely time, and making the most of other resources such as their clients and their abilities.

SETTING SALES GOALS AND OBJECTIVES
The importance of goals

Sales representatives must have sales goals to give themselves direction in self-management. These must reflect their personal ambitions and wants, and they must be set, otherwise energy and time are wasted, which leads to poor performance.[5] Career goal setting can be used effectively as a time-management tool to aid in organisational goal setting and planning.

The defining, description or identification of goals implies that the salesperson is focused, knows where he or she wants to go and how to get there, and has the self-discipline to take action to do so. By focusing, the sales representative creates a personal mission and vision, and sets the objectives he or she wants to reach in life. Self-management requires self-discipline. The goals help the salesperson to apply self-discipline, make self-management easier, and provide a target to aim at, i.e. they give meaning and direction, and supply a yardstick against which to measure what progress has been made. Goals lead to happiness and fulfilment.[6]

The following guidelines must be followed to set effective goals:[7]

- They must be realistic and reachable, and must provide challenges.
- They must be measurable and serve as a form of feedback to help identify progress.
- They must be written down so that the salesperson does not forget them, and this helps him or her to think about each one.
- They should be prioritised so that tasks can be accomplished according to their importance.
- They should be evaluated.

Next, the type of goals that sales representatives set will be briefly discussed, because this is part of self-management.

Types of goals

Sales representatives must write down their goals before they are ready to start selling. There are 12 categories of goals, namely family goals, health goals, fitness goals, personal development goals, travelling goals, material goals, financial goals, productivity goals, career goals, emotional goals, social goals and spiritual goals. To assist themselves in setting these goals, sales representatives can use a computer.

The goals can be divided into three categories, namely performance goals, activity goals and conversion goals. This will be briefly discussed below.[8]

- *Performance goals* are those that relate to outcomes. These goals are set first because attaining certain performance levels is of primary importance to both the sales representative and the organisation. They are mostly quantifiable because outcomes such as bonus cheques, number of products sold or commission received are always measured in units. These goals should be specific, challenging and time based.
- *Activity goals* are behavioural objectives such as the number of calls made in a day, the number of presentations done, and so on. They reflect how hard the sales representative intends to work. Activity goals are intermediate goals: if achieved, they are translated into performance goals. Activity and performance goals are not enough, and therefore sales representatives also need to set conversion goals.

- *Conversion goals* are measures of a sales representative's efficiency. They reflect how efficiently or smartly the sales representative would like to work. For example, such goals may set the number of sales to be made relative to the number of calls – the higher the ratio, the more efficient the sales representative. They also indicate how efficiently the sales representative spends time in order to accomplish performance goals. Working harder would reflect in an increase in activity; working more smartly should be reflected in conversion goals.

Goal setting means that the salesperson must focus. When focused, salespeople know where they are and where they are going. Salespeople must set goals because:[9]
- It gives them a target to aim at
- It gives them direction
- It gives them something to measure progress against
- It leads to happiness, contentment and fulfilment

The goals must be written down and prioritised, and they must also be carried around mentally. They must be translated into action plans so that they can be attained. They must be specific, measurable, attainable and relevant, and they must have time frames. To be successful in the execution of the sales task, each sales representative must set sales call objectives. Although the sale is the ultimate objective, it is not the objective for every call because other objectives are for sales representatives to introduce themselves, to leave literature and samples, or to get information from the client. These are objectives that lay the groundwork for future calls.[10]

Without goals and objectives, sales representatives will not be able to measure their progress. Goals and objectives must be managed and time based. When sales representatives are using quotas, objectives must be set, otherwise they will not know if they have reached the set quota. This implies that sales representatives must manage their time because time management is part of the self-management process.

TIME MANAGEMENT
Introduction
Time is the core of selling and is one of the most valuable commodities in personal selling. It is a valuable resource because it is in limited supply. Once lost it cannot be reclaimed, and this is what makes time management so important. The sales representative must be an excellent time manager. Appointments must be made so as to utilise the available time, and the sales representative must avoid spending time in waiting rooms. To save time the sales representative must use a cellphone to confirm appointments while driving from one client to another.[11]

Time is also important to the clients and consumers, and they are beginning to insist more and more on the availability of products and services after normal working hours.

Consumers now have multiple options available for purchasing and doing business: they can use the telephone, the Internet and interactive television. These multiple options influence salespeople's time management.[12]

Sales representatives have a great need to manage their time because selling requires a lot of self-motivation and self-discipline. The objective of time management is to utilise the available time productively. If the sales representative manages time efficiently and effectively, it leads to profitability because less time is spent on low-profit-margin calls. The additional time generated can be utilised to visit prospects. Electronic technology such as a laptop enables sales representatives to spend less time with their clients. Up to one day's sales time a week is gained by using such technology.[13]

Time management have five dimensions, namely (1) setting goals; (2) analysis; (3) planning; (4) practising; and (5) follow-up.[14] These five dimensions are interwoven; especially as regards time and territory, but they will be separated for the purposes of this discussion. Before sales representatives can carry out their plans, they must commit themselves to changing their approach to time management, which can only happen if they have the urge to be successful.

Setting goals

The core of setting goals in time management is the ability of the sales representative to identify and control activities and events that waste time, such as telephone interruptions; unscheduled visits; lack of self-discipline; crises; meetings; lack of objectives, priorities and deadlines; indecision and procrastination; attempting too much at once; leaving tasks unfinished; and unclear communication. To manage timewasters, salespeople must set sales goals that also provide some means to achieve personal career objectives. Goals are guidelines for sales representatives to ensure that they know they are on the right track and that they are keeping within the time frame they have set for themselves. Goal formulation requires sales representatives to have clarity about what they want to achieve. They must set their personal goals, career goals and sales call goals because they provide guidelines that help them to decide which activities to carry out, when to carry them out, whom to call on and how to sell.[15]

Analysis

Sales representatives should analyse how they currently spend their time. The goals they have set serve as guidelines to analyse the time spent on each one. To be able to make proper analyses, the sales representatives must record each activity on a time log sheet every day for one month, using a laptop. At the end of the month the sales representative analyses the sheets, which will give a good indication of how the time for that month was spent.[16] This information is then used to do future planning.

It is important to remember that sales results depend on the utilisation of time. The sales representative must establish which part of time in a workday is the most valuable. In some cases the morning and afternoon are the best time for appointments, while lunchtime is the worst, but the opposite can also be true. The sales representative can also establish which hours, days, weeks and seasons are the most productive time, which can only be done by an analysis of how time is being spent. [17]

The planned time versus the actual time spent is recorded, and those activities on which more time is spent than had been planned for must be identified, so that the situation can be rectified. With this information in hand, sales representatives can start to plan the future utilisation of their time. For sales representatives to plan time they must make a written and not a mental list of all activities. This is a somewhat complicated process. Joseph Trickett developed such an activity analysis in the 1960s. [18] He identifies five activities that require analysis, namely:

1. A list of activities that are part of the selling job, such as:
   - Talking to a new prospect
   - Checking secondary sources for new leads
   - Checking that orders have been executed
   - Contacting customers to ensure that they are satisfied
   - Planning the route
   - Preparing sales presentations
   - Handling paperwork
   - Contacting the supervisor and the office
   - Travelling
   - Reading literature
2. Activity analysis for communication
   - People I must talk to every day. List of names and telephone numbers
   - People I must talk to frequently. List of names and telephone numbers
   - People I must talk to regularly. List of names and telephone numbers
   - People I must talk to infrequently. List of names and telephone numbers
3. Activity analysis for intrinsic importance
   - Activities that are important and must be done
   - Activities that are important and should be done
   - Activities that are not so important, but are useful to do
   - Activities that are unimportant and can be eliminated
4. Activity analysis for urgency
   - Very urgent; must be done now
   - Urgent; should be done soon
   - Not urgent; can be done at a later time and period
   - Time is not a factor
5. Activity analysis for delegation
   - Must be done by me
   - Delegate to ...

Because the task of the sales representative is interaction with the clients, the pattern of time spent on a working day's tasks is analysed to establish what percentage of the time spent was active time and which part was passive. Passive time is time that salespeople spend by themselves, such as travelling and waiting time. Active time is time that they spend on interaction with clients. This must be kept in mind when doing the planning.

Planning

The sales representative's aim with regard to future planning must be to spend as much time as possible on activities that help to reach goals. Sales representatives tend to think about the present and not about the future when they do their planning. When they do think about the future they think about those broader long-term goals that are normally the activities that pay the best. To think into the future is the basis of planning. If time planning is inefficient, the sales representative experiences problems such as waste of effort, waste of time, deadlines not reached and frustrations. Planning ahead helps to avoid these problems. [19]

By establishing how many selling days are available in a certain year, the sales representative can calculate the available selling time. This is important for planning ahead. The sales representative must remember that there are only so many hours in one day and so many days, weeks and months in a sales career, and therefore tomorrow's sales calls must be planned today, and next season's sales calls must be planned this season in order to get the full benefit of them. [20]

It is important that sales representatives plan for the future in order to fully utilise the selling time available to carry out the activities through which they will reach their goals.

Practising

Seeing that each day has a limited numbers of hours, the starting point of planning is the calendar, where each day is divided into time slots of 15 or 30 minutes. Each day should have a definite starting time and a tentative stopping time. The most important calls must be scheduled for the best selling hours in a working day. Enter all the appointments into a calendar, which can be in book or electronic format. The most useful aspect of a calendar is that each appointment is written in as soon as it is confirmed, and the sales representative must predetermine the time to be spent with the client. The representative must draw up a to-do list, and go through each day's list first thing every morning, determining priorities and making sure that the first tasks to be completed are the high-priority ones. [21]

FOLLOW-UP

The follow-up is the final step in time management. It is used to ensure that all goals have been accomplished, that progress has been made, that the calendar was kept and updated, and that the priorities of the day were achieved. [22]

Ways of saving time

The time wasters are telephone interruptions; unscheduled visits; lack of self-discipline; crises and meetings; lack of objectives, priorities and deadlines; indecision and procrastination; attempting too much at once; leaving tasks unfinished; and unclear communication. The sales representative must manage these time wasters and this requires planning.

Sales representatives can use a framework to manage their time and to plan how to spend their time efficiently. The frame is divided into four quadrants, namely emergencies, time wasters, personal growth and leisure. The importance and urgency of each activity is noted within each quadrant. *Importance* refers to the degree to which an activity is necessary in order to accomplish goals, while *urgency* refers to the time pressure that is experienced to carry out a certain activity. An activity is an emergency when both the urgency and the importance are high. When the activity is a time waster, the urgency is high but the importance is low. With personal growth, the urgency is high while the importance is low. When it comes to leisure, both the urgency and importance are low. Each activity can be classified according to this template, and the sales representative will be able to act accordingly.[23]

Electronic information and communication technology can be used to utilise time better while the sales representative is working in his or her territory. The telephone or cellphone can be used to replace a personal call to customers whose accounts are marginal in terms of profitability. Some clients prefer telephone contact, for instance when placing a reorder. The phone can be used to call in advance to make an appointment, to keep the customer informed, and to build customer relationships. Voicemail and email are often used instead of a phone call, especially when the client is too busy to answer the phone. The fax machine is used to send documents or product specifications in advance so that the client can study them before the salesperson's visit. They normally contain information that is given to the client by the salesperson during the visit. These actions save time when the sales representative calls on the client, because by then the client has all the information at hand and less time needs to be spent on explaining it to the client.

TERRITORY MANAGEMENT

Introduction

Territory management is an important task because sales representatives must plan their own time and routes, and work most of the time without supervision. Territory management involves the geographic designation of selling boundaries, the establishment of call patterns, and the planning of sales routes. A sales territory is a geographic area encompassing present and potential customers that is assigned to a sales representative to sell in. The sales territory enables the sales representative to be aware of each client's needs, which can lead to better service with orders and deliveries. To be able to manage the territory, the sales manager and the sales representative must first work together to establish the territory itself and secondly, analyse each account to assign it to a sector and identify the accounts that generate the most sales.[24]

Territory design

Management normally designates the sales territory for the sales representative. There are several reasons why this is done. Firstly, sales territories are established to assure coverage of the market. Secondly, designating territories helps to establish the responsibilities of sales representatives and to measure their performance. Thirdly, it decreases the selling cost. Lastly, sales territories have other benefits such as improving customer relationships; matching the needs of the salesperson and the clients; and giving both the sales representative and the company an advantage. Sales quotas are established and are expressed in quantities (volume) or money amounts to guide the sales representatives on how much of a product must be sold in a day, a week, a month or a year. Once this is done, the sales representative divides the accounts into extra-large, large, medium and small, and this division is then used to plan visit patterns.[25]

The management sets various sales and profit goals, and establishes expense budgets for each territory, so that it can manage and keep track of profitability. Management allocates resources such as money, transport, samples and promotional material so that their sales representatives keep within their expense budgets, and have the resources to achieve the sales goals. Management also estimates the sales potential of each client from past information and establishes how many prospective customers there are in the territory. The number of existing customers and potential prospects affects the time allocated to serving the various customers and prospects.

Classification of customers

Customers are classified according to their sales potential. Not all customers in a territory have the same sales potential and they are therefore classified according to short- or long-term profitability. A common rule of thumb called the 80/20 principle (also called Pareto's Rule) suggests that as much as 80% of the sales in a territory involve as little as 20% of the customers. Regardless of whether the percentages are accurate, the principle can be applied to most sales territories. Many companies use computer programs to assist their salespeople in account analysis, planning and control.

The simplest approach to account classification is called the ABCD analysis. ABCD analysis ranks accounts by sales potential. Industries that require regular contact normally use the ABCD classification, as per the example in Table 5.1. The most important accounts are the A accounts, which are extra-large accounts, also referred to as key accounts. These are the very profitable and good customers, and they need weekly attention. The B accounts are large accounts that are profitable and need to be called on regularly. The C accounts are medium accounts that offer potential sales. If such accounts are lost, the effects will not be dramatic, but they will influence the salesperson's quota. The D accounts make occasional purchases but are not very profitable and they are limited. If the average number of working days a month is about 20, the sales representative should make about 4 to 5 calls per day. This procedure makes it easy to plan and route the sales territory.[26]

Table 5.1 *Example of classification of accounts*

Sales representative: Pete Maseko

Company: BEE Electronics

Classification of accounts	Annual sales in rand per account	Total no. of accounts	Monthly recommended calls	Monthly calls per class
A	500 000+	4	4	16
B	250 000–500 000	11	3	33
C	50 000–250 000	19	2	38
D	10 000–50 000	6	1	6
TOTAL		**40**		**93**

The amount of time spent on each account may vary from 15 minutes to hours to days or even a week. Therefore the sales representative must allow for flexibility when planning the frequency of calls.

Break-even analysis

To employ a representative for a given territory, enough income must be generated to cover the fixed cost. A break-even analysis is used to determine the sales volume that a sales person must generate to meet the cost of the territory he or she is working in. The gross profit of the territory is calculated by subtracting the cost of the goods sold from the total amount of goods sold, e.g. :

Sales for the territory	R1 200 000
Less: the cost of goods sold in the territory	(R800 000)
= Gross profit for the territory	R400 000

The gross profit must be calculated as a percentage and therefore it is:

$$R400\ 000 \div R1\ 200\ 000 \times 100 = 33.33\%$$

The break-even point can be calculated using the following formula:[27]

Break-even point in rand = sales representative's fixed cost $\div$ gross profit %

Calculate the sales representative's direct cost.

Assume that the sales representative's direct costs are as follows:

Salary:	R180 000
Expenses:	R10 000
Transportation:	R18 000 (total expenses R208 000)

Now substitute these figures in the formula:

$$\text{Break-even point} = R208\ 000 \div 33.33 \times 100 = R624\ 062.41$$

The sales representative must therefore produce a turnover of R624 062.41 or a gross margin of 33.33% to meet the sales volume that must be generated to meet the direct cost in the territory.

There are 252 working days in a year and if you subtract six days for holidays, 15 working days for vacations, and five days for sick leave, you are left with 226 working days. A working day consists of eight hours less 30 minutes for lunch. Assume the salesperson works 1 808 hours a year and the average call takes one hour, then he or she can make eight calls per day. This comes to 40 calls a week or 93 a month, as shown in Table 5.1. The salesperson's cost per hour is calculated by dividing the direct cost by the number of hours worked. That is:

$$R208\ 000 \div 1\ 808\ \text{hours} = R115.04\ \text{per hour.}$$

Therefore the break-even rand volume per hour = cost per hour ÷ gross profit %. That is:

$$R115.00 \div 0.3333 = R345.03$$

Thus the salesperson must sell an average of R345.03 per hour or R2 760.00 per day to break even to cover direct costs in the territory. This calculation firstly enables the sales manager to establish if a route is profitable and secondly, it gives the salesperson guidelines on how to manage the territory better.[28]

Routing and visiting patterns

The daily visits must be scheduled in such a way that travelling time and distance are kept to a minimum, and that provision is made for re-visits if clients are not available. Visiting patterns are a planning tool that helps the sales representative to establish how regular and with what intervals customers must be visited. A sales route is the travel pattern that a sales representative follows in the territory where he or she sells, and it must be executable, adjustable and economical. Route planning is done to ensure that the territory is covered, time is saved, and that communication channels between management and the sales representative are accomplished.[29]

Variable call patterns are used when the sales representative must call on accounts in an irregular order. There are four basic routing plans that salespeople can use, namely the straight-line pattern, the cloverleaf pattern, the spiral pattern and the zone pattern. These visit patterns are illustrated in Figure 5.1. Depending on the type of client and products, the sales representative can vary the visiting pattern. One week the sales representative can follow a circular route, and the next week a cloverleaf route. It all depends on the type of clients and the size of the accounts.

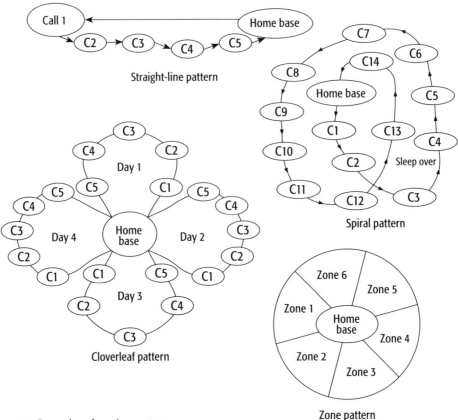

Figure 5.1 *Examples of routing patterns*

- *The straight-line pattern* is used where the customers that the sales representative calls on are situated more or less in a straight line. Early in the morning the sales representative drives to the customer who is situated furthest away for his or her first appointment, and this helps to reduce travel time during business hours.
- *The cloverleaf pattern* is used when the sales representative has to travel extended distances to cover the territory over a number of days. ·
- *The spiral pattern* is used if the accounts are widely dispersed. This is done to cover several accounts along the way. The salesperson will spend the night close to the account he or she will call on the next morning, and will continue calling on clients while on the return route back to the home base. The method is frequently used where sales representatives cover accounts in country areas.
- *The zone pattern* is used where the sales territory is divided into zones to reduce travel time and where the customers are concentrated. The sales representative may have to spend more that one day in a zone in order to call on all the customers there. Once a zone has been covered, the sales representative moves to the next zone, and repeats this until all the zones are covered.

Computer programs can be used to plan selling routes efficiently, and there are several large models available to assist in planning routes to save cost and time. Call plan is a computer-based model that is used for complicated route planning and is of great help in establishing how clients will react to different sales call frequencies. Computer-based models can help in solving routing problems and in establishing better and more profitable visiting patterns. If the software that is available is integrated and used with video-conference and digital communication technology, it can help to increase the productivity of the sales representative, and the concept of a fixed sales territory is no longer valid.[30]

Record management

The sales representative must keep a record of each client regardless of the product that he or she sells. Record management is essential for successful selling and the sales representative must have first-hand knowledge about the accounts he or she services. The information in a client record varies but should be up to date on past sales, the client's last order, recent developments and problems, and the most recent correspondence. A correct up-to-date record is important because it saves a lot of time. The sales representative must be on top of things in the entire selling area and must have access to and manage information that concerns sales, trends, leads, expenses and call reports.[31]

Sales representatives must organise data that deals with leads, their clients and their own time allocation so that they can sell efficiently. Computers play an important role in record keeping. The development of technology such as computers and software has helped sales representatives to manage information about their clients, to their own benefit. Computers are used to manage databases. A database is any information gathered, such as information on the purchases made by clients, appointment lists and sales call records. The most common records that a sales representative should keep are customer and prospect files, call reports, expense records and sales records.

Customer and prospect files can also be kept on printed cards, though these have become outdated with the automation of the sales force. Nowadays they are usually kept in an electronic format that contains the same information as that on the printed cards. Each record has a space for the client's name, address and telephone number(s), the appropriate time to call, the buyer's personal characteristics and preferences, and the names and positions of people who might influence the purchase decision. Electronic records in a notebook computer are accessible at the touch of a button, and are not on a number of loose cards that could get lost. Call reports are records of the members of the customer organisation that the sales representative has called on and what took place during the call. They indicate what the sales representative must do in the future. They contain information about the customer's profiles and their long- and short-term buying plans. Expense reports reflect the selling expenses and include meals, travel, accommodation and entertainment. These records are necessary because, as required by income tax law, the company controls the expenses. Sales records are used to analyse the sales representative's performance, and they vary according to the company's requirements. In some cases the sales records must be completed immediately, and in others they are completed daily or even weekly. The records must be accurate, neat and legible, and must be updated often to reflect the current state of things.[32]

The attitude of sales representatives to their job and themselves establishes their success or failure. The obstacles to success are identified as stress, procrastination, fear of failure and unhappiness.

STRESS MANAGEMENT
Introduction

Stress can be defined as the response of the body or mind to demands on it, in the form of either psychological or physiological strain. Stress is feelings of frustration, pressure, fear, conflict, confusion, guilt and inadequacy. The causes of stress are called stressors and can be internal (e.g. thinking you are unable to convince the client) or external (e.g. not closing the sale). The stressors can be conscious or unconscious. If stress is not managed properly, it leads to strain, which damages the sales representative's ability to deal with everyday sales situations. A survey in America has shown that 25% of the workforce suffers from stress and 3% suffer from depression. It is estimated that 16 working days per worker per year are lost due to stress. Selling produces a certain amount of stress because the non-routine nature of the job brings new experiences daily, therefore salespeople should know how to manage stress.[33]

Reasons for stress

Sales representatives work in isolation and independently, are bound by limits that cause conflict, stand between the client and the organisation, and are exposed to stress. The pressure to close a sale, meet quotas, find new clients, absorb rejection by clients and care for their family make life difficult for the sales representative, therefore selling must be viewed as an up-and-down experience that evokes feelings ranging from cheerfulness to depression. Above all, the sales representative must keep track of competition within and outside the organisation.[34]

Stress is caused when the sales representative cannot keep an appointment, has to make a presentation to a large group, has to meet sales quotas, or tries to stay on time with the travelling schedule. Uncontrollable factors such as large fluctuations in the market, the stage of market development and intensity of competition can contribute to work stress. It is ironic that time-saving devices such as the fax machine, the cellphone and email make it difficult for sales representatives to escape the pressure of their job. The term 'techno-stress' is used to describe the illness that is caused by the inability of the workforce to keep up to date with all the new technologies. Some people have an unreasonable urge to upgrade their technology all the time, and the effect of this is the opposite of time saving. The reasons for stress are hassles, helplessness, hurriedness and burnout (exhaustion).[35] Each of these will be briefly discussed.

Hassles

Hassles are the irritating and frustrating little annoyances that happen every day, like traffic jams, inability to find parking, bad weather, pollution and petty arguments. Although the hassles are small, they accumulate and the effect is stress, therefore the sales representative must learn how to relax.

Helplessness

Sales representatives sometimes feel helpless because they have to depend increasingly on other people, bureaucratic organisations, machines and technology to function, which makes them vulnerable. For example, the notebook computer may give problems during a presentation. This makes the sales representative feel helpless and out of control, and leads to stress.

Hurriedness

Many sales representatives are chasing the clock to accomplish such things as meeting a quota or a deadline. Some personality types are naturally in a hurry. They schedule too many calls a day, and need to learn to schedule their tasks better and to manage time. Hurriedness is also a cause of stress.

Burnout

Stress without proper management can lead to burnout. Burnout is caused by stress that lasts too long without being managed successfully, and has several kinds of effects, namely physical, emotional, mental, psychological, behavioural and organisational. Physical exhaustion is characterised by low energy, chronic fatigue and weakness. Emotional exhaustion involves feelings of helplessness, hopelessness and entrapment. Mental burnout manifests in the development of negative attitudes toward oneself, one's work and even life itself. Psychological effects include shallow breathing, numbness, tingling, cold hands and feet, tight muscles, back and head pain, dry mouth, headaches and hypertension. Behavioural effects are smoking, over- or under-eating, loss of appetite, drug abuse, alcoholism, impulsive or aggressive outbursts, crying, complaining, accident proneness, restlessness, withdrawal and isolation. Organisational effects are job burnout, low morale, absenteeism, poor performance, mistakes, job dissatisfaction, lawsuits, sabotage, a high use of medical facilities, accidents and poor working relationships.

It is clear that stress has a tremendous impact on people and therefore it is important that the sales representative must manage it. Stress management will be discussed next.

Stress management

The use of electronic technology can help to reduce stress for sales representatives because it enables them to coordinate personal schedules and work schedules. Stress must be handled during the sales call, especially in cases where the sales representative is aware that the client is a difficult person to deal with.[36] When dealing with stress, the sales representative must:[37]

- Take control of the situation.
- Become aware of the symptoms, the feeling and the stressful situation.
- Analyse what is really going on.
- Act rather than worry.
- Change the situation.
- Accept what cannot be changed.
- Stick to his or her viewpoint but do not step on others'.
- Change the negative things into positive things.
- Develop a support system.
- Recognise the danger signs of stress.

It is important that sales representatives reserve time to relax with their family, to do physical exercises, to be alone, and not to work during lunch hours. This must be part of their time management programme. Stress must be managed just like time, records and sales territory. From the above discussion it is clear that the things mentioned cannot be viewed as separate entities. Sales representatives must manage the whole of their life in order to become more successful, acquire greater personal satisfaction, and be more productive.

SUMMARY

Self-management in selling is an integrated process of managing career, territory, time and stress. It requires salespersons to set objectives for themselves, their time and their territory. Goals play an important role in selling. Certain guidelines must be followed to set effective goals. Goals can be divided into three categories, namely performance goals, which relate to outcomes; activity goals, which relate to daily activities; and conversion goals, which measure efficiency. Without goals and objectives, sales representatives will not be able to measure their progress.

Time management is important because it relates to managing the territory, the self and stress. It is an integral part of planning. The activities and events that waste time must be identified, and include such things as telephone interruptions, unscheduled visits, lack of self-discipline, meetings, and lack of objectives, priorities and deadlines. Time management has five interwoven dimensions, namely setting goals, analysing time, planning time, following the time plan, and follow-up. To do effective planning the sales representative must make a written list of the activities that are part of the selling job, aid communication, are of intrinsic importance and are urgent. To manage time more effectively, that sales representative can make use of electronic information and communication technology.

Territory design is important because it ensures that the market is covered, that selling costs are reduced, that the salesperson's responsibilities are established, that performance is measured, and that customer relationships are improved. In designing a territory, firstly all accounts must be classified according to their potential, so that call frequency can be established. Then a break-even analysis is done to determine the sales volume that a salesperson must generate in the territory to cover the cost of the territory. Once this is done the routing and visiting patterns are established. There are four basic visiting patterns that can be applied, namely the straight-line pattern, the cloverleaf pattern, the spiral pattern and the zone pattern.

Stress is the response of the body or mind to demands on it in the form of either psychological or physiological strain, and must be managed just like time, records and sales territory. Stress management is necessary because stress influences the productivity of the salesperson. The most common reasons for stress are hassles, helplessness, hurriedness and burnout. To cope with stress sales representatives must reserve time to relax with their family, to do physical exercise, to be alone, and not to work lunch hours, which must be part their time management programme.

CASE STUDY

Jay's Foods, producers and distributors of a range of food products and soft drinks, has appointed you as the representative for the Mpumalanga/Limpopo territory. The route covers a travel distance of approximately 1 250 kilometres per week (see Figure 5.2). The average driving time is calculated as 13 hours a week or three hours a day. The average time spent with the A accounts is one hour, with the B accounts 45 minutes, with the C accounts 30 minutes and with the D accounts 30 minutes (see tables 5.2 and 5.3). The sales volume for the territory is approximately R8 300 000 per year, which equals an average of R692 000 per month. The average cost of sales is R75 000 per month. The A accounts are situated in Polokwane, Potgietersrus, Phalaborwa and Nelspruit (the home base), and must be serviced weekly. The average salary plus commission for the territory costs the company R280 000 per year, other expenses amount to R62 000 per year, and transportation amounts to R76 000 per year. There are about 226 working days a year, and eight working hours a day, thus the salesperson works about 1 808 hours a year.

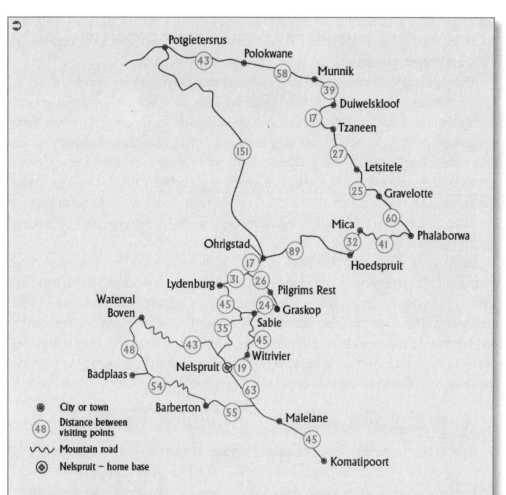

Figure 5.2 *Mpumalanga/Limpopo route*

Table 5.2 *Current ABCD classification of accounts*

Account type	Sales volume per year	Calling rate per month	No. of Accounts	No. of sales calls per month
A	R400 000+	4	9	36
B	R200 000–R400 000	3	16	48
C	R50 000–R200 000	2	21	42
D	Less than R50 000	1	11	11

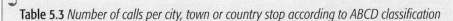

Table 5.3 *Number of calls per city, town or country stop according to ABCD classification*

City, town or country stop	A	B	C	D
Potgietersrus	1	1	2	1
Polokwane	2	1	1	
Munnik				1
Duiwelskloof			1	
Tzaneen	1	2	1	1
Letsitele				1
Gravelotte			2	
Phalaborwa	1	1	3	1
Mica				1
Hoedspruit				1
Ohrigstad				1
Lydenburg		1	1	1
Pilgrims Rest		2		
Graskop			1	
Sabie		1	1	
Witrivier			2	
Waterval Boven				1
Badplaas		1		
Barberton			2	1
Komatipoort			1	
Malelane			1	
Nelspruit	4	6	2	
TOTAL	**9**	**16**	**21**	**11**

Assignment

1. Replan your route so that it fits in with the ABCD classification of the accounts.
2. Indicate your travelling time as well as the time spent with customers.
3. Calculate the break-even point for the route in rand.
4. Motivate the routing patterns that you have decided on.

SELF-ASSESSMENT QUESTIONS

1. Why is self-management important?
2. What is the purpose of sales goals and objectives?
3. What types of goals must be set?
4. Why is time management important to salespeople?
5. What activities need to be analysed in order to plan your time?
6. What ICT applications can be used to utilise time better?
7. Why do managers normally design the sales territory for the salespeople?
8. Why is the classification of clients necessary in territory planning?
9. What is the purpose of a break-even analysis in territory design?
10. What are the five dimensions of time management?
11. When will you use:
    - The straight-line pattern?
    - The zone pattern?
12. What is stress?
13. How does stress influence the salesperson?
14. What are the reasons for stress?
15. How can stress be reduced?

DISCUSSION QUESTIONS

1. You have recently been promoted to senior representative and have been transferred from Pietermaritzburg to Welkom, where there are a few key accounts that need the attention of a senior person. The sales manager asks you to write a report on how you will set goals for managing yourself in this new territory. What will you say?
2. Fully discuss the five dimensions of time management that you will consider in planning your time in the new territory.
3. Arriving in Welkom, you go through the records and find the following: there are eight key accounts that purchase R500 000+ a year, three accounts that bring in between R200 000 and R500 000 per year, 24 accounts that bring in between R40 000 and R200 000 per year, and two accounts that bring in between R5 000 and R40 000 per year. The sales for the territory amount to R1 500 000 per year, the cost of goods sold to R900 000. Do an ABCD classification in table format and calculate the break-even point in rand.
4. Discuss the different routing patterns that you will consider.
5. Discuss stress management.

NOTES

1.   Faria, A.J. & Johnson, H.W. 1993. *Creative Selling.* (Fifth edition). Cincinnati: South-Western, p. 331.

2.   Jobber, D. & Lancaster, G. 1997. *Selling and Sales Management.* (Fourth edition). London: Pitman Publishing, p. 102.

      Soldow, G.F. & Thomas, G.P. 1991. *Professional Selling: An Interpersonal Perspective.* New York: Macmillan, p. 434.

3.   Pollack, A. 1997. Information technology and socialist self-management. *Monthly Review: An Independent Socialist Magazine.* [Online]. September. 49. 4: 32–50. Available at: (Sabinet).../fulltext. asp?resultSetId=R00000000&hitNum=162&booleanTerm=Self%20management% (accessed on 26 April 2002).

      Taylor, T.C. 1994. Making more time to sell. *Sales and Marketing Management*, pp. 94–99. Available at: http:////infotrac. london. gale.../purl=rc1_GBIM_0_ A15230265&dyn=52!ar_fmt?sw_aep=tp_it (accessed on 7 May 2002).

4.   Palmer, G. 1999. Cellular communications: a vital marketing tool. *The South African Journal of Marketing and Sales*, 5.1, pp. 4–7.

5.   Weitz, B.A., Castleberry, S.B. & Tanner, J.F. (Jr). 2001. *Selling: Building Partnerships*. Boston: McGraw-Hill Irwin, pp. 482–483.

6.   The Sales & Marketing Foundation. 1995. *Basic Sales Skills – Business to Business*, p. 118.

7.   Ibid., pp. 125–129.

      O'Connor, J. & Galvin, E. 1997. *Marketing and Information Technology: The Strategy, Application and Implementation of IT in Marketing*. London: Pitman, p. 38. Weitz et al., op. cit., p. 484.

8.   Weitz et al., op. cit., pp. 485–487.

9.   Faria & Johnson, op. cit., p. 202.

10.   The Sales & Marketing Foundation, op. cit., p. 118.

11.   Curtis, J. 1997. Out of time, out of mind. *Marketing*. [Online]. October 16: 22. Available at: http:// infotrac.london.gale.../purl=rcl_EIM_0_A20057368&dyn=6!ar_fmt?sw_aep=tp_it (accessed on 15 April 2002).

      Shook, R.L. 1994. *How to be the Complete Professional Salesperson*. Hollywood: Lifetime Books Inc., pp. 71–73.

12.   Curtis, op. cit., p. 23.

13.   Taylor, op. cit., p. 40.

14.   Rix, P., Buss, J. & Herford, G. 1999. *Selling – A Consultative Approach.* (Second edition). Sydney: McGraw-Hill, p. 171.

15.   Dalrymple, D.J. & Cron, W.L. 1998. *Sales Management – Concepts and Cases.* (Sixth edition). New York: John Wiley & Sons, p. 191.

      Manning, G.L. & Reece, B.L. 1998. *Selling Today – Building Quality Partnerships*. (Seventh edition). New Jersey: Prentice Hall, p. 343.

16.   Rix et al., op. cit., p. 174.

17.   Shook, op. cit., pp. 68–71.

18.   Trickett, J. 1962. A more effective use of time. *California Management Review*, 4: 4–15.

19. Gordon, D. 2000. *Self-Management and Goal Setting*. Cincinnati: South-Western, p. 59.

20. Coppet, J.I. & Staples, W.A. 1994. *Professional Selling – A Relationship Management Process*. Cincinnati: South-Western, p. 280.

    Shook, op. cit., pp. 73–76.

21. Futrell, C.M. 2002. *Fundamentals of Selling: Customers for Life*. (Seventh edition). Boston: McGraw-Hill, p. 167.

22. Rix et al., op. cit., p. 177.

23. Dalrymple & Cron, op. cit., p. 192.

24. Dalrymple & Cron, op. cit., p. 419.

    Quigg, B. & Wisner, B. 1998. *Selling the Right Way*. New Jersey: Prentice Hall, p. 435.

25. Blem, N. 1997. *Achieving Excellence in Selling – The South African Approach*. Johannesburg: Thompson, p. 212.

    Zoltners, A. & Lorimer, S.E. Sales territory alignment: An overlooked productivity tool. *Journal of Personal Selling & Sales Management*. XX. 3: 139–150. Available at: http://mkt.cba.cmich.edu/jpssm (accessed on 10 November 2004).

26. Faria & Johnson, op. cit., pp. 345–346.

27. Improving decision making with simple break-even analysis. [Online] Available at: http:www.coba.panam.edu/fbshell/breakevenanalysis.html, p. 1–17 (accessed on 10 November 2004).

28. Blem, op. cit., pp. 216–217.

29. Noonan, C. 1998. *Sales Management*. Johannesburg: Butterworth-Heinemann, p. 247.

    Quigg & Wisner, op. cit, p. 436.

30. Donaldson, B. 1998. *Sales management – Theory and Practice*. (Second edition). London: Macmillan Press, p. 175.

    Stanton, W.J. & Spiro, R. 1999. *Management of a Sales Force*. (Tenth edition). Boston: Irwin McGraw-Hill, p. 441.

31. Quigg & Wisner, op. cit., p. 75.

    Manning & Reece, op. cit., p. 350.

32. Rix et al., op. cit., p. 184.

    Soldow & Thomas, op. cit., p. 393.

33. Anderson, R. 1991. *Professional Personal Selling*. New Jersey: Prentice Hall, p. 536.

    Manning & Reece, op. cit., pp. 354–355.

34. Jolson, M.A., Dubinsky, A.J., Yammarino, F.J. & Comer, L.B. Transforming the salesforce with leadership. *Sloan Management Review*, 34. 3: 95–105. Available at: http://infotrac.london.gale.../purl=rcl_EIM_0_ A14412243&dyn=18!ar_fmt?sw_aep=tp_it (accessed on 24 April 2002).

35. Manning & Reece, op. cit., pp. 353–355.

    Moncrief, W.C., Babakus, E., Cravens, D.W. & Johnson. 1997. Examining the antecedents and consequences of salesperson job stress. *European Journal of Marketing*. 31. 11: 786–798. Available at: http://web1.infotrac.lo.../purl=rcl_GBIM_0_A20357604&dyn=9!ar_fmt?sw_aep=tp_it (accessed on 26 October 2001).

36. Taylor, op. cit., pp. 90–94.

37. The Sales & Marketing Foundation, op. cit., pp. 269–308.

FURTHER READING

Journal of the Academy of Marketing Science.

Harvard Business Review.

The South African Journal of Marketing and Sales.

Any related textbook covering the topic 'Sales management and selling'.

6

PROSPECTING

LEARNING OUTCOMES

After studying this chapter, you should be able to:

- Define the terms 'prospecting' and 'prospect'
- Discuss the importance of prospecting
- Discuss how leads can be changed into prospects
- Identify and discuss different prospecting methods
- Provide the different prospecting methods in tabular form
- Discuss how prospects are qualified
- Illustrate and discuss the referral cycle
- Discuss the process of making an appointment with a prospect or customer in person or by telephone
- Discuss how a salesperson can overcome the reluctance to prospect

INTRODUCTION

To be successful in selling, a salesperson should know how to deal with customers and how to sell to them. The sales manager therefore must ensure that once salespeople have sufficient knowledge about the business and its products, they are taught the basic selling skills and methods. Prospecting is the first step in effective and successful personal selling. It enables the salesperson to compile a list of potential customers who are highly likely to need or have a use for the product or service and the ability to buy it. Prospecting is perceived as the most important process of locating potential customers for a product or service and is critical whether you are a new or an experienced salesperson. In fact, many experts note that prospecting is the most important activity a salesperson does.

Effective prospecting enables the salesperson to spend more time on sales presentations and the successful closing of transactions. The salesperson's search for new customers and for increased business from existing ones never ends. With an average of almost 20% of an organisation's customers leaving the market every year, it is not surprising that prospecting is considered to be the lifeblood of selling.

In this chapter the focus will be on a definition of the sales process. The steps in the sales process will be identified and discussed. The importance of prospecting will be emphasised and the different prospecting methods will be identified and discussed in detail. Reference will be made to the referral cycle, and the process of making an appointment with a prospect or customer – in person or by telephone – will be highlighted.

A BACKGROUND STUDY TO PROSPECTING

Defining the terms 'prospect' and 'prospecting'

A prospect is a qualified person or business that has the potential to buy the salesperson's product or service. Prospecting is the foundation on which the sales process is built. Why? The reason is that it identifies potential customers.

There are two reasons why it is necessary to keep looking for new customers: to increase sales and to replace customers who will be lost.

Prospecting is the process of acquiring basic demographic and psychographic knowledge of potential customers for your product. A prospect should not be confused with a 'lead'. The name of a person or business that might be a prospect is referred to as a lead. A lead can also be called a 'suspect'. This term indicates that the person or business is 'suspected' of being a prospect. Once the lead has been 'qualified', it becomes a prospect.[1]

The importance of prospecting

Think of prospecting – pursuing leads that you hope will develop into customers – as a way to fill your pipeline of future business. Today's business generated by current customers is well and good, but a good salesperson always has to be thinking ahead to where business will come from next week, next month and even next year. Prospecting is not a part-time process in selling. Good salespeople are always engaged in prospecting in one form or another. They always have their sights set on where tomorrow's business is coming from.

Prospecting is important because a business can only grow if it expands its customer base. It is estimated that, on average, a business continually loses about 20% of its customers through competition, transfer, death, retirement, takeovers, liquidation and dissatisfaction with the organisation. This emphasises the need to find new customers all the time. The two main reasons for prospecting are to increase sales and to replace lost customers.[2]

Beyond this general growth perspective, several reasons may necessitate prospecting for new customers being an even higher priority. These reasons are:

- A customer gets into financial difficulty or goes out of business entirely.
- A salesperson's contacts in the client organisation leave or change position.

- A salesperson's organisation needs to increase revenues to pay for expansion or other items.
- A customer moves to a new location outside the salesperson's area of sales responsibility.

Prospecting is therefore a key activity of successful selling. How leads are developed from which prospects (and ultimately customers) is discussed in the next section.

Characteristics of a good prospect

Prospecting is where the selling process begins. It is a brutal but inescapable fact that the best salesperson in the world will starve if he or she does not have any prospects. Selling is about numbers. It is about prospecting for new customers, about selling repeat business to current customers, and about revitalising inactive settled accounts. How does the salesperson find more customers? Simply by prospecting in an intelligent way and by working hard. All salespeople know the importance of sales leads, of investigating every sales prospect.

To be successful, the salesperson's search for business should be planned. It is vital for salespeople to know what they want to do and achieve, which areas and which types of customer they will visit, and when they will visit them.

Prospecting methods

Prospecting methods vary for different types of selling. The methods used will depend on the industry, for example the motor vehicle industry (e.g. Volkswagen, Toyota) versus the insurance industry (e.g. Sanlam, Old Mutual) versus the property industry (e.g. Pam Golding, Seeff) versus retail (e.g. Edgars, Pick n Pay), the size of the organisation; the product or service on offer (e.g. travel insurance; Tupperware), the competitors operating in the market place, the types of customers and the salesperson.

A wide variety of sources and methods can be used to identify potential prospects. The salesperson will prefer the technique which best suits his or her personality, knowledge and field of experience. Table 6.1 illustrates seven categories of prospecting methods that can be used by a salesperson when recruiting new customers.

Table 6.1 *Prospecting identification categories*

Source	How used
Satisfied customers	Current and previous customers are contacted for additional business and leads
Endless chain	Salesperson attempts to secure at least one additional lead from each person he or she interviews
Centre of influence	Salesperson cultivates well-known, influential people in the territory who are willing to supply lead information ⮌

Networking	Salesperson uses personal relationships with those who are connected and cooperative to secure leads
The Internet	Salesperson uses websites, email, bulletin boards, forums and newsgroups to secure leads
Advertisements, direct mail, catalogues, publicity	Salespeople use these forms of promotional activities to generate leads
Seminars	Salespeople use trade shows and conferences for lead generation
Lists and directories	Salesperson uses secondary data sources, which can be free or fee based
Data mining and CRM	Salesperson uses sophisticated data analysis software and the organisation's customer relationship marketing (CRM) system to generate leads
Cold calling	Salesperson tries to generate leads by calling on totally unfamiliar companies or individuals
Spotters	Salesperson pays someone for lead information
Telemarketing	Salesperson uses phone and/or telemarketing staff to generate sales
Sales letters	Salesperson writes personal letters to potential leads
Other sources	Salesperson uses non-competing salespeople (people in his or her own organisation, friends, etc.) to secure information

Source: *Weitz, Castleberry & Tanner (2004:185)*

Satisfied customers

Satisfied customers, particularly those who are truly partners with the seller, are the most effective sources for leads. In fact, one authority claims that successful salespeople should obtain 75% of their new business through referrals from customers. Referrals of leads in the same industry are particularly useful because the salesperson already understands the unique needs of this type of organisation.

To maximise the usefulness of satisfied customers, salespeople should follow several steps. First they should make a list of potential references (customers who might provide leads) from among their most satisfied customers. This task will be much easier if they have maintained an accurate and detailed database of customers. Next, they should decide what they would want each customer to do (e.g. write a personal letter of introduction, take phone enquiries, contact prospects directly, or provide a generic letter of reference). Finally, salespeople should ask the customer for the names of leads and for the specific type of help he or she can provide. Since people can have trouble coming up with a list of good leads, salespeople should allow their customers time to consider this.

The endless-chain technique

This technique can be used for prospecting customers for any type of product or service. It amounts to the salesperson getting the names of friends and acquaintances from every customer to whom he or she sells a product for future use in prospecting. It is important that the salesperson is professional and ethical in his or her handling of prospects obtained in this way. This technique must be deliberately built into each sales presentation. Ask a satisfied buyer for names of friends or acquaintances who have a similar need or use for the product and can afford it. The salesperson can also obtain names from prospects to whom he or she has not sold. However, it is easier to get names from satisfied customers. It is also a good opportunity to get names of prospects for follow-up when actual follow-up and after-sales service visits are made.

This technique offers the salesperson various advantages:

- Prospecting and approach times are reduced.
- Appointments are more easily obtained.
- The prospect has to an extent already been qualified in terms of need or use and ability to buy by the person who refers him or her to the salesperson.
- A satisfied customer is a good reference.

Centre of influence

In the centre-of-influence methods, the salesperson cultivates a relationship with well-known, influential people in the sales area (covered by the salesperson) who are willing to supply the names of leads. A centre of influence is therefore usually a person (e.g. Gary Kirsten) or an organisation (e.g. Woolworths) which has gained honour, respect and admiration in the community, business and industry, or a public figure others look up to. People respect such people's judgement and are keen to follow their example in everything they do. Salespersons must use their existing customers who qualify as centres of influence or as references once they have obtained permission to do so. Examples of centres of influence are attorneys, doctors, ministers, successful businesspeople and sports personalities.

Networking

Networking is the utilisation of personal relationship by connected and cooperating individuals for the purpose of achieving goals. In selling, networking simply implies establishing connections to other people and then using them to generate leads, gather information, generate sales, etc. Networking can also include centres of influence and satisfied customers.

The Internet

Probably the fastest-growing method of generating leads is through the Internet. Successful salespeople are using websites, email, bulletin boards, forums and newsgroups to connect to individuals and companies that may be interested in their products and services. New technologies, which are unfolding at a fast pace, allow a selling organisation to use various methods, including audio, video (such as showing product demonstrations or organisational tours) and text (letters of reference, product specifications, special lists of contacts) to provide information to prospects.

Advertising, direct mail, catalogues and publicity

Organisations have developed sophisticated systems to generate enquiries from leads by using advertising and direct mail. For example, Hewlett-Packard (HP) sends out direct mail to potential customers for its colour copiers. The organisation also places advertisements in business and industry publications, such as *Finance Week* and *Finansies & Tegniek*. An interested reader can request additional information by calling a toll-free number in the advertisement or by returning the reader service card at the back of the magazine.

Many organisations operating in the insurance and banking industries, for example, mail and distribute brochures, advertisements, catalogues, price lists and special offers on a regular basis. This technique attracts telephone, letter or email enquiries about the organisation's products or services, which the secretary or switchboard operator gives to the salesperson as leads (possible customers) for follow-up.

Newspapers are full of news reports and other leads such as the list of promotions and retirements in the business columns, announcements of engagements, births and weddings in the social columns, and other matters which provide leads. The alert salesperson will scour all the newspapers daily for leads to possible prospects. Awards of new contracts, openings of new businesses and business complexes, expansions of existing businesses, and staff moves and appointments are news reports salespeople must watch out for. Magazines and trade, industrial, technical and professional publications may also lead to prospects.

Shows

Many organisations display or demonstrate their products at trade shows or exhibitions in South Africa. Sales representatives are present to demonstrate products to visitors, many of whom salespeople have not called on before. Often, the primary focus of salespeople at trade shows or exhibitions is to qualify leads for future follow-up. Typically, having only five to ten minutes with a prospect, they need to get down to business and qualify the visitor quickly.

People visit various specialised shows such as Design for Living, the Outdoor Expo, and the Market and Media Expo. Those who show interest and make enquiries can be followed up as prospects. A practical way organisations can do this is by running a competition at their stall for the duration of the show. To enter for these competitions, participants must drop their business cards in a competition entry box. At the close of the show, salespeople can phone all these people to determine if they are interested in buying their organisation's products.

Lists and directories

There are organisations that sell prospect lists to other organisations and salespeople. Organisations also provide their salespeople with such lists. Prospect lists can be lists of members of:

- Social and sports clubs (e.g. Virgin Active)
- Societies
- Professions
- Chambers of commerce
- Municipal ratepayers
- Newspapers
- Public records

All these can also be used as possible sources of prospects by salespeople.

The telephone directory gives names, addresses and telephone numbers of private individuals, businesses, medical practitioners, schools and other professional people, and is another important source for prospects.

Data mining and CRM systems

Sophisticated organisations are developing interactive databases that contain information on leads, prospects and customers. Progressive organisations are using data mining, artificial intelligence and statistical tools to discover insights hidden in the volumes of data in their databases.

Cold calling

This technique is also known as cold canvassing and door-to-door selling. The salesperson approaches an individual without any pre-knowledge of him or her, and without making sure that the person actually is a prospect. The technique does not work for very expensive products, like speciality goods, and shopping.

Only after the salesperson has met the possible prospect and has briefly conveyed the reason for his or her visit can it be determined whether or not the prospect is a good one.

Direct selling will not work with all products and prospective customers, and not even with all salespersons, with the same effective results. The technique must be applied correctly; the planning must be effective; the short sales talk must stimulate the attention and interest immediately; and the salesperson's appearance, personality and the first impression given must inspire confidence and trust.

This also applies to direct prospecting by telephone, where the salesperson's voice and tone and the image he or she conveys will determine if the prospect will listen to the presentation.

Examples of direct selling are:

- House-to-house selling
- Direct telephone selling
- Systematic visits to schools and hospitals

Spotters

Some salespeople use spotters, also called bird dogs. These individuals will, for a fee, provide leads for the salesperson. The salesperson sometimes does pay the fee simply for the name of the lead, but more often pays only if the lead ends up buying the product or service. Spotters are usually in a position to determine when someone is ready to make a purchase decision. In other words, people working for large organisations such as Old Mutual or in professions such as education (e.g. teachers or lecturers) or the medical profession (e.g. nurses or doctors) can act as spotters. They provide salespeople with the names, addresses and telephone numbers of prospects that they hear about at work. It is usually salespeople who sell property, cars, domestic appliances and services such as insurance who use spotters.

Telemarketing

Increasingly, organisations are relying on telemarketing to undertake many tasks that sales representatives used to perform. Telemarketing is a systematic and continuous programme of communicating with customers and prospects via the telephone. In outbound telemarketing, telephones are used to generate and then qualify leads. These calls may be initiated directly by the salesperson or by inside sales representatives. Inbound telemarketing makes use of a telephone number (usually a toll-free one) that leads and/or customers can call for additional information. Again, the call may be answered by several types of persons; the salesperson, an inside salesperson, or a customer service representative.

The telephone is one of the most important aids to the salesperson in obtaining, finding and contacting prospects. It should be used only if the target market is defined as a specific group such as hospitals, or people in the medical, teaching or legal profession, etc. Insurance companies and companies selling timeshare sell their products over the telephone.[3]

A telephone call can identify the prospect; be used to gather and provide information; arouse interest in the product; and also help to overcome objections. The telephone call can be followed up with a personal visit to make the sales presentation. The telephone can also be used to contact existing customers who have not bought anything for some time, to determine the reason.

Do you know what *affiliate marketing* or *direct selling* is? How do people *make extra money* through this form of selling? Direct selling or affiliate selling is a way of making extra money by marketing someone else's products to potential consumers in their homes, at a central office (many direct sellers hire halls or offices for meetings) or even online. Instead of carrying all the overheads of owning your own business, you receive a percentage of the earnings in the form of commission. Some fantastic affiliate network businesses that have proven their success in the years they have been operating would include Amway, Sportron, Herbalife and even GNLD.

The affiliate marketing and direct selling industry has come a long way over the years, starting out as a business opportunity that was viewed with scepticism, and has ended up changing the lives of thousands of people who get involved in it. Many affiliate network businesses have rescued people from the grip of poverty and helped them rebuild their lives. Their foolproof method of creating a huge network of filter-through income by introducing new members and earning a portion of their earnings has been helping people all over the world to live the *financially free* and luxurious lives they have always dreamed of.

Affiliate marketing and direct selling businesses take dedication, hard work and effort. In order to be a success in this industry you will need to treat the business as your own.

This type of business is suited to just about anyone; the stay-at-home mom, the full-time secretary looking for some extra money, the student with some *extra time* each day – anyone. Not many skills are required for affiliate marketing or direct selling, but people skills and confidence are definitely an advantage. Having good communication and literacy skills can also spur one's direct selling business to success. Legitimate affiliate marketing and *direct selling networks* are worked by new members selling products and brands to potential consumers and receiving a commission in return. The selling doesn't stop here. Each member is encouraged to recruit new members to promote and sell the same products in order to also earn a commission on the products that the new members sell. Affiliate marketing and direct selling are great ways of *earning residual income.*

If you are serious about getting involved in affiliate marketing and direct selling, then it is to your advantage to have your own computer, internet access and telephone. The *affiliate program you are buying into should be able to supply you with all relevant marketing and promotional materials* needed to enable you to get your direct selling business up and running smoothly. Being ready to enter into a state of financial freedom, not without hard work and extra effort, means you have taken the first step towards owning and running your own affiliate marketing and direct selling business. Take the plunge and *start earning extra money* or an extra income today!

Other sources
Personal observation

One of the most successful methods of prospecting is that of personal observation by salespeople of everything that happens around them, and personal contacts they make daily. A salesperson's friends; neighbours; fellow club members; soccer, cricket, or golf partners; fellow church members; and business acquaintances are good prospects if they need the salesperson's product or service. If they do not, they are good sources for references to other prospects. The salesperson must treat these people in the same professional way as other prospects.

The 'eye and ear' approach which the wide-awake salesperson uses is an excellent source of prospects. By listening during conversations to what people are saying and talking about, you can spot sales opportunities. For example, if you hear someone say that they have opened a new business, ask yourself:

- What are the needs and requirements of the new business?
- Will they need some products from our product range, e.g. office furniture, or a fax or photocopying machine?
- What sales opportunities might arise from the following?
    - 'Building a new house' or 'doing alterations'
    - 'The washing machine broke'
    - 'New baby'
    - 'Pension'
    - 'Inheritance'
    - 'Being promoted'

These are all leads to prospects with a need for specific products or services which must be satisfied.

Observation of the environment and changes which occur, such as a new office complex being built, new houses being built, residential areas getting rezoned as business areas, accidents, and personal observation of things around the salesperson and of other people and their possessions can provide leads to good prospects.

Organisational records

Information stored in the organisation's files and on its computers can provide valuable information about previous sales to specific customers. The salesperson must analyse this information and try to derive a so-called 'itch cycle' for each customer. An 'itch cycle' is derivable from previous purchasing dates; e.g. every two years a particular customer 'itches' to buy a new bike. What can the salesperson do with this information? A few months before the customer starts 'itching', the salesperson must phone and inform the prospect about the launching of a new bike or even invite him or her for a test drive.

The service reports of the service staff can also provide information about prospects. For example, a Nashua salesperson must stay in close contact with the organisation's technical staff who service photocopying machines. Why? Because these service staff can give the salesperson some excellent leads on which customers will need new machines in the near future.

The accounts department keeps records of inactive accounts and customers who have not bought from the organisation for quite a while. The salesperson must phone these customers and find out the reason for this.

All of the organisational leads above can provide excellent prospects.

Referrals by other salespersons

You can get referrals from:

■ *Salespeople in your own organisation who sell other product lines.* For example, you may be a salesperson for Volkswagen, selling their Golf product line, but you are aware that one of your customers is expecting triplets, and you refer her to your colleague who is selling the Kombi product line

■ *Salespeople in your own organisation who work in other areas.* For example, as an estate agent for Seeff Properties in Cape Town, you are aware of a customer who is moving to Pretoria so you refer this customer to your colleague there.

Non-competing salespeople of other companies are also good sources of leads

For example, consider salespeople who work for four different organisations that sell paint, carpets, blinds and cupboards respectively. All of them have the same target market in common, namely customers who are building new houses or renovating their existing ones. When salespeople visit customers, they often hear of products which the customer needs but which their organisation does not sell.

A practical way of handling these cases is to organise a meeting once a week with these non-competing salespeople where you can share names, addresses and telephone numbers of possible customers.

If you are working for a short-term insurance organisation, you should stay in contact with salespeople who are selling cars on hire purchase, because customers who use this type of financing are legally required to insure these vehicles. These salespeople can therefore supply you with some excellent leads.

If you are employed by an organisation such as Tiger Wheel & Tyre, you should keep in touch with salespeople selling second-hand cars.

Comment

Salespeople must show resourcefulness and originality in order to find prospects. Different salespeople who sell different products and services find prospects in different ways from different sources. The most important prospects are always existing customers. A salesperson can never devote too much time and effort to them. Salespeople who give themselves exposure by moving around, meeting people and joining clubs and societies; who are involved in their communities; and who are always on the lookout for new business will never have a shortage of prospects.

QUALIFICATION OF PROSPECTS

Qualification is the evaluation by the salesperson of possible consumers of the salesperson's product or service to determine whether the person or institution has an immediate need for the product or service, has the authority to buy, and has the means to pay for the product.

Qualifying criteria are need or use, ability to buy, the size or importance of the sales transaction, frequency of need, urgency of need, and authority to buy. Each of these criteria will now be discussed in more detail.

Need or use

Prospects who are only interested in a product or service, but do not have a use or a need for it for themselves or for a relative, a friend, a colleague or their organisation, do not qualify as a prospect. For example, a person who has a facebrick house does not need paint for the outside maintenance of the house.

During the qualification process, it is necessary for the salesperson to determine the prospect's reasons for his or her possible interest in the product. The salesperson must find out what the prospect's real motives are. For example, a prospect may want to buy a pair of sunglasses. What possible reasons are there for this? Does he or she want them for eye protection or for the image associated with the specific brand, e.g. Ray-Ban?

Prospective buyers are sometimes not aware that a need for a product exists; for example they may not know that there is a need in their organisation for a colour printer. The salesperson must present the use of his or her product in such a way that the prospect develops a need for the product and can find a use for it.

Ability to buy

The ability to buy means that the prospect has cash available, or can pay by cheque or credit card, or has credit facilities available, or qualifies for credit arrangements (e.g. a specific amount for a bond).

The qualification of a prospect therefore includes an investigation into his or her financial position and creditworthiness. The salesperson must examine the prospect's credit record with the help of credit agencies such as the Information Trust Corporation, or must request a bank report or follow up a trade reference.

When price is mentioned in the sales transaction, the salesperson can also set out the terms for payment:

- The required deposit, if any
- The time period (24, 36 or 48 months)
- The amount of the monthly instalment
- The interest rate charged
- The qualifications for credit facilities (to qualify for a credit limit of R5 000 at Edgars, for example, you must earn at least R8 000 per month)

If the prospect wishes to make use of credit facilities, the necessary credit application forms must be filled in, credit references must be checked, and approval must be obtained from the accounts department.

Size and importance of the sales transaction

The income of salespeople is directly related to the volume of their sales if they receive straight commission. It would be more profitable for a salesperson to concentrate on a prospect who may place a larger order than on a lot of smaller prospects. In terms of time, cost and the avoidance of problems, it will pay the salesperson to attend to a prospect who will place a larger order before one who places a smaller order.

Frequency of need

How often a customer purchases also plays a role in determining a salesperson's time and effort.

Does one spend one's time on the buyer who purchases often or on the one who buys now and then? The answer depends on the industry, the distance from the suppliers, the size and financial strength of the customer, and his or her potential.

Salespeople prefer to get larger and more frequent orders because the customer will then purchase less from competitors.

Urgency of need

Much of a salesperson's valuable time may be lost in sales transactions if the urgency of the prospect's need has not been established. Salespeople must use their discretion in not devoting too much of their time to prospects who only wish to buy at some time in the future.

For example, a couple who have no children yet will only be interested in purchasing a BMX bicycle within the next five years. In cases like these the salesperson must only leave brochures, other information on the product and a business card after a personal visit. A telephone conversation followed by mailing, faxing or emailing the above-mentioned details and documentation to the prospect can be sufficient and will save the salesperson a lot of time.

Authority to buy

This refers to the authority the so-called final decision maker on the purchasing team has in making purchasing decisions, especially in the industrial market. It can also refer to the authority people (husband and wife) or parties (partners in the case of a partnership) have to sign cheques.[4]

REFERRALS DURING THE REFERRAL CYCLE
Referrals are popular

Referrals come from prospects. Different sources of prospects form the prospect pool, which is a group of names gathered from various sources. The source used by the salesperson, for example, may be a mailing list, the telephone directory, referrals, so-called 'orphans' or visiting customers. A prospect pool is usually created from four main sources, as follows:

Table 6.2 *Referral sources*

Source	Description
Leads	People and organisations salespeople know nothing or very little about
Referrals	People or organisations salespeople frequently know very little about other than what they have learned from the referral
Orphans	Customers whose salesperson has left the organisation. Organisational records provide the only information about these past customers
Customers	The most important prospects for future sales

Most salespeople required to create customers through prospecting do not like to cold call, i.e. contact strangers. They have the goal of using a prospect pool composed of customers, friends and, when available, orphans. Referral from customers is the very best way to increase the chances of selling to a stranger (prospect). People want to do business with, and refer business to, people they know, like and trust. Relationship building becomes more important since a satisfied customer will provide the salesperson with a constant supply of prospects.[5]

MAKE AN APPOINTMENT WITH A PROSPECT OR CUSTOMER IN PERSON OR BY PHONE
Introduction

The quickest and most cost-effective way to get around is to travel by phone. This does have a downside in that you cannot see the customer or the expressions on his or her face. The telephone is, nonetheless, a good way of obtaining an appointment. A telephone call can be unwelcome – you may be intruding on the prospect's time – so whatever you say to the prospect should be short, relevant and of interest to him or her.

Comment

Unless the salesperson operates in a business environment that has a well-established client list from whom regular telephonic orders can be taken, it is not recommended that he or she try to sell over the telephone. This approach rarely works. The salesperson's aim should be to get an interview with the prospect 'even if it is just for ten minutes'. If the prospect agrees to ten minutes, provided that he or she is genuinely interested, the salesperson can be sure that the appointment will last considerably longer.

Note

When making an appointment over the telephone always consider the following three questions:

- Is there a best time to see the prospect?
- What is the best place to see the prospect (e.g. his or her office or your showroom)?
- What is the best product to show your prospect?

Examples of telephone conversations

There are many ways to open a telephone conversation. Below are four examples of opening statements:

Example 1: Convey a benefit

'Good morning, Mr Chapedi. My name is Anele Boqwane of Healthcare Systems. Every organisation is interested in reducing the cost of medical aid and in obtaining improved benefits for their members. Our organisation has just launched a new product that does just this. If you will give me ten minutes of your time, I can show you some statistics that will illustrate how companies just like your own have made the savings. Our research will really make you sit up and take notice. Just ten minutes?'

Example 2: Ask a question

'Mr Louw, my name is Jacques and I am phoning from an organisation called Phone Call Systems. Have you found that staff members are using the phone for private calls?'

Example 3: The good news approach

'Mrs Thethwa, are you aware that there is a new sales game on the market that has been shown to make sales staff more productive?'

Example 4: The solution approach

'Mr Johnson, I noticed that you were advertising for a secretary in the *Oosterlig*. Our, organisation, Assisting Hand, specialises in providing secretarial assistance on a short-term basis. Perhaps while you are screening candidates we could arrange for someone to help you with your workload. '

Getting appointments

The use of the telephone to make appointments is the most efficient method of getting to see the customer. However, some salespeople dislike using the phone because they tend to get rejected.

Why do prospects say 'no' over the telephone?

There are several reasons for this.

- *All phone calls are an interruption.* Whether people are phoned at work or home, they are not sitting there waiting for you to call. They may reject you for the simple reason that they do not want to be bothered. This has nothing to do with you, your ability or your product. They are simply reacting negatively to being interrupted.
- *Salespeople are not interesting.* Suppose you were to call someone to say: 'Hello, Mr van der Walt. My name is Leon Vermeulen, with the XYZ organisation. I wonder if we could get together so that I could show you some of our products?' If you were to use this approach, the only people who would readily agree to an appointment would be those who already wanted your product and had been thinking of calling you (the chances of this would be slim) or the lonely or depressed (who are not likely to be your best-qualified prospects).

Prospects are afraid that the salesperson will waste too much of their time. In an interview, salespeople who do not respect their prospect's time will use up hours blathering on and on.

Also, prospects are busy people and they have other interests in their lives which are stronger than their desire to spend much time with longwinded salespeople. They do not want to get tied up in long telephone conversations. This concern ties in with the previous point, but refers to time on the phone rather than time spent on an appointment. To avoid a long phone call, it is easier to cut it off at the beginning by saying 'No'. Prospects are also tired of unprofessional salespeople. Too many salespeople just pitch products rather than providing a valuable service that would be of benefit to the prospect. Again, prospects do not want their time wasted.

Guidelines for using the phone

In preparing to use the phone to set up appointments, keep in mind some rules that will help you to beat the rejection factor.

- Do some mental exercises before phoning. Give yourself a pep talk. For example: 'I am confident in my approach. The service I can offer this prospect is of such value that I would be hurting her by not giving her the opportunity to know about it. She needs this service and she needs me. She will become a customer and a friend. '

- Make your calls in a standing position. You will come across as more confident and focused.

- Keep your calls short and to the point: each telephone call to get an appointment should take less than three minutes.

- Remember, if you provide your prospects with too much information on the phone, they may have enough to decide they do not want to see you. Do not volunteer information: save this for the meeting with them.

- Make your approach interesting. Spend time coming up with benefits and ideas that will make the prospect want to hear more.

- Use the prospect's name frequently. Make sure you know the prospect's name and how to pronounce it properly before making a call.

- Put a smile on your face and in your voice. The warmth and friendliness you project can be picked up on the other end of the line. Try putting a mirror in front of you while you make the calls as a reminder to smile.

- Dress in your business attire when you phone. Do this even if you are making your calls from home. Being in a suit or business outfit makes you feel more professional, confident and prepared to do business.

- Be polite to a fault. Use 'Please' and 'Thank you' often in your conversation.

- Do not attempt to sell your product on the phone if your purpose is to get an appointment. You can achieve only one thing at a time. If you try to sell your product to a new prospect over the phone, your chances of getting the appointment are slim. The more time you spend talking with someone, the more information you give and the less chance you have of making the appointment.

- Be extremely well organised before you dial. Have all your prospects' names, phone numbers and addresses in front of you. Have several names and numbers ready to call. Have your calendar ready, and block the times you want to set up appointments. Once you start phoning, do not stop until you have met your appointment objectives. Never stop phoning to look up a number, get a cup of coffee, chat with an associate or anything else. *Do not let anyone or anything interrupt your momentum.*

- Do not waste time thinking between calls. Just keep phoning. Make sure the place you phone from is quiet and free from interruptions. Avoid distractions by clearing everything not related to your calls off your desk.

- Set your appointments at ten minutes to the hour; for example 7:50, 8:50 or 9:50. Never ask for an appointment on the hour or the half hour. Prospects will assume you will take only ten minutes of their time if you ask for an appointment at 1:50. If you wish to add some levity to the discussion, ask for the appointment at 1:49. You are sure to get a reaction! Be cautious, though. If you set such a specific time, you must be there on time.

■ Develop and practice a telephone script until you know it by heart.

■ No matter what business you are in, seeing people with the purpose of solving their problems is how you become successful.

■ Do whatever needs to be done to see enough of the right people at the right time in order to meet your sales objectives.[6]

SELF-EVALUATION: HOW WELL DO YOU USE THE TELEPHONE?

This self-test will help you to evaluate how effectively you use the telephone and will also highlight some of the dos and don'ts of telephone selling.

Table 6.3 *Evaluation list for telephone application[7]*

Step	Activity
Preparation	■ Plan what you are going to say ■ Write down key points as memory aids, if necessary ■ Identify whom you should be speaking to ■ Review the results of previous telephone calls made, if any
The call	Do you: ■ Greet the customer pleasantly? ■ Identify yourself and your organisation? ■ Check that you are speaking to the right person (such as the buyer)? ■ Have a reason for calling – perhaps a written-out opening statement, designed to be of interest to the listener? ■ Use the phone only to try to secure an appointment, not to sell? ■ Stress the main benefit you are selling as early as possible in the course of your call?
Your telephone technique	Do you: ■ Try to smile down the phone? ■ Keep the conversation friendly, yet businesslike? ■ Speak slowly and clearly, yet confidently and positively? ■ Use the prospect's name while talking to him or her? ■ Respect the other person's time? ■ Show enthusiasm in a genuine way? ■ Speak more slowly than usual if the concept or product is new? ■ Check that you are communicating effectively? ■ Try to ask a few probing questions that will get the prospect talking? ■ Listen without interrupting, and answer questions? ■ End the conversation politely? ■ Offer to call back at another time if the prospect is busy? ■ Keep your conversation reasonably short? ⮎

The summary	Do you:
	■ Summarise whatever arrangements you have made before ringing off?
	■ Ask if the prospect has any questions?
	■ Thank the prospect for his or her time?
	■ Allow him or her to hang up first?
	■ Put the phone down gently?

OVERCOMING A RELUCTANCE TO PROSPECT

People often stereotype salespeople as bold, adventurous and somewhat abrasive. The view that salespeople are fearless is more fiction than fact. Salespeople often struggle with a reluctance to prospect that persists no matter how well they have been trained and how much they believe in the products they sell. Many people are uncomfortable when they initially contact other people, but for salespeople reluctance to call can be a career-threatening condition.

Research shows a number of reasons for reluctance to call. Reasons include worrying about worse-case scenarios; spending too much time preparing; being overly concerned with looking successful; being fearful of making group presentations, of appearing too pushy, of losing friends or losing family approval, and of using the phone for prospecting; feeling intimidated by people with prestige or power, or feeling guilt at having a career in selling; and having a compulsive need to argue, make excuses or blame others.

Reluctance to call can and must be overcome to sell successfully. Several activities can help:

■ Start by listening to the excuses other salespeople give to justify their call reluctance behaviour. Evaluate their validity. Then identify the excuses you use to avoid making calls and evaluate the validity of those excuses. In most cases, the excuses are simply not valid.

■ Engage in sales training and role-playing activities to improve your prospecting skills and your ability to handle questions and rejections that arise.

■ Make prospecting contacts with a supporting partner or sales manager. Just their presence will often provide additional needed support (you will not feel so alone).

■ Set specific goals for all your prospecting activity.

■ Realise the economic value of most prospecting activities. For example, if you keep good records, you may discover that every phone call that you make results in an average of R150 commission in the long run.

■ Stop negative self-evaluations from ruling your behaviour. Learn to think positively about the future instead of focusing on past blunders.

■ Remember that you are calling on prospects to meet their needs, not just so that you can line your pockets with money. You are performing a helpful and vital service to your prospects by calling on them.

■ Control your perceptions of what prospects might say about you, your organisation or your products. You do not know what their reactions will be until you meet with them.

■ Learn and apply relaxation and stress-reducing techniques that you can implement before and during prospecting.

■ Recount your own prospecting success, or those of others. Read books by people who have prospected successfully or creatively. Realise that persistence pays off in the long run.

DISCUSSION QUESTIONS

Discuss the following assessments in groups and with your facilitator, who will evaluate your assessments during the discussion.

1.   You are a sales representative for one of the country's largest paper mills. You have an appointment for your first visit to the production manager of a successful printing organisation. You are on time for the appointment, but have to wait 20 minutes. On entering the production manager's office, you immediately notice that she seems very businesslike and pressed for time. Explain how you would approach this prospect to ensure that she listens to your sales presentation.

2.   What prospect source(s) would you recommend that salespeople use when selling the following products or services?

   ■ Life insurance
   ■ Computer software
   ■ An exclusive range of cosmetics
   ■ Photocopiers
   ■ Cars
   ■ Vacuum cleaners
   ■ A medical aid scheme

   Clearly state why you would recommend a particular source.

3.   Illustrate clearly the difference between a prospect's need to buy and the ability to buy.

4.   The methods used for prospecting will depend on the industry, the size of the organisation, the product and service, the competitors, the types of clients and the salesperson. List and discuss five possible prospecting methods a person selling computers could use in order to get new clients.

5.   You are appointed as an estate agent at Property Are One and will specialise in the selling of townhouses. Name and discuss four prospecting methods you will use in order to find new customers. Name two criteria you will use to qualify prospective clients as customers, and motivate these criteria with examples.

6.   List and discuss six possible prospecting methods a person selling Tupperware products (containers for household use) can use in order to get new clients. List the criteria you will use to qualify someone as a potential client.

South African Equipment Corporation[8]

You work for the South African Equipment Corporation selling office equipment. Imagine entering the lobby and reception room of a small manufacturing company. You hand the receptionist your business card and ask to see the purchasing agent. 'What is this in reference to?' the secretary asks, as two other salespeople approach.

Questions

Which of the following alternatives would you use and why?

(a) Give a quick explanation of your equipment, ask whether the secretary has heard of your company or used your equipment, and again ask to see the purchasing agent.

(b) Say: 'I would like to discuss our office equipment.'

(c) Say: 'I sell office equipment designed to save your company money and provide greater efficiency. Companies such as yours prefer our products. Could you help me to get in to see your purchasing agent?'

(d) Provide a complete presentation and demonstration.

Johannesburg Satellites[9]

As a salesperson for Johannesburg Satellites, you sell satellite dishes for homes, apartments and businesses. After installing a satellite in John Gabriel's home, you ask him for a referral. John suggests you contact Riaan Immelman, his brother-in-law.

Mr Immelman is a well-know architect who designs and constructs unique residential homes. Your objective is to sell Mr Immelman a satellite dish for his office and home in the hope that he will install them in the homes he builds. Certainly he is a centre of influence, and a good word from him to his customers could result in numerous sales, thus another objective is to obtain referrals from Mr Immelman.

Questions

1. After eight attempts, you now have Mr Immelman on the telephone. What would you say in order to get an appointment and set the stage for getting referrals?

2. You get the appointment and are now in Mr Immelman's office trying to get him to buy a satellite dish for his home and office. Sometime during the presentation you are going to ask for a referral. What would you say? ➲

3. Mr Immelman buys a satellite dish for his home, but not for his office. You install it yourself and then spend 15 minutes showing Mr and Mrs Immelman and their teenage son how to use it. Before you leave, how would you ask for a referral?
4. Three months after the installation you are talking to Mr Immelman. How would you ask for a referral?

SELF-ASSESSMENT QUESTIONS[10]

1. What is the difference between a lead and a prospect?

2. What should you, as a salesperson, do to qualify a potential customer?

3. This chapter termed prospecting the 'lifeblood of selling'.

    ▪ Where do salespeople find prospects?

    ▪ Discuss any five prospecting methods discussed in this chapter. Can you think of any other ways to find prospects?

4. Assume that you have started a business to manufacture and market a product line selling for between R2 500 and R5 000. Your primary customers are small retailers. How would you uncover leads and convert them into prospects without personally contacting them?

5. You are a new salesperson. Next month your regional sales manager will be in your city/town to check your progress in searching for new customers for your computer software line of products. You have learned that Technology Inc., a high-technology company, requires a supplier of your product. A friend has also told you about 12 local manufacturing companies that could use your product. The sales potential of each of these companies is about one-fifth of Technology Inc. Knowing that your sales manager expects results, explain how you will qualify each lead (assuming that the 12 smaller firms are similar).

NOTES

1. Futrell, C. 1993. *Fundamentals of Selling*. Boston: Irwin.

2. Visser, op. cit., p. 113.

3. Roelofse, A. & Van der Vyver, D. 2000. *Sales Management*. Observatory: Future Managers, pp. 52–58.

4. Roelofse & Van der Vyver, op. cit., pp. 58–59.

5. Stanton, W.J. & Spiro, L.R. 1999. *Sales Management in Action: A Practical Guide for Learners and Practitioners*. Sandton: Heinemann, pp. 59–62, 429.

6.   Vanwyck, W. 1996. *Pure Selling: The Basics.* North Vancouver: Self-Counsel Press, pp. 36–37.

7.   Clarke, H. 1995. *Secrets of Successful Selling: An Essential Guide for South African Salespeople.* Sandton: Struik Book Distributors, pp. 102–103.

8.   Futrell, C.M. 2006. *Fundamentals of Selling – Customers for Life through Service.* New York: McGraw-Hill-Irwin, p. 251.

9.   Ibid., p. 252.

10.   Ibid., p. 248.

i   Franchise Finder, Online Directory of Franchises and Business Opportunities in South Africa. Franchisefinder. co. za (accessed on 4 April 2010).

ADDITIONAL SOURCES

Johnston, M.W. & Marshall, G.W. 2005. *Relationship Selling and Sales Management.* New York: McGraw-Hill, pp. 134–141.

Weitz, B.A., Castleberry, S.B. & Tanner, J.F. 2004. *Selling – Building Partnerships.* (Fifth edition). New York: McGraw-Hill-Irwin, pp. 184–202.

7

PLANNING THE SALES CALL (PRE-APPROACH)

LEARNING OUTCOMES

After studying this chapter you should be able to:

- Explain the importance of planning a sales call
- Discuss the pre-approach process when planning a sales call
- Discuss the setting of call objectives
- Discuss and compile a prospect profile

INTRODUCTION

Many salespeople are excellent public speakers; that is to say, they can present to a prospect and speak in front of a crowd confidently and convincingly. These same salespeople will often spend many hours preparing a fantastic presentation with great PowerPoint slides and stunning product demonstrations and will be ready to present it at the drop of a hat. The problem is that being able to present well is only one small piece of the personal selling puzzle. You will have heard it said that failing to plan is planning to fail. Well, this old adage has never been as true as it is in the field of selling. In this chapter we will look at planning the sales call, sometimes referred to as the 'pre-approach', the set of tasks that salespeople have to perform before they get around to seeing the prospect for the first time. These steps are summarised in Figure 7.1.

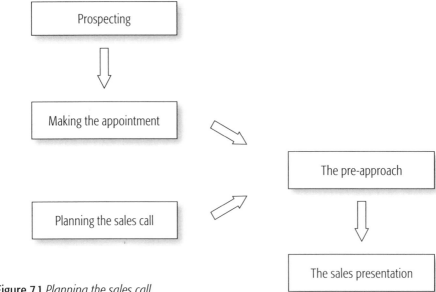

Figure 7.1 *Planning the sales call*

MAKING THE APPOINTMENT

One of the oldest, most recognised and often the hardest form of sales is known as cold calling. Cold calling is when salespeople present themselves to a prospect without making an appointment and dive straight into their sales pitch

In some industries or with regard to some products, cold calling might work and is still the preferred tactic of some salespeople. However, when the prospect is a busy businessperson whose time is as valuable as the salesperson's then an appointment is often the only way to ever get in to see them. Let us consider some of the benefits of making an appointment with a prospect[1]

1. Making appointments will save the salesperson hours, and even days, in selling time every year. If salespeople do not make an appointment and try cold calling, they will inevitably spend time waiting for the right decision maker to become available, and that person may not even be on the premises! Unplanned visits by salespeople rarely get treated quickly and efficiently.[2]
2. Prospects are normally in a more open frame of mind when they are expecting the salesperson. A prospect that is caught by surprise by a salesperson who just arrives unannounced may be more negative, and even hostile, making the sales pitch harder than it ought to be.

Remember: Arriving without an appointment makes you an 'interruption' not a 'bringer of benefits'.

3. Serious businesspeople make appointments (and keep them). An appointment made in advance and confirmed closer to the time projects an image of professionalism that already sets the salesperson apart from the average.
4. Appointments aid in planning. Appointments that are set in advance allow salespeople to plan their time efficiently. This not only aids in time management but also in route planning. Salespeople who know where and when their next two or three appointments are going to be can plan their travel in the most fuel- and time-efficient manner.

Making an appointment with a prospect for the first time can be a daunting and sometimes discouraging task. A lot like making a presentation, when calling to make an appointment, there is only one chance to make the right impression! Professional buyers will often be easier to reach because they are constantly looking out for ways to improve their own organisations. Amateur buyers tend to be more difficult when it comes to making appointments as they are struggling under the barrage of salespeople trying to see them. Let us look at some tips for making appointments.

1. Making the appointment with the right person
When purchase decisions are made, especially in organisations, there are a variety of people involved in the decision. There are gatekeepers (people who protect the decision makers); influencers (people who influence the decision); decision makers (people who have the final say); and payers (the people who actually pay for the purchase). There is no golden rule as to which one of these should be seen first. In most selling situations the salesperson will have to deal with each of them at some point or the other. Getting to the correct person almost always involves speaking to a gatekeeper first, and each salesperson has a different way of dealing with them. Gatekeepers could be a secretary (most often), a security guard or even a lower-level manager. Some salespeople recommend getting friendly with the gatekeepers first, as time spent on this is an investment that will reward handsomely when appointment time comes around.

Dropping the right names

One technique that most salespeople have used at one time or another is to call the CEO's office directly. The secretary will inevitably know who the correct person is to speak to, which provides the salesperson with the best referral available.

Consider this situation: James (the salesperson) has no idea who the correct person is to speak to in the organisation, or he has had trouble getting past the buyer's gatekeeper. He calls the CEO's office and the following conversation takes place:

James: 'Good morning, my name is James Weed from Acme Oils. I am convinced that using Acme Oils would save your organisation 15% per annum on lubrication costs. I

➲

⮎

believe that Mr Avis (the CEO) is the correct person to speak to in this regard.'
The secretary: 'Well, Mr Weed, that sounds very interesting. The correct person to speak to regarding oils is actually not Mr Avis but Mr Good, our purchasing manager.'
James: 'Thank you. Would you happen to have his direct line?
The secretary: 'It's xxx-xxx xxx.'

Now, James calls Mr Good's gatekeeper…

James: 'Good morning. I have just spoken to Mr Avis's secretary, who has referred me to Mr Good and suggested that I speak with him directly regarding the replacement of oil supply…'

Notice how a referral from the boss's office can lead to doors being opened?

Some golden rules for making appointments with the right people:[3]
- Believe in yourself and that it can be done.
- Make friends in the prospect organisation (gatekeepers, etc.).
- Don't waste time calling the wrong people.

2. Making the appointment over the phone

Most appointments are made over the phone. Email or fax may also be used, but the personal touch is always a winner. When making an appointment over the phone always be prepared. The more time spent planning, the better the call will go. (Telephoning for an appointment is discussed in detail in Chapter 6.)

3. Selecting the right time

When calling to make appointments there are two issues regarding time – firstly, when to make the call, and secondly, when to schedule the appointment. Both of these issues can be solved by carefully planning the appointment call. Some salespeople recommend calling after hours when the prospect is not likely to be distracted by work;[4] others recommending not calling in the first or the last few hours of the working day as those are usually the busiest times.[5] Once again, in personal selling there is no golden rule. Each prospect is different and it is up to salespeople to do their homework well enough so that they know when to call.

The time for the appointment is a very similar situation. Buyers and purchasing managers are extremely busy people and making time to see salespeople had better be worth the effort! Bear in mind that these prospects are seeing many salespeople each day and that you need to make yourself stand out if you want to get that appointment.

4. Selecting the right place

Depending on the type of appointment, the location of the appointment can vary. If the salesperson requires a lot of space for a demonstration then meeting at the prospect's premises might not be the best option. Some salespeople believe that getting the prospect to come to another location signifies commitment on the part of the prospect and gives them hope for closing the sale. If time is an issue for the prospect then maybe a breakfast meeting at a coffee shop on the way to work should be considered.

> If your product or service requires a messy demonstration, remember to warn the prospect beforehand. You don't want them caught unawares.

Now that the appointment has been made, the real pre-sales work begins ...

PLANNING THE SALES CALL

There is no substitute for good planning. In every aspect of life, the better prepared we are, the more successful our results. Soccer players who work well together as a team and who are all familiar with the coach's plans will be successful, and the same goes for a sales call. The salesperson that is better prepared will close more sales and ultimately earn more commission. In this next section we will look at the four steps in the planning of a sales call.

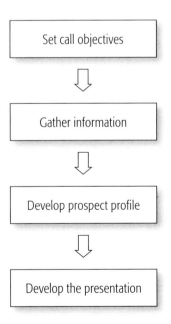

Figure 7.2 *The steps in the planning of a sales call*

Good planning will definitely increase the salesperson's chances of success. Consider some of these reasons for planning properly for a sales call:

- Planning builds self-confidence. If the salesperson has planned for all possibilities and is fully prepared for the presentation, then there is less that can go wrong.
- Planning projects a professional image. If prospects can see that the salesperson is well prepared, they know they are dealing with someone who takes them seriously as a potential customer.
- Planning saves both the prospect's and the salesperson's time. A well-prepared salesperson will be on time for the presentation, set up quickly and not waste time by looking for information or equipment.
- Planning helps the salesperson to remain flexible. If salespeople take all situations into account when preparing for the sales call, they can easily adapt the presentation based on what the prospect is looking for.
- Planning improves the chances of a long-term relationship with the prospect. Prospects are impressed by well-prepared salespeople and are more willing to listen to someone who shows them respect by being well prepared.

The first step in preparing for a sales call is to set call objectives.

Setting sales call objectives

The objectives for the sales call are those things that the salesperson wants to achieve from it. They may be as simple as selling the product or service, or they could be loftier like establishing a relationship with the prospect. The sales call objectives will, of course, vary with each selling situation, but the most important thing is that salespeople take the time to establish what the objectives are before they embark on a sales call.

Sales call objectives should be:[6]

- *Specific.* Objectives should focus exactly on what the salesperson has to do on the sales call. 'Introduce product X' is not as specific as 'Make sure that the prospect is aware of all of the features and benefits of product X'

- *Quantified.* Objectives should have a quantity assigned to them. 'To get an order' is not quantified, but 'To sell five units' is

- *Realistic.* Objectives should aim to push the limits but must still be attainable. 'Meeting the new prospect and selling them 100 units and signing a contract for ten years' does not seem like a realistic objective

Once salespeople have a clear idea of what they want to achieve with the sales call, they can move on to step 2, which is gathering information.

Gathering information

Most of the information that the salesperson has about the prospect will have been gathered during the prospecting stage. Now that the appointment has been made and objectives set for the call, the salesperson needs to gather as much detailed information about the prospect (individual or organisation, or both) as possible.

> Name:
> Title and responsibilities:
> Attitude towards company:
> Attitudes towards competitors:
> Views and opinions about the product or category:
> Personality and social style (lifestyle):
> Background (education, training):
> Personal interests (hobby, sports):

Figure 7.3 *Typical information needs for planning the sales call (individual)*

If the salesperson's research into the prospect indicates that they follow an organisational decision-making process, implying that there will be multiple decision-making units, influencers and gatekeepers, they may need additional information, such as is indicated in Figure 7.4.

> Type of organisation and position in distribution channel:
> Customer base:
> Competitors:
> Buying situation:
> Purchase history:
> Policies:
> Reasons for current supplier choice:

Figure 7.4 *Typical information needs for planning the sales call (organisation)*

The resourceful salesperson will gather this information from as many sources as possible to verify facts and to identify inconsistencies. Much of the information is available in the public domain (libraries, the Internet, magazines, etc.) but a few well-placed questions to gatekeepers and contacts within an organisation can provide the salesperson with a wealth of information.

The purpose of gathering as much information as possible is to determine a profile of the prospect.

Developing the prospect profile

Prospect profiles are a complete picture of prospects, their situation and their needs, so that sales calls can be customised.[7] The more detailed the prospect profile, the better the chance of successfully closing the sale. A prospect profile should tell you:[8]

- Who makes the final purchase decision – an individual or a committee?
- What is the buyer's background? What is the organisation's background?
- What is the buyer expecting of the salesperson?
- What are the desired business terms and needs of the prospect – delivery, quantities, etc.?
- What competitors are doing business with the organisation and why?
- What are the prospect's purchasing policies?
- Do we have a history with the account?

> For individual buyers, some salespeople go further and develop personality or brain profiles of the prospects so that they can anticipate how the prospect will think and react to certain stimuli.

The prospect profile is then used to develop a backbone for the sales presentation. The backbone of a presentation is the core benefit that the salesperson is trying to sell and the means to do so. The backbone should, for example, consider the following:

1. What is the core benefit that this prospect is looking for? By clearly answering this question (the answer might already have been found during prospecting), salespeople know whether or not they can meet the prospect's needs fully. Some desired benefits/needs might be latent and once salespeople have identified them, they can be sure to highlight them in the presentation The amount of research done will have the added benefit of impressing the prospect.

2. What is the business proposition to this prospect? What will the salesperson ultimately propose to the prospect in terms of the business deal? This answer should include potential quantities, delivery times, service level agreements, payment plans, etc.

Once salespeople have a clear idea of what they want to achieve with the presentation, it comes down to developing the actual presentation.

Developing the presentation

The last pre-call planning step is that of preparing the sales presentation. The idea behind the sales presentation is to guide the prospect through the AIDA model, i.e. getting their *attention,* generating *interest* in the product or service, stimulating *desire* for the product or service and finally initiating *action,* by purchasing or agreeing to purchase the product or service. The salesperson needs to answer the following questions:[9]

- How much technology should be employed? Should PowerPoint, notebooks, etc. be used?
- How formal should the presentation be?
- How long should the presentation be, and how much time must be allocated for questions and answers?
- What materials should be sent to the prospect in advance?
- What should the salesperson bring to the presentation?

The presentation will be discussed in more detail in the next chapter.

This chapter has looked at the steps that a salesperson should follow before even beginning to design a sales presentation namely the pre-call planning. A well-designed plan backed up by intensive research will ensure a better chance of a successful sale.

CASE STUDY

AMWAY[i]

Amway is a direct selling company and manufacturer that uses multi-level marketing to sell a variety of products, primarily in the health, beauty, and home care markets. [3] [4][5] Amway was founded in 1959 by Jay Van Andel and Richard DeVos. Based in Ada, Michigan, the company and family of companies under Alticor reported sales growth of 2.3%, reaching US$8.4 billion for the year ending December 31, 2009. [1] Its product lines include home care products, personal care products, jewelry, electronics, Nutrilite dietary supplements, water purifiers, air purifiers, insurance and cosmetics. In 2004, Health & Beauty products accounted for nearly 60% of worldwide sales. [6] Amway conducts business through a number of affiliated companies in more than ninety countries and territories around the world.[7] It is ranked by Forbes as one of the largest private companies in the United States[8] and by Deloitte as one of the largest retailers in the world.[9]

History

Jay Van Andel and Richard DeVos, friends since school days, had been business partners in various endeavors including a hamburger stand, air charter service, and a sailing business. In 1949 they were introduced by Neil Maaskant (Van Andel's second cousin) to the *Nutrilite Products Corporation*. Nutrilite was a California-based direct sales company founded by Dr. Carl Rhenborg, developer of the first multivitamin marketed in the United States. In August 1949, after a night-long talk, DeVos and Van Andel signed up to become distributors for

Nutrilite food supplements.[10] They sold their first box the next day for $19.50, but lost interest for the next two weeks. Shortly thereafter, at the urging of Maaskant, who had become their *sponsor*, they traveled to Chicago to attend a Nutrilite seminar. The meeting was at a downtown hotel, with over a hundred people in attendance. After seeing promotional filmstrips and listening to talks by company representatives and successful distributors, they decided to pursue the Nutrilite business opportunity with enthusiasm. They sold their second box of supplements on their return trip to Michigan, and rapidly proceeded to develop their new business further.[10]

In 1949, DeVos and Van Andel had formed **Ja-Ri Corporation** (abbreviated from their respective first names) for importing wooden goods from South American countries; after their trip to the Nutrilite seminar, they dropped this business and Ja-Ri became their Nutrilite distributorship.[11] In addition to profits on each product sold, Nutrilite also offered commission on the sales of products by new distributors introduced to the company by existing distributors – a system today known as multi-level marketing or network marketing. By 1958, DeVos and Van Andel had built an organization of over 5 000 distributors. However, following concerns about the stability of Nutrilite, in April 1959 they and some of their top distributors formed *The American Way Association* to represent the distributors and look for additional products to market.[12]

Their first product was called *Frisk*, a concentrated organic cleaner developed by a scientist in Ohio. DeVos and Van Andel bought the rights to manufacture and distribute Frisk, and later changed the name to LOC (Liquid Organic Concentrate).[13] They subsequently formed *Amway Sales Corporation* to procure and inventory products and to handle the sales and marketing plan, and *Amway Services Corporation* to handle insurance and other benefits for distributors (Amway being an abbreviation of American Way).[14] In 1960 they purchased a 50% share in *Atco Manufacturing Company* in Detroit, the original manufacturers of LOC, and changed its name to *Amway Manufacturing Corporation*.[15] In 1964 the Amway Sales Corporation, Amway Services Corporation, and Amway Manufacturing Corporation merged to form a single entity, *Amway Corporation*.[16] Amway bought control of Nutrilite in 1972 and full ownership in 1994.[17]

International expansion

Amway expanded overseas to Australia in 1971, to Europe in 1973, to parts of Asia in 1974, to Japan in 1979, to Latin America in 1985, to China in 1995, to Africa in 1997, to India and Scandinavia in 1998, to Russia in 2005, and to Vietnam in 2008.

Quixtar

In 1999 the founders of the Amway corporation established a new holding company, named Alticor, and launched three new companies, 1) a sister (and separate) Internet-focused company named Quixtar, 2) Access Business Group, and 3) *Pyxis Innovations*. Pyxis, later replaced by Fulton Innovation, pursued research and development and Access Business Group handled manufacturing and logistics, for Amway, Quixtar, and third party clients. [18]

After virtually all Amway distributors in North America switched to Quixtar, Alticor elected to close Amway North America after 2001. The main difference was that all distributors, now called *Independent Business Owners* (IBOs) could order directly from Amway on the internet, rather than from their upline 'direct distributor', and have products shipped directly to their home. The Amway name continued being used in the rest of the world, and the home of the Orlando Magic was named the Amway Arena in 2005. The Orlando Magic is owned by Amway founder Richard DeVos. [19] In 2006, Quixtar published *The Quixtar Independent Business Owner Compensation Plan*, in which the company reported that the average monthly gross income for 'Active' IBOs was $115. [20] In June 2007 it was announced that the Quixtar brand would be phased out over an 18- to 24-month period in favor of a unified Amway brand worldwide.

Global markets

In 2008 two thirds of Amway's 58 markets reported sales increases, including strong growth in the China, Russia and India markets. [21] Amway India sales grew 40% to 1128 crore (US$230 million). [22]

Amway China

Amway grew quickly in China from its market launch in 1995. In 1998, after abuses of illegal pyramid schemes led to riots, the Chinese Government enacted a ban on all direct selling companies, including Amway. [23] After negotiations, some companies like Amway, Avon, and Mary Kay continued to operate through a network of retail stores promoted by an independent sales force. [24] China introduced new direct selling laws in December 2005, and in December 2006 Amway was one of the first companies to receive a license to resume direct sales. At the time they had a reported 180 000 sales representatives, 140 stores, and $2 billion in annual sales. [25] In 2007 Amway Greater China and Southeast Asia Chief Executive Eva Cheng was ranked #88 by Forbes magazine in its list of the World's Most Powerful Women. [26] In 2008 Amway Greater China was Amway's largest market, reporting 28% growth and sales of ¥17 billion (US$2.5 billion). [27]

Brands

Amway's product line grew from LOC, with the laundry detergent SA8 added in 1960, and later the hair care product Satinique (1965) and Artistry (1968). Today Amway manufactures over 450 products, with manufacturing facilities in Ada, Michigan, China, and India, as well as Nutrilite organic farms in California, Washington State, Mexico, and Brazil. In addition Amway affiliates market products from hundreds of other manufacturers offering everything from books (e.g. Barnes & Noble, North America) to wine (World of Wine, Europe). [28]

Household cleaners

Amway is best known in North America for its original cleaning products, LOC, SA8 clothes washing products and *Dish Drops* dish cleaning products. In the January 2007 issue of Consumer Reports, *SA8 with Bioquest* was rated as the best performing laundry detergent, scoring 99 out of a possible 100.[29] Consumer Reports did however criticise SA8's pricing, which was disputed by Amway.[30] In 2008, Amway's cleaning products were named *Favourite of Experts* by an independent consumer survey in Ukraine.[31]

Health and beauty

The majority of Amway's sales today come from the Health & Beauty sector and in North America the Amway Global/Quixtar website is ranked the #1 Health & Beauty website by Internet Retailer.[32] In South Korea Amway is ranked one of the top two companies in toiletries and cosmetics. Amway's health & beauty brands include Artistry, Time Defiance, Satinique, Tolsom, Body Series, Glister, *Moiskin* (South America),[33] Nutrilite, *Nutriway* (Scandinavia and Australia/New Zealand), eSpring, *Atmosphere* and *iCook* as well as XL and XS Energy drinks.

Artistry

Main article: Artistry (cosmetics)

Amway's Artistry products include skin care, cosmetics, and anti-aging creams and serums. Euromonitor International, an independent researcher and publisher of market reports, business reference books and online information databases, ranks Artistry as one of the world's top 5 best selling brands in the *prestige brand* category, alongside Clinique, Estee Lauder, Lancôme, and Shiseido.[34][35] Artistry is the only direct sales brand classified in the 'prestige' category.[34][36]

Nutrilite

Amway's largest selling brand is the Nutrilite range of health supplements (marketed as Nutriway in some countries), and in 2008 Nutrilite sales exceeded US$3 billion globally[37] Nutrilite products incorporate organically grown whole-plant concentrates. Euromonitor has for several years ranked Nutrilite the world's best selling nutritional brand in tablet or capsule form.[38] In 2001, five Nutrilite products were the first dietary supplements to be certified by NSF International.[39] Surveys by independent group Consumerlab.com since 2002 have rated Nutrilite as having the highest customer satisfaction rating (96% in 2006) in the direct selling/MLM brand category.[40][41] In 2006, 2007, 2008, and 2009 in the nutrient and health food category, Nutrilite won 'Platinum' and 'Gold' awards in Malaysia, China, Taiwan, Thailand, and Asia overall in the Reader's Digest 'Trusted Brands of Asia' survey.[42] In 2008 Nutrilite scientists, in partnership with Alticor subsidiary Interleukin Genetics won the 12th *John M. Kinney Award for Nutrition and Metabolism* for their research into the interaction between nutrition and genetics.[43]

eSpring

Amway's eSpring water filter, introduced in 2000, was the first home water treatment system to incorporate a carbon block filter and Ultraviolet disinfection unit, becoming the first home system to achieve certification for ANSI/NSF Standards 42, 53 and 55.[44] The unit was also the first commercial product to include sister company Fulton Innovations eCoupled wireless power induction technology. Fulton Innovation introduced the technology in other consumer electronic products at the 2007 International Consumer Electronics Show. Companies licensing this technology include General Motors, Motorola and Visteon.[45][46] In 2006 eSpring was named *Product of the Year* by the Poland-based non-profit *World Foundation of Health, Heart and Mind*.[47] eSpring has won numerous *Gold* and *Platinum* awards in the *Reader's Digest Most Trusted Brand Asia* surveys.[48]

Atmosphere

In 2008 Amway's HEPA air filtration system became the first air cleaner certified Asthma and Allergy Friendly by the Asthma and Allergy Foundation of America.[49]

Ditto Delivery

Amway owns a patent on the online shopping method of Ditto Delivery, which allows consumers to specify an automatic monthly delivery of each product.[50] In May, 2001, Ditto Delivery accounted for 30% of Quixtar's North American sales.[28]

Business model

Amway combines direct selling with a multi-level marketing strategy. IBOs may both market the products directly to potential customers and also recruit (sponsor) and train other people who become IBOs themselves and in turn have the same opportunity. Each IBO may earn income both from the retail markup on any products they sell personally, plus a performance bonus based on the sales volume they and their downline have generated.[3] People may also register as IBOs to buy products at a discounted rate.[51]

Orlando Arena naming rights

In December 2006, Alticor secured the naming rights for the 17 000-seat basketball arena in Orlando, Florida – home of the Orlando Magic, which are owned by the family of Rich DeVos. The arena, formerly known as the TD Waterhouse Centre, is now called Amway Arena.

San Jose Earthquakes

Prior to the 2009 Major League Soccer season, Amway Global signed a three-year deal with the San Jose Earthquakes to become the team's official jersey sponsor.

A major part of the partnership is focused on community initiatives in the Bay Area. As a result, Amway Global is now also the official sponsor of the team's *Kicks for Kids* program that focuses on fitness and healthy lifestyles, as well as bringing underprivileged children to Earthquakes games.

The partnership also saw the creation of the Amway Global Street Team, which appears at all Earthquakes home games and at a number of soccer and non-soccer events throughout the Bay Area. The members of the Amway Global Street Team give away Earthquakes-branded merchandise and provide soccer skills demonstrations at each event.[52]

Los Angeles Sol

In March 2009, Amway Global signed a multi-year deal to become the official presenting partner of the Los Angeles Sol of Women's Professional Soccer.[53]

Politics and culture

Commentators have identified Amway as supporting the U.S. Republican Party,[54] and its founders contributed $4 000 000 to a conservative 527 group in the 2004 election cycle.[55] Amway states that its business opportunity is open to people regardless of their religious and political beliefs.[56]

Rolling Stone's Bob Moser has contended that former Amway CEO and co-founder Richard DeVos is connected with the dominionist political movement in the United States. Moser states that DeVos was a supporter of the late D. James Kennedy, giving more than $5 million to Kennedy's ministry.[57]

Multiple high-ranking Amway leaders such as Richard DeVos and Dexter Yager are also owners and members of the board of Gospel Films, a producer of movies and books geared towards conservative Christians as well as co-owner (along with Salem Communications) of Gospel Communications.[58]

One of Amway's most successful distributors, Dexter Yager, has criticized Democratic President Bill Clinton. *Mother Jones* reported that Yager stated in voice mail to his downline network of distributors, 'If you analyze Bill Clinton's entire inaugural address, it is nothing but a New Age pagan ritual. If you go back and look at how it was arranged and how it was orchestrated, he talked about forcing the spring. So what they're trying to do is ... force the emergence of deviant lifestyles, of a socialist agenda, and force that on us as American people.'[59] Yager also allowed Republican George W. Bush to send messages through that voicemail system to thousands of distributors.[60]

Doug Wead, who was a Special Assistant to U. S. President George H. W. Bush, is a successful IBO who is a regular speaker at group rallies. In 2000, President George W. Bush appointed Timothy Muris, a former anti-trust lawyer whose largest client was Amway to head the FTC, which has direct federal regulatory oversight over multi-level marketing plans.

Amway co-founder, Jay Van Andel (in 1980), and later his son Steve Van Andel (in 2001) were elected by the board of directors of the United States Chamber of Commerce as chairman of that organization.[61]

In May 2005, former Amway President Dick DeVos, one of the wealthiest men in Michigan, announced that he would run against Governor Jennifer Granholm in Michigan's 2006 gubernatorial election. DeVos, running as a Republican, won 42% of the popular vote, while Granholm won 56%.[62]

Amway touts the environmental benefits of many of its products, and in June 1989 the United Nations Environmental Program's Regional Office for North America recognized it for its contributions to the cause of the environment.[63]

Controversy
Pyramid scheme accusations

Amway has several times been accused of being a pyramid scheme. A 1979 FTC investigation in the United States (see below) and a 2008 court judgment in the United Kingdom dismissed these claims.[64]

FTC investigation

In a 1979 ruling,[16][65] the Federal Trade Commission found that Amway does not qualify as a pyramid scheme since Amway compensation system is based on retail sales to consumers, not payments for recruiting.

It did, however, order Amway to stop retail price fixing and allocating customers among distributors and prohibited the company from misrepresenting the amount of profit, earnings or sales its distributors are likely to achieve with the business. Amway was ordered to accompany any such statements with the actual averages per distributor, pointing out that more than half of the distributors do not make any money, with the average distributor making less than $100 per month. The order was violated with a 1986 ad campaign, resulting in a $100 000 fine.[66]

Amway Andhra Pradesh (India)

In September 2006, following a public complaint, Andhra Pradesh state police (CID) initiated raids and seizures against Amway distributors in the state, and submitted a petition against them, claiming the company violated the *Prize Chits and Money Circulation Schemes (banning) Act*.[67] They shut down all offices of firm Amway, and Arijit Saha writes that 'with it the fate of 80 000 distributors of the company has been indefinitely sealed'. The enforcement said that the business model of the company is illegal.[68] The Reserve Bank of India (RBI) had notified the police that Amway in India may be violating certain laws regarding a 'money circulation scheme' and the IB Times article writes that 'some say ... Amway is really more about making money from recruiting people to become distributors, as opposed to selling products'.[68] The complaint was initiated following a dowry dispute between a local man and his wife, an Amway distributor.[69] Following a petition by Amway, the state High Court issued an injunction against the CID and stated the Act did not *prima facie* apply, [70] however after Amway requested the CID petition be dismissed the High Court declared that if police allegations were true, Amway's Indian subsidiary would be in violation of the act and the investigation should continue. On August 14, 2007 the Supreme Court of India ordered the state police to complete the investigation against Amway in 6 months.[71] In 2008, citing the High Court decision, the Andhra Pradesh state government enacted a ban on Amway media advertisements.[67] Amway challenged the ban and in July 2009 the AP High Court refused a petition the ban should be enforced.[72] As of June, 2009 the original 2006 CID case was still pending at the Chief Metropolitan Magistrate Court in Hyderabad.[73]

Canadian tax case

In 1983, Amway pleaded guilty to criminal tax evasion and customs fraud in Canada, resulting in a fine of $25 million CAD, the largest fine ever imposed in Canada at the time. In 1989 the company settled the outstanding customs duties for $45 million CAD.[74][75] In a 1994 interview, Amway co-founder Rich DeVos stated that this incident had been his greatest 'moral or spiritual challenge', first in 'soul searching as to whether they had done anything wrong' and then for pleading guilty for technical reasons, despite believing they were innocent of the charges. DeVos stated he believed that the case had been motivated by 'political reasons'.[76]

RIAA lawsuit

The Recording Industry Association of America (RIAA), as part of its anti-piracy efforts, sued Amway and several distributors in 1996, alleging that copyrighted music was used on 'highly profitable' training videotapes.[77] Amway denied wrongdoing, blaming the case on a misunderstanding by distributors, and settled the case out of court for $9 million.[78] In a related lawsuit initiated by the distributors involved, the Court established that Mahaleel Lee Luster, who had been contracted to make the videotapes, had violated copyright without the knowledge of three of the five of those distributors.[79]

Procter & Gamble

Some Amway distributors were involved with an urban legend that the (old) Procter & Gamble service mark was in fact a Satanic symbol or that the CEO of P&G is himself a practicing Satanist. (In some variants of the urban legend, it is also claimed that the CEO of Procter & Gamble donated 'satanic tithes' to the Church of Satan.)[80] Procter & Gamble alleged that several Amway distributors were behind a resurgence of the urban legend in the 1990s and sued several independent Amway distributors and the parent company for defamation and slander.[81] The distributors had used Amway's Amvox voice messaging service to send the rumor to their downline distributors in April 1995. After more than a decade of lawsuits in multiple states, by 2003 all allegations against Amway and Amway distributors had been dismissed. In October 2005 a Utah appeals court reversed part of the decision dismissing the case against the four Amway distributors, and remanded it to the lower court for further proceedings.[82] On 20 March 2007, Procter & Gamble was awarded $19.25m by a U.S. District Court jury in Salt Lake City, in the lawsuit against the four former Amway distributors.[83][84] On November 24, 2008 the case was officially settled.[85]

Other issues

A *Dateline NBC* report from 2004 picked up the criticism against some Amway distributor groups.[86] Amway subsequently published a website with a response to the Dateline report.[87]

Some Amway distributor groups have been accused of using cult-like tactics to attract new distributors and keep them involved and committed.[88][89][90][91] Allegations include resemblance to a Big Brother organization with paranoid attitude to insiders critical of the organization,[91] seminars and rallies resembling religious revival meetings[88][91] and enormous involvement of distributors despite minimal incomes.[88][90][91] An examination of the 1979–1980 tax records in the state of Wisconsin showed that the *Direct Distributors*, comprising less than 1% of all distributors, reported a net loss of $918 on average.[90][92]

Sociologist David G. Bromley calls Amway a *quasi-religious corporation* having sectarian characteristics.[92][93] Bromley and Shupe view Amway as preaching the Gospel of Prosperity.[94] Economists Bhattacharya and Mehta propose an alternative economic explanation to negative claims, concluding that distributors' continued involvement despite minimal economic return results from social satisfaction compensating for less economic satisfaction.[95] Amway disputes stigma charges, and states that meetings with enthusiasm, excitement and energy are a proven way to motivate salespeople.[96]

Amway UK

On 9 January 2006 the Secretary of State for Trade and Industry (then known as the DTI – Department of Trade and Industry, later changed to BERR – Department for Business Enterprise and Regulatory Reform) initiated an investigation into the operations of Amway UK, Britt World Wide (BWW), and Network TwentyOne.[97] On 11 April 2007 the Secretary of State presented a petition to the UK Company Court for the winding up of all three companies. After negotiations, BWW elected to cease operations in the UK and the case was dropped. After agreeing to abide by the findings of the investigation into Amway, the case against Network 21 was also dropped.

Upon filing of the petition Amway immediately called a moratorium on all new sponsoring and a ban on the distribution of all non-Amway produced Business Support Materials. Shortly after, Amway introduced a number of fundamental changes to the business model in the United Kingdom and Republic of Ireland. The case was found in the favour of Amway UK and the revised business model was allowed to trade on in the UK.

Amway UK also now has to make available an earnings disclosure for prospective Business Owners to enable them to evaluate the opportunity. The most recent official statement can be found here on the Amway UK (website. http://www.amway.co.uk/cms/opportunity/earnings_disclosure).

References

1. [a][b] http://www.reuters.com/article/pressRelease/idUS173002+05-Feb-2009+PRN20090205
2. Amway GC Lives the Dream.
3. [a][b] Xardel, Dominique (1993). *The Direct Selling Revolution. Understanding the Growth of the Amway Corporation*. Blackwell Publishing. pp. 1–4. ISBN 978-0631192299.
4. About Amway – Global Leader in Direct Selling.
5. The Times 100 Business Case Studies: Amway – Direct selling and supply chain.
6. NBJ's 2004 Business Achievement Awards & Executive Review.
7. Amway (uk) – Who is Amway?

8.   Forbes. com – America's largest Private Companies.

9.   Deloitte 2008 Global Powers of Retailing.

10. [a][b] Conn, Charles Paul (1977). *The Possible Dream: A Candid Look At Amway*. Revell. ISBN 0800708571.

11. Van Andel, Jay (1998). *An Enterprising Life*. HarperCollins. pp. 37–39. ISBN 0-88730-997-6.

12. Robinson, James W. (1997). *Empire of Freedom: The Amway Story and What It Means to You*. Prima Publishing. p. 11. ISBN 0761510885.

13. *Profiles of the American Dream: Rich DeVos and Jay Van Andel and the Remarkable Beginnings of Amway.* [Documentary]. Premiere Films. 1997.

14. Interview with Bill Hybels at the Willow Creek Association Global Leadership Summit in 2000.

15. Van Andel, Jay (1998). *An Enterprising Life*. HarperCollins. pp. 58–60. ISBN 0-88730-997-6.

19. [a][b] From MLM Law Library: FTC Final Order from May 8, 1979 (93 F.T.C. 618).

17. Orange County, Calif., Firm Goes Back to Dawn of Vitamin Age.

18. Amway marque to be revived; Quixtar label scrapped.

19. 'N.B.A. Orlando Team Sold'. *The New York Times*. 1991-09-20. http://query.nytimes.com/gst/fullpage.html?res=9D0CEED8163AF933A1575AC0A967958260. Retrieved 2008-03-10.

20. http://www.quixtar.com/documents/iwov/vis/010-en/pdf/IBO%20Support/BusForms/SA4400.pdf

21. Amway Parent hits 50th year running recording 15% sales growth.

22. Amway India records turnover of Rs. 1128 crore in 2008.

23. 'Chinese officials ban direct marketing', April 22, 1998 *Associated Press*, The Associated Press.

24. 'Once-barred Amway becomes booming business in China', Leslie Chang, March 12, 2003, *Wall Street Journal*.

25. 'Amway, Mary Kay get long-awaited direct-selling licenses in China' Rob Kirkbride, December 24, 2006, *Kalamazoo Gazette*.

26. Forbes' The 100 Most Powerful Women; #88 Eva Cheng.

27. 安利中国销售额增28%.

28. [a][b] Amway.com

29. Consumer Reports – Laundry Detergents.

30. Rob Kirkbride / The Grand Rapids Press (December 12, 2006). 'Amway's old reliable cleans up'. Grand Rapids Press, The (MI). p. A1.

31. Favourite of Experts.

32. Internet Retailer.

33. Amway do Brasil.

34. [a][b] The World Market for Cosmetics and Toiletries.

35. The World of Artistry.

36. Artistry – Beauty, Science, Synergy.

37. NUTRILITE passes $3 billion mark in annual sales.

38. *The World Market for OTC Healthcare*. Euromonitor. January 2008. http://www.euromonitor.com/reportsummary.aspx?folder=The_World_Market_for_OTC_Healthcare&industryfolder=OTC_Healthcare.

39. NSF International Announces Dietary Supplements Certification Program.

40. ConsumerLab.com Survey.

41. Consumerlab.com 2009 Report on Vitamin & Supplement Users.

42. Reader's Digest Trusted Brands Asia.

43. John M Kinney Winners 2008.

44. NSF International: Who they are what they do.

45. In-Vehicle Wireless Power Transfer Unveiled.

46. Startup Jump-Starts Wireless Power.

47. Amway Poland receives 'Product of the Year' for eSpring.

48. Reader's Digest Trusted Brands Asia.

49. Helping to Clear the Air for Consumers – New Certification Standard for HEPA Filters Will Help Millions of People Make More Educated Choices.

50. U.S. Patent 7, 359, 871.

51. Amway in China: factory in Guangzhou.

52. San Jose Earthquakes Media Relations, *Quakes, Amway Global reach sponsorship deal*, http://sjearthquakes.mlsnet.com/news/team_news.jsp?ymd=20090127&content_id=214090&vkey=news_sje&fext=.jsp&team=t110, retrieved 2009-01-27

53. Los Angeles Sol, *Amway Global becomes Los Angeles Sol presenting sponsor*, http://www.womensprosoccer.com/la/news/press_releases/090305-amway-global, retrieved 2009-03-05.

54. Vlasic, Bill; Mary Beth Regan (February 16, 1998). 'Amway II: The Kids take over'. *BusinessWeek*. http://www.businessweek.com/archives/1998/b3565099.arc.htm?chan=search. Retrieved 2007-07-05.

55. From opensecrets.org: Progress for America – Top Contributors, 2004 Cycle.

56. Amway Corporation Website – Frequently Asked Questions.

57. 'The Crusaders' Bob Moser, April 7, 2005, *Rolling Stone*.

58. 'Billy Zeoli and Doug DeVos Named Co-Chairman of GCI Board'. Gospel Communications. http://www.gospelcommunications.org/press/?p=4. Retrieved December 27, 2008.

59. Burstein, Rachel; Kerry Lauerman (September/October 1996). 'She Did It Amway'. *Mother Jones*. http://www.motherjones.com/news/special_reports/1996/09/myrick.html. Retrieved 2007-07-05.

60. Berkowitz, Bill (April 24, 2005). 'Amway's GOPyramid Scheme'. *mediatransparency.org* http://www.mediatransparency.org/pdastory.php?storyID=4. Retrieved 2007-07-05.

61. Steve Van Andel Bio – U. S. Chamber of Commerce Board of Directors.

62. State of Michigan, Department of State; Terry Lynn Land, Secretary of State (2007-05-10). '2006 Michigan Gubernatorial General Election'. *Governor 4 Year Term (1) Position*. http://miboecfr.nictusa.com/election/results/06GEN/02000000.html. Retrieved 2007-11-09.

63. Motavalli, Jim; Leslie Pardue (April 1994). "Multilevel' marketing goes green – Amway Corp. and Shaklee see profits from environmentally safe products – includes related article on 'green' networking'. *The Environmental Magazine*. http://findarticles.com/p/articles/mi_m1594/is_n2_v5/ai_14896030. Retrieved 2007-07-05.

64. U.K. judge dismisses claims against Amway.

65. 'Pyramid Schemes'.

66. *Amway Corp. To Pay $100, 000 Civil Penalty, Settling FTC Charges*.

67. [a][b] Ban on Amway Chits, Schemes.

68. [a][b] Saha, Arijit (13 December 2006). 'Amway in hot water in Hyderabad over 'business model' controversy'. IB Times. http://www.ibtimes.co.in/articles/20061213/amway-mlm-business-model.htm. Retrieved 17 January 2010.

69. [1].

70. Amway back to business in state.

71. SC asks Andhra to finish Amway probe in 6 mths.

72. No Direction on Amway Ads.

73. Writ against Amway.

74. 'Amway of Canada Drops Tax Appeal'. *New York Times* (Reuters). February 7, 1984. http://query.nytimes.com/gst/fullpage.html?res=9D04E3D81039F932A15750C0A962948260. Retrieved 2007-07-05.

75. 'Amway, Canada Reach Settlement In Customs Dispute'. *The Wall Street Journal* (The Wall Street Journal). September 25, 1989. http://pqasb.pqarchiver.com/wsj/access/860493942.html?dids=860493942:860493942&FMT=ABS&FMTS=ABS:AI&date=Sep+25%2C+1989&author=JOHN+URQUHART+Staff+Reporter+of+THE+WALL+STREET+JOURNAL&pub=Wall+Street+Journal++(1889-Current+file)&edition=&startpage=C17&type=historic&desc=Amway%2C+Canada+Reach+Settlement+In+Customs+Dispute. Retrieved 2008-06-04.

76. Capitalism with Compassion, *Religion and Liberty*, Volume 4, Number 5.

77. Record Labels Sue Amway over its videos.

78. Amway pays $9 million to settle copyright infringement suit.

79. *Foley v Luster*.

80. Urban Legends Reference Pages: Procter & Gamble and Satanism Rumor.

81. *Proctor & Gamble v. Amway*, 280 F. 3d 519 (Fifth Circuit Court of Appeals July 19, 2004).

82. 03-4234 – Procter & Gamble Co. V. Haugen – 19 October 2005.

83. 'Procter & Gamble Awarded $19.25 Million in Satanism Lawsuit'. *Fox News.com/AP*. March 20, 2007. http://www.foxnews.com/story/0,2933,259877,00.html. Retrieved 2007-07-05.

84. Kirdahy, Matthew (March 22, 2007). 'The Devil Didn't Make Them Do It'. *Forbes.com*. http://www.forbes.com/facesinthenews/2007/03/22/procter-gamble-faces-markets-equity-cx_mk_0320autofacescan02.html. Retrieved 2007-07-05.

85. 'P&G Satanic Rumors Case Settles After Marathon Battle'. *onpointnews.com*. December 16, 2008. http://www.onpointnews.com/081216.asp. Retrieved 2008-12-18.

86. Hansen, Chris (May 7, 2004). 'In pursuit of the almighty dollar'. *Dateline NBC* (NBC News). http://www.msnbc.msn.com/id/4375477/. Retrieved 2007-07-05.

87. Quixtar – Dateline Quixtar Response to NBC Dateline Quixtar Story.

88. ᵃ ᵇ ᶜ *Amway: the cult of free enterprise*, by Stephen Butterfield, South End Press, 1985.

89. *Dangerous persuaders* by Louise Samways. Penguin Books, 1994.

90. ᵃ ᵇ ᶜ *Hidden persuaders*, by Tony Thompson. Time Out, June 22–29, 1994.

91. ᵃ ᵇ ᶜ ᵈ *The power of positive inspiration* by Paul Klebnikov. *Forbes*, December 9, 1991.

92. ᵃ ᵇ *Quasi religious corporations: A new integration of religion and capitalism?* by David G. Bromley. In *Religion and the Transformations of Capitalism: Comparative Approaches*, edited by Richard H. Roberts, pages 135-160. Routledge, 1995.

93. *Transformative movements and quasi-religious corporations: the case of Amway*, by David G. Bromley. In *Sacred Companies: Organizational Aspects of Religion and Religious Aspects of Organizations*, edited by Nicholas Jay Demerath, Peter Dobkin Hall, Terry Schmitt and Rhys H. Williams, pages 349-363. Oxford University Press, 1998.

94. *Rebottling the Elixir: The Gospel of Prosperity in America's Religioeconomic Corporations*, by David G. Bromley and Anson Shupe. In *In Gods we trust: new patterns of religious pluralism in America*, edited by Thomas Robbins and Dick Anthony, pages 233-254. Transaction Publishers, 1990.

95. *Socialization in network marketing organizations: is it cult behavior?* by Patralekha Bhattacharya and Krishna Kumar Mehta, Journal of Socio-Economics, Volume 29, Issue 4, pages 361–374.

96. FAQ on Amway's website.

97. Lupo, Lee (July 1, 2007). 'UK threatens to ban Amway'. *The Muskegon Chronicle* (Grand Rapids). http://blog.mlive.com/chronicle/2007/07/united_kingdom_investigates_am.html

NOTES

1. Futrell, C. 1999. *Fundamentals of Selling*. (Sixth edition). Boston: Irwin McGraw-Hill, p. 230.

2. Rix, P., Buss, J. & Herford, G. 1999. *Selling: A Consultative Approach*. Roseville: McGraw-Hill, p. 224.

3. Futrell, op. cit., p. 233.

4. Cooper, S. 1997. *Selling: Principles, Practice and Management*. London: Pitman, p. 86.

5 Rix, op. cit., p. 226.

6 Rix, op. cit., p. 219.

7 Rix, op. cit., p. 221.

8 Futrell, op. cit., p. 239.

9 Johnston, M.W. & Marshall, G.W. 2005. *Relationship Selling and Sales Management*. McGraw-Hill International edition. New York: McGraw Hill, p. 148.

i Retrieved from http://en.wikipedia.org/wiki/Amway on 2 April 2010.

8

APPROACH AND SALES PRESENTATION METHODS

| LEARNING OUTCOMES |

After studying this chapter, you should be able to:
- Discuss the various sales approach methods
- Distinguish between the various sales presentation methods
- Explain the elements of the FAB sequence
- Discuss the elements of the SELL sequence

INTRODUCTION

We have all heard the saying that 'first impressions last'. This is so true in the world of professional selling – salespeople often only have one chance to make a good impression on the prospect that they are selling to. This is why sound sales approach and presentation techniques are vitally important to the success of the sale!

In this chapter we will be discussing the various sales approach and presentation techniques that a sales person could employ. The elements of the FAB and SELL sequences will also be discussed.

WHAT IS AN APPROACH?

In terms of selling, the approach refers to the time from when the salesperson first sees the buyer to when they begin discussing the product. Bear in mind that the approach could last anything from a few seconds to a few hours depending on how long it takes to build up a rapport with the prospect. Sales approach methods are very important to the success of the sales presentation as they make the first impression that the rest of the process is built around.

The various approach methods that a salesperson could employ will be discussed next.

Sales approach methods

The various approach methods consist of:

- The introductory approach
- The complimentary approach
- The referral approach
- The product approach
- The customer benefit or question approach
- The opinion approach
- The shock or dramatic approach

Each of these will now be discussed.

The introductory approach

This approach is needed when meeting the prospect for the first time, and usually opens with the salesperson's name and the business that he or she is representing, for example: 'Hello Mr X, my name is Justin Surname and I represent the ABC Photocopy Organisation'. Bear in mind that this approach is not very effective unless combined with one of the other approaches.

The complimentary approach

Here the salesperson compliments the prospect on his or her business or work ethic, for example: 'Mr X, I have used your business many times for my printing requirements and have always found your staff to be friendly and efficient'. It is very important, however, that the compliments paid to the prospect are sincere.

The referral approach

Here the salesperson uses another person's name in order to establish a rapport with the prospect, for example: 'Mr X, Mrs Y of the Wedding Printing Company suggested that I contact you with regards to our latest range of photocopy machines'.

The product approach

Here the salesperson uses the actual product to start a conversation by placing it on the table in front of the prospect without saying a word in order for the product to 'do the talking'. This is an especially useful method if the product is exciting or interesting, or has changed in appearance.

The customer benefit or question approach

When using this approach method the salesperson makes a statement or asks a question that implies that the prospect will be benefiting from using the product, for example: 'Mrs Z, wouldn't it benefit your printing organisation to save up to 20% on your overall printing costs?'

The opinion approach

Here the prospect is asked for an opinion. This approach is useful as it shows that the salesperson values the prospect's opinion, for example: 'Mrs A, I would like to know your honest opinion on our range of copier'.

The shock or dramatic approach

Here the prospect is made to think seriously about a subject related to the salesperson's product. Products that this sort of approach would suit include home security systems, life insurance and home insurance, for example: 'Mrs B, have you thought about what would happen to your family if you were to be killed in an accident today?'

In the section that follows, the various sales presentation methods will be discussed.

WHAT IS A SALES PRESENTATION?

A sales presentation is a vocal and visual explanation of an organisation's products and services on offer. The main goal of a sales presentation is to sell the product to the prospect. In order to do this, various sales presentation methods exist. These will be discussed next.

Sales presentation methods

Five main types of sales presentation methods can be utilised by the salesperson.[1] These are:

- Memorised presentation
- Formula presentation
- Need-satisfaction presentation
- Problem-solution presentation
- Group presentation

Each of these methods, as well as their advantages and disadvantages will now be discussed in more detail.

The memorised presentation

When using this method, the salesperson does approximately 80–90% of the talking, and only allows the prospect to answer questions that were prepared before the presentation began.

The salesperson does not try to determine the prospect's specific needs, but delivers the same prepared talk to all his or her prospective clients, and only discusses the benefits of the product. The sales presentation is concluded with a purchase request.

Advantages of utilising this method include the following:

- This approach ensures that the same information is presented to all the organisation's clients
- It enables the inexperienced salesperson to feel more confident
- It is an effective method to use when the selling time available is short, such as during telephonic sales
- It is effective to use when the product is non-technical, such as in the case of encyclopaedias

Disadvantages of this method include the following:

- It does not allow for enough participation by the prospect
- It may present product benefits that are not important to the prospective buyer
- It is not suitable for the sale of technical products that require input from the prospect
- The sales presentation does not last long, and requires that the salesperson request an order more that once, which the prospect may see as high-pressure selling

The formula presentation

Unlike the memorised presentation, the formula presentation requires that the salesperson must first find out information about the prospective buyer's needs, and then base his or her presentation on them. This presentation method follows a less-structured approach, in which the salesperson dominates the first part of the presentation, and then solicits questions and comments from the prospect. The salesperson then regains control over the conversation and moves in to close the sale. This method is appropriate in situations where prospects need to make a straight repurchase or a slightly modified one.

The formula presentation method offers the following advantages:

- It ensures that all information is presented logically
- It allows for interaction between buyer and seller
- It allows for the handling of pre-identified questions and objections

Disadvantages of this method include the following:

- It is not adaptable to a number of complex selling situations
- Customers' objections often arise early on in the presentation

The need-satisfaction presentation

This presentation method is more creative, flexible and interactive than the memorised and formula methods. The presentation begins with the salesperson asking the prospect a probing question such as: 'What are your organisation's computer training needs at present?'

This probing question then starts a discussion between the salesperson and the prospect about the prospect's various needs, and allows the salesperson to determine if any of the products currently on offer would satisfy them. This type of presentation method is suited to the sale of technical and industrial products.

Here advantages include that:

- Based on the prospect's response, the salesperson can quickly determine what needs to be done
- If the buyer requests more information it can quickly be provided

Disadvantages include that:

- Care must be taken when attempting to uncover a prospect's needs as too many questions can alienate them
- Some salespeople are uncomfortable with this method as they feel less in control of the selling situation

The problem-solving presentation

Before beginning the sales presentation, the salesperson develops a detailed analysis of the prospect's needs. This presentation method is suited to the sale of highly complex or technical products such as insurance packages, computers and office equipment. This is a flexible method, as it involves an in-depth study of the prospect's needs before the sales presentation can be prepared.

This type of presentation usually consists of the following steps:

- Firstly the prospect must be convinced to allow the salesperson to conduct the needs analysis
- The actual analysis is made
- The prospect and salesperson agree on the problems and also determine that the prospect wants to solve them
- A proposal is prepared as a solution to the prospect's needs
- The sales presentation is then prepared based on the analysis and proposal made
- The sales presentation is then made

An advantage of this method is that it is a flexible and customised approach, while disadvantages include that an in-depth study of the prospect's needs is needed and a well-planned presentation is always required, which can be time consuming for the salesperson.

The need-satisfaction and the problem-solving presentation methods are often used to present proposals to groups. These group presentations will be discussed next.

The group presentation

In this kind of presentation, the salesperson addresses a group of individuals. The group presentation is less flexible than one made to an individual prospect. The larger the group being presented to, the more structured the presentation, because the presentation will not work if everybody interrupts with his or her own ideas throughout it.

When making a presentation to a group, you should accomplish the following during the first part of your presentation:

- Always provide a proper introduction, where your name and the name of your organisation are clearly stated, and the purpose of your visit is clearly explained
- Establish the credibility of your organisation by briefly discussing its history, and by naming a few organisations that you have successfully worked with in the past
- Provide a complete list of these organisations, and hand it out while you are providing some background details about your organisation and yourself
- State your organisation's competitive advantages, and illustrate what advantages it has over its competition
- Give quality assurances and show why your organisation is qualified to provide the product or services. Here you should indicate the guarantees offered by your organisation, such as an unlimited money-back guarantee
- Always cater to the specific group's behavioural style. Good salespeople are able to determine the presentation style that is going to hold the audience's attention. Remember that some prospects are more impatient than others and will become bored if your presentation is not adapted to their needs

After you have provided background details about your organisation and the necessary information regarding guarantees and quality assurances, you should involve the entire group in your presentation by asking for their input on factors such as success criteria and benefits sought from the particular product or service. Once you have obtained some input from the entire group, you may proceed with the presentation as if it were one-on-one.

In the sections that follow, the elements of the FAB and SELL sequences will be discussed. These sequences should be used throughout the presentation of products to prospects.

CASE STUDY

Having a party – the Tupperware way[i]

The **party plan** is a method of marketing products by hosting a social event, using the event to display and demonstrate the product or products to those gathered, and then to take orders for the products before the gathering ends. The primary lead generation system for home party plan sales is through the home party itself. The sales professional uses the home party business model as a source for future business.

ELEMENTS OF THE FAB SEQUENCE

The FAB (*features*, *advantages* and *benefits*) selling sequence is a selling method that relates the product's benefits to the customer's needs using the product's advantages and features to support claims made. The terms are defined as follows:

- *Features* refer to the physical characteristics of the product such as the size, shape and colour
- *Advantages* refer to the performance characteristics of the product, such as that the copier can print in both black and white, and colour
- *Benefits* refer to the favourable result that the buyer will receive from using the product, such as a vacuum cleaner reducing the amount of sweeping that a cleaner has to do

ELEMENTS OF THE SELL SEQUENCE

The use of the SELL sequence is very important as it helps the salesperson to stress product benefits important to prospects. Remembering the four elements, namely S (*show feature*), E (*explain advantage*), L (*lead into benefit*) and L (*let the customer talk*), is a great method to determine if the FAB discussed above is of interest to the buyer. The SELL sequence is therefore a very effective form of persuasive communication, and should be used before the sale is closed, which is discussed in Chapter 10 of this book.

The launch of Windows XP in South Africa[3]

Microsoft SA encountered problems with the launch of the newest Microsoft operating system called Windows XP in South Africa. The reason for this was that its main retail supplier of software (Siltek) was put under provisional liquidation in October 2001, just before the launch. Siltek's largest division was Siltek Distribution Dynamics, a high-volume, low-profit margin distributor that supplied thousands of resellers and retail stores in South Africa. Microsoft SA has another distributor, Comztek, which obtained the rights to distribute Microsoft's products and licences in the retail sector after the problems of Siltek. Previously Comztek was a distributor of corporate software products. Comztek also obtained sole distribution rights to publishing and graphics software companies Adobe and Vivendi Universal's products.

Other channels of distribution that are used by Microsoft SA to sell Windows XP in South Africa are corporate computer suppliers Mustek and Rectron. These two distributors are licensed by Microsoft SA to sell Windows XP only as preinstalled software in new computers.

Microsoft SA has developed the marketing strategy for Windows XP based on the premise that they must create awareness among the customers in South Africa and then take the campaign to their corporate customers. The mother company plans to spend more than $1 billion on a global marketing campaign.

Question

If Microsoft SA were considering using personal selling to promote Windows XP, which method would you advise them to use? Give reasons for your choice.

Tupperware[ii]

Tupperware is the name of a home products line that includes preparation, storage, and serving products for the kitchen and home, which were first introduced to the public in 1946. Tupperware develops, manufactures, and internationally distributes its products by its parent company Tupperware Brands Corporation and it is marketed by means of direct sales through an independent sales force of approximately 1.9 million consultants.[1] Tupperware is a wholly owned subsidiary of Tupperware Brands Corporation.

Company history

Tupperware was developed in 1946 by Earl Silas Tupper (1907–1983) in the USA. He developed plastic containers used in households to contain food and keep it airtight. The formerly patented 'burping seal' is a famous aspect of Tupperware, which distinguished it from competitors.

Tupperware pioneered the direct marketing strategy made famous by the Tupperware party. Brownie Wise (1913–1992), a former sales representative of Stanley Home Products, developed the strategy. During the early 1950s, Tupperware's sales and popularity exploded, thanks in large part to Wise's influence among women who sold Tupperware, and some of the famous 'jubilees' celebrating the success of Tupperware ladies at lavish and outlandishly themed parties. Tupperware was known – at a time when women came back from working during World War II only to be told to 'go back to the kitchen' – as a method of empowering women, and giving them a toehold in the post-war business world. The tradition of Tupperware's 'Jubilee' style events continues to this day, with rallies being held in major cities to recognize and reward top-selling and top-recruiting individuals, teams, and organizations.

In 1958, Earl Tupper fired Brownie Wise over general difference of opinion in the Tupperware business operation. It is believed that Tupper objected to the expenses incurred by the jubilee and other similar celebrations of Tupperware.[2]

Tupperware spread to Europe in 1960 when Mila Pond hosted a Tupperware party in Weybridge, England, and subsequently around the world. In 2003, Tupperware closed down operations in the UK, citing customer dissatisfaction with their direct sales model as an issue[3], and relaunched after a restructuring in 2005.

Rexall bought Tupperware in 1958. Rexall sold its namesake drugstores in 1977, and renamed itself Dart Industries. Dart merged with Kraftco to form Dart & Kraft. The company demerged, with the former Dart assets named Premark International. Tupperware Brands was spun off from Premark in 1996; Premark was acquired by Illinois Tool Works three years later.

Tupperware is now sold in almost 100 countries, after peaking at more than a hundred after 1996.[4] The top ten consumers[5] of Tupperware are: Germany, USA, France, Mexico, Russia, Australia/New Zealand, Italy, Austria, South Africa, Japan.

Tupperware parties

Tupperware is still sold mostly through a party plan, with rewards for hosts. A Tupperware party is run by a Tupperware consultant for a host who invites friends and neighbors into his or her home to see the product line. Tupperware hosts are rewarded with free products based on the level of sales made at their party. Parties also take place in workplaces, schools, and other community groups.

In most countries, Tupperware's sales force is organised in a tiered structure with consultants at the bottom, managers and star managers over them, and next various levels of directors, Legacy Executive Directors at the top level. In recent years, Tupperware has done away with distributorships in the US. This has allowed Tupperware more flexibility, and more generous commission and rewards for their consultants.

In recent years, Tupperware in North America has moved to a new business model, which includes more emphasis on direct marketing channels and eliminated its dependency on authorized distributorships. This transition included such strategies as selling through Target stores in the US, and Superstores in Canada, with disappointing results. Tupperware states this hurt direct sales. [6] In countries with a strong focus on marketing through parties (such as Germany and Australia/New Zealand), Tupperware's market share and profitability continue to grow.

In many countries, Tupperware products come with a lifetime guarantee. In India, there are some restrictions on the lifetime guarantee clause. In the UK/Ireland the guarantee is 10 years. [7] The company is best known for its plastic bowls and storage containers, however in recent years has branched out into stainless steel cookware, fine cutlery, chef's knives and other kitchen gadgets. After experiencing a slump in sales and public image in the mid-1990s, the company created several new product lines to attract a younger market.

In some countries including Belgium, Australia and the US, Tupperware market their parties and career opportunities through mall kiosks from time to time. In China, Tupperware products are sold through franchised 'entrepreneurial shop fronts', of which there were 1900 in 2005, due to laws enacted in 1998 aimed at pyramid selling. [8][9] The Chinese characters 特百惠 are used as the brand name, and translate as 'hundred benefit'.

Cultural and Historical Impact

Tupperware created a means for the housewife to maintain her obligations in the domestic sphere of the household while creating an independence from the home in a sociable atmosphere. [10] The Tupperware Party allowed for women of the 1950s to work and enjoy the benefits of earning an income without completely taking away the independence granted to women during the Second World War when women first began entering the labor market, all the while keeping their focus in the domestic domain. [11] The 'Party' model builds on characteristics generally developed by being a housewife (e.g. party planning, hosting a party, sociable relations with friends and neighbors) and created an alternative choice for women who either needed or wanted to work. The reciprocity that emerges at the 'parties' which are traditionally composed of friends and family members of the hostess create a nurturing atmosphere without a direct sales feeling. Studies show that the creation of the 'Tupperware party' is a gendered construct aimed at appeasing the general ethos of the domestic arrangements of the era where men were the sole earners and it was the women's responsibility to manage the housework. Earl Tupper invented the plastic for Tupperware in 1938, however the product only worked with the emergence of the sale through presentation in a party setting. This reflects in the empowerment it gave women in a setting of gossip and game playing the ability to sell and create a role for individuals outside of the domestic realm. It has been argued that the repercussions of the Tupperware boom in American households and the American economy is the elevation of the status of women in the labor market along with status within the home and facilitating their entrance into the labor market in further years.[12]

Feminist views vary regarding the Tupperware format of sales through parties, and the social and economic role of women portrayed by the Tupperware model. Opposing views state that the intended gendered product and selling campaign further domesticates women, and keeps their predominant focus on homemaking. [12] The positive feminist views consider that Tupperware provided work for women who were pregnant or otherwise not guaranteed their position at work due the unequal gender laws in the workplace. The company promoted the betterment of women and the endless opportunities Tupperware offered to women; whereas the negative view includes the restriction of women to the domestic sphere and limiting the real separation between running the household and a career.[11] The emergence of Tupperware on the American market created a new kind of opportunity to an entirely underrepresented labor demographic; women, and especially suburban housewives, which subsequently facilitated the calls for equal rights between men and women in the workplace.

Product lines

Tupperware's product ranges are often marketed under different names in different markets, and the product ranges and colors themselves differ between markets. Some of Tupperware's most popular lines include:

- **FridgeSmart** (US, UK, AU), **PrimaKlima** (DE): With air control vents, FridgeSmart containers are modular containers intended for refrigerated fruits and vegetables. FridgeSmarts which have air control vents intended to allow different levels of airflow around different types of fruits and vegetables, as well as a corrugated bottom to allow them to store securely on a refrigerator shelf.
- **UltraPro** (AU, UK), **UltraPlus** (DE): Plastic casseroles advertised as being safe when used in a microwave or a conventional oven, with heat resistant properties.
- **Eleganzia** (UK, DE), **Illusions** (AU): A 'glasslike' range of serving dishes

- **FlatOut!** (US), **MiniMax** (UK, DE, AU): Bowls that flatten for storage, and can be expanded when needed
- **Stuffables** (US), **Bungee** (DE): refrigerator storage with flexible lids for overfilling

'Chain of Confidence' program

On May 9, 2007, Tupperware announced Brooke Shields as the celebrity spokesperson for Tupperware's 'Chain of Confidence' campaign in the USA. The campaign invites women to celebrate the strong bonds of female friendships and the self-confidence derived from those relationships. ChainOfConfidence.com serves as an online community where women can share their confidence stories with one another and join an online discussion about the importance of female friendships and confidence. As part of *Chain of Confidence*, Tupperware is donating over one million dollars to the Boys & Girls Clubs of America to sponsor SMART Girls – a program dedicated to promoting confidence in young girls ages 8–17.

References

1. 'Tupperware Freshens Up the Party'. The New York Times. July 7, 2007. http://www.nytimes.com/2007/07/07/business/07interview.html. Retrieved May 19, 2009.

2. 'How Tupperware has conquered the world'. The Daily Mail. January 18, 2007. http://www.dailymail.co.uk/femail/article-429672/How-Tupperware-conquered-world.html. Retrieved May 19, 2009.

3. 'Party is over for Tupperware UK'. BBC News. January 22, 2003. http://news.bbc.co.uk/1/hi/business/2685755.stm. Retrieved May 19, 2009.

4. 'Is Tupperware Dated? Not in the Global Market'. The New York Times. May 26, 1996. http://www.nytimes.com/1996/05/26/business/investing-it-is-tupperware-dated-not-in-the-global-market.html?pagewanted=all. Retrieved May 19, 2009.

5. As reported at Tupperware's New South Wales State conference, 19 Feb 2008.

6. 'Tupperware to End Partnership with Target Stores'. The New York Times. June 19, 2003. http://www.nytimes.com/2003/06/19/business/company-news-tupperware-to-end-partnership-with-target-stores.html. Retrieved May 19, 2009.

7. 'Customer Service'. Tupperware UK & Ireland. http://www.tupperware.co.uk/service/1539.html. Retrieved 2009-05-19.

8. 'Tupperware Party's Over, Says China'. The Los Angeles Times. April 24, 1998. http://community.seattletimes.nwsource.com/archive/?date=19980424&slug=2747051. Retrieved May 19, 2009.

9. 'Tupperware adapts to serve diverse markets'. Plastics News. November 17, 2005. http://www.plasticsnews.com/china/english/printer_en.html?id=1131755394. Retrieved May 19, 2009.

10. Susan Vincent, 'Preserving Domesticity: Reading Tupperware in Women's Social, Domestic, and Economic Roles, ' Canadian Review of Sociology and Anthropology 40 no. 2 (2003): 176. doi:10. 1111/j. 1755-618X. 2003. tb00242. x

11. [a b] Allison J. Clarke, Tupperware, Washington: Smithsonian Institution Press (1999), 192–193.

12. [a b] Susan Vincent, 'Preserving Domesticity: Reading Tupperware in Women's Social, Domestic, and Economic Roles,' Canadian Review of Sociology and Anthropology 40 no. 2 (2003): 180-184. doi:10. 1111/j. 1755-618X. 2003. tb00242. x

External links

1. Tupperware USA official website

2. Tupperware's Chain of Confidence official website

3. Links to national Tupperware websites around the world

4. 'Selling Tupperware results in a full salad bowl of problems'. Times Union. October 12, 2008. http://www.timesunion.com/AspStories/story.asp?storyID=728713. Retrieved May 19, 2009

5. 'Why Short Sellers Want to Crash the Tupperware Party'. *The New York Times*. November 17, 2006. http://www.nytimes.com/2006/11/13/business/13short.html. Retrieved May 19, 2009

NOTES

1. Futrell, C.M. 2004. *Fundamentals of Selling: Customers for Life*. (Eighth edition). Boston: Irwin.

2. Futrell, C.M. 2003. *ABCs of Relationship Selling*. (Seventh edition). New York: McGraw-Hill Irwin.

3. Futrell, op. cit., pp. 237-240.

4. Strydom, J. (Ed.) 2004. *Introduction to Marketing*. (Third edition). Lansdowne: Juta, p. 134.

i   http://en.wikipedia.org/wiki/Party_plan (downloaded on 8 April 2010).

9.

OBJECTIONS AND
THE TRIAL CLOSE

LEARNING OUTCOMES

After studying this chapter, you should be able to:
- Identify the reasons that prospects object
- Prepare to handle objections
- Identify the type of objection being raised
- Evaluate the various methods of dealing with objections
- Effectively answer objections in a sales situation
- Discuss the trial close and the timing of the trial close
- Discuss trial closing techniques

INTRODUCTION

In times gone by, salespeople were taught that if the prospect showed any sign of sales resistance, it was bad and that the salesperson had obviously not done a good job of explaining the product benefits.[1] In fact, sales resistance or objections to the sale are still the most intimidating aspect of a sales call. It is a salesperson's worst nightmare: the presentation is going well when all of a sudden the prospect blurts out that the product is too expensive and that the salesperson is wasting their time! What do you do now? Do you pack up and leave? Do you argue? Do you pretend not to have heard? While these might be our first responses, in this chapter we will look at objections in a new light and come to expect and even welcome them. We will look at various types of objections and finally we will discuss how to handle them. We will close off the chapter by looking at the 'trial close'. The trial close is what salespeople use to gauge the attitude of the prospect before they ask for the actual order. As you can imagine, the trial close must be used very carefully and can quite easily backfire on the salesperson. Let us begin by looking at objections.

WHY DO PROSPECTS OBJECT?

With every purchase, whether it is a large, important purchase such as a house or a car, or a relatively cheaper one such as a new television or refrigerator, there is some degree of nervousness or tension. We are never sure of the wisdom of our purchase until after the money has changed hands and we have spent some time with the product. The larger the amount of money or the more important the consequences of the purchase, the more apprehensive we become. The desire for all of the information and the fear of making a mistake sometimes drive us to put off a decision or even cancel a transaction altogether. It even happens that sometimes we are suspicious of salespeople and believe that they want to force us into a decision that benefits them and does not meet our needs. Sometimes we want to discover salespeople's real motives, so we question them and object until they reveal their 'true colours'.[2]

All of these reasons apply to our prospects as much as they apply to us. Prospects object because:[3]

- *They want to avoid the sales call or salesperson.* Time constraints or a busy schedule can often discourage prospects from meeting salespeople
- *The salesperson has failed to qualify the prospect properly.* Do you remember our discussion of the qualification of prospects in Chapter 6?
- *Objecting is a matter of custom.* Many buyers will say no on the first sales call to test the salesperson's persistence. In other companies, intensive negotiations are part of the culture, so objections are customary
- *Resistance to change.* Many companies are not keen to change or even to listen to new ideas. Buyers tend to be loyal to their suppliers and will not even meet with other sales representatives
- *The prospect fails to recognise the need.* A qualified prospect may not realise the need or the fact that the salesperson is presenting a product or service that will satisfy the need. This reason for objection ties in to good qualification of the prospect and overcoming resistance to change
- *Lack of information.* The prospect might not have enough information to make a decision, so he or she raises objections in order to gather more facts

It is important to remember that if prospects sit through a presentation in silence, they may be daydreaming or thinking about your competitor or keeping quiet in order to get the sales call over as soon as possible. An objection implies that they are at least listening and showing some interest in your sales call. Also, salespeople should always welcome objections, because they are predictable. Most objections follow similar patterns and can be categorised in two main types, namely the smokescreen and the genuine objection.[4] The smokescreen is raised by prospects when they are either trying to stall for time to put off making a decision or to hide the real reason for not going ahead with the sale. The genuine objection is raised when the prospect has a legitimate reason for not wanting to purchase the product or service, or they are looking for more clarification about some or other issue. Genuine objections could result from an error on the part of the salesperson or from a misunderstanding by the prospect. The list of objections raised is endless, but within the two main types six groups can be distinguished, which we will discuss later in the chapter. Common objections are listed in the box below.

Common objections[5]

'Your price is too high.'
'We are satisfied with our current supplier.'
'We have already budgeted for that this year.'
'The decision maker is on leave.'
'We need head office approval.'
'Our advertising/PR agency handles that for us.'
'You are not on our approved list of suppliers.'
'We can get it cheaper on the Internet.'
'I can't make that kind of decision right now.'
'We do not have the money.'

PREPARING FOR OBJECTIONS

One of the most useful and productive techniques for handling objections is careful and thorough preparation. Salespeople can develop knowledge and skills which will help them respond to objections by:

- Learning to recognise common objections
- Being prepared for objections
- Developing the skill of responding appropriately to objections

No matter what objection is raised by the prospect, the following eight basic points will ensure that the objection is handled in a professional manner:[6]

- Plan for objections
- Anticipate and forestall
- Acknowledge the objection
- Handle objections as they arise

- Be positive
- Listen
- Understand objections
- Meet the objection

Plan for objections

Most objections occur frequently and can be foreseen by the salesperson. It is important to plan for objections while preparing the sales presentation. Consider not only the reasons for buying the product but also the reasons *for not* buying it. By looking at the sale from the prospect's perspective, the salesperson can anticipate where the objections will come from and what they will be about. It is important that the salesperson is thoroughly informed about the competitive offerings and is an expert on his or her own offerings.

Anticipate and forestall

Good preparation enables a salesperson to anticipate common objections and to forestall them by addressing them in the presentation *before* the prospect has a chance to do so. This is easy in the case of common objections, but because each prospect is different to the previous one and is an individual with individual needs, some objections will be unique to a specific situation. Common objections like price can easily be handled at the beginning of a sales presentation by saying something like: 'Right up front, I would like tell you that our price is a little higher than others because of the Xenon technology that we have incorporated into our product. This technology enables the product to ...' In this example, a price objection which would probably have occurred later in the presentation has been anticipated and converted into a benefit statement.

Acknowledge the objection

Remember that when a buyer raises an objection, he or she believes it to be a genuine problem or reason not to buy. It is important that the salesperson acknowledge the objection. This validates the objection in the mind of the prospect and helps to reduce defensiveness on the part of the salesperson.

Handle objections as they arise

In certain situations it is pertinent to postpone the handling of the objection, but only when you are going to handle it later in the presentation or when you are building up to that specific point. Generally, however, it is best to handle the objection as soon as it arises. This ties in strongly to the issue of acknowledging the objection. If a salesperson does not acknowledge or handle the objection immediately, the prospect might feel that the salesperson is trying to hide something or perhaps that he or she does not have much regard for the prospect's opinion.

Be positive

In most cases, when prospects raise an objection, they are expressing confidence in the salesperson. Either they have a problem and are trusting the salesperson to solve it for them, or they are testing the salesperson's knowledge or expertise. It is essential, therefore, to develop a positive attitude towards objections. A good salesperson's goal is to provide prospects with genuine assistance, not to win an argument with them.

Listen

Listening closely to what the prospect has to say is critical to the successful handling of an objection. A famous error is to begin speaking or even formulating a response before the prospect has stopped objecting. Never assume that you know what the prospect is about to say: you may be totally on the wrong track and highlight an objection that the prospect never thought of! If prospects trust you enough to tell you what is bothering them, then have the courtesy to hear them out. Do not address every sentence they say, but rather let them finish and then address the entire issue. This is especially important in the case of emotionally charged objections. It sometimes happens that prospects become irritated or angry, and feel very strongly about the objection. In these cases, the salesperson must make a concerted effort to be silent until they have finished. This allows them to release pent-up frustrations and vent their true feelings. These can then be addressed by the salesperson in a calm and collected manner.

Understand objections

Continuing on the subject of listening, it is critical that the salesperson understands the objection and has clarity about the actual issue. When prospects object, they are usually doing one of the following things:

- *Requesting more information.* If a prospect requests more information, it usually means that the salesperson has created a desire for the product, but that the prospect is still a little unsure
- *Setting a condition for the sale.* If a prospect's objection addresses issues that pose certain conditions under which a sale might take place, the salesperson must quickly move to attempt to meet those conditions.
- *Highlighting a genuine objection.* An effective tool is to repeat the objection to the prospect in the form of a question. For example:
  Prospect: 'But our current supplier delivers in two weeks.'
  Salesperson: 'Would you be happy if we could deliver in a week-and-a-half?'

Meet the objection

Once the salesperson understands the objection and has empathy with the prospect's situation, he or she is ready to meet the objection. Techniques for dealing with objections will be discussed later in this chapter.

TYPES OF OBJECTIONS

Most objections fall into six major categories. Each of these will now be discussed and we will look at ways of dealing with them when they arise in a selling situation.

The hidden objection

The most difficult objection of all is the hidden objection. Prospects who have hidden objections often hide behind small, trivial objections that can lead the salesperson astray or they blatantly lie to cover up the real objection. Prospects hide their true feelings for a number of reasons: sometimes they feel that the truth is none of the salesperson's business; at other times they do not want to offend the salesperson; in some cases they just do not feel that the sales call is worthy of their attention. Developing the skill of uncovering true objections beneath a web of deceit is a lifelong journey that each salesperson must undertake. Reading between the lines and asking appropriate probing questions are common tools used to uncover hidden objections. In some cases the prospect does not even know what the real objection is: the salesperson needs to peel away the psychological layers in an effort to understand the prospect's real motivations. By asking probing or leading questions the salesperson could reveal true objections, for example:[7]

- What would it take to convince you?
- What causes you to say that?
- Tell me, what is really on your mind?

The direct approach, for example asking a prospect directly what the real objection is, can be very dangerous and detrimental to the sales call. In effect, the salesperson is calling the prospect a liar, and this can only be harmful to the relationship. Salespeople eventually can intuitively tell, by reading between the lines, what the real reason behind the 'smokescreen' objection is. The box below lists some common 'smokescreen' objections and the truth behind them.

Smokescreen objections

Lie: I would love to talk about it, but I really don't have the time right now.

Truth: I am not actually the decision maker and my boss is already in a bad mood.

Lie: We budget for that kind of expense at the beginning of the year, so right now we don't have any funds available.

Truth: We have enough budget, but I am screening the boss's calls.

Lie: Mr Khumalo would handle that, but unfortunately he's away on holiday.

Truth: I am Mr Khumalo but I just want to go home and not spend any more time at work than I have to.

The stalling objection

Prospects often use stalling objections in order to postpone the decision and to avoid having to take immediate action.[8] This is sometimes motivated by fear in that the prospect is afraid that by making a quick decision he or she will be disadvantaged in the transaction. In other cases the prospect is just looking for a polite way to say no. This sometimes takes the form of indefinite postponement. It can be that the stall is a genuine request to seek further advice from a superior or mentor. Some examples of the stalling objection are listed below.

<table>
<tr><td colspan="2">Stalling objections</td></tr>
<tr><td>Buyer:</td><td>'We have enough of the product right now, but thanks for coming by.'</td></tr>
<tr><td>Buyer:</td><td>'I can see the merit in your proposal but I just don't think that now is the right time for us to be changing suppliers.'</td></tr>
<tr><td>Buyer:</td><td>'We have already budgeted for that this year. Why don't you give me a call next year?'</td></tr>
<tr><td>Buyer:</td><td>'I cannot make a decision like that right now. I am going to need some time to think about it.'</td></tr>
</table>

The salesperson needs to identify the motive behind the stalling objection. If the motive is deemed genuine and the prospect really does need time, then it is appropriate for the salesperson to schedule another appointment. If a prospect raises a second or even third stalling objection in succession, it may just be a polite way of saying no. Let us look at some ways to handle the stalling objection.

Buyer: 'I need some time to think about this.'

Salesperson: 'I understand that you need more time to think and I would be very interested in hearing your thoughts. What items do you need to know more about?'

Or

Salesperson: 'We have been thinking about this since the first time I called. You know that this is a terrific opportunity and you know you like the product, so why don't we go ahead right now?'

Buyer: 'We are planning to purchase next year, not now.'

Salesperson: 'Why?'

Or

Salesperson: 'What if I delivered now, but you only had to pay next year?'

Or

Salesperson: 'Some of my best customers also said that – once they bought they were sorry that they had waited.'

Buyer: 'I will have to get approval from my manager.'

Salesperson: 'If you had the authority, you would go ahead with the purchase, wouldn't you?'

It is imperative that salespeople do not accept stalling objections, but rather press on tactfully until they have uncovered the real motives behind them.

The lack-of-interest or no-need objection

Prospects might state that they have no need for the product or that they are not interested in changing suppliers. This type of objection might be a smokescreen or a genuine reason for not buying. If the prospect has been qualified correctly then the salesperson knows that the need exists – the prospect might just not be aware of how the product can meet that need as yet. Prospects raise the no-need objection when they do not see sufficient reason to buy, when they have recently purchased a similar product, or when they are happy enough with the current situation not to go to the effort of changing suppliers. The box below lists some common no-need objections.

No-need or lack-of-interest objections

Buyer: 'I am not interested.'

Buyer: 'We are happy where we are now. A change would require too much work and hassle for me and for the production department.'

Buyer: 'Your offer sounds good, but we are not interested right now.'

While a no-need objection is not always genuine and can be overcome, in most cases it indicates the end of a sales call.[9] Some ways of dealing with the no-need objection:

Prospect: 'I am not interested.'

Salesperson: 'May I ask why?'

Or

Salesperson: 'Some of my best customers also said that until they heard about the …'
[state a special benefit]

Prospect: 'There is nothing wrong with our existing product.'

Salesperson: That is exactly why you should buy now – you can get an excellent trade-in.

Prospect: 'We are satisfied with our current product.'

Salesperson: 'Most of our customers were happy with what they had until they saw our product. They purchased because [state some benefits].'

Or

Salesperson: 'I have studied the product that you are using and would like to compare products and show you how our [state some benefits].'

The financial objection

Financial objections take two forms: they are either price related as in: 'Your price is too high' or money related as in: 'We cannot afford that right now'. Financial objections can be legitimate, for example in cases where the prospect really can get the product more cheaply somewhere else. Financial objections could also just be smokescreens that are hiding real objections, or even stalls, for example: 'That kind of money needs to be budgeted at the beginning of the year. Why don't you come back then?' Occasionally, price objections are very strong selling signals.[10] They indicate that the prospect is ready to buy and is trying to negotiate a lower price. Objections that relate to the prospect not being able to afford the product should never occur if the prospect has been qualified correctly. The box below lists some common money objections.

Money objections

Buyer: 'That is too expensive.'
Buyer: 'I can't afford it.'
Buyer: 'Your price seems a little high for that size/quantity.'
Buyer: 'We have been buying from another supplier who meets our budget constraints.'

Price objections should be anticipated because they are probably the most common objections raised.[11] Inexperienced salespeople can blow the price objection up from a minor issue to a major one. A well-prepared salesperson should turn a price objection into an opportunity to display the product benefits and to demonstrate the greater value received from the product. Let us look at some ways of dealing with the financial objection.

Prospect: 'You are too expensive.'
Salesperson: 'What is too expensive? The installation costs? The running costs?'
Or
Salesperson: 'How much were you expecting to pay?'
Or
Salesperson: 'Our price is higher than our competition because of the value-added features such as [state some features].'

Prospect: 'It is outside my budget.'
Salesperson: 'Let us look at your budget and find a solution that fits it.'
[Salesperson should attempt to remove extra features, reduce quantities, etc.]
Prospect: 'Give me a discount and I will order right now.'

Salesperson: 'I always quote my best possible price.'

Or

Salesperson: 'If you give me an order for ten, I can give you a 10% discount. Do you want to order ten?'

It is sometimes pertinent to deal with the price objection later in the presentation; however, delaying an objection might be construed as avoidance.[12] Use a confirming sentence such as: 'I can see that you are concerned about the product's price and if it's okay with you, I have made a note of it and will come back to it shortly. I hope that I will be able to dismiss your worries.' It is then obviously imperative that the salesperson should return to the issue and address it later. It would be advisable to discuss the product benefits and value during this time.

The product-related objection

No product will ever meet all of the needs of all buyers. The salesperson's product may offer a feature that the prospect does not need, there may be features that the prospect does need that the product does not have, or there may be questions about the reliability of the product. The box below lists some common product objections.

Product objections

Buyer: 'Your product needs ISO certification.'

Buyer: 'Your product comes in 5 kg containers, but we need deliveries in bulk containers.'

Buyer: 'Our existing machine is still good.'

Buyer: 'I believe that your competitor's product is more reliable.'

The salesperson's response to a product objection should be positive and not debasing towards the competition. The use of testimonials, independent research reports and demonstrations can often overcome the product objection. Here are some examples of ways of dealing with the product objection:

Prospect: 'The competitor's product is better.'

Salesperson: 'I see that you have had a chance to look at their product. What about it impressed you?'

[The salesperson should then listen for important features and demonstrate how his or her product performs on those same features.]

Prospect: 'I am not sure that the quality of your product meets our needs.'

Salesperson: 'Let me demonstrate the product's durability ...'

Or

Salesperson: 'Independent tests by the SABS have shown that our product can handle ten times more pressure than our closest competitor's product can.'

Remember that you are selling against a competitor. Many prospects are put off by sales-people who run down the competition and spread negative rumours or unfounded opinions.

The company objection

Prospects may have developed a dislike for your company or for you. They may have had a bad experience with you or your company or they may be loyal to their current supplier. Company objections can be very difficult to overcome and must be handled with tact and care. The salesperson must never become personally or emotionally involved and take offence at the objection. This type of objection takes time to overcome and will probably involve many repeat visits to build bridges or establish legitimacy. The most difficult part is to identify the company objection because many prospects will cover it up with a smokescreen to avoid offending the salesperson. While salespeople do not expect to get on well with everybody, they do not always realise that the problem may be themselves and not the product or price.[13] Some common company objections are listed below.

Company objections
Buyer: 'I have heard that you guys are all promises until the customer signs, and then you don't deliver. How do I know that you will follow up on your promises?'
Buyer: 'When we were looking for this kind of product three years ago, we approached you and you weren't interested. We decided that we would never deal with your company again.'
Buyer: 'We want to work with a more established company.'
Buyer: 'You are rather young to be selling this kind of product, aren't you?'

It takes time to break down a resistance barrier, and salespeople should demonstrate a genuine interest in the prospect. It becomes the salesperson's responsibility to correct past errors and to suggest a way forward that benefits the salesperson and the prospect. Some common responses to the company objection are:

Prospect: 'We won't buy from you.'

Salesperson:	'You must have a reason for feeling this way. May I ask what it is?'
Or	
Salesperson:	'What would it take for us to win your business?'
Or	
Salesperson:	'I respect the fact that you aren't buying from us right now, but I am convinced that if you were aware of some of our new products and benefits, you would purchase something from us in the future. Would you mind if I dropped in periodically to tell you about our specials?'

Prospect:	'You are rather young to be selling this kind of product, aren't you?'
Salesperson:	'Would you prefer to work with someone else from our company?'
Or	
Salesperson:	'Yes, I am younger than most of the people in this industry, but I have worked very hard to gain my customers' respect. Why don't you give some of them a call and see if they are happy with my service?'

Not all objections can be handled. It may be that the salesperson has to leave and consult with a superior or technician, or it may be that the prospect really does need to take some time off and think about the decision. Experienced salespeople realise when they have done all they can and need to back off. In the next section we will look at common techniques for dealing with objections.

TECHNIQUES FOR DEALING WITH OBJECTIONS

We have already looked at some basic pointers for handling objections. Let us recap:

- Welcome the objection
- Listen carefully
- Rephrase and repeat the objection
- Uncover hidden objections
- Ask 'what' and 'why' questions
- Be tactful
- Discover the hidden objections

It is important to answer all of the objections that prospects might raise. A good salesperson will anticipate objections and incorporate techniques for handling them into the sales presentation. Common techniques for handling objections are listed in the box below:

- Direct denial
- Indirect denial
- Let it go
- Compensation
- Boomerang
- Third-party

Let us look at each of the techniques in some more detail.

Direct denial

Occasionally the salesperson will face an objection that is factually incorrect. In such a case, it may be pertinent to deny the statement and correct the prospect; however, the salesperson needs to be very careful and extremely tactful when doing so. Nobody likes to be corrected or (in extreme cases) made out to be a liar.[14] It is essential that the salesperson acknowledges the prospect's statement or opinion and then moves on to a denial that is not arrogant or sarcastic. An arrogant or sarcastic reply could very easily alienate the prospect.[15] Let us look at some examples.

Prospect: 'I am not interested in your product because your competitor was here and he said that your product is known to break down after a few months.'

Salesperson: 'That salesperson was not aware of all of the facts. Our products are in fact known for their reliability and that is one of the reasons we have introduced our unique three-year guarantee.'

Did you notice that the salesperson did not call the prospect or the competitor a liar? Let us look at another example.

Prospect: 'I believe that your company does not deliver on its promises.'

Salesperson: 'I don't know where you heard that, but it is simply not true. I could easily provide you with a list of satisfied customers that you are welcome to call.'

This response is much more aggressive, yet still enlightens the prospect without alienating him or her.

Direct denial is fairly dangerous as it can easily be misunderstood. The prospect's feelings and pride must always be taken into consideration when using direct denial.

The salesperson must have hard evidence or facts that can back up any direct denial. A somewhat softer approach is to use indirect denial.

Indirect denial

Indirect denial is similar to direct denial except that the salesperson initially appears to agree with the prospect's objection. This method of handling objections is softer, more tactful and more courteous than direct denial. Indirect denial is characterised by the 'yes, but …' phrase. Let us look at some examples.

Prospect: 'Your price is much higher than the competition's.'

Salesperson: 'I agree, our price is higher, but we do offer the extended warranty …'

Did you notice that the salesperson agreed with the prospect and then subtly highlighted a competitive benefit of the product? Let us look at one more example.

Prospect: 'You only offer the product in 5 kg tubs, but we need 250 kg bulk containers.'

Salesperson: 'I can understand you thinking that we only supply in 5 kg tubs, because that is what we sell the most of, but I may not have made myself clear. We do have the ability to supply in bulk; in fact several of our larger customers purchase 250 to 300 kg containers regularly.'

Did you notice how the salesperson gently corrected the prospect's misconception? In some cases the objection might not be serious enough to warrant attention. In these cases it may be best to 'let it go'.

Let it go

Occasionally, objections are made out of frustration, fear or anger. They are sometimes neither genuine objections nor smokescreens; they are simply a vent for the prospect to express his or her views. In such situations it permissible, sometimes advisable, for the salesperson to pass over the objection and not address it at all. As with all objections it is important to acknowledge the prospect's opinion.

Prospect: 'The service I received from your company last time made me decide never to purchase from you guys again.'

Salesperson: 'It sounds like we really treated you badly last time. I am sorry that you had that experience. I hope you will find me better to deal with. What I was hoping to address was …'

In this example the salesperson acknowledged the prospect's opinion and expressed empathy with the situation. The salesperson did not address the objection by offering to take care of the issue or fix it in any way, but simply let it go.

Compensation

Compensation is necessary when the prospect has highlighted a competitive weakness in your product offering. It becomes necessary for the salesperson to offer another benefit or feature that compensates for the weakness. The most common use of compensation is when trying to justify a higher price. Look at the following scenario:

Prospect: 'Your product costs 5% more than the competition's.'

Salesperson: 'That's true; our product is 5% more expensive. Our product is also 50% more reliable and the payment terms are very convenient.'

In this example the salesperson acknowledged the price objection and then compensated for the higher price by highlighting pertinent benefits of the product. Sometimes the prospect's objection can be turned into a selling point. This is known as the boomerang method for dealing with objections.

Boomerang

The boomerang method involves 'sending' the objection back as an advantage or a reason to buy. An experienced salesperson can identify the objection as a potential boomerang and then reply with an indication of just how positive the raised point really is. Let us look at the following example:

Prospect: 'Your product seems to work well, but the fact that the lid is so difficult to open is really putting me off.'

Salesperson: 'I am glad you mentioned that because it is one of our key safety features. The lid prevents air from reacting with the product and creating dangerous fumes.'

Or

Prospect: 'I think that my employees will struggle to sell a product that is so difficult to open.'

Salesperson: 'The lid is a very important safety feature. Imagine how difficult it will be for a little child to open.'

The boomerang approach requires a quick-thinking and self-assured salesperson who is very familiar with the product and the prospect's needs.

Referrals are not only a good way of identifying prospects, but also an excellent method for overcoming objections.

Third-party

The third-party or referral method of addressing objections requires the cooperation of a previous customer or other reliable source. This method is used when the objection has already been raised in the past by a previous customer and successfully overcome. (Obviously if the objection was not satisfactorily dealt with, that customer would not be a good referral!)

Salespeople should always be ready with statistics, research and favourable figures that can support their sale. A third-party commendation often carries more weight and seems more reliable than only the salesperson's word. Consider the following situation:

Prospect: 'Our current machine runs eight hours a day and we haven't had a malfunction in weeks.'

Salesperson: 'That's pretty good, but ABC manufacturing is running our X400 model 24 hours a day and they have this to say about it ...'

Or

Prospect: 'I have heard that your product has fewer vitamins in it than your competitors'.'

Salesperson: 'Independent research conducted by the CSIR indicates that our product contains 30% more vitamins than our closest competitor's.'

Remember that the third-party method must only be used when you have valid figures and permission from the third party to use their name. The old adage about honesty being the best policy is very important when dealing with objections. Fake results will always be found out and can lead not only to a lost sale but also to a career-damaging loss of credibility.

THE TRIAL CLOSE

An objection cannot be resolved until the prospect says it is. For this reason salespeople use what is commonly known as a trial close to try to establish the prospect's attitude or frame of mind at that point in the presentation.[16] The trial close should not be viewed in the same light as the final close where the salesperson asks for the actual order, but rather as a question to make sure that the salesperson and the prospect are on the same page. The final close will be discussed in an upcoming chapter. The trial close takes the form of a question and is most effectively used at any of the following points during a presentation:[17]

- After the salesperson has made a strong selling point
- After the salesperson has answered an objection
- After the salesperson has completed the presentation
- Immediately before the salesperson moves to close the sale

If a trial close is used immediately after addressing an objection, you have a clear idea of whether or not you understood the objection properly and whether or not you have dealt with it satisfactorily. Some important tips for the trial close are:

- *Summarise.* Especially in the case of a complex product or more specifically a complex objection, first summarise the issue as you understood it and then summarise your answer. By doing this you are refreshing the mind of the prospect about your solution and also clarifying if you understood the objection correctly.
- *Do not focus more attention on the objection than necessary.* Salespeople are sometimes tempted to overdo the solution or spend too much time explaining an objection away.

This added attention could have the opposite effect and cause the prospect to remember the objection above all else!

- *Get the prospect's confirmation and then move on*. Following on from the previous tip, if you have summarised the objection and the solution, and the customer nods in agreement, then move on with the presentation and do not overemphasis the point.

Let us consider some examples of the types of questions that can be used in a trial close to establish where the prospect sees themselves relative to your product or presentation.

The trial close question	What we can learn from it
How does that sound to you?	We would normally ask this question just after a unique selling point and can determine if the prospect values the point or not
What do you think?	With this question we can tell if the prospect is actually listening to us or if there is a potential objection on the horizon
Is this important to you?	Again, with this question we can gauge the importance of a selling point for the prospect
I have a hunch that you like the money-saving features of this product. Am I right?	By making a bold statement like this one, the salesperson is drawing attention to the money-saving qualities of the product, stating an obvious advantage, making sure the prospect perceives the money-saving features, and then asking for affirmation

Try to think of some more questions that you could ask as a trial close.

SUMMARY

A good salesperson does not fear or avoid objections. A good salesperson will prepare for objections, identify them when they arise and handle them in a manner that reassures the prospect and sets the scene for a positive close. In the next chapter we will be looking at the closing of the sale.

Situation

You are the salesperson for Radical Insurance Services. You have worked hard recently on prospecting and have a meeting with Mr O Bama regarding his household insurance. You have sent some information to him prior to your call. You are about to begin your sales call, and your objective is to sell the client an all-inclusive short-term insurance policy. Complete the following tasks:

- Mr O Bama raises the following objection: 'Your insurance policy seems very expensive'. How would you handle it? (There are four ways to handle this objection.)
- You have reached the end of the sales call. How would you close the deal for the insurance policy with Mr O Bama? (There are three ways to close this deal.)

Solution

Mr O Bama raised the following objection: 'Your insurance policy seems very expensive'. This is how to handle it:

- 'Yes, but the final insurance policy is much better in comparison with other policies, when you actually claim.' (i.e. 'yes, but...')
- 'Why do you think the insurance policy is expensive?' (i.e. ask why)
- 'Our insurance policy is too expensive?' (i.e. restate)
- 'I appreciate your point. However, in comparison to the cover offered by our competitors, our policy is much more extensive' (i.e. contradiction)

You have reached the end of the sales call. This is how to close the deal for the insurance policy with Mr O Bama:

- 'Shall I arrange the policy for you?' (i.e. ask for the business)
- 'You like the easy monthly payments, the payment holiday if needed, the frequent payback bonus for remaining with us and not cancelling your policy, and the free travel clock. So shall I arrange the policy for you?' (i.e. trial close)
- 'Would you like to pay by cash weekly, or by regular monthly salary deductions?

SELF-ASSESSMENT QUESTIONS

1. During your sales presentation, the prospect suddenly interrupts you by saying: 'Your product looks good, but we are not going to be buying until the next financial year'. How should you respond?

2. Price objections are the most common objections raised. Discuss how you would react to price objections in the following scenarios:

   - You are selling high-priced industrial conveyor belts and the prospect claims that your competition's product is 20% less expensive.

   - Your product is a relatively cheap industrial staple gun that is on a par with the competitive products. The customer is pushing for a discount.

   - While you are selling a new flu vaccine, the prospect argues that the price is too high.

3. Discuss which method of dealing with objections you would use in the following situations:

   - While you are selling computer networking peripherals, the prospect objects to the delivery times that you offer.

   - During a sales presentation for office copy machines, the prospect comments about a problem that was experienced by one of your other customers.

   - The prospect to whom you are presenting your new desktop printers claims that your competitor has presented research that demonstrates reliability superior to that of your product.

4. You are a salesperson who is selling recycled paper for use in industrial printing presses. The prospect has clearly stated that he or she is not prepared to deal with your company because of a previous bad experience. It seems that your predecessor presented false evidence during a sales presentation. Evaluate the different methods that could be used to deal with this situation.

5. Let us assume that you have answered a prospect's objection and now feel that you want to move on with the presentation. Discuss the importance of the trial close and provide some examples of questions that you would ask.

NOTES

1. Ingram, T.N., LaFroge, R.W., Avila, R.A., Schwepker, C.H. & William, M.R. 2001. *Professional Selling: A Trust-based Approach*. Orlando: Harcourt, p. 221.

2. Rix, P., Buss, J. & Herford, G. 1999. *Selling: A Consultative Approach*. Roseville: McGraw-Hill, p. 261.

3. Ingram et al., op. cit., p. 222.

4. Cooper, S. 1997. *Selling: Principles, Practice and Management*. London: Pitman.

5.   Adapted from Gitomer, J. 23 June 2003. Look at sales objections from the customer's perspective. *Cincinnati Business Courier.*

6.   Futrell, C. 1999. Fundamentals of Selling. (Sixth edition). Boston: Irwin McGraw-Hill, p. 337.

7.   Futrell, op. cit., p. 342.

8.   Ingram et al., op cit., p. 223.

9.   Futrell, op. cit., p. 345.

10. Futrell, op. cit., p. 347.

11. Rix et al., op. cit., p. 265.

12. Rix et al., op. cit., p. 274.

13. Rix et al., op. cit., p. 264.

14. Rix et al., op. cit., p. 269.

15. Futrell, op. cit., p. 358.

16. Rix et al., op. cit., p. 272.

17. Futrell, C. 2003. ABCs of Relationship Selling. (Seventh edition). Boston: Irwin McGraw-Hill, p. 72.

10

CLOSING THE SALE

LEARNING OUTCOMES

After studying this chapter, you should be able to:

- Explain the various buying signals
- Understand when to ask for the order
- Recognise the appropriate time to close the sale
- Identify the factors that make a salesperson a good closer
- Understand how many times a salesperson should close a sale
- Discuss the various problems encountered in closing a sale
- Explain the essential elements of closing a sale
- Identify several closing techniques

INTRODUCTION

It has been said that a salesperson who cannot close a sale is merely a conversationalist! And naturally, no employer would employ someone to go out and 'make conversation' with prospects. Closing is therefore an important part of the personal selling process. However, just as many other aspects of the personal selling function and the personal selling process have changed dramatically in the last two decades, so too has the 'closing' element. It is therefore appropriate to comment on and debunk some of the myths about 'closing'.

A noted sales trainer, Landy Chase, commenting on the 'old-style' closing techniques said:[1]

> The idea of 'closing' has long been regarded as applying pressure to get a person to buy. This is complete nonsense, and there is no place for this definition of closing in today's business environment. The irony of 'closing' is that good closing skills have nothing to do with being pushy.

In this chapter, emphasis is placed on methods, or closing techniques, of getting the customer to say 'yes'. The focus is on the salesperson's need to make a sale.

Selling emphasises the *relationship* between seller and buyer, and the process they work through to satisfy the customer's needs. Asking for a commitment (the closing) becomes a much less pivotal event and evolves naturally from the consultation that has preceded it – a solution to a problem has been found and the order, or other commitment, is confirmation of this mutual achievement.[2]

This is not to say that asking for a commitment is not important or necessary in selling. It is the salesperson's *duty* to ask for the order, or agree to give the customer an opportunity to try the product, or to arrange to meet again, or whatever the objective of the call is. *Asking* focuses the attention of both buyer and seller on the underlying reason they are together. The seller's question and the buyer's answer let both know where they are in the process of satisfying the buyer's need.[3]

Outstanding salespeople do not give a presentation and then ask for the order; rather, they cultivate selling techniques that help develop a natural instinct, sensitivity and timing for when and how to close with each buyer. In this chapter we discuss when to close and what makes a good closer. After that, we will focus on the number of times you should attempt to close a sale, along with some problems associated with closing. Closing techniques are then presented, followed by an explanation of the importance of being prepared to close several times, depending on the situation. To be a good closer, you must be able to handle objections, which frequently arise as the salesperson nears the end of the presentation.[4]

Although, technically, 'closing' a sale takes place when products or services are delivered to the customer's satisfaction and payment is received, we will define closing as 'asking for the order'. There are many closing techniques as well as many ways to ask trial closing questions. A trial question may take the following form: 'Now that I've addressed your concerns, what other questions do you have that might affect your decision to purchase?' Closing does not always mean that the sales professional literally *asks* for the order – it could mean, for example, asking prospects how many products they would like, what colour they would prefer, when they would like to take delivery, etc. Too many sales professionals are either too weak or too aggressive when it comes to closing. If you are closing a sale, be sure to ask for the order. If the prospect gives an answer other than 'Yes', it may be a good opportunity to identify new objections and to continue selling.[5] Closing, therefore, can be seen as the time when the prospect is ready to commit. The time to close is the time when the buyer gives a buying signal to the salesperson.

BUYING SIGNALS

Buying signals are not always easy to read and understand, and this has been the centre of many discussions on the topic. No one can predict how and when a prospect will give a buying signal during the sales presentation. It is, however, the task of the salesperson to be vigilant and to be wary of anything that might indicate that the prospect is in the conviction stage of the buying process. Generally speaking, however, buying signals come in the form of questions such as: [6]

- Can you clarify the price calculation?
- When can you deliver?
- Do you offer finance terms?
- Who will do the installation?
- Do you provide training?
- Where can I see a similar unit in operation?

Not only must the salesperson be on the lookout for verbal buying signals, but also for the more subtle, yet equally valid, non-verbal ones, such as up-and-down nodding of the head. This also includes being attentive to the facial expressions of the buyer, hand movements, a relaxed and complacent atmosphere, and so forth to detect an inclination to buy.

A buying signal can be defined as anything that prospects say or do that indicates that they are ready to buy. Futrell describes a number of such signals and states that a prospective buyer:[7]

- *Asks questions:* 'How much does it cost?'; 'What is the earliest time that I can receive it?'; 'Do you have an exchange policy?'. It is good strategy in some instances for you to ask some questions based on the buying signals received. This helps you to get more clarity and to understand the product better. If the question is answered positively, the prospect is showing a high interest level and you are nearing the close.
- *Asks somebody else's opinion:* A businessman calling on others in the company for their opinion, for example, is sending out a clear buying signal.
- *Relaxes and becomes friendly:* Once the prospect decides to purchase a product, the pressure of the buying situation is reduced. A state of visible anxiety changes to relaxation as the new customer sees you as a friend.
- *Pulls out a purchase order form:* If the prospect reaches for the order book, it is time to move towards the close.
- *Carefully examines merchandise:* When a prospect carefully scrutinises the product or seems to be contemplating the purchase, this may be an indirect request for prompting. Given these indications, attempt a trial close: 'What do you think about ...?' If you obtain a positive response to this question, move on to close the sale.

A prospective buyer may send verbal or non-verbal buying signals at any time before or during a sales presentation and it is the task of the salesperson to look out for these signals and to react to them (see Table 10.1). A trial close should focus on the more important points that are relevant to the potential buyer.

Table 10.1 *Answering a prospect's question with a question[8]*

The buyer says:	The salesperson replies:
What's your best price?	Would that be for 50 units?
When can you make the earliest delivery	When do you need it by?
Can I get this special price on orders placed now and next month?	Would you like to split your shipment?
Do you carry 2.5-, 4-, 12- and 18-metre pipe?	Are those the sizes you commonly use?
How large an order must I place to receive your best price?	What size order do you have in mind?
Can the payment be made over two months?	Do you want to stagger the payments?

The next section focuses on how to go about preparing to ask for an order.

PREPARING TO ASK FOR THE SALE/ORDER[9]

Generally, customers expect a salesperson to ask them for a commitment. How they respond to the request will, in part, depend on the salesperson's manner, attitude and approach. Some thoughts on how a salesperson can manage this stage of the sales call or interview are given below.

Be confident

Self-assurance in a salesperson goes a long way towards building the customer's confidence, and a well-delivered presentation will help instil this confidence. Remember that there are only two possible outcomes of the sales call, namely that a sale will happen or it will not. If you lose a sale now it is not the end of the world, and next time the product may better solve the needs of the customer.

A salesperson must remember that not all presentations will lead to a sale, but that all presentations can help to build confidence. This is part of the learning experience.

Be assertive

It is easier for confident salespeople to be more assertive than it is for those who are unsure of themselves or their product. Confidence will also enable the salesperson to be more aggressive. Remember that a subtle aggressiveness is also a sign of confidence.

Unduly aggressive behaviour at this stage can also alienate the buyer, and the salesperson must avoid this. For example, a salesperson might say: 'It's really very simple – this is the best model on the market and you just won't get a better price than the one I'm offering you ...'

A potential buyer could see this type of comment as negative and even arrogant, and this may even make him or her more defensive.

Merely agreeing with the customer all the time may also be viewed in a negative light and could lead to a negative reaction from the customer, who may think that the salesperson is only saying what he or she wants to hear.

An assertive approach is a balance between being aggression and submission, and is an integral part of confidence and the ability to solve customers' problems.

TIMING: WHEN TO CLOSE[10]

When to ask for the sale is always a fine balancing act. If you ask too soon, you may get a firm 'No'. The idea is to choose the time in such a way as to maximise the chances of a 'Yes'.

It is important that salespeople learn when to guide the customer to the next stage of the decision-making process. This is important both in order to maintain the trust established between buyer and seller and to ensure that the process takes as much time as it needs but no more.

As a general rule, customers will emit buying signals when they are ready to buy. These can be verbal or non-verbal signs of satisfaction with the proposal being offered. Some of these are outlined below:

Customer questions

Certain questions posed by a customer serve as an indication that the major benefits of a particular product or service have been accepted. Some typical questions are as follows:

- 'You do take trade-ins, don't you?'
- 'Is the software included?'
- 'What will the total cost be?'
- 'You say you can deliver tomorrow – is that right?'
- 'Do you have red ones in stock?'

In asking questions such as these, the customer is determining the minor benefits or commercial terms that will confirm the intention to buy.

Customer requests

Requests by customers are also an indication of acceptance, and generally they confirm certain conditions or aspects of the deal:

- 'Can I pay with a debit card?'
- 'Can I have the extra cover in writing?'
- 'If your technician confirms ...?'

Customer agreement

When a customer is close to buying, there will generally be a more easy agreement on benefits. This can be expressed as follows:

- 'This colour goes well with my eyes.'
- 'It is good enough for my children.'
- 'I have been looking for this model for years.'

Non-verbal signals

A customer who feels confident that his or her needs or problems are being addressed relaxes more. Facial expressions may change, frowns disappear, and nervous smiles or looks of apprehension give way to a genuine smile.

A customer may move closer to the salesperson and talk in a low voice, as if sharing a confidence. This can be seen as a sort of 'conspiracy' between them. On the other hand, people who have decided not to buy are likely to start distancing themselves, both physically and mentally. These customers may look at any option to end the conversation and to leave.

In some cases a customer comes across as already owning the product. After fitting a garment, for example, the customer may fold it neatly and hold onto it. This is a sign that he or she has decided to buy.

Responses to trial closes

In order to assess a customer's readiness to commit, the salesperson may ask questions to gauge the customer's thinking at that stage. The responses to these questions are an indication as to how close the customer is to committing:

- 'How do you like the features so far?'
- 'Should I explain anything else?'
- 'How do you feel about the ability of this product to meet your needs?'
- 'Do you feel confident about the features?'

The responses to these questions should further enhance discussion and lead towards finalising the sale.

COMPLETING THE SALE[11]

Completion of the sale can happen in various ways. Some tips on how to mastermind the close follow.

Keep the customer part of the process

The salesperson should not adapt or change the way of working as the sale draws to a conclusion. Changing the approach may result in the buyer losing confidence in the salesperson's ability, or feeling that the salesperson is hiding something.

The salesperson must constantly show an understanding of the customer's needs and problems, which will further instil confidence.

Reconfirmation

By restating and confirming the benefits, the salesperson shows his or her understanding of the customer's needs and confirms the customer's choice.

A good salesperson will focus on those benefits of most interest to the customer. This, however, does not mean that all the benefits must be repeated – only those that are important.

Solve any outstanding issues

If last-minute problems are not adequately resolved, a sale may be lost. Even though the problems may be minor, they are important to the customer.

Any unresolved issue needs to be attended to – even if it is deemed to be minor. Deal with it quickly and effectively without giving it undue attention, even though it may cost you the sale.

Do not look for problems

Do not look for problems as you move to close. Costs and price are usually areas where problems may occur but these should have been dealt with at the beginning of the transaction. Make sure that all matters regarding costs are covered then – the customer will expect to pay what has been quoted and does not want any hidden costs.

Help the customer to justify the decision

The higher the unit price of an item, the greater the possibility that customers may seek to justify their decision. Last-minute questions on price or brand must not be seen as negative but rather as an indication of customers' need for more information to convince themselves that they have made the right decision. Salespeople should ensure that they supply all the information needed, as this may well lead to a successful sale.

Avoid interruptions

Untimely interruptions by other salespeople, the telephone, etc. may jeopardise a sale. Buyers expect the undivided attention of the salesperson, who should show the necessary interest to ensure an environment free from interruptions.

ATTRIBUTES OF A GOOD CLOSER

Some individuals are better than others at closing sales. Some attributes of good closers are the following:

- They have a strong desire to close each sale.
- They prepare for each sales call.
- They do not stop with the prospect's first 'No'.
- They ask for the order and then remain quiet.
- They get the order – then move on!

Generally speaking, a good closer will try at least three to five times to close a sale and does not give up after the first rebuttal. Attempting several closes in one call challenges a salesperson to employ wit, charm and personality in a creative manner.

PROBLEMS WITH CLOSING

The closure of a sale should be the easiest part of a presentation as it affords the salesperson time to evaluate and assess the needs of the customer, yet salespeople sometimes have difficulty closing the sale, for several reasons:

- One reason may be a lack of confidence in themselves. If they have failed before, it may place pressure on them.
- A second reason may be that the salesperson may not feel that his or her solution is correct any more, and thus does not ask for the order. When in doubt, remember that the final decision rests with the customer.
- Finally, the salesperson may have offered a poor presentation. Often a poorly prepared presentation falls apart.

ESSENTIAL ELEMENTS WHEN CLOSING THE SALE[12]

To improve the chances of a successful sale, the following elements need to be considered:

- Be sure that the prospect understands you.
- Present a complete story and not only parts of it.
- Tailor your close to each prospect. Prepare to give the expert customer all the facts requested, to give the egotistical customer praise, to lead the indecisive customer, and to slow down for a slow thinker.
- Everything that is said and done should take the customer's point of view into consideration.
- See the first 'No' as simply a hesitant 'Yes'.
- Learn to recognise buying signals.
- Attempt a trial close before closing.
- After asking for the order, keep quiet.
- Develop and maintain a positive, confident and enthusiastic attitude towards yourself, your products, your prospects and your close.

Often, salespeople believe that there is some mystical art to closing a sale – if they say the right words in the appropriate manner, the prospect will buy. What is needed most is a thorough understanding of the entire selling process and of the critical role that closing plays in it.

It often happens that the customer through his or her actions closes the sale by saying: 'I'll take two'. This leaves the salesperson to write up the order. If this does not happen, there are some closing techniques that can help finalise the deal.

Futrell[13] identifies the following 12 keys to a successful closing.

> ## Twelve keys to a successful closing
>
> 1. Think success! Be enthusiastic.
> 2. Plan your sales call.
> 3. Confirm your prospect's needs in the approach.
> 4. Give a great presentation.
> 5. Use trial closes during and after your presentation.
> 6. Smoke out a prospect's real objections.
> 7. Overcome real objections.
> 8. Use a trial close after overcoming each objection.
> 9. Summarise benefits as related to buyer's needs.
> 10. Use a trial close to confirm step 9.
> 11. Ask for the order and then be quiet.
> 12. Leave the door open. Act as a professional.

CLOSING TECHNIQUES[14]

There are various techniques that the salesperson can follow to close a sale. The type of customer, type of product and/or type of industry will impact on the type of technique to use in each situation. Some of these techniques are discussed below.

Direct request

This method says exactly what it is – ask for the order! If, however, this has been done the salesperson should be *silent*, and wait for the prospect's response. It may happen that if the salesperson says anything at all immediately after asking for the order (and before the prospect has time to reply), the magic may be broken as the prospect will not feel the pressure to make a decision. Asking for the order is, however, not as easy and straightforward as it sounds – in fact it is much more complicated than that. Even the most experienced salespeople experience some anxiety in most situations as there is always the possibility of rejection.

Benefits summary

It must be remembered that potential buyers or prospects aim to buy something that will offer specific benefits to them or certain solutions to opportunities or threats, therefore it is logical in some cases to give them a summary of the benefits or solutions the product offer. The FAB approach is often used in such a situation. This implies the following:

- *F = Features.* This refers to the product itself and what it offers.
- *A = Advantages.* This refers to the advantages or solutions the features offer to the prospect
- *B = Benefits.* This refers to the benefits the prospect will obtain from these advantages.

This method is a very popular and obvious way to conclude a presentation as it leaves prospects with a clear understanding of how the product addresses their needs.

Balance sheet method

Just as a balance sheet has a debit and credit side, or an asset and a liabilities column, so does a product offer certain positives (pros) and negatives (cons). This method aims to help the prospect to weigh the pros and cons and to make a decision in a logical way. It is the task of the salesperson to identify and highlight as many positives as possible for the prospect, and also to point out disadvantages. Hopefully, the salesperson will be able to identify more pros and offer options or solutions as to how the cons can be overcome to lessen their importance.

In order for this method to be effective, the salesperson must get the prospect's agreement on the pros identified as by doing so the prospect has a higher level of commitment. Whenever a valid concern is raised by the prospect, the salesperson should not just ignore it but agree that it is a limitation. This method can be very effective if used properly and in the appropriate circumstances. Nervous and unsure buyers can be convinced by this step-by-step approach as it helps them to analyse the whole buying situation. A word of caution is, however, needed here. It may be that a particular con or limitation may be the result of the sale not going through. In such cases the salesperson needs to have alternatives available or ways to reduce the potential impact of such a limitation, or be able to indicate how the positives outweigh the negatives.

The assumptive method

In this method, which is based on the assumptions of the salesperson, the salesperson assumes that the prospect is going to make a commitment, and uses positive statements throughout the presentation to reinforce this assumption. This method should ideally be followed only if there is some sort of an indication that the prospect has given some sort of positive indication towards the presentation/product. Where a product has been bought in the past, this method can be more easily employed as it is likely to be a repeat order – if the client was satisfied.

The alternative choice method

It is not always possible for the salesperson to offer alternatives to a prospect but if it is possible this method can be very effective. The rationale behind this method is that the prospect is not making a commitment on the 'major issue' – i.e. placing an order – but is simply making a decision on a 'minor issue', a choice between alternatives A or B. By offering a choice, the salesperson will either receive a 'Yes' decision or discover an objection not raised before. Assuming that the objection can be successfully overcome, the salesperson is close to obtaining a commitment from the prospect.

The agreement on minor points method

A complicated decision or one that is seen to be a big decision by the prospect may require a different approach. This may be by means of obtaining a number of 'Yeses' or agreements from the prospect on minor points. This may make it easier for the prospect to make a final commitment as the salesperson builds on each agreement to obtain an ultimate commitment on the 'big' decision, namely to place an order.

This process progresses slowly but surely toward obtaining the final commitment.

The compliment method

Many prospects can be persuaded to purchase a product by means of a correctly judged compliment or two. The opposite is, however, also true where an insincere or ill-judged compliment may sound deceitful or patronising, and may lead to a negative reaction from the prospect. It is therefore important that salespeople do not engage in dishonest or forced flattery as this can have the totally opposite effect. It is the task of the salesperson to ensure that, when giving a compliment, he or she knows for certain that the compliment is indeed based on fact and not on assumption. This can only be done if the salesperson has done the necessary research on the prospect and ensured that the compliment is justified. The reputation, for example, of the prospect in the business world may be a case where a compliment is given. This acknowledgement is in many cases an indication to the prospect that he or she is obviously qualified to make such a decision to purchase the product being offered by the salesperson. This technique is also referred to as the 'soft sell' approach. It comes down to the salesperson 'seeking' the advice of the prospect on the features, benefits and advantages of the product being offered, and effectively allows the prospect to sell him- or herself on the product!

The negotiation method

One can arguably say that every sale is a negotiation as all negotiations focus on two major themes – perceived value and price. The end result of this process is that both parties must feel that there has been a win-win situation and that they have achieved a good deal. The salesperson may use any one or more of the methods mentioned in this section in combination with the negotiation method, and with practice and experience this will blend seamlessly into a very professional conclusion to the sales presentation.

All of these alternatives may be used individually or with any other one, depending on the circumstances. At best these options are tools to be used by the salesperson in the correct sales situation.

COMMON MISTAKES IN SALES CALLS

There are many mistakes that prevent sales calls from being successful. Some have been identified by means of research and are listed below.[15]

Tells instead of sells; does not ask enough questions
A salesperson who talks too much and does not allow the customer to contribute is talking him- or herself out of a sale.

Over-controls the call; asks too many closed questions
This sales dialogue resembles an interrogation, and the customer has limited opportunities to express needs.

Does not respond to customer needs with benefits
The salesperson lets the customer infer how the features will satisfy his or her needs.

Does not recognise needs; gives benefits prematurely
A customer discussing telephone equipment may, for example, mention that some clients complain that the line is always busy. The salesperson demonstrates the benefits of his or her answering service, but the customer responds that busy lines are not important since people will call back. In such a case, the customer is not concerned enough to want to solve the problem.

Does not recognise or handle negative attitudes effectively
The salesperson fails to recognise the customer's statements of objection (opposition), indifference (no need) or scepticism (doubts). What is not dealt with effectively remains on the customer's mind. Left with a negative attitude, the customer will not make a commitment.

Makes weak closing statements; does not recognise when or how to close
Successful salespeople are alert to closing opportunities throughout the call. The most powerful way to close a sales call is to give a summary of benefits that interest the customer.

FACTORS TO PLAN BEFORE THE SALE
Before the salesperson attempts to sell, the following need to be considered and be prepared:

Customise the approach strategy
Not all strategies or approaches are the same. There is no one correct approach and therefore the salesperson needs to evaluate the customer and plan his or her approach accordingly. The salesperson must do proper research regarding the prospect's requirements, and plan the sales presentation accordingly. In this way a customised proposal to the prospect can be offered. There is nothing more off-putting to prospective buyers than a standard or generic approach to sell to them.

Positive attitude

If there is one thing that can kill a presentation and potential sale it is a defeatist or fatalistic attitude. If the salesperson does not come across as positive and upbeat about the product, he or she cannot expect the prospect to buy it.

The salesperson must come across in a positive way – a positive attitude is contagious and rubs off on the prospect. Customers like to deal with salespeople who have confidence in themselves, their products and their companies. Care must, however, be taken not to come across as arrogant.

Let prospects set the pace

Over-eager salespeople often try to force the prospect to commit to a deal. This can be counterproductive as many prospects want to feel that they are making the decision. The salesperson needs to ensure that the prospect is ready to make the decision, and not half way there. The salesperson is the one in charge and should keep it that way while at the same time being aware of the verbal and non-verbal cues, and the concerns of the prospect.

Be assertive, not aggressive

The assertive salesperson is self-confident and positive, and maintains proper perspective by being responsive to customer needs.

Sell the right product for the job to be done

One of the fundamental aspects of selling is for the salesperson to sell the right product to the prospect. Failure to do so might have long-term implications for the business in terms of boycotting of their products, refusal to buy from them, and so forth. The company does not want to develop a perception in the market of one that is only focused on the sale and not the needs of the customer. This approach may lead to short-term success but may result in long-term disaster.

SUMMARY

Closing the sale is the final conclusion of all the efforts of the salesperson. It is the culmination of ferreting out the needs of the customer, matching the characteristics of the product with those needs, answering questions and handling objections – and in some cases, losing the sale.

Closing techniques must be practised, used and refined. A good closer has a strong desire to close each sale. Rarely should salespeople accept the first 'No' as the final answer. If they are professional, they should be able to close a minimum of three to five times.

Remember that a good salesperson always stays calm and collected, no matter what the provocation.

Tupperware[16]

Promotions are a vital part of Tupperware's marketing.

The most visible part of the promotional process is personal selling or, more specifically, a demonstration where information is shared with guests. The demonstrator shows Tupperware items in a non-competitive environment, adding value by explaining to the guests how to make full use of the product in a non-pressurised, non-retail setting. Brochures, including invitations, flyers, catalogues and order forms, are readily available for the demonstrator to use as sales tools, to promote the product range and to assist in the recruiting process.

A Hostess Gift Catalogue is also used to help hostesses identify the particular gift they wish to earn when they host a demonstration. This catalogue helps the demonstrator to motivate hostesses to try for additional sales in order to qualify for a higher level gift.

Demonstrators and managers are continually motivated at weekly distributor rallies, at which new and promotional products, sales incentives and recruiting challenges are launched.

Tupperware also runs international travel and other recognition programmes for distributors, who are continually competing against one another to achieve both short- and longer term goals.

Questions

1. Explain different buying signals a prospect may display once a demonstration has been done.
2. Discuss the various techniques a salesperson can use to close a sale.

NOTES

1. Abratt, R., Connett, B.I. & Cant, M.C. 2009. *Sales Management*. (Third edition). Sandton: Heinemann.

2. Rix, P., Buss, J. & Herford, G. 1999. *Selling: A Consultative Approach*. Sydney: McGraw-Hill, p. 281.

3. Ibid., p. 281.

4. Futrell, C.M. 1996. *Fundamentals of Selling: Customers for Life*. (Fifth edition). New York: Irwin, p. 337.

5. http://www.davedolak.com

6. Abratt et al. Ibid., p. 139.

7. Futrell, op. cit., p. 338.

8. Adapted from Futrell, op. cit., p. 339.

9. This section based largely on Futrell, op. cit., pp. 340–350.

10. Loosely based on Futrell, op. cit., pp. 284–285.

11. Loosely based on Futrell, op. cit., pp. 286–287.

12. Based on Futrell, op. cit., p. 342.

13. Ibid., p. 344.

14. Loosely based on/taken from Abratt, Connett & Cant, 2009.

15. Xerox Learning System, taken from Futrell, op. cit., pp. 356–358.

16. Cant, M.C. & Machado, R. 2002. *Marketing Success Stories*. (Fourth edition). Lansdowne: Juta, p. 310.

11

FOLLOW-UP

LEARNING OUTCOMES

After studying this chapter, you should be able to:

- Discuss the steps to be taken when following up a sale
- Explain what is meant by the term *post-purchase dissonance*
- Identify the techniques to use when no comment is received from a prospect
- Explain how to keep the customer
- Discuss the importance of relationship building when following up a sale

INTRODUCTION

The sales task is not yet finalised once an order has been secured. In many instances this is when the sale actually starts as the salesperson must ensure that the order is filled and that the customer's expectations are managed. In fact, following up is crucial to the whole process and to ensuring long-term relationships with customers. Good follow-up helps to satisfy the needs of customers, and a good salesperson can convert a follow-up call into a sale.

The next section deals with the steps involved in following up the sale.

STEPS IN FOLLOW-UP[1]

A number of steps need to be taken to ensure that sales are correctly followed through. Some of these are discussed below.

Correct order

It is of utmost importance for salespeople to ensure that the order of a new client especially is correct as this may be the only chance they have to prove that they deserve to be a supplier.

Sometimes a prospect may decide to give a new supplier a chance and if this is not executed correctly it can jeopardise all future possibilities. Similarly, it is important for the supplier (salesperson) to maintain good relationships with existing customers to ensure long-term commitment and orders. The aim of this step is to ensure that buyers get what they want. The salesperson needs to reassure them about this, especially when large purchases are made.

Contracts

A deal is not finalised until the contract is signed, and if the salesperson neglects to complete the contract, which should be a routine and easy matter, a sale can be lost. Many sales have also fallen through due to authorisation that was not obtained. Further to this, it is important that all agreed-upon terms and conditions are in this contract. This also implies that the salesperson should not have made promises which he or she cannot keep.

Thanking the customer

It is common practice for the salesperson to thank the prospect for placing an order. By thanking customers for their support, much goodwill can be generated. Sending a card to a customer who has made a large purchase can be an effective way of building on a relationship.

Service can keep customers

Salespeople can sometimes work weeks or months to secure a sale and must now ensure that their relationships with their customers last for future sales. Some things that can be done to help customers are the following.[2]

- Focus on improving customer service.
- Contact new customers often.
- Handle any complaints promptly.
- Do what you say you will do
- Provide excellent service.
- Show appreciation for support from customers.

By offering good service, the salesperson keeps on reinforcing the positive image the customer may have. The salesperson must always be on the lookout for methods and means to make contact with the customer and to identify new opportunities for sales.

POST-PURCHASE DISSONANCE

Most people tend to have doubts after making a major purchase. Generally this refers to a feeling of: 'Did I make the right decision?'; 'Can I afford it?'; 'Was it too high a risk?'. This is known as post-purchase dissonance (see Table 11.1). The salesperson must be aware of this uneasy feeling and help to reduce it, or, in psychological terms, to change the dissonance into *consonance*. Below are some ways salespeople can help their customers to bring about this change.

FOLLOWING UP WHEN THERE IS NO COMMITMENT[3]

Salespeople need to realise that failure is part of selling. In fact, a salesperson can expect more failures than successes. The worst thing a salesperson can do is to take lack of commitment personally. In such cases there are two options the salesperson can exercise – to evaluate the possible reasons for this or to withdraw:

Evaluating possible reasons

The salesperson should ferret out reasons why no commitment has been made. The following are some possibilities:

- The salesperson may have failed to understand the buyer's needs.
- The presentation may have been unclear.
- The salesperson may have been ineffectual.

The real reason (even though it may hurt) must be determined. Only then can the salesperson move forward confidently.

The salesperson should analyse each stage of the call, remembering what seemed to go well or badly, and how the buyer reacted at different stages. This applies to both successful and unsuccessful sales.

Throwing in the towel – gently

Salespeople win some sales and lose others. If you have lost a sale, the loss is not necessarily permanent. Quit gracefully and work on the next one. You must evaluate why the sale was not made and see how you can improve in future.

Table 11.1 *Methods to change dissonance to consonance[4]*

Strategies to overcome post-purchase dissonance	Reflecting on your dissonance
Be realistic If you have oversold the benefits of a product, you can expect trouble from the customer whose needs have not been satisfied to the extent you promised. It is very difficult to solve this	Were you honest and straightforward about the product your customer was considering?
Show the buyer how to use it Explain how to use the product in different situations. This is particularly important when, from the customer's point of view, the purchase is complex. The product application may be easy for you to understand but it may not be so for the customer	Did you provide any extra advice, help or instructions? How did this make the buyer feel?

Strategies to overcome post-purchase dissonance	Reflecting on your dissonance
Continue to reinforce the buyer's decision Reiterate how well the product performs and meets people's needs. Concentrate on the benefits appropriate to the particular customer. Advertisements and sales promotions can also be used to confirm the customer's choice. Testimonials and endorsements not only attract new buyers, but they also offer confirmation to buyers that they have done the right thing	Did you do or say anything to reassure the buyer about his or her choice?
Exchange policy Have a firm policy concerning the exchange of goods and cash refunds. Then you will know where you are, and so will the customers. If people know you are prepared to exchange goods, they will be more adventurous in their purchases, which can be to your advantage. If you are not prepared to exchange certain items, put up a notice that clearly says so, then buyers will not be disappointed	Did you raise or clarify any risk-reduction policies?

KEEPING THE CUSTOMER

Customer retention is extremely important today. This can be attained in various ways and must be managed.

Providing service after the sale to customers is important in all types of businesses. Failure to do so will lead to more lost sales. A salesperson must understand that to keep a customer (retention), all aspects of the sale must be good, i.e. the product and value-added aspects must meet the needs of the customer in order to ensure repeat orders.

Figure 11.1 shows the process and the steps to be monitored.[5]

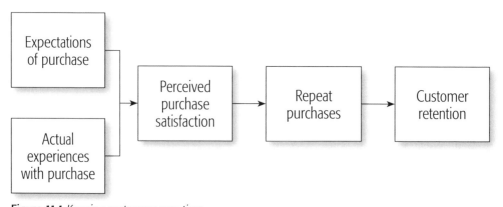

Figure 11.1 *Keeping customers over time*

The quality of service an organisation offers must be based on customers' expectations. More often than not, these expectations are formed by what the salesperson says and promises. It is therefore imperative that the salesperson does not over-promise. If the promised service materialises, this keeps customers satisfied. When a customer is satisfied, this equates to expectations being met, which leads to loyalty and, eventually, retention, which is crucial to the long-term success of the salesperson.

For the salesperson to render good service, technology is becoming increasingly important. Technology today assists salespeople to receive up-to-date information, to perform administrative tasks faster, and to serve clients better. In using technology and other means that are available, salespeople broaden their customer base, attract more customers and sell more to existing customers.

Good salespeople can convert follow-up and service situations into sales. Small things like a thank-you note, a telephone call or a visit can establish a positive image with buyers, which will lead to their coming back when the need arises – and happy customers also usually refer new customers.

Keeping customers through service

Salespeople may spend months cultivating a sale, but need to ensure that their customers will buy again in future. Futrell suggests the following behaviour after a major sale:[6]

- Concentrate on improving the account penetration. Account penetration is critical in uncovering prospect needs or problems, and consistently recommending effective solutions in terms of products that can be purchased. This shows the salesperson is really interested in the customer.
- Contact new customers often. In determining the frequency of calls, consider:
  - Present sales and/or potential future sales to the account
  - The number of orders over a year period
  - The range of products sold
  - The complexity of the products purchased by the customer

How much time is spent on a customer can vary tremendously, and it is up to the salesperson to work on an optimal ratio. The best way to do this is to be able to determine when additional calls are not in fact leading to an increase in sales.

Losing a customer: what to do

Losing a customer happens in all kinds of business. Salespeople will always lose a customer at some stage and how the salesperson handles this is important. Some ways that can be used are as follows:

- *Personal contact*. Find out the reason why the sale was lost.
- *Professionalism*. Being professional even when losing an account can stand the salesperson

in good stead in future. The salesperson must always show that he or she would like to be considered for future business.

- *Refrain from criticism.* Even if the salesperson knows that the decision made by the customer is not the best one, he or she should not criticise it. The customer can find this out for him- or herself.
- *Keep in contact.* Keep in touch with the customer. When something new comes up, it will benefit the salesperson.

The way the salesperson handles defeat will determine future business at the company.

Handle complaints fairly[7]

Customers may be dissatisfied with products for any number of reasons. These may include the following:

- The wrong product is delivered.
- The order is incorrect.
- Delivery is late.
- The manufacturer does not give the discounts agreed on.
- The product specification is not what the customer expected.
- The product does not perform as the customer believed it would.

It is the responsibility of the salesperson to judge whether a complaint is because of an honest mistake or not. Even if the customer made an honest mistake, it would be futile to argue with him or her, and you may even lose an account in such a case.

Customers should get the benefit of the doubt and the salesperson must have a solution. Some guidelines are as follows:[8]

- Obtain details and relevant information from the customer.
- Express sincere regret about the problem.
- Show the customer your willingness to help.
- Confirm the sale through sales records.
- If the customer is right, handle the complaint quickly and positively.
- Follow up to make sure that the problem has been properly resolved.

The salesperson must know who the more important customers are and see to it that they are looked after. Losing a big customer can be catastrophic.

SUMMARY

The salesperson, through follow-up, must ensure that the customer is satisfied and that any uncertainties, doubts and dissatisfaction are cleared out of the way. By doing this a relationship is formed for long-term business.

Avroy Shlain[9]

One of the biggest advantages to marketing in a direct-selling organisation (as opposed to its competitors in the retail sector) is the instant line of communication to the final consumer through the sales force. At present, Avroy Shlain Cosmetics boasts some 15 000 sales representatives throughout South Africa. The success or failure of a product line, promotion, advertising campaign or pricing policy is instantaneous. To this end, responsiveness and flexibility on behalf of the marketing team can counteract any negativity, or further drive any success. This powerful network makes for accurate identification of target markets and needs, thereby increasing the likelihood of successful marketing programmes.

The Avroy Shlain marketing vision is to provide 'exceptional yet affordable products'. This means identifying early trends and capitalising on them to provide the market with a leading-edge, world-class product offering. The challenge is to offer products at highly competitive price points and at the same time offer the shareholders a healthy return. This strategy has served to build market share as well as the image of the company.

It has been said that customer orientation means that 'the customer has to be satisfied because he is king' (although in this case the customer is usually 'queen'). In fact, the aim of an enterprise must be to delight the customer. In order to meet and exceed customers' expectations (and to delight them), Avroy Shlain concentrates on the following:

- Providing a high level of training to ensure that their salespeople are experts in the field of beauty care
- Focusing on motivation to ensure regular calls on customers and thus good service
- Offering a seven-day, money-back guarantee
- Giving personal consultations and facials in customers' homes
- Holding exciting, money-stretching promotions
- Holding regular client competitions and giving gifts to clients
- Providing a high-quality product by using leading-edge technology

Questions

1. What strategies can Avroy Shlain use to overcome post-purchase dissonance among their customers?
2. Into what level of relationship marketing do you think Avroy Shlain falls? Motivate your answer.

NOTES

1. Based on Futrell, C.M. 1996. *Fundamentals of Selling: Customers for Life.* (Fifth edition). New York: Irwin, pp. 293–297.

2. Futrell, C.M. 1999. *Fundamentals of Selling: Customers for Life.* (Sixth edition). Boston: Irwin McGraw-Hill, p. 408.

3. Loosely based on Futrell, 1996, p. 297.

4. Adapted from Futrell, 1996. Ibid., p. 296.

5. Based on Futrell, 2003. *The ABCs of Relationship Selling.* (Seventh edition). Boston: McGraw-Hill, p. 366.

6. Ibid., p. 369.

7. Futrell, 1996, op. cit., p. 381.

8. Futrell, 2003, op. cit., p. 376.

9. Cant, M.C. & Machado, R. 2002. *Marketing Success Stories.* (Fourth edition). Cape Town: Lansdowne: Juta, p. 310.

12

ETHICAL AND LEGAL ISSUES IN PERSONAL SELLING

LEARNING OUTCOMES

After reading this chapter you should be able to:

- Distinguish between ethics and ethical behaviour
- Understand the factors that influence ethical behaviour
- Explain a sales code of conduct
- Understand the different unethical situations that a salesperson can be exposed to
- Know which business laws affect the sales industry

INTRODUCTION

The sales industry should be viewed as a noble profession, given that one of the main functions of salespeople is to provide solutions to their customers' problems. Unfortunately this profession has been tainted due to the unethical and illegal practices of salespeople such as:

- Getting ignorant customers to sign contracts of sale without reading it or explaining the fine print
- Promising gifts that are not part of the company's policy
- Exaggerating the benefits of a product
- Call centre salespeople signing customers up for insurance contracts without their permission

WHAT IS ETHICS?

Ethics can be defined as the principles governing the behaviour of an individual or a group.[1] These principles establish appropriate behaviour, indicating what is right and wrong. Ethical behaviour, on the other hand, can be described as follows:[2]

- Being honest and truthful
- Maintaining confidence and trust
- Following the rules
- Conducting yourself in the proper manner
- Treating others fairly
- Demonstrating loyalty to company and associates
- Carrying your share of the work and responsibility with 100 percent effort.

Ethical behaviour stems from various positive moral influences that we have had in our lives. Our moral compass serves as a guide to the choices we make in our personal and business lives.

ETHICS AND BUILDING RELATIONSHIPS

Ethical principles are extremely important in personal selling. Being able to distinguish between what is right and wrong will have a direct impact on the success of your sales. Salespeople are the face of their organisation and if they engage in unethical practices, they could tarnish the image of that organisation. Furthermore, they could scar their own reputation and lose business, as customers want to deal with salespeople that are honest and fair. If a salesperson promises early delivery knowing that it cannot be done on the said date, there is not only a risk of losing the customer, but a negative opinion could also be formed about the company.

Being trustworthy is an essential component in developing long-term relationships. It is always easier and less costly to make a sale with an existing customer than to go to all the effort of recruiting a new one.

FACTORS THAT INFLUENCE ETHICAL BEHAVIOUR

Two significant influences that have an impact on the ethical choices of salespeople are employees and the organisation itself .[3]

The individual's role

It can be accepted that the ethics displayed by an individual will be as a result of a number of factors and influences on that person's life. Personal experiences, culture, religion and personality are factors that would influence our core belief system, therefore everyone is unique, as we all view the world differently. As we mature, we develop the ability to differentiate between what is right or wrong and therefore most people's moral development progresses as they grow older. These developments may not necessarily be positive.

The organisation's role

Most companies have a code of conduct to guide the behaviour of their staff members, the objective being to eliminate or reduce unethical and unlawful behaviour.

Table 12.1 is an example of Distell's Corrective Action Code. This code matches the organisational values to the practice that is expected from their employees. It also indicates what the organisation views as unacceptable behaviour. False promises, bad customer service, misusing company assets, moonlighting and the submission of false reports are examples of unacceptable behaviour that salespeople should refrain from engaging in.

Table 12.1 *Distell's Corrective Action Code*

Organisational values	Standards/best practice	Deviations from best practice
We acknowledge and accept that we must act proactively and responsibly in all customer-related activities	Treat internal/external customers as special	Passing on substandard work
		Failing on promises without good cause
	Deliver on customer promises	Not anticipating, raising, communicating and dealing with problems
We must anticipate needs. We must consistently meet our promises	Confront, collaborate and communicate over problems	Not supporting/cooperating with supply chain partners
We must increase levels of customer satisfaction	Support others and cooperate with our supply chain partners	Leaving undone what can be done today
	Act with urgency in all customer dealings	Not resolving customer problems to satisfaction point
	Customer tasks only end at the point of satisfaction	Not adhering to SOP [standard operating procedure]
We passionately promote the name, business, reputation and products of the company		Failure/refusal to carry out reasonable instructions
	Adhere to standard operating procedures	Ineffective promotion of company products
We are involved and accountable	Carry out reasonable instructions	Abusing/misusing company resources/property/assets
		Fraud/theft/bribery
	Take pride in our products	Unauthorised use/ possession of company resources/property/assets
	Proper and best use of company resources/property/assets	

Organisational values	Standards/best practice	Deviations from best practice
We realise the importance of sharing the right information	Being in the right place at the right time	Unauthorised absenteeism/ attendance
We are dedicated to and will be accountable to perform more and better	Conveying correct information timeously	Moonlighting/clocking irregularities
	Protect sensitive/confidential information	Abuse of sick leave
We are driven by a sense of urgency		False/incorrect reports
We will persist in overcoming obstacles	We promise to deliver on our KPIs [key performance indicators] and KPAs [key performance areas]	Disclosing sensitive/ confidential information without authority or allowing this to happen
Our competitive edge depends on us learning faster than our opposition	Best utilisation of inputs to ensure best quality outputs	Resorting to unproductive work activities
	Understand the way we work and challenge the current practices to ensure improvement	Inferior performance
We train harder and learn faster. We do not rest on past achievements nor blindly repeat yesterday's practices		Substandard performance
	Care, attention and dedication even over 'the little things'	Not supporting others to excel
		Negligence/carelessness
	Listening to the ideas of others	Gross negligence
	We continuously learn	Not supporting/collaborating with team effort/not being a team player
	We challenge and deal collaboratively with problems	
		Not learning from mistakes
	We encourage new ideas and ways of doing things	Failing to maximise training opportunities
		Not cooperating with change
		Missing opportunities to do better
		Avoidable idleness

Organisational values	Standards/best practice	Deviations from best practice
We encourage new thoughts and ideas. We take calculated risks	We learn from our mistakes. We celebrate and communicate our successes	Wasting time, energy, money and resources Excessive use of inputs
We always show care and respect for others We act with dignity and help others to do so as well Alertness and sensitivity for colleagues under stress or in difficulties	Actively respect individuals Seek effective working relationships Giving and listening to open/ honest feedback Appreciate the cultural richness and uniqueness of diversity	Unauthorised interference with supervision Physical, verbal interference or harassment Assault Insubordination/disrespect Gross insubordination Carrying/possession of unauthorised/dangerous weapons Rudeness, letting personal differences affect work Untruthfulness and rumour mongering and withholding information Racial, sexual and gender abuse or harassment

ETHICAL AREAS THAT SALES PERSONNEL REGULARLY DEAL WITH

Salespeople not only interact with customers, but also with their employers and colleagues, and with competitors' products. Unethical situations can occur in relationships that salespeople have with their employers, customers, competitors and colleagues. Each of these areas will be discussed in detail.

Ethics in dealing with employers

If every salesperson abuses his or her company, even in a small way, this could lead to substantial financial losses. Imagine the cost a company could incur should most of their staff members take home stationery, or take their spouse out on their expense account or claim for petrol used for personal purposes. The company could lose profits, which could result in higher prices of their products. Here are examples of some of the methods used by salespeople that can be regarded as being unethical:

Unauthorised use of expense accounts

This is an area abused by many salespeople. Not only are legitimate expenses claimed, but also expenses that have nothing to do with the job at hand. These include taking out their spouse or friends and claiming it as a legitimate expense. Many salespeople also use their cellphone allowances to make personal calls. Abusing an expense account may be viewed as stealing and could lead to dismissal. Many companies make provision for some personal calls, but these are limited to a set number. Remember that an expense account is not a personal perk, but should be used to improve your sales.

Misusing company resources

Salespeople have access to their company's resources and can easily take advantage of them. Using company copiers to print their child's assignments, giving company samples to friends and taking home stationery from the office for personal use are unethical activities that can significantly add to an employer's cost. These resources should only be used to do their jobs effectively.

Moonlighting

As many salespeople work flexi-hours and do not have to report back to the office, they are in a position to use their company time for personal use. Salespeople should use their spare time to prospect, do their paperwork or for after-sales service, and not enrol for a full-time course or take on a part-time job. Should they decide to study part time or take on a second job, this should be in line with company policy and not interfere with their primary function.

Cooking the books

As most companies are target and incentive driven, some salespeople do not play fair in competitions. They may hold back sales that they were supposed to hand in at the end of a month to give them a healthy start to the following month. They may also sell stock that a customer does not need or persuade them to over-order and then return it when the competition is over.

It is unethical when a salesperson wins unfairly as this prevents the legitimate winner from enjoying the prizes. This could also have a negative impact on the other salespeople's morale.

Badmouthing employers

When you are experiencing problems with your superior or other departments, do not share this with your customers. After all, your company pays your salary and you should display a degree of loyalty. Rather sort out the problems internally as airing dirty linen is unprofessional. Customers also dislike doing business with salespeople who are negative.

Ethics in dealing with customers

It is common practice today for customers to try to entice the salesperson to engage in unethical behaviour, and the bigger the deal, the greater is the temptation to try to influence a decision. Promises of a kickback are usually used as a method to try and influence a decision. Some of the more common methods used are the following:

Bribes

The sales industry is very competitive and some salespeople will do almost anything to close a deal. Always resist the temptation to offer the customer unauthorised gifts, financial kickbacks or free holidays to secure a sale. When a salesperson offers money under the table, a weekend away or even a bottle of the customer's favourite alcohol, this is not only unethical, but also illegal. Salespeople must familiarise themselves with their company's policies regarding gifts.

Salespeople should also refuse bribes if the customer is the instigator. It is preferable to lose business in the short run, and to retain one's integrity and the company's reputation in the long run.

Misrepresentation

Salespeople should not distort the truth about the features, benefits and advantages of their products. They should also not take advantage of a customer's ignorance and make promises that they cannot keep.

Promising early delivery dates that the company cannot keep or adding capabilities that the product does not have is wrong. Sales staff should educate themselves about their products and sell the strengths and weaknesses of their products.

Price discrimination

It is standard practice to provide bigger discounts on bulk purchases, but when different discounts are given to customers buying the same quantity, then this illegal. Thus it is wrong to give one customer a 10% discount and another 15% when they both are purchasing for exactly the same amount.

Favouritism

Salespeople are bound to develop closer relationships with some customers than others, but should not allow this to affect their professionalism. They therefore should not give them preference to deliveries, scarce products or specials.

Reciprocity

This occurs when a company will only buy from you if you buy from them. Thus if a industrial cleaning company tells a stationery company that they will only buy stationery from them if they place an order for cleaning products, this is reciprocity. This practice is deemed as illegal if it should hurt or eliminate competition.

Customer confidences

Sometimes salespeople end up being their customer's mother, brother or psychologist. Customers tend to share very personal information with them and it is important to keep this information confidential. If you know that customer is getting divorced or struggling financially, do not discuss it with a colleague or in the staff room.

Ethics in dealing with competitors

It is not acceptable for any salesperson to talk negatively about their competitors. Care should be taken by a salesperson to focus on the facts and not on the negative aspects of competitors' products or the company. By doing this there will always be the possibility that it can have an adverse effect on your company. Some examples in this regard are as follows:

Criticising the competition

Badmouthing your competitors and their products is bad sales practice. Always sell the strengths of your products as opposed to the weaknesses of other companies' products. Customers do not appreciate it when salespeople gossip about other companies as they can also spread rumours about them.

Rearranging/damaging competitors' products

Salespeople should not interfere with their competitors' displays or point-of-sale materials, nor break their products. It is unethical if a potato chip salesperson crushes a few chip packets, or if a coffee salesperson persuades the store manager to place his products at eye level claiming that the other coffee is of bad quality.

Ethics in dealing with colleagues

Salespeople do not work in silos. They have to cultivate a team spirit even though this industry is a very competitive one. They should also be careful about their non-verbal and verbal interactions with other staff members. Aggressive behaviour by some salespeople does not only lead to uncomfortable situations, but could also lead to a reduction in job satisfaction and employee morale. It could also counter the company's goals and objectives. The following are deemed to be unethical practices pertaining to colleagues:

Sexual harassment

Given that salespeople are in contact with so many people there are many opportunities for them to be victims or perpetrators of sexual harassment. They should refrain from telling sexual jokes, flirting or making sexual comments to staff members or customers.

Stealing customers

Overstepping territorial boundaries or convincing customers to do business with you when they have made initial contact with a colleague of yours is unethical. This type of behaviour will not only lead to animosity among employees, but culprits will also be reprimanded by their manager.

Undermining co-workers

Sometimes salespeople become so competitive that they deliberately fail to pass on a message from a customer, or make negative comments about another salesperson. Not only is this discourteous, but these negative acts eventually come to light and can cause an uncomfortable situation.

LEGAL ISSUES

We have looked at unethical standards, but there are also legal standards that salespeople have to consider.

The sales industry is affected by numerous laws, which salespeople and their companies should be familiar with as they could get into serious trouble. Illegal activities can result in costly legal fees and millions of rand in fines. Unfortunately some salespeople believe that if their actions are still legal they can get away with them.

Here are examples of laws that salespeople and companies should adhere to:

Contracts of sale

There are many instances where a contract needs to be signed when a salesperson closes a sale. The sale of bulk raw materials, component parts, and maintenance and repair services over a period of time are a few examples where contracts are required. Contracts need to comply with the general requirements of a contract in order to be valid. Parties entering into agreements must be clearly stated, as well as the delivery of a particular product at a stipulated price.

Salespeople should also not get their customers to sign blank documents and should also explain all the clauses and the fine print to them.

What you need to know is as follows, from an overview by Rosalind Lake, attorney at Deneys Reitz:

- According to the Department of Trade and Industry, the primary purpose of the new act is to prevent exploitation or harm to consumers.
- The law regulates the way businesses relate with consumers and how they market their products and services. The act therefore applies not only to 'every transaction occurring within the Republic' (subject to certain exemptions) but also to the marketing and supply of goods and services.
- The act touches on many aspects of supply relationships, including warranties, pricing, standards of service and quality, advertising, labelling, marketing and others. The act introduces a bill of rights, granting consumers wide-ranging powers to cancel contracts within 'cooling-off' periods, to refuse to purchase 'bundled' products or services, to cancel fixed-term agreements if not satisfied with their terms and to block approaches by direct marketers, amongst many others.
- There is also a distinct focus throughout the act on clear and understandable language and ensuring that the consumer is not misled by suppliers.
- Most controversially, the act introduces a system of product liability on suppliers for damage caused by the supply of defective goods. A consumer can therefore claim damages from producers, distributors or suppliers for any death, injury, loss, damage to property and economic loss, without having to prove negligence.
- Contraventions of the act will not be treated lightly and there is provision for hefty penalties for non-compliance.

While the Advertising Standards Authority (ASA) code may already cover many of these areas, the consumer now has a big stick: 'the consumer may hold at their whim any or all persons in the supply chain liable for damages ...', as described by experts at *Hahn & Hahn Law*. (And by the way, a consumer doesn't actually have to *buy* your product: they can complain even if it's on a shelf and it offends them.)

Substantial legal and financial risk

Thus, marketers now are exposed to substantial legal and financial risk, over and above being rapped on the knuckles by the ASA for breach of the code.

From what I can see, the professional marketing community is on top of this legislation and its consequences. Communication agencies, whether advertising, packaging design, PR, digital – whatever – need to be working closely with their clients on their brand claims and promises, their advertising messaging, the copy on their packaging.

They should also be chatting to a friendly attorney who understands this stuff (I'm just the messenger) and buttoning down their role in this Act. The Association for Communication and Advertising (ACA) says it has sent out quite a bit of information to its members and is running a workshop on the Act.

Supply chain of information

The communication agency is a key part of the supply chain of information from manufacturer to consumer, so this knowledge is critical, for all disciplines in the agency, from management and account management, to strategy and, very importantly, creative, in developing claims and ad campaigns that may keep your client out of trouble.

If it can mislead, you could be putting yourself and your client at risk.

Credit Agreement Act

A credit agreement is an agreement where a product or service use is made available immediately, even though payment is made over a period of time. The National Credit Act 34 of 2005 regulates credit agreements.

This Act protects consumers in that it reduces reckless lending as the credit grantor must take reasonable steps to qualify the customer before selling anything to them. This Act has had a negative impact on the car, property and furniture industries, as stringent guidelines need to be used to qualify customers. Even though customers may be unhappy because they cannot purchase an item that they really wanted, it is in their best interest not to purchase something that they cannot afford.

Competition law

Unlawful competition occurs when a rival company's conduct amounts to unlawful interference with the competitor's trade. The purpose of competition law is to regulate the economy of a country. The current competitive legislation adopted by South Africa is the Competition Act 89 of 1998. The rationale for this Act is that competition is good for business, and that businesses will not act competitively if there is no regulation in place. The main objective of the regulation is consumer welfare.

In horizontal relationships, which are relationships between direct competitors like car dealers, this law stipulates that companies are prohibited from price fixing, market sharing and collusion. In vertical relationships, which are relationships that a company has with its channel members, a supplier cannot insist that a retailer may not sell a product for less than a certain amount.

Sadly, even though there are laws that prohibit the above-mentioned practices, companies are constantly found guilty of them and are fined heavily. This is illustrated in the following articles extracted from http://www.capetimes.co.za

Firms pay high fines, prices keep climbing
15 July 2009

This year alone, the competition authorities have imposed total fines of over R344 million on companies that have contravened the Competition Act, but one leading law firm questions what deterrent effect fines are having and "to what extent these huge penalties are really benefiting the consumer?"

A note issued to clients by law firm Deneys Reitz points out that, while consumers may derive a sense of satisfaction from seeing huge penalties being paid by companies such as Sasol, Foodcorp and Tiger Brands, the fines are paid into the national revenue fund, so consumers do not directly benefit.

The fines are not applied directly to the consumers that bore the brunt of the higher prices. They simply go into the fiscal government coffers.

Deneys Reitz refers to the bread and milk cartels. In both cases, the firms concerned admitted guilt and huge fines were imposed. However, consumers who walked into the stores the day after the tribunal's order did not financially benefit; indeed, it seemed that prices continued to rise.

Tiger Brands implemented price hikes on its Albany bread brand – soon after the competition commission hit it with a R99 million fine for admitting its role in a bread price-fixing cartel. It is now charging more for a loaf of bread.

Commission fines Sasol R188m for price-fixing
7 May 2009

Sasol had agreed to pay a R188 million settlement to the competition commission after admitting to colluding with Yara South Africa and Omnia Fertiliser to set fertiliser prices, the firm said yesterday. This is the highest sum any South African company has agreed to settle a competition matter. The highest fine imposed by the competition tribunal was R692m on ArcelorMittal South Africa, which the company is appealing.

The Sasol settlement was a result of a complaint lodged with the commission in May 2005 by KwaZulu-Natal fertiliser company Nutri-Flo. The company alleged that Sasol, Yara and Omnia had colluded to fix fertiliser prices.

"The commission found that Sasol and its competitors, Omnia and Yara, divided markets and fixed prices," said the commission. The three companies had set up committees to co-ordinate business practices. The commission said: "Arrangements between these competitors resulted in Sasol becoming the sole wholesale supplier of an important fertiliser product, limestone ammonium nitrate.

"Sasol's compliance review uncovered further collusive practices between Sasol, Omnia and Yara, including price-fixing, market allocation and collusive tendering in the supply of a wide range of fertiliser products … (from) 1996 to 2004."

Sasol said that an internal competition law compliance review had revealed evidence of "potentially collusive conduct" at Sasol Nitro's fertiliser business.

SUMMARY

Salespeople should know the differences between what is right and wrong when dealing with customers, employers, colleagues and competitors. They should always be honest, fair and reliable if they want to develop long-term relationships with their customers. They should not only conduct their business by their personal standards, but also adhere to the company's code of ethics if they want a future in selling. Salespeople should be familiar with the laws that affect the sales industry and the impact that they could have on their sales. Salespeople and their managers should strive to conduct their business in an ethical, legal and moral way.

CASE STUDY

Pyramid schemes[ii]

A **pyramid scheme** is a non-sustainable business model that involves the exchange of money primarily for enrolling other people into the scheme without any product or service being delivered. Pyramid schemes are a form of fraud.

Pyramid schemes are illegal in many countries including Albania, Australia,[1] Brazil, Bulgaria, Canada, China,[2] Colombia,[3] France, Germany, Hungary, Iceland, Iran[4], Italy,[5] Japan,[6] Malaysia, Mexico, Nepal, The Netherlands,[7] New Zealand,[8] Norway[9], the Philippines,[10] Poland, Portugal, Romania,[11] South Africa,[12] Sri Lanka,[13] Switzerland, Thailand,[14] the United Kingdom, and the United States.[15]

These types of schemes have existed for at least a century, some with variations to hide their true nature and there are people who hold that multilevel marketing, even if it is legal, is nothing more than a pyramid scheme.[16][17][18][19]

A successful pyramid scheme combines a fake yet seemingly credible business with a simple-to-understand yet sophisticated-sounding money-making formula which is used for profit. The essential idea is that the mark, Mr. X, makes only one payment. To start earning, Mr. X has to recruit others like him who will also make one payment each. Mr. X gets paid out of receipts from those new recruits. They then go on to recruit others. As each new recruit makes a payment, Mr. X gets a cut. He is thus promised exponential benefits as the "business" expands.

Such "businesses" seldom involve sales of real products or services to which a monetary value might be easily attached. However, sometimes the "payment" itself may be a non-cash valuable. To enhance credibility, most such scams are well equipped with fake referrals, testimonials, and information. The flaw is that there is no end benefit. The money simply travels up the chain. Only the originator (sometimes called the "pharaoh") and a very few at the top levels of the pyramid make significant amounts of money. The amounts dwindle steeply down the pyramid slopes. Individuals at the bottom of the pyramid (those who subscribed to the plan, but were not able to recruit any followers themselves) end up with a deficit.

The "Eight-Ball" model

Many pyramids are more sophisticated than the simple model. These recognize that recruiting a large number of others into a scheme can be difficult so a seemingly simpler model is used. In this model each person must recruit two others, but the ease of achieving this is offset because the depth required to recoup any money also increases. The scheme requires a person to recruit two others, who must each recruit two others, who must each recruit two others.

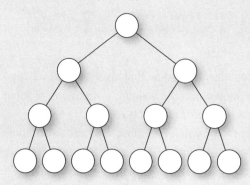

"Captain" paid when 8 "passengers" arrive at the bottom.

"Co-Pilot"

"Crew"

8 "Passengers" must pay into scheme before the layers above can advance.

The "eight-ball" model contains a total of fifteen members. Note that, unlike in the picture, the triangular setup in the cue game of *eight-ball* corresponds to an arithmetic progression $1 + 2 + 3 + 4 + 5 = 15$. The pyramid scheme in the picture in contrast is a geometric progression $1 + 2 + 4 + 8 = 15$.

Prior instances of this scam have been called the "Airplane Game" and the four tiers labeled as "captain," "co-pilot," "crew," and "passenger" to denote a person's level. Another instance was called the "Original Dinner Party" which labeled the tiers as "dessert," "main course," "side salad," and "appetizer". A person on the "dessert" course is the one at the top of the tree. Another variant, "Treasure Traders", variously used gemology terms such as "polishers", "stone cutters", etc. or gems like "rubies", "sapphires", "diamonds", etc.

Such schemes may try to downplay their pyramid nature by referring to themselves as "gifting circles" with money being "gifted". Popular scams such as the "Women Empowering Women"[20] do exactly this. Joiners may even be told that "gifting" is a way to skirt around tax laws.

Whichever euphemism is used, there are 15 total people in four tiers $(1+2+4+8)$ in the scheme – with the Airplane Game as the example, the person at the top of this tree is the "captain", the two below are "co-pilots", the four below are "crew", and the bottom eight joiners are the "passengers".

The eight passengers must each pay (or "gift") a sum (e.g. $1 000) to join the scheme. This sum (e.g. $8 000) goes to the captain who leaves, with everyone remaining moving up one tier. There are now two new captains so the group splits in two with each group requiring eight new passengers. A person who joins the scheme as a passenger will not see a return until they exit the scheme as a captain. This requires that 14 others have been persuaded to join underneath them.

Therefore, the bottom 3 tiers of the pyramid *always lose their money* when the scheme finally collapses. Consider a pyramid consisting of tiers with 1, 2, 4, 8, 16, 32, and 64 members. ... No matter how large the model becomes before collapse, approximately 88% of all people will lose.

If the scheme collapses at this point, only those in the 1, 2, 4, and 8 got out with a return. The remainder in the 16, 32, and 64 tiers lose everything. 112 out of the total 127 members or 88% lost all of their money.

During a wave of pyramid activity, a surge frequently develops once a significant fraction of people know someone personally who exited with a $8 000 payout for example. This spurs others to seek to get in on one of the many pyramids before the wave collapses.

The figures also hide the fact that the confidence trickster would make the lion's share of the money. They would do this by filling in the first 3 tiers (with 1, 2, and 4 people) with phoney names, ensuring they get the first 7 payouts, at 8 times the buy-in sum, without paying a single penny themselves. So if the buy-in were $1 000, they would receive $56 000, paid for by the first 56 investors. They would continue to buy in underneath the real investors, and promote and prolong the scheme for as long as possible in order to allow them to skim even more from it before the collapse.

Other cons may also be effective. For example, rather than using false names, a group of seven people may agree to form the top three layers of a pyramid without investing any money. They then work to recruit eight paying passengers, and pretend to follow the pyramid payout rules, but in reality split any money received. Ironically, though they are being conned, the eight paying passengers are not really getting anything less for their money than if they were buying into a "legitimate" pyramid which had split off from a parent pyramid. They truly are now in a valid pyramid, and have the same opportunity to earn a windfall if they can successfully recruit enough new members and reach captain. This highlights the fact that by "buying" into a pyramid, passengers are not really obtaining anything of value they could not create themselves other than a vague sense of "legitimacy" or history of the pyramid, which may make it marginally easier to sell passenger seats below them.

Matrix schemes

Matrix schemes use the same fraudulent non-sustainable system as a pyramid; here, the participants pay to join a waiting list for a desirable product which only a fraction of them can ever receive. Since matrix schemes follow the same laws of geometric progression as pyramids, they are subsequently as doomed to collapse. Such schemes operate as a queue, where the person at the head of the queue receives an item such as a television, games console, digital camcorder, etc. when a certain number of new people join the end of the queue. For example, ten joiners may be required for the person at the front to receive their item and leave the queue. Each joiner is required to buy an expensive but potentially worthless item, such as an e-book, for their position in the queue. The scheme organizer profits because the income from joiners far exceeds the cost of sending out the item to the person at the front. Organizers can further profit by starting a scheme with a queue with *shill* names that must be cleared out before genuine people get to the front. The scheme collapses when no more people are willing to join the queue. Schemes may not reveal, or may attempt to exaggerate, a prospective joiner's queue position which essentially means the scheme is a lottery. Some countries have ruled that matrix schemes are illegal on that basis.

Connection to multi-level marketing

The network marketing or multi-level marketing business has become associated with pyramid schemes as "Some schemes may purport to sell a product, but they often simply use the product to hide their pyramid structure."[21] and the fact while some people call MLMs *in general* "pyramid selling"[22][23][24][25][26], others use the term to denote an illegal pyramid scheme *masquerading* as an MLM.[27]

The FTC warns "Not all multilevel marketing plans are legitimate. Some are pyramid schemes. It's best not to get involved in plans where the money you make is based primarily on the number of distributors you recruit and your sales to them, rather than on your sales to people outside the plan who intend to use the products"[28] and states that research is your best tool and gives eight steps to follow:

1) Find — and study — the company's track record.
2) Learn about the product
3) Ask questions
4) Understand any restrictions
5) Talk to other distributors (beware shills)
6) Consider using a friend or adviser as a neutral sounding board or for a gut check.
7) Take your time.
8) Think about whether this plan suits your talents and goals[29]

Some believe MLMs in general are nothing more than *legalized* pyramid schemes[30][31][32][33] making the issue of a particular MLM being legal or not moot.

Notable recent cases
Internet
In 2003, the United States Federal Trade Commission (FTC) disclosed what it called an internet-based "pyramid scam". Its complaint states that customers would pay a registration fee to join a program that called itself an "internet mall" and purchase a package of goods and services such as internet mail, and that the company offered "significant commissions" to consumers who purchased and resold the package. The FTC alleged that the company's program was instead and in reality a pyramid scheme that did not disclose that most consumers's money would be kept, and that it gave affiliates material that allowed them to scam others.[34]

Others
In early 2006 Ireland was hit by a wave of schemes with major activity in Cork and Galway. Participants were asked to contribute 20 000 each to a "Liberty" scheme which followed the classic eight-ball model. Payments were made in Munich, Germany to skirt Irish tax laws concerning gifts. Spin-off schemes called "Speedball" and "People in Profit" prompted a number of violent incidents and calls were made by politicians to tighten existing legislation.[35] Ireland has launched a website to better educate consumers to pyramid schemes and other scams.[36]

On November 12, 2008 riots broke out in the municipalities of Pasto, Tumaco, Popayan and Santander de Quilichao, Colombia after the collapse of several pyramid schemes. Thousands of victims had invested their money in pyramids that promised them extraordinary interest rates. The lack of regulation laws allowed those pyramids to grow excessively during several years. Finally, after the riots the Colombian government was forced to declare the country in economical emergency in order to seize and stop those schemes. Several of the pyramid's managers were arrested, and these are being prosecuted for the crime of "illegal massive money reception".[37]

November 2008: The *Kyiv Post* reported on November 26, 2008 that American citizen Robert Fletcher (Robert T. Fletcher III; aka "Rob") was arrested by the SBU (Ukraine State Police) after being accused by Ukrainian investors of running a Ponzi scheme and associated pyramid scam netting $20 million in US dollars. (The *Kiev Post* also reports that some estimates are as high as $150m USD.)

The DSA warns as follows: Don't make a costly mistake! Thousands of people have lost a substantial amount of money by participating in pyramid schemes. Pyramid selling is a fraud. Many of the victims knew they were gambling (although they didn't know the odds were rigged against them). Many others, however, thought they were paying for help in starting a small business of their own. These people were fooled by pyramid schemes disguised to look like legitimate businesses. **The purpose of this warning is to help you avoid falling victim to pyramid schemes,** whether simple or disguised, and from breaking the law as participating in such schemes is illegal. Simple pyramid schemes are similar to chain letters, while disguised pyramids are like "wolves in sheep's clothing", hiding their true nature in order to fool potential investors and evade law enforcers. For further information on what to look out for and how to avoid illegitimate pyramid schemes go to the WFDSA website link: http://www.wfdsa.org/about_dir_sell/index.cfm?fa=schemes1

References

1. Trade Practices Amendment Act (No. 1) 2002 Trade Practices Act 1974 (Cth) ss 65AAA - 65AAE, 75AZO

2. Regulations for the Prohibition of Pyramid Sales

3. http://news.bbc.co.uk/1/hi/world/americas/7736124.stm

4. Key GoldQuest members arrested in Iran Airport

5. Legge 17 agosto 2005, n. 173 (in Italian)

6. 無限連鎖講の防止に関する法律 (in Japanese)

7. Sentence by the High Council of the Netherlands regarding a pyramid scheme

8. Laws and Regulations Covering Multi-Level Marketing Programs and Pyramid Schemes *Consumer Fraud Reporting.com*

9. http://www.lovdata.no/all/tl-19950224-011-004.html#16

10. [1] Investors in Philippine Pyramid Scheme Lose over $2 Billion

11. Explozia piramidelor *Ziarul Ziua*, 12.07.2006

12. [2] Pyramid Schemes

13. Pyramid Schemes Illegal Under Section 83c of the Banking Act of Sri Lanka Department of Government Printing, Sri Lanka

14. ข้อมูลเพิ่มเติมในระบบธุรกิจขายตรงและธุรกิจพีระมิด by Thai Direct Selling Association (in Thai)

15. Pyramid Schemes *Debra A. Valentine, General Counsel, Federal Trade Commission*

16. Carroll, Robert Todd (2003). *The Skeptic's Dictionary: A Collection of Strange Beliefs, Amusing Deceptions, and Dangerous Delusions*. Wiley. pp. 235. ISBN 0471272426

17. Coenen, Tracy (2009). *Expert Fraud Investigation: A Step-by-Step Guide*. Wiley. pp. 168. ISBN 0470387963.

18. Ogunjobi, Timi (2008). *SCAMS - and how to protect yourself from them*. Tee Publishing. pp. 13–19.

19. Salinger (Editor), Lawrence M. (2005). *Encyclopedia of White-Collar & Corporate Crime*. 2. Sage Publishing. pp. 880. ISBN 0761930043.

20. Pyramid selling scam that preys on women to be banned

21. Pyramid Schemes, May 13, 1998. *Federal Trade Commission*

22. Edwards, Paul (1997). *Franchising & licensing: two powerful ways to grow your business in any economy*. Tarcher. p. 356. ISBN 0874778980.

23. Clegg, Brian (2000). *The invisible customer: strategies for successive customer service down the wire*. Kogan Page. pp. 112. ISBN 074943144X.

24. Higgs, Philip; Smith, Jane (2007). *Rethinking Our World*. Juta Academic. pp. 30. ISBN 0702172553.

25. Kitching, Trevor (2001). *Purchasing scams and how to avoid them*. Gower Publishing Company. pp. 4. ISBN 0566082810.

26. Mendelsohn, Martin (2004). *The guide to franchising*. Cengage Learning Business Press. pp. 36. ISBN 1844801624.

27. Blythe, Jim (2004). *Sales & Key Account Management*. Cengage Learning Business Press. pp. 278. ISBN 1844800237.

28. Facts for Consumers; The Bottom Line About Multilevel Marketing Plans and Pyramid Schemes *Federal Trade Commission*

29. Facts for Consumers; The Bottom Line About Multilevel Marketing Plans and Pyramid Schemes *Federal Trade Commission*

30. Carroll, Robert Todd (2003). *The Skeptic's Dictionary: A Collection of Strange Beliefs, Amusing Deceptions, and Dangerous Delusions*. Wiley. pp. 235. ISBN 0471272426.

31. Coenen, Tracy (2009). *Expert Fraud Investigation: A Step-by-Step Guide*. Wiley. pp. 168. ISBN 0470387963.

32. Ogunjobi, Timi (2008). *SCAMS - and how to protect yourself from them*. Tee Publishing. pp. 13-19.

33. Salinger (Editor), Lawrence M. (2005). *Encyclopedia of White-Collar & Corporate Crime*. **2.** Sage Publishing. p. 880. ISBN 0761930043.

34. FTC Charges Internet Mall Is a Pyramid Scam *Federal Trade Commission*

35. Gardaí hold firearm after pyramid scheme incident *Irish Examiner*

36. National Consumer Agency Ireland

37. *Colombians riot over pyramid scam.* Colombia: BBC news. Nov 13, 2008. http://news. bbc.co.uk/2/hi/americas/7726069.stm.

■ *The Fraudsters - How Con Artists Steal Your Money Chapter 9, Pyramids of Sand (ISBN 978-1-903582-82-4)* by Eamon Dillon, published September 2008 by Merlin Publishing, Ireland

Books

■ *American Victory: The Real Story of Today's Amway* published April, 1997 by Chapel & Croft Publishing; ISBN 0-96451716-7

■ *Amway: The Cult of Free Enterprise* published December 1, 1985 by South End Press; ISBN 0-96487951-4

■ *Amway: The True Story of the Company That Transformed the Lives of Millions* published September 1, 1999 by Berkley Publishing Group; ISBN 0-42517040-3

■ *An Enterpising Life* published 1998 by HarperCollins; ISBN 0-88730-997-6

■ *An Uncommon Freedom, the Amway Experience and Why It Grows* published 1982 by Revell; ASIN B000HFJE1Y

■ *Commitment to excellence: The remarkable Amway story* published 1986 by Benjamin; ISBN 0-875021360

■ *Compassionate Capitalism: People Helping People Help Themselves* published September, 1994 by Penguin Books; ISBN 0-452-27051-0

■ *Empire of Freedom: The Amway Story and What It Means to You* published September 3, 1997 by Prima Lifestyles; ISBN 0761510885

■ *How to Be Like Rich DeVos. Succeeding with Integrity in Business and Life* published 2004 by Health Communications, Inc; ISBN 0-7573-0158-4

■ *The First Eleven — The growth of Amway in Britain through the lives of its local heroes* published 1984 by AM Publishing; ISBN 0-9509593-0-8

■ *Promises to Keep: The Amway Phenomenon and How It Works* published 1986 by Berkley Books; ISBN 0425098567

■ *The Direct Selling Revolution: Understanding the Growth of the Amway Corporation* published 1993 by WileyBlackwell; ISBN 978-0631192299

■ *The Possible Dream: A Candid Look at Amway* published 1977 by Revell; ISBN 0800708571

NOTES

1. Weitz, B.A., Castleberry, S.B. & Tanner, J.F. 2007. *Selling: Building Partnerships.* (Sixth edition). New York: McGraw Hill/Irwin.

2. Futrell, C.M. 2006. Fundamentals of Selling. (Ninth edition). New York: McGraw Hill/Irwin.

3. Futrell, op. cit.

i   http://www.bizcommunity.com/Article/196/423/45743.html (16 Mar 2010 11:23) (accessed on 2 April 2010).

ii Retrieved from http://en.wikipedia.org/wiki/pyramid scheme on 2 April 2010.

FURTHER READING

Anderson, R.E., Dubinsky, A.J. & Mehta, R. 2007. Personal Selling. (Second edition). Boston: Houghton Mifflin Company.

Blem, N. 2007. Achieving Excellence in Selling. (Third edition). Cape Town: Oxford University Press.

Collier-Reed, D. & Lehmann, K. 2006. *Basic Principles of Business Law.* Cape Town: LexisNexis Butterworths.

Manning, G.I. & Reece, B.L. 1995. Selling Today. (Sixth edition). New Jersey: Prentice Hall.

13

SELLING OF SERVICES

LEARNING OUTCOMES

After studying this chapter, you should be able to:

- Distinguish between a product and a service
- Distinguish between the selling of a product and the selling of a service
- Classify services according to career opportunities, a product/service continuum, benefits, and service provider/customer contact
- Outline the characteristics of a service
- Discuss intangibility; inseparability of production and consumption; heterogeneity; perishability; and fluctuating demand; and outline the problems associated with these, and suggest solutions
- Examine the impact of the characteristics of a service on the distribution of services

INTRODUCTION

In this chapter the unique principles involving the selling of services will be discussed. Various ways to classify services are described and the unique characteristics of services highlighted. The chapter concludes with tips on selling services. First, however, the difference between a product and a service needs to be clarified.

THE DIFFERENCE BETWEEN A PRODUCT AND A SERVICE

When sales as a career is mentioned, most students think of selling products such as encyclopaedias or second-hand vehicles. So what is a product? A *product* is a bundle of tangible and intangible attributes, including packaging and branding. When people buy a product, they buy more than just a set of physical attributes. They also buy satisfaction, for example the satisfaction of knowing what the product will do, appreciating its quality and enjoying the image of owning or consuming it.[1]

Salespeople have gone from selling products to selling products and services, and now to selling products, services and value-added services. A *service* is an action or activity, or an act or performance, that one party offers to another, at a fee, that is essentially intangible and does not result in the ownership of anything (except for an experience, a memory or an intangible perceived benefit).[2] Lawyers, plumbers, teachers and taxi drivers perform services.

The term *value-added* refers to benefits received that are not included in the purchase price of the individual product or service. A retailer may offer customers free financing, free gift wrapping, and well-trained and knowledgeable sales staff[3] who can offer advice on services, features and benefits.

The number of rand spent on services will continuously rise, and as household expenditure increases a higher percentage of it will be spent on services. Job opportunities in selling services will therefore also grow as consumers expand their demand for insurance, real estate, holidays, recreation and leisure opportunities, and banking services. Business customers will increasingly feel the need for advice and assistance in office automation and communication, business security, marketing services such as advertising; and hotel and hospitality services such as those found in the meetings, incentives, conventions and exhibitions (MICE) industry.

The contribution of tertiary services (electricity, gas and water; wholesale and retail trade, hotels and restaurants; transport, storage and communication; finance, real estate and business services; general government services; and personal services) contributed just under 70% to South Africa's GDP in 2007.[i] Finance, real estate and business services' share of the GDP was just over 20%. This indicates how large the potential is for selling services in the economy.

CLASSIFYING SERVICES[4]

In this section, services are classified according to career opportunities, a product/service continuum, benefits, and service provider/customer contact.

Classifying services according to career opportunities

There are many types of sales positions, found in many industries, for literally thousands of products and services. The examples below illustrate the wide variety of sales jobs available in a few industries. A major task for any salesperson in any industry is to introduce the customer to the services offered by the company and to build a long-term relationship between the service provider and the customer. A long-term relationship builds brand loyalty and is much more profitable because it is usually more expensive to recruit new customers than to keep current ones loyal. Career opportunities are available in the industries discussed below.

Insurance

Selling insurance can be a lucrative proposition and is very rewarding. Common forms of insurance sold include life insurance (e.g. Sanlam, Old Mutual), health insurance (e.g. Bestmed, Discovery), and household insurance (the so-called short-term insurance, e.g. Dial Direct, OUTsurance). Companies may also buy into a group medical scheme on behalf of their employees.

Real estate

Buying a home is usually the largest purchase in the average consumer's lifetime. The acquisition of business and commercial properties by individual investors or business firms is also a major investment decision. People who sell real estate therefore assume a very important role, and offer services such as property valuation, bringing prospective buyers to view the property, advertising in local media, giving legal advice on contracts, and holding property exhibitions. The middle- to higher-income sections of the South African population have become very mobile, which leads to a greater turnover in real estate deals. Selling cluster housing and golf estate units are prime examples of the kinds of lucrative sales jobs that can be found in this industry.

Holiday, recreation and leisure

The tourism industry is regarded as the largest and fastest-growing industry in the world. According to Statistics South Africa, the tourism industry is a potential source of huge economic growth in South Africa. South Africa's tourism business is overwhelmingly leisure oriented, with three-quarters of overseas visitors being leisure tourists. The local industry's competitive advantages depend on four pillars of tourism: physical scenery, modern infrastructure, cultural diversity and wildlife. This industry is dynamic and diverse, and comprises various subsectors including accommodation and catering (hospitality), travel, transport and attracting tourists. All subsectors require dynamic and enthusiastic salespeople to sell destinations, tour packages and 'experiences'.

Hotel and hospitality services

Thousands of meetings, promotions, conferences and exhibitions such as trade shows are held annually throughout South Africa. Most of these events are hosted at specialised venues such as conference centres, but hotels and holiday resorts are also active players in this market. Rooms, food, beverages and transport services are needed for successful meetings and conferences. It often happens that travel agencies support businesses in hosting successful events. According to a report by Grant Thornton Kessel Feinstein, commissioned by SA Tourism in 2000, the value of the meetings industry internationally can be estimated at US$90 billion per year, while its growth rate is estimated at between 8 and 10% per annum, which makes it the fastest-growing sector in the hospitality and hotel industry in the world.

Banking services

The importance of the banking industry in the South African economy is unquestionable. South African banks comply fully with international banking standards and offer one of the most sophisticated banking systems in the world, with 24-hours-a-day, 365-days-a-year, online real-time nationwide access to bank accounts. Service capabilities further include more than 7 000 ATMs nationwide, and overnight cheque-clearing facilities. A few key imperatives are currently forcing change in the South African banking industry. The first is the power of technology, such as Internet banking. The second is the changing dynamics of the South African customer. Upmarket customers' needs are changing from standardised to customised and specialised. Relationship managers and personal bankers create closer relationships with those customers who want, and expect to get, more than the bank has traditionally offered. The other side of the coin is the emergence of new low-cost service providers, such as short-term money-lending concerns, whose success has forced the major South African banks to become involved with such operators. Banks are also under pressure to expand their delivery of financial services to the growing informal small-business industry, and the previously disadvantaged communities.

Marketing of banking services has grown dramatically in the past decade or so. Most banks have a sales promotion programme, and personal selling is one of their key focus areas. Individual bank customers, small entrepreneurs and professionals such as doctors and dentists are now even afforded the opportunity to consult personal bankers. In fact, nearly every employee in a market-driven bank is faced with selling situations daily.

Bank officials can no longer afford just to sit behind a desk waiting for business opportunities to walk in. Some have to spend a large portion of their day involved in selling activities, developing new accounts and servicing existing ones.

Office automation and communication

Major emphasis is placed on after-sales service where a technician or engineer does a 'relationship-selling job'. The professional maintenance, repair and upgrading of office equipment such as computer systems, photocopiers, fax machines and PABX technology may keep customers loyal to the service provider. A few strong brands such as Xerox, Canon, Minolta, HP, Nashua and Samsung are active in South Africa.

Financial planning

Lucrative opportunities exist for those who excel at selling money management plans, stocks, bonds or mutual funds. You have to be clued up on the state of the economy and the workings of the stock exchange, and be well experienced and properly trained in order to prosper in this field.

Marketing services such as advertising

Revenue from advertising supports a large number of media such as the SABC, M-Net, e.tv, magazines and newspapers. Every media vehicle (radio station, magazine, newspaper or television channel) employs a sales team to call on existing and prospective advertisers. Each advertiser's needs are unique, and working closely with brand and product managers is one of the most interesting careers in sales. In addition there is a creative side to media sales because many advertisers are not able to create their own marketing material.

Advertising and specialist agencies also offer advertisers additional services such as media planning, media research and sponsorship execution. Advertising executives and creative directors handle advertising presentations, but a continuous effort is needed from all employees of the agency to retain key advertising accounts.

Other examples of services are home and business security (e.g. armed response), pest control, gardening services, transportation (the taxi industry), health and fitness, and the wellness industry (creating a feeling of well-being – e.g. aromatherapy treatments).

This classification only identifies career opportunities but it does not provide any help in setting up an appropriate approach to selling the services mentioned.

Security

Criminal activities have created a huge market for personal and business security services such as providing guards, alarm and security systems, and armed response. Companies such as Chubb, ADT, Netstar and Tracker are, inter alia, using sales reps to gain customers. There are also companies specialising in personal security services such as providing bodyguards.

Home improvement

This industry often relies on attracting customers through advertisements placed in free publications dropped in suburban mail boxes. The prospect contacts the advertiser who then sends a sales consultant to the homeowner. Examples are building contractors and renovators, interior decorators, roof repairers and garden designers.

Classifying services according to a product/service continuum[5]

Figure 13.1 shows a mix of goods and services on a continuum ranging from relatively pure goods to relatively pure services. Few truly pure products or pure services exist. When enrolling for a course in personal selling you may buy a textbook (a product) in addition to attending the course (which constitutes a service, as it provides you with the opportunity to gain knowledge and skills). Similarly, when buying tangible products, support services are required, such as after-sales maintenance and repairs.

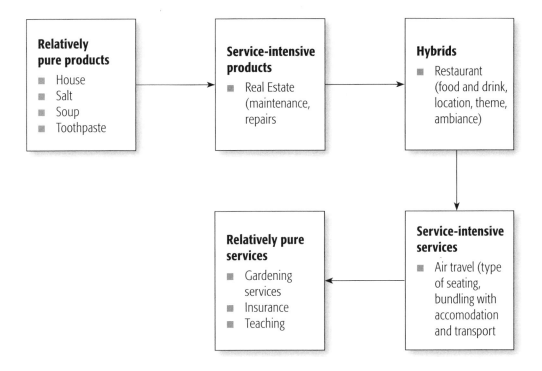

Figure 13.1 *A mix of goods and services on a continuum ranging from relatively pure goods to relatively pure services*[6]

The following two classifications delve more deeply into the uniqueness of services. They may prove to be more helpful in allowing sales managers to develop selling strategies that are appropriate to services.

Classifying services according to core benefits[7]

Table 13.1 shows that some services are physical acts and some are intangible, and a service can be performed on a person or on an object. This classification alludes to the implication of selling core benefits to the consumer. An insurance salesperson may emphasise the benefits of a policy in terms of the guaranteed payment of a child's university expenses, or a retirement income of so many rand per month. A Telkom salesperson may stress service benefits such as how a business can cut telephone costs by using a customised Telkom cost-saving system.

Table 13.1 *Understanding the nature of the service act (who or what is the recipient of the service?)*[8]

	People	Things
What is the nature of the service act?	**Services directed at people's bodies**	**Services directed at goods and other physical possessions**
Tangible actions	Health care (doctors, hospitals) Passenger transport (air, rail, road) Beauty salons (nails, facelifts) Exercise venues (gyms, health clubs) Restaurants (French, grill) Hairdressers (unisex, men's, ladies')	Freight transport (air, rail, road) Equipment repair and maintenance Janitorial services Laundry and dry cleaning Landscaping/lawn care Veterinary care
	Services directed at people's minds	**Services directed at intangible assets**
Intangible actions	Education (tertiary, short courses, adult learning) Broadcasting (radio, television) Information services (consultants, advertising and research agencies) Theatres (plays, movies) Museums	Banking Legal services Accounting Securities Insurance

It also helps to understand that differentiation opportunities in services marketing can be created in four dimensions (tangible actions on people, tangible actions on people's possessions, intangible actions on people, and intangible actions on people's possessions). This classification also indicates what level of contact will exist between service provider and customer. The selling approach would differ for each example.

Classifying services according to service provider/customer contact[9]

Table 13.2 contains another view on how to classify services. Three distinct methods of contact between the service provider and the customer exist: requiring the customer to come to the firm; going to the customer; and conducting service transactions at 'arm's length' by mail, telephone or electronically. Service outlets can also be situated in a single location or at multiple sites.

Table 13.2 *Method of service delivery*[10]

Availability of service outlets		
Nature of interaction between customer and service organisation	**Single site**	**Multiple sites**
Customer goes to service organisation	Theatre Barber shop	Bus service Fast-food chain
Service organisation goes to customer	Lawn care, pest control Taxi	Mail delivery AA emergency repair
Customer and service organisation transact at arm's length (mail or electronic communication)	Credit card (banking) company Local TV (radio) station (SABC)	Broadcast network (M-Net) Telephone company (Telkom)

Sales managers should carefully study the last two classification schemes before designing their selling approach. The following section discusses the unique characteristics of a service.

THE CHARACTERISTICS OF A SERVICE

The more complex the service, the more difficult it will be to make the sale. The sale of a complex service often requires a great deal of creativity if it has to be made on some basis other than the merit of the product, or multiple sales have to be made to get the order and continual effort is needed to keep the account.[11] The easiest deals to close are self-service sales where the customers are aware of their needs, know which services or service provider satisfies their needs best, are themselves sellers, and go through a checkout line.

Certain characteristics make the selling of a service different from the selling of physical products. These are intangibility, inseparability, heterogeneity and perishability, and they influence the success of the selling process. In the following section, each of these characteristics will be discussed in more detail.[12]

Characteristic 1: Intangibility

Goods are tangible and physical objects that can be seen, held, smelled and tasted, while services are intangible deeds, acts or performances. There may be physical consequences of the service such as a new hairstyle, but the customer often experiences the service itself in intangible ways. In some services, physical objects are used to perform the service, such as using electronic equipment to set the carburettor of a motor vehicle. The type of equipment used is of secondary importance to the actual act of servicing a vehicle.

Prospective customers are usually not able to try or experience the service before committing themselves to purchasing it. Intangibility is the main source of differences between goods and services, and is also the source of the other three characteristics. Services are intangible because it is often impossible to taste, smell, feel, see or hear a service. This attribute can make it difficult for customers to comprehend what they are paying for.

To better illustrate the basic concept of intangibility read the following illustration of the differences perceived by the customer when purchasing a dress as opposed to renting a video. When purchasing a dress, the consumer can try it on, feel the fabric, view the fit in the mirror, decide on the suitability of the colour, purchase it, take it home to wear occasionally, and derive satisfaction from it over a period of time. The customer renting a video, by contrast, cannot evaluate the video prior to the purchase and has to rely on information from others with different expectations from his or her own. After watching the video the customer does not keep anything except for the memory of the experience.

The explanation shows that service marketers are typically challenged to make the intangible more tangible. The salesperson's task is therefore to add physical evidence of the possible satisfaction created by the service and to allow the customer to obtain a genuine feeling for the benefits it has to offer. From being a big black box, the personal computer has been transformed into a multimedia tool. Prospective hospital patients are given a 'hotel guest' experience in upmarket hospital clinics. Salespeople must concentrate on the benefits derived from the product to reduce the intangibility aspect of a service.

Problems in selling services associated with intangibility

- As the service is intangible it cannot be stored. This leads to a problematic balancing act between the demand for and the supply of the service.
- The lack of physical features means that services cannot be patented. Only tangible machinery involved in the service process can be patented, but not the process itself. This leads to new and existing services being copied with ease, which in turn leads to difficulty in attaining and maintaining a competitive advantage or a unique differentiation in the market.
- The intangibility of the service complicates the communication process as there is essentially nothing to 'show' the customers in advertising or promotion, except, for example, a colour brochure of a holiday destination. Customers purchasing insurance policies are paying monthly instalments for a service offering that they cannot see, that in essence holds no benefit for the present and that cannot be taken home, and is sometimes difficult to comprehend fully. Insurance companies, therefore, have to be extremely creative in their selling approach – they have to sell the eventual long-term benefits.
- The pricing of services also poses a challenge, as the cost element involved is mainly labour. The problem with labour pricing is that it places a monetary value on time spent in the production of the service, and this is difficult to evaluate. Selling services can be the most challenging sales job when prospects do not understand the intangible characteristics of services, especially for insurance, financial investments and health services such as surgery.

Reducing the selling problems created by intangibility

- *Salespeople should emphasise tangible cues.* To reduce uncertainty, buyers will look for signs or evidence of the quality of the service provided. They will draw conclusions about the service by paying attention to the place, the people, the communication material, the symbols used and the price of the service offering. Service providers have to manage this evidence as it will impact on the customers' perception of quality and their satisfaction with the service.
- *Using personal sources of information.* As customers of services lack objective means of evaluating services, they often rely on the subjective evaluations of friends, family or colleagues. When moving to a new town a person will often ask other people for a referral to doctors and dentists. These personal sources of information become far more important to service customers than non-personal sources such as advertisements in the mass media.
- *Stimulating personal sources of information.* Organisations can use service excellence to stimulate word-of-mouth referrals. Customers who are extremely satisfied with a service tend to tell other people about their experience. Word-of-mouth advertising campaigns can also be used and usually include incentives, sales promotions and customer testimonials.
- *Creating a strong corporate image.* In an attempt to combat the increased levels of perceived risk associated with the purchase of services, much time and effort are often spent developing a recognisable organisational image. A well-known and respected corporate image reduces perceived risk and lowers the reliance on personal sources of information when choosing a service provider.
- *Encouraging employees to communicate with customers.* Encouraging salespeople to call on customers invites and stimulates two-way personal communication. The information gained by the organisation can be viewed as primary data that can be used to increase the value of the service offering and build a relationship with customers.

Characteristic 2: Inseparability of production and consumption

The second characteristic is inseparability, meaning that services are often produced, delivered and consumed all at once; in other words, the service cannot be separated from the seller. In the case of goods manufacturing, employees hardly ever see any of their customers. This is different for service organisations, as there is often constant contact between the service providers and their customers.

Inseparability has two important dimensions. Firstly, the production of a service and its consumption often occur at the same time. Travelling by air between Johannesburg and Cape Town, attending a sporting event and watching a movie on television are examples of the consumption of services while they are being produced. The second dimension concerns whether consumers participate in the production process of services. Customers 'enter' the service 'factory' of the service provider. Dentists and hairstylists cannot perform their services without the physical presence of the customer.

Inseparability also means that a direct sale is the only possible channel for distributing many services. The direct provider–customer interaction is a special feature of service marketing and can be referred to as the critical incident or moment of truth. The outcome of this critical incident represents the greatest challenge with regard to customer satisfaction or dissatisfaction. Customer retention and loyalty depend on how positive or negative the interaction was.

Problems associated with inseparability

- The service provider's physical connection to the service provided causes the provider to become part of the tangible cues that influence the customers' evaluation of quality. Service providers, therefore, are evaluated on the basis of their use of language, their body language, their clothing, their personal hygiene, their personal interaction and their communication skills.
- The involvement of the customer in the service production process varies from a requirement that the customer be physically present to receive the service (e.g. dental services), to a need for the customer to be present only to begin and end the service (e.g. auto repair and dry cleaning), to a need for the customer to be mentally present (e.g. university correspondence courses). The service organisation thus has to design its operations to accommodate the degree of customer presence. When customers are present, the facilities become part of the tangible cues of quality and the customer has an input into the service production process. This input can positively or negatively influence the outcome of the delivery process.
- Interaction among customers during the service production process can be either a positive or a negative experience. This shared experience occurs because of the simultaneous production and consumption of a service. To explain this phenomenon we will take a look at the experience of a sporting event. At such an event, examples of negative experiences will be smokers violating the space of non-smokers, intoxicated fans, long queues at food outlets or any other situation causing dissatisfaction. On the positive side, the atmosphere at an event or fan reaction such as cheering can add to the social experience.
- The final problem associated with inseparability is the challenge surrounding mass production. Here the problem is twofold. Firstly, since the service provider is directly linked to the service produced, an individual service provider can only produce a limited supply of the service. Secondly, due to customer presence during production, the process may be slowed down. This poses a problem when it comes to providing a service to a geographically widespread target market.

As an exception to the inseparability feature, a person representing the creator of the services may sell the services. Travel agents, insurance brokers and rental agents represent, promote and sell services on behalf of service providers.

Reducing the selling problems created by inseparability

- *Selection and training of personnel.* To handle possible inseparability problems, organisations should emphasise effective selection and training of contact personnel. Variations in contact personnel's behaviour can affect the customer's experience of the service positively or negatively.
- *Effective customer management.* Customer management includes, for example, training customers on how to use technology such as ATMs or ticket-buying machines at cinemas, and ensuring that a group on a bus tour is homogeneous.
- *Mass production.* Here service providers can try to find ways to work with larger groups of customers at once. Some psychotherapists, for example, have introduced small group sessions rather than one-on-one sessions to increase the supply of their service.

Characteristic 3: Heterogeneity

Heterogeneity means that it is often difficult if not impossible to achieve standardisation of output in services. Unlike the production of physical products, which can be quality-controlled in the factory, services are mostly delivered by people. The quality tends to vary with each encounter and may not be perceived as being consistent with previous experiences.

Different employees within the same service firm or even the same employee at different times of the day may vary in the ability or willingness to perform the service according to the expectation of the customer. Standardisation and quality control are extremely difficult to maintain in service firms. Some firms, such as McDonald's and City Lodge, have built marketing differentiation on their ability to deliver consistent and standardised service levels.

Problems in selling services associated with heterogeneity

External influences may also impact on the perception of quality, for example parking problems at the airport, flight delays, and a bumpy flight due to turbulence. Most of these things might be totally out of the control of the airline and its staff.

The major obstacle is that service standardisation and quality control are difficult to achieve because different people might be involved in the service encounter. When observing the service encounter you realise that each contact personnel member has a different personality and interacts with customers differently. From one day to the next they may have mood swings, or be subject to numerous other factors ultimately influencing the service experience. The problem is that it does not matter whether the organisation has the best processes in the world; if the employee is having a bad day the service encounter will be adversely affected and the customer's perception will be negative.

Reducing the selling problems created by heterogeneity

There are two possible solutions to this problem, namely customisation or standardisation.

- *Customisation.* This occurs when the service offering is adapted to the individual customer's specific needs and instructions. On the positive side, customisation can lead to the ability to satisfy different needs and provide the opportunity to set a higher price, thereby increasing profits. The downside, however, is threefold: customers may not be willing or able to pay a higher price for a customised service; the speed of service delivery may be slowed down, since customised services take extra time to provide and deliver; and customers may not be willing to face the uncertainty associated with customised services. If price, speed and consistency of performance are factors driving customers' perception of value, they will probably be happier with a standardised service.
- *Standardisation.* Service organisations can address extreme variations in personnel performance by standardising their offering through intensive training of contact and frontline staff. One major way to eliminate the variability in service quality is to replace humans with machines. Examples include automated car washes and automatic teller machines (ATMs). Standardisation leads to lower customer prices, consistency of performance and faster service delivery. On the negative side, some customer groups believe that standardisation sends the message that the organisation does not care about individual customer needs and is attempting to distance itself from the customer. Replacing humans with machines may also be regarded as socially irresponsible in that it may increase already high unemployment. Another major difficulty is forecasting the quality of a service. A fan may buy a ticket to a match without knowing whether the match will be exciting, be worth the entrance fee or have a dull result. It may even be rained out.

Characteristic 4: Perishability and fluctuating demand

Services are highly perishable as they cannot be stored – inventory holding is impossible. Periods of increased demand can therefore not be handled through inventory, as is the case with tangible goods.

Since the demand for ice cream increases over the summer months, manufacturing is increased during the months preceding summer. Additional stock may be stored until the demand increases, whereupon it is distributed to retailers. However, this strategy is impossible with services, and peak demand periods need to be handled with alternative strategies. Sellers should therefore attempt to match service capacity and demand. Because of the potential loss in income, medical practitioners like dentists charge patients if they do not turn up for an appointment or do not cancel an appointment timeously.

Once a service is produced, it is no longer available to be sold until production occurs a second time. When kulula.com's flight from Lanseria International Airport departs and there are a number of empty seats on the flight, those empty seats represent a lost sales opportunity that can never be recovered. Unsold tickets to a music festival, empty seats at a soccer match, mechanics standing idle at a repair shop – all these represent lost business. Service providers face a dilemma because they need to match capacity to a demand that tends to vary a lot.

Problems in selling services associated with perishability

Owing to the lack of inventory and the need for the service provider to provide the service physically, three supply-and-demand scenarios arise:

- *Scenario 1: A demand higher than available supply.* This situation means that there are too many customers to serve, so long queues and increased waiting time are inevitable. This can cause customer dissatisfaction and potential loss of business, as customers may decide to support the competition.
- *Scenario 2: A demand lower than available supply.* Here, resources are underutilised and operating costs are increased as employees stand around unproductively.
- *Scenario 3: Supply and demand at optimum level.* In this case, demand is equal to supply; customers do not have to wait in long queues, and employees are utilised at optimum levels.

The first two scenarios are usual but the last is rarely found. Customers do experience lengthy waits at times, while at other times service providers have no one to serve.

Reducing the selling problems created by perishability

The following strategies can be employed to help the organisation balance supply and demand.

On the demand side:

- Differential pricing can be used to shift some demand from peak to off-peak periods. An example is a leisure resort that offers lower holiday tariffs during low-season periods, creating an incentive for people who are not season bound to visit the resort during off-peak times.
- Non-peak demand can be handled by offering special promotions during lower demand periods. The management of a takeaway outlet knows that business is slow on Monday and Tuesday evenings and so introduces a hamburger or chicken-burger special for those nights.
- Complimentary services can also be developed during peak times to provide alternatives to waiting customers. Such services include cocktail bar facilities or a free glass of wine at restaurants to accommodate waiting customers. The banking industry relies on automatic banking services such as the ATMs available inside and outside the banks, which are designed to decrease customer reliance on in-bank services at the counter and during business hours.

On the supply side:

- Part-time staff may be hired to support peak demand. Retail stores can employ casual sales staff for Saturday mornings when the demand for sales advice is substantially higher than during the rest of the week. This way the organisation does not have to carry the burden of extra permanent staff that may not always be optimally utilised.
- Peak-time efficiency routines can be introduced where employees perform only essential tasks during peak periods. For example, Wimpy's breakfast menu is only available between 07:00 and 10:00.
- Increased customer participation can be activated. For example, banks encourage customers to make use of Internet banking facilities, so that there will be fewer people in the bank, and the bank will not lose customers.
- Shared services can be developed. For example, several medical practices can share medical equipment such as sonar scanners. Such equipment may not be fully utilised by one doctor, but if utilised by several doctors it can yield a higher return to each.

A notable exception to the generalisation about the perishability and lack of storage for a service is the buying of an insurance policy, for example. In a sense the policy is bought and held by the insurance company (the seller) until needed by the buyer or beneficiary (e.g. a study policy bought by parents and used when their child goes to university).

The above characteristics are the main reasons why services prove to be such an enormous challenge to any organisation. Sales managers should be sensitive to this and plan for these situations.

The impact of the characteristics of a service on the distribution of services[13]

The characteristics of services can have two important implications for the distribution of services. Firstly, because services are intangible and production occurs simultaneously with consumption, there is little need for logistical functions for many services.

It is not possible to build inventories of intangible acts. In other words, services cannot be stored, warehoused or stocked on retailer shelves awaiting customers' demand. Inventory, storage and transportation are ignored in the design of distribution channels for services. Certain secondary products, such as oil and lubricating grease, are stored in anticipation of the demand for the servicing of vehicles.

Secondly, the lack of logistical functions in the distribution of services means that there is a lack of merchant intermediaries in service channels. Service channels tend to be relatively direct from service provider to user. Manufacturers can appoint agents as approved dealers to offer services on their behalf, such as repairing and maintaining Samsung or Philips electronic appliances.

In Table 13.3, three guidelines are suggested as an approach to designing a channel for services, namely seeking physical manifestations of services, developing alternative contacts, and developing logistics channels where none have existed before.[14]

Table 13.3 *Guidelines for designing service channels*[16]

Distribution alternatives and strategies		
Seek physical manifestation of services	Airline tickets	■ Purchase in person at airline's own outlet(s) ■ Purchase by telephone from airline ■ Purchase by telephone from travel agent ■ Purchase via Internet ■ Delivery to customer
	Education	■ Direct classroom contact ■ Televised lectures ■ Web-based training ■ Combining contact with a distance-learning approach ■ Material made available on videotape, CD-ROM or on a course website
Develop alternative contacts	Library services	■ Travelling library bus ■ Mail-order of books ■ Interlibrary loan systems (especially academic libraries) ■ Web-based access to periodicals and journals
	Banking	■ Personal banker interacting with customer away from banking premises ■ Internet banking ■ Purchase of cellular airtime at an ATM
Develop logistics channels where none existed before	Repairs	■ Repair of electrical appliances on the customer's property ■ Handyman services at the customer's property
	Collection and delivery	■ Collect clothing to be dry-cleaned ■ Online grocery shopping such as Pick n Pay's and Woolworths' online service ■ The executive wardrobe – purchase of clothing and other personal items by executives from their offices (via telephone or catalogue, or by selecting from samples brought to their office)

TIPS FOR SERVICES SALESPEOPLE[15]

The special characteristics of services described above also have implications for the specific personal selling tasks services salespeople perform. Here are some tips to improve your skills in selling services.

1. Use brochures, photographs or videos that clearly show the outcome of utilising the service. When selling services, you need to think of these visual aids as samples.

Encourage the customer to hold and inspect them, add further tangibility by specifically pointing out details of interest and leave them with the customer to remind him or her of what the service provides.

2. Add evidence of performance, such as reservation confirmation or tickets (for hotels and airlines), policies or contracts (for insurance or security services), or programmes or specifications (for training, maintenance or professional services). Each of these pieces of documentation makes the service more tangible, as it were, and can act to reassure the customer.

3. If the service is equipment based (e.g. carpet cleaning, car maintenance or goods handling), give the customer a demonstration, again encouraging involvement with the equipment and its attributes, especially those that distinguish it from the services of your competitors.

4. Always aim to seek the customer's commitment to the first available time the service can be provided. For example, if you have the choice of booking a customer onto today's flight or into today's concert, or tomorrow's, always take the former option. You have another 24 hours to sell tomorrow's seat, whereas by tonight today's seat, if unsold, is a sale lost forever.

5. Use price and other special incentives or services to increase demand during slack periods. A small free gift, a pick-up or delivery service, or a discount on a future purchase can all motivate customers during low-demand times.

6. Prepare yourself physically and mentally for the peak-demand periods. You may feel you need an extra pair of hands and a few additional hours in each day and there may be little you can do in a practical sense to increase your supply except work harder and longer. It can help to reduce the stress if you (and your family and friends) simply accept that these rush times are part and parcel of your job. It can be useful also during these times to recall the slack periods when you wondered where your next order was coming from.

7. The inseparability of the service provider and the service product means that for many services, such as cleaning, installations, repairs and maintenance, and professional services, you are really selling time; the cost of using people and equipment to provide the service is calculated on an hourly or daily rate. It is important, therefore, that you become experienced and skilled in estimating the time required to complete each particular job. A useful discipline is to keep a record of your time estimates for each job and the actual times taken.

8. Where a service is time based and an estimate must be made before it is provided, high levels of trust must be established between you and your customer. You are asking your customer both to accept your initial estimate of the time the service will take and to accept that this amount of time was actually spent on the task. Obtain references and recommendations from other customers to help build this trust. Also, it is always better to under-promise and over-deliver than the other way round. Imagine the increased trust

and goodwill you create by being able to present the customer with a lower cost for the service than your original estimate.

9. Use consulting skills to determine exactly what the customer needs from the service you are selling. Consultation is even more important when selling services than when selling physical goods. Often customers themselves may be unsure of their need. A young married man, for example, might wish to protect his family in the event of his death but does not know what type of insurance will best do this. Be prepared to take the time to discover customers' needs and to bring them to an understanding of the benefits you can offer.

10. Develop an attitude of measuring the quality of the service you are providing by the degree of customer satisfaction you can achieve. Learn to understand what aspects of the service are important to your customers – speed, friendliness, expertise, and so on – and focus on these. In this way the variability of your service can be converted from a potential disadvantage into an advantage. Each service is customised to your customers' individual needs in a way that is often very difficult with a physical good.

SUMMARY

In this chapter we introduced the field of selling services, paid attention to the classification of services and attempted to help you to understand that there are major differences between the selling of physical goods and the selling of intangible services. An understanding of the distinguishing characteristics of services was also cultivated, and possible strategies introduced to help handle these challenges. Sales professionals in service organisations need to fully comprehend the basics of selling a service before they can optimise the impact of their selling campaigns.

CASE STUDY

The following scenario outlines the actions of a medical insurance salesperson who has just closed a sale with a businessman who plans to travel to the People's Republic of China (PROC). South African businesspeople are increasingly travelling to overseas destinations such as the PROC and it is estimated that very few take health and medical insurance seriously. The insurance bought by the businessman will cover him in the event of illness and injuries sustained during the business trip.

After closing the deal the salesperson attempts to build a lasting relationship and also probes for future referrals. 'Congratulations on your purchase! I can see that you will have peace of mind during your trip now that your health and medical needs are adequately covered! Thanks so much for purchasing the medical insurance from my company; it is most appreciated. Please feel free to call before you leave if you require anything else. I will call you after your trip, if you don't mind, to check that everything was fine. Looking forward to being of service to you again in the future and to a beneficial relationship. Goodbye!'[17]

The salesperson provided the following essentials for a stress-free business trip: advice on travel insurance and proof of health insurance; information on vaccines and an updated international vaccination card; and a reminder to the customer about taking his daily medication along.

To make the service more tangible the salesperson included the following free of charge as part of the health insurance package: a travel medicine chest (painkillers and products to relieve diarrhoea, constipation, travel sickness, itching, sunburn and inflammation), a first-aid kit (plasters, thermometer, bandages, needles, syringes, tweezers and scissors), water sterilisation tablets, insect spray, mosquito repellent and sun-block cream.

The salesperson also recommended that the businessman apply for an international driving licence at the Automobile Association in Menlyn shopping centre; and should get money and travellers' cheques at American Express. The salesperson advised the customer to enquire about the following from the travel agent: travel information, maps, and whether the appropriate visas had been attended to, and also advised that a copy of his passport, driving licence, etc., should be carried separately from the originals.

In building long-term relationships with customers, salespeople should keep the following in mind:[18]

- They should value the relationship with the customer beyond merely closing the sale.
- They should invest time and money in their customers by remaining in constant contact with them, and sending birthday and other appropriate greeting cards from the company.
- They should constantly be attentive to their customers' needs in order to get repeat business.
- They should regularly ask about their customers' needs, and then see if they can be satisfied.
- They should demonstrate through action that they are their customers' need satisfiers, which will build a solid foundation for their loyalty.
- They should ask their customers for referral leads from their immediate family, relatives, friends, colleagues and acquaintances.

Questions

1. Identify the core advantage of the medical insurance and its ultimate benefit.
2. Analyse the way the salesperson offered value-added services.
3. Examine the way in which the problems created by the unique characteristics of a service were addressed.
4. In the case study, other service providers were also mentioned. List them and offer other examples that may apply to the case study.

SELF-ASSESSMENT QUESTIONS

1. Explain the difference between a product and a service. Provide examples of each.

2. Services can be classified according to a variety of classification schemes. Explain the premise behind each one discussed in this chapter.

3. Name and briefly explain each of the unique characteristics of a service. Use examples from any one of the industries discussed in the early part of the chapter to explain each one of these characteristics.

4. Explain how the problems in selling services associated with each of the four unique characteristics of a service could be applied to any one of the industries discussed in the early part of the chapter. Also, outline the way a salesperson could reduce the selling problems created in a particular industry by each of the four unique characteristics of services.

5. Find other sources to add to the list of 'Tips for services salespeople' provided in this chapter.

6. Return to Chapter 1 and study the steps in the selling cycle carefully. How would a salesperson's approach differ/be similar between selling a product and selling a service at each step?

FURTHER READING

Marketing – selling a product vs a service[ii]
Leo Lingham – 10/16/2006

Question
I am interviewing for a software sales position and would like to be able to explain the difference between selling a product and a service.
Thanks,
Tommy

The difference between product selling ....
- tangible
- buyers can see/feel
- use a product brochure to reinforce
- buyers judge the value
- brochures can help to support

- leave a product for test trial
- companies must market a point of (USAGE BENEFITS) concerning how they can help customers achieve the desired benefits

To convince prospective customers that your product is different and better on some meaningful dimension, marketing should be focused around the communication of a particular philosophy of FEATURES/BENEFITS/AFTER SALES SERVICE/DELIVERY (and benefits of the PRODUCT to the buyer).

…….. and service selling
- intangible
- buyers can only sense it
- it is more like concept selling
- buyers cannot judge the value
- testimonials will be useful
- free service for a period
- companies must market a point of view concerning how they can help customers achieve the desired benefits

To sell services, businesses must make intangible offerings real for customers. To do so, marketing and sales have an array of real artefacts at their disposal; everything from samples of recent work, case studies, testimonials, white papers, and so on. This evidence can be used to make the case for purchase. The trouble is, many services companies speak in broad generalities when it comes to presenting their case. To differentiate themselves, and to build their brands, services companies must market a point of view concerning how they can help customers achieve the desired benefits

To convince prospective customers that a service is different and better on some meaningful dimension, marketing should be focused around the communication of a particular philosophy of service delivery (and benefits of the service to the buyer).

The pink Post-It note of an excellent salesperson[iii]

Douglas Kruger

As a professional speaker, I spend more time at airports than I do eating, sleeping or singing in the shower. Recently, after dragging my bags across the semi-dark of the OR Tambo parking garage, I found a little pink Post-It note attached to the side-view mirror of my car. It had a name and a phone number, and, ominously, nothing more.

My immediate reaction was a small pulse of adrenaline, and the thought, "Oh great! Someone's bashed into my car."

So I made the call as I drove home along the N1. A female voice answered, and said, "I saw that you had a crack on your windscreen. I was wondering whether you might like to bring that to our company to have it repaired." She then offered to call my insurer on my behalf, and ask what the excess would be.

Had to smile

In addition to a small sigh of relief, I had to smile as well. This was precisely what I had been teaching in one of my sales courses that day: Make it easy for your customer to buy from you. This lady was already one step beyond prospecting. She was showing me how little effort it would require from my side to 'let her' solve my problem. She was making it easy for me. Now that's salesmanship!

It's worth using that philosophy to re-examine our own businesses. For instance, log onto your website. Like every site, I'm sure it has all the pertinent information about how great your company is, and what it is that you offer. Sterling stuff! But here's a question: can customers easily buy from you? If the site is all they have, does your site make it easy? Or do they have to search for contact details, and, having found them, will they call through to a switchboard, where the receptionist isn't sure how to handle the call? If so, you are putting up barriers to your sales.

Another simple example

Another simple example, at retail level, is the almost innumerable stores that don't put price tags on things. That drives me nuts! I might have bought your product, but now I'll have to stand in a queue to find out whether I can afford it. I guess I'll just leave it. Barrier. Business lost. It's worth your while to think of ways in which you can make it easier for customers to do business with you. Are you selling financial products that require your client to take a medical exam? Offer to set it up for them. Whenever your business model faces logistics that can be an obstacle to purchase, you should be the one that provides the solution. Don't just hope your customers will do the work. Find a way to do it for them.

Catnip is to kitty

Not only is that a clever approach, but it's the beginning of a relationship. And relationships are to sales what catnip is to kitty. Start today. Do an audit of the ways in which customers can approach you. Find out whether there are any opportunities to make it easier for them. Then use it as a competitive advantage. The lady with the pink Post-It notes understands that principle. And for that reason, her company will be repairing my windscreen.

Jellybeans and Tabasco: a recipe for loyal customers, memorable brands[iv]

Jo Duxbury

Your customers are potentially your best salespeople. If you want to get them talking positively about your brand, consider thoughtful, low-cost, high impact touches that will surprise and delight them.

Pinelands in Cape Town is a sleepy suburb. People joke that if you move to Pinelands, you'll never leave. It's home to Old Mutual's head office, schools named after colours, lots of families with 2.5 kids and a fair number of old age homes. It's nice enough, but not the sort of place where you'd expect to be wowed by, well, anything.

Which is why Joe Fish is such a pleasant surprise. This little seafood restaurant on the edge of the suburb's only notable shopping centre is not fancy, but it is a delight. Your chips arrive on your plate wrapped in a 'newspaper' cone – and when you ask for the bill, it's delivered with marshmallow fish in a little tin 'treasure' chest. Quirky, memorable, fun – and the sort of thing you'd tell your friends about.

At Col'Cacchio pizzerias, customers get to take home miniature Tabasco bottles. Ideal, says now-loyal Col'Cacchio fan@candieo via Twitter, who keeps hers on hand in case of 'emergency oyster-eating'.

Thoughtful

When you check your car in at the Long Beach Car Wash at the mall in Noordhoek, the staff record your cell phone number and hand you a voucher for a free coffee at Wimpy and a discount voucher for the mall's Spur restaurant. When your car's ready, they send you an SMS. How thoughtful! The cost to the car wash? Probably about 12c. The results? I'd guess high repeat-business rates and customers who tell their friends about it.

In London in the mid-1990s, ordering stock images meant that the photo libraries would have to bike over the transparencies, which agencies would scan and return. One of the libraries used to send a small bag of sweets with each order. Guess who we bought images from most often? Yup, the photo library with the 10p jellybeans.

When you're next considering how you can integrate online and social media with your traditional advertising and branding activity, take a step back and think about how you can add thoughtful little touches into your brand mix. Do it right and you'll build amazing customer loyalty – and you might be surprised at the impact on your bottom line.

Launching a brand: Walking tall in land of the small[v]

The world changes when small people ignore their insignificance and do what others tell them can't be done, says Ondina Kuhn.

Small people with big ideas are interested in why it can't be done and so they start doing it. And once it's done no-one remembers it was once impossible because now it simply makes sense. And so it is with the brand I work with, SureSwipe.

If you think of credit cards a few big names immediately come to mind: MasterCard, Visa, AmEx, Diners ... but few of us observe the machines we swipe our cards through, unless they persistently don't work and then we soon learn which are most likely to work. If we think about these small little workhorses, glowing with the exertions of our galloping credit cards, we tend to think of them as the preserve of the big banks.

But in a world where many more of us work from home and outsourcing has become business sense, the same applies to banking tools like credit card swipe machines. SureSwipe is not outsourced, it's independent and works within the limitations imposed by the SA Reserve Bank and has as its banking associate, Capitec.

Marketing the skinny new boy on the block next to the big guys isn't easy

Initially SureSwipe was an adjunct to our sister company, Healthbridge, an electronic medical and payment company servicing doctors, hospitals and medical aids. Early thinking was that SureSwipe should have a testing ground in specialist medical practices. The clients of a plastic surgeon, as an example, are rarely covered by a medical aid and pay upfront, but as novices, we did not know there was an existing specialist company already offering a similar service to high end medical practitioners.

We learnt enough about the challenges of small businesses to realise that there was a desperate need for really good service and competitive rates. Although small and medium businesses generate a third of South Africa's gross domestic product and employ two-thirds of the workforce, they often battle to get decent service and reasonable rates.

It's an irony of the world that where small businesses globally are the biggest employers and contributors to GDP – 66% of jobs in the European Union as an example and far higher contributors in Africa and Asia – banks and companies will jump to attention for the big companies and make the real drivers of economic growth (SMMEs) stand in line.

We are small and most of our clients, but for big brands like BMW and Ducati dealerships are small, so there was an obvious synergy. We were battling, as they had, to establish ourselves, to get great staff, to get our name known. Even if a company could save as much money as it would require to pay his electricity bill each month, by using our service, they were initially slow to switch.

Being a new brand in the financial services market is loaded with challenges. Research shows that only 10% of consumers will change their bank in any given year, and similar conservatism is shown in any other area where money management is necessary. And no-one sits around waiting for marketing messages to hit them. We tried an array of marketing channels to reach them; for example a campaign using email, mobile and post did not reap the results required so we resorted to good old footwork and personal selling tied in with quirky marketing.

Recently we launched our tiered client service package, which offers anti-fraud blue UV lights (an important asset in the run-up to the World Cup with 23% of credit card fraud on foreign cards), 24-hour technical support and rates of up to half those of the big guys.

We called the packages Cocoa and Citrus (similar to our brand colours of orange and black). What are the images those names conjure for you? Comforting cocoa is our top offering with additional service, great rates, fraud training and guaranteed technical assistance within two hours of a problem occurring. It best suits businesses that are open long hours and probably serve relatively high-end clientele. Tangy orange represents the speed of our service tied to zesty technology and is ideal for businesses with conventional working hours and a solid base of clients.

Interestingly enough, retailers responded well to the quirky offering. Retailers work long hours and need consistent creative input to lure in trade and then to keep clients with great service. And so it is critical that our service to them echoes that commitment to creativity and excellent service.

And so what we are learning is that the greatest advantage is not in being big. Many walk tall in this small world by consistently looking for ways to please and by giving great customer service. After all, the biggest name in brands is loyalty. And that is our aim.

Ondina Kuhn is marketing and brand manager for SureSwipe www.sureswipe.co.za

More to value propositions than meets the eye[vi]
Peter Gilbert

Since the emergence of organised selling, generations of salespeople have been steeped in the traditions of FAB (features, advantages and benefits) and the old favourite, the USP (unique selling proposition). These simple concepts served generations of salespeople well. However, markets have changed, rendering these familiar, rather product-centric tools all but obsolete.

In markets characterised by plentiful supplies, a wide range of options, shrewd, well-informed buyers and ferocious competition, the usefulness of these tools is greatly diminished. A new generation of skilled salespeople understand that they must make the transition from walking catalogue to that of business consultant, and value creator.

Raised the bar

In a recent project, HR Chally interviewed over 80 000 senior business executives, and it became abundantly clear that they have raised the bar in terms of their expectations of salespeople. They expect salespeople to have in-depth knowledge of the buyer's business, as well as the ability to craft offerings around their product/services that deliver demonstrable financial value to the buyer's business.

Marriott Hotel's proposition to one of its key international clients, Siemens, is not simply about renting out hotel rooms. It is all about reducing staff turnover among middle and senior management with gruelling travel schedules by creating technologies and systems that facilitate the creation of a customised, user friendly, hassle-free travel experience.

Boise Cascade Office Products are not simply purveyors of office consumables. It brings its expertise in procurement and supply chain management to bear in creating a web-enabled buying process that centralises control, makes buying easy, generates usage reports, reduces shrinkage, and uses bulk buying to lower prices and save the client a great deal of money.

Must become adept

Successful modern sales forces must become adept at formulating and communicating creative value propositions for their customers, and salespeople must be equipped with the knowledge, the tools and the templates to enable them to do this.

OUTsurance helps OUT over the holiday season[vii]
Issued by OUTsurance

Over the recent festive season, short-term insurance company OUTsurance was expecting its all-hours emergency call centre operation, Help@OUT, to really be put to the test. And tested it was, with over 1 300 OUTsurance insurance clients receiving emergency assistance for home emergencies and more than 3 150 clients that were assisted for emergencies that left them stranded on South Africa's national roads.

All OUTsurance clients automatically receive access to its 24-hour emergency roadside and home assistance service, aptly dubbed Help@OUT, free of charge. Managing director of OUTsurance, Ernst Gouws, commented: "It's awesome to be able to help our insurance clients out when they are in need. Be it a locksmith to unlock your car or a glass fitter to repair a window damaged in a freak storm or even a plumber to solve a late night burst geyser, we go out of our way to send the emergency assistance our clients need when they need it. Best of all is that it is a free service to our clients. This means it actually saves them the cost of subscribing to a paid-for service which offers the same benefits."

In the Roadside Assistance category, by far the majority of cases were opened for towing of vehicles, but over 700 cases were opened for locksmiths, flat car batteries, assistance in tyre changing and fuel deliveries for vehicles that had run out of fuel. With concerns over the safety of motorists that are broken down or stranded on the side of the road, roadside assistance from Help@OUT has really proven to be a valuable product benefit.

An OUTsurance client, Mr Madikwe of Garsfontein, Pretoria, recently requested Help@OUT emergency assistance when his car broke down just outside Durban. "The people at this insurance company were simply amazing – they took care of everything! That's not something you see every day."

OUTsurance Insurance Company is also very proud of the level of service achieved in the delivery of these services. Mr Gouws commented in closing: "To have over 90% of our clients that used the Help@OUT service over the festive season rate the service they received as 'good' or 'awesome', is a fantastic achievement, especially given that many of our service providers are closed at this time of year. There is however room to improve and we will be working hard at getting that number closer to 100% in future."

About OUTsurance: OUTsurance Insurance Company has established itself as the leader in the direct insurance market offering car insurance, household insurance and business insurance. For awesome service and affordable insurance premiums get an insurance quote from OUTsurance now and experience insurance cover with a difference.

NOTES

1. Futrell, C.M. 1998. Sales Management. (Fifth edition). Dryden Press, p. 87.

   Futrell, C.M. 2001. Sales Management: Teamwork, Leadership, and Technology. (Sixth edition). Harcourt College Publishers.

2. Jordaan, Y. & Prinsloo, M. 2004. *Grasping Service Marketing*. Vine News, p. 6.

3. Futrell, C.M. 1999. Fundamentals of Selling. (Sixth edition). Boston: Irwin McGraw-Hill, p. 45. Also see Futrell, C.M. 2004. Fundamentals of Selling. (Eighth edition). Boston: Irwin McGraw-Hill.

4. This section draws from Manning, G.L. & Reece, B.L. 1987. Selling Today – A Personal Approach. (Third edition). Boston: Allyn & Bacon, pp. 48–50.

5. Based on Futrell, op. cit. 1999, p. 460; and Futrell, C.M. 2000. ABCs of Relationship Selling. (Sixth edition). Boston: Irwin McGraw-Hill, p. 437. Also see Futrell, C.M. 2004; and Futrell, C.M. 2008. ABCs of Relationship Selling Through Service. (Tenth edition). Boston: Irwin McGraw-Hill/Irwin.

6. Based on Lovelock, C.H. 1983. Classifying services to gain strategic marketing insights. Journal of Marketing, 47(3): 9–20; and Lovelock, C.H. 1986. Marketing of services, in Handbook of Modern Marketing, (ed. Buell, V.P.) (Second edition). New York: McGraw-Hill, pp. 5–13.

7. Ibid.

8. Ibid.

9. Ibid.

10. Ibid.

11. Ibid.

12. Rix, P., Buss, J. & Herford, G. 1999. Selling: A Consultative Approach. (Second edition). Sydney: Irwin McGraw-Hill, pp. 421–422. Also see Rix, P., Buss, J. & Herford, G. 2001. Selling: A Consultative Approach. (Third edition). Sydney: Irwin McGraw-Hill.

13. Based on Futrell, op. cit. 1999, pp. 460–461; Rix et al., op cit., p. 422; Futrell, op. cit. 2000, p. 437; Jordaan & Prinsloo, op. cit., pp. 12–25; and Boshoff, C. & Du Plessis, F. op. cit., pp. 5–8; Baron, S., Harris, K. & Hilton, T. 2009. *Services Marketing – Text and Cases.* New York: Palgrave MacMillan, pp. 31–39; Zeithaml, V.A., Bitner, M.J. & Gremier, D.D. 2009. *Services Marketing – Integrating Customer Focus across the Firm.* Boston: McGraw-Hill International Edition, pp. 20–23.

14. Drawn from Bowersox, D.J. & Cooper, M.B. 1992. *Strategic Marketing Channel Management.* New York: McGraw-Hill, p. 421.

15 Ibid., pp. 423–426. Also see Bowersox, D.J. & Cooper, M.B. 2004. *Strategic Marketing Channel Management.* New York: McGraw-Hill.

16. Rix et al., op. cit., pp. 422–423.

17. Based on Fisher, K. 2004. *Simply Successful Selling.* Pretoria: Van Schaik, p. 130.

18. Fisher, op. cit., p. 130.

i   Boshoff, C. & Du Plessis, F. 2009. *Services Marketing – A Contemporary Approach.* Cape Town: Juta, p. 3.

ii   http://en.allexperts.com/q/Marketing-1090/selling-product-vs-service.htm#b (accessed on 8 April 2010).

iii http://www.bizcommunity.com/Article/196/20/41754.html (accessed on 8 April 2010).

iv   http://www.bizcommunity.com/Article/196/20/37551.html (accessed on 8 April 2010).

v   http://www.marketingweb.co.za/marketingweb/view/marketingweb/en/page71654 (accessed on 8 April 2010).

vi   http://www.bizcommunity.com/Article/196/20/36524.html (accessed on 8 April 2010).

vii http://www.bizcommunity.com/Article/196/20/32118.html (accessed on 8 April 2010).

14

PERSONAL SELLING IN BUSINESS MARKETS

LEARNING OUTCOMES

After studying this chapter, you should be able to:

- Explain the difference between personal selling in consumer markets and personal selling in business markets
- Discuss the various terms used to describe business markets
- Describe the unique characteristics of personal selling in business markets
- Explain the different types of business markets
- Discuss the different roles of personal selling in business markets
- Explain the link between the marketing concept and selling in business markets
- Discuss the impact of the Internet on personal selling in business markets
  - e-procurement
  - activity points
  - sales force deployment

INTRODUCTION

The focus of this book so far has largely been on personal selling within the retail or 'business-to-consumer' environments. This is because business-to-consumer personal selling is far more 'visible' than the personal selling that takes place in business markets (also known as 'business-to-business' or 'industrial' markets). As consumers ourselves, we seldom see the interactions that occur between the many buyers and sellers that are involved in the long process of transforming raw materials into final consumer goods in the business environment.

We are generally far more familiar with the salesperson across the counter in a retail outlet trying to sell us a camera or a bottle of perfume in the business-to-consumer situation.

Unlike in the consumer market, however, in business markets few sales are closed solely as a result of the advertising, sales promotion or publicity that is so common in retail marketing. In business markets, the complexities of organisational needs often demand complex personal forms of communication before, during and after a purchase decision. The result of this is that personal selling in business markets is often a team effort. What is more, while in consumer markets the buyer will frequently seek out the supplier's product by going to a particular store, in business markets it is more common for the salesperson to seek out the customer. To this end, the selling organisation's salesperson or team and the selling efforts of intermediaries play a central role, while other forms of promotion play a supporting one. Finally, business markets are also characterised by stronger relationships and shorter channels, emphasising the importance of personal selling.[1]

We begin this chapter by exploring the difference between consumer and business markets. We define personal selling in business markets; we go on to identify the various features of the selling task in business markets; and we close the chapter by examining the steps involved in managing the business sales force.

THE DIFFERENCE BETWEEN CONSUMER MARKETS AND BUSINESS MARKETS

It is essential, if we want to study personal selling in business markets, that we understand what the difference is between consumer markets and business markets. Business markets are defined by Vitale and Giglierano as consisting of 'all organizations that purchase goods and services to use in the creation of their own goods and services'.[2] These goods and services are then sold to the organisation's own customers. These customers can, in turn, be other businesses or consumers.

Let us examine this definition in more detail. Organisations operating in business markets buy goods and services for one of three purposes:[3]

1. *To make other goods or services.* For example, KWV buys grapes from farmers to make wine. Similarly, the Holiday Inn hotel group buys beds and linen from suppliers so that it can supply its clients with accommodation.
2. *To sell to consumers or other business users.* Edgars buys finished clothing from suppliers to sell to consumers, while Cecil Nurse Furnishers buys desks from suppliers which it mainly sells to other businesses.
3. *To conduct the organisation's business.* Almost every organisation buys office supplies (such as stationery) to keep its business running.

It is important to note from the above that we are referring to the sale of goods or services to businesses and not to the final consumers, although it may well be that these businesses that buy the goods or services sell them on to the final consumer.

UNDERSTANDING THE SEMANTICS

In the literature on business marketing, you may come across various terms such as business-to-consumer, business-to-business and industrial marketing. Business-to-consumer marketing refers to a situation where sales, usually retail, are made to individual consumers. The term *industrial marketing* is generally used when sales are made to 'blue collar' businesses (such as factories) that use the products or services to manufacture other goods directly. Business-to-business marketing includes industrial marketing but expands the types of businesses to which goods or services are sold to include all other types of non-manufacturing businesses (e.g. retailers, tourism providers, accounting firms, distributors, importers, designers, consultants, etc.). Business marketing is taken to mean essentially the same as business-to-business marketing. In this book we will use the term *business marketing*.

WHAT IS DIFFERENT ABOUT BUSINESS MARKETS?

There are numerous differences between business markets and consumer markets. Business markets are often characterised by:[4]

- *Their geographic location*. They are frequently clustered around specific locations. Retailers may all be located in a single mall such as the V&A Waterfront in Cape Town, while manufacturers may be located near to suppliers of a strategic resource, or near an airport.
- *Their relatively small numbers*. Business markets may comprise as little as a single monopoly entity (such as Telkom for telephone exchanges), or several thousand companies in the case of shirt manufacturers, whereas consumer markets often number in the hundreds of thousands or even millions.
- *Their generally large buying capacity*. The buying potential of businesses often reflects their huge size and cannot really be compared with the buying potential of an individual consumer.
- *Their employment of professional buyers*. Businesses generally appoint qualified and experienced buyers to handle their purchasing activities. What is more, they know what they want and they keep abreast of what is on offer in the marketplace.
- *The level of buyer behaviour*. Businesses commonly spend large amounts on their purchases and so the risk to them of what they buy is quite significant. They are also more concerned with the future relationship with their suppliers and the support they are likely to get from these suppliers, as this is an important component of their competitive offering to their buyers or consumers.
- *Complex products*. The products that are sold in business markets are often complex in nature (e.g. bottling machines).
- *Customisation to meet user needs*. Products are often developed uniquely to meet the specific requirements of a single customer.
- *Wide fluctuations in demand*. The loss of single contract can have enormous effects on the buying capacity of the business in question and, in turn, on their suppliers.

- *Derived demand*. It is important to note that the ultimate source of demand in business markets is often far removed from the buyer–seller interactions that occur in these markets. For example, the manufacturer of fertilisers for grape-growing farmers is quite far removed from the derived demand which stems from wine drinkers. Should there be a drop in demand for wine, this will ultimately affect the fertiliser manufacturer, but unfortunately the fertiliser manufacturer can do little to influence the demand for wine.
- *Inelastic demand*. Futrell suggests that demand for many industrial products is inelastic.[5] In other words, an increase or decrease in the price of the product will not result in a proportionate decrease or increase in the sales of the product in question. The reason for this is that buyers are often committed to a particular type of product or supplier. Changing suppliers would be more costly than absorbing an increase in the price of the product or products. This does not mean that suppliers can abuse the situation and keep on increasing prices. Buyers will not tolerate such actions and the supplier will quickly get a bad name in the industry.
- *Joint demand*. At the same time, Dibb et al. suggest that many industrial products are affected by joint demand.[6] This occurs when two or more products are used together to produce a single product; for example, computers contain hard drives, memory chips and motherboards (among other components). Business salespeople need to understand the role of joint demand, as it is possible that their sales can be affected positively or negatively by the sales of the associated products. For example, if there is a sudden shortage of motherboards, this may affect memory chip suppliers.

All of these factors impact quite significantly on the selling that takes place in these markets.

PERSONAL SELLING IN BUSINESS MARKETS

Given the points made above, it is obvious that personal selling in business markets will take a form different from that of personal selling in consumer markets. After all, the salesperson will need to contend with professional buyers, fewer customers, larger orders, greater scrutiny of orders, the need to establish longer term relationships and the threat of wide fluctuations in demand, which he or she cannot influence.

Furthermore, personal selling is the most frequently used and effective way of promoting goods and services in business markets. With the need to establish long-term relationships with its customers, the business sales force needs to understand its clients and their needs in some detail. This suggests a two-way interaction with customers. To this end, personal selling facilitates dialogue, as well as rapid and accurate feedback to the supplier. It makes sense, therefore, for business suppliers to invest in an effective and professional sales force.

This sales force will need to consider the following factors:

- *Doing a considerable amount of homework on customers*. In the consumer market, personal selling is often undertaken with little or no knowledge of the customer. Salespeople make use of their experience of human nature in general in their personal interaction with the customer. This is not the case in business selling, where the salesperson (often a 'sales team') will spend considerable time and effort learning about the customers and what their needs are. The preparation and effort involved is thus much greater in business markets.

- *Preparing extensive presentations.* In consumer markets, salespeople often make their presentation up 'on the fly'. Using considerable knowledge of the product, consumer salespeople are normally able to handle most of the queries that the customer will direct to them. In business markets, however, the sales team will normally prepare an in-depth presentation based on the needs of the customer (gathered earlier), the strengths of the supplier and the unique features of the product.
- *Understanding customers' needs.* In consumer markets, personal selling is often focused on the product and what it offers. In business markets, the emphasis is different. The sales team will focus on the needs of their customers and how they and their organisation's products will help customers meet these needs. This is commonly referred to as 'needs-based selling'.

In business markets, if the salesperson or sales team tries to 'hard sell' a product without taking the needs of customers into consideration, they are doomed to failure. Business customers are always seeking solutions to their own problems and the salesperson who wants to succeed in business markets must consequently focus on problem solving.

To this end, the salesperson or sales team may often work together with their clients in attempting to find these solutions, or even help them find new markets. They may sit in on meetings, help with the firm's long-term planning, assist with design issues, provide support and technical staff that will work with the customer's own staff, do research on the customer's behalf, help develop new products, and much more. This may involve one or more of the supplier's technical staff (who often form part of the sales team), working together – either part time or full time – with the client (occasionally even being located at the client's premises). It may even involve finding and passing on business leads to the customer. While all of this effort is aimed at selling products and services, what is more important is these products and services will have been developed or adapted to meet the customer's needs and to solve his or her problems.

- *Teamwork.* In consumer markets, personal selling is a lonely task, with the salesperson interacting with the customer on a one-to-one basis. The sales approach is often a 'hard sell' one, where the salesperson uses his or her considerable skills to convince the customer to buy the product in question. In the case of business selling, the focus is on teamwork, with the entire sales team working together to convince customers that the product can meet their needs. Each member of the sales team may be responsible for a part of the presentation (e.g. gathering the facts, compiling graphs and drawings, preparing the presentation, doing the physical presentation, arranging the discussions, watching the reaction of the customers, communicating with head office, leading the team, etc.). In such instances, head office is often drawn into the negotiations and there may be several interactions back and forth between the sales team and the support staff at their head office.

■ *Establishing long-term relationships with the customer.* In consumer markets, often little effort is made to establish a relationship with the customer (although this is changing with the advent of customer relationship marketing). However, in business markets it becomes essential to develop a long-term relationship with the customer. The value of the sale, the importance of each customer and the effort put into acquiring the sale, as we mentioned in the point above, are generally so great that no business can afford one-off sales. Businesses need to know that they can depend on their suppliers to meet future demand. We discuss this point in more detail below.

■ *Investing in their customers.* In the light of the above, it is clear that business selling involves a far greater investment in customers.

Considering the points we have made above, it becomes clear why personal selling is a more expensive but more relevant and effective form of communication in business markets.

Business personal sales expenditures can be as much as two to ten times as high as those for consumer sales. These costs can be attributed to the technical nature of business products, the longer buying process, and the larger size of the typical client organisation. In business markets, there are fewer organisational customers and they place larger rand orders for large volumes of products. Business customers are more involved with their purchases than the average consumer because the purchased items will affect the customer's operations, end products and profits.

Moreover, business customers spend more time, effort and money making purchasing decisions than those in the consumer market, and are themselves often technically qualified individuals. Business markets also tend to be characterised by more direct, shorter channels, which places more responsibility on a vendor's own sales force.

FROM TRANSACTIONS TO RELATIONSHIPS

There is a trend today towards focusing on building relationships in marketing rather than just generating single transactions; this is referred to as 'relationship-based selling'. This is especially true in the area of personal selling in business markets. As we have highlighted above, the complexities of business markets underscore the need for cooperation and two-way interactions that result in value being generated for both parties – the buyer and the seller. Business sellers cannot afford to lose a sale of hundreds of thousands or even millions of rand, and the solution is to focus on building long-term relationships that lock the buyer to specific sellers. It is fair to say, therefore, that relationship marketing is the goal of effective personal selling in business markets.

At the same time, it should be said that sellers cannot afford to work at establishing a relationship with a customer, and then sit back and do nothing once this has been achieved. A relationship needs to be worked at constantly over the longer term – it is an ongoing process, not a once-off target.

REVISITING THE MARKETING CONCEPT

You will recall that one of the main components of the marketing concept is the satisfaction of customer needs. In business markets, the sales force plays a greater role in actualising the marketing concept. This is so because of the necessity of making many mutual adjustments while working through the decision processes involved in buying and selling over long periods of time. As business customers face increasing competition and shorter deadlines, marketing managers must discover more effective ways to meet their needs. It is the business salesperson, working in conjunction with engineering and manufacturing staff, who offers the potential for developing the necessary creativity to satisfy customer needs.[7]

Thus the sales force is the physical link between the selling and buying organisations in the business market. Not only do salespeople communicate information on the attributes of the firm and its products or services to customers, they also report back to the firm on customer problems or changing needs. In this manner, those in research and development, production, quality control, shipping, order processing, collections and other key areas can adapt their operations to better serve the customer.

In addition, the salesperson frequently serves to negotiate price and delivery terms, including discounts, returns policies, shipment quantities, and supplies and transportation forms. The sales force often services customer accounts, as well as providing demonstrations and training in the use of the vendor's products.

To sum up, a business salesperson can be characterised as playing at least four roles: crusader for the organisation's cause, market researcher, negotiator, and consultant or solver of the customer's problems. To actualise the marketing concept effectively, however, the sales force must include well-trained experts in areas involving the choice and applications of products.

DIFFERENT TYPES OF CUSTOMERS AND BUYERS

In business markets, the salesperson is often confronted with sales to three main types of customers.[8] These are:

1. *Sales to resellers.* These occur when one organisation or individual sells goods to another organisation that in turn sells the goods to other organisations without any changes being made to the goods in question. An example of this is when a manufacturer or sales intermediary sells products to a retailer that in turn sells these products to consumers.
2. *Sales to other business producers.* These take place when a supplier or manufacturer sells goods to another organisation, which then uses these goods (which could be raw

materials or components) to manufacture or produce another product. For example, printed circuit-board (PCB) manufacturers sell PCBs to telephone companies such as Siemens or Philips, which use these PCBs to manufacture telephone switchboards.

3. *Sales to business users.* These occur when an organisation sells a product (such as a photocopier) to an institution, such as a hospital or government department, that uses the photocopier in its daily activities, but for which the copier is not a core product or input (i.e. it is not used directly to produce or provide other goods or services).

Not only does the salesperson have to deal with different types of customers, but among these customers there are often different types of buyers. Bingham et al. identify six different types of individual buyers that the salesperson is likely to encounter.[9] These are:

1. *The hard bargainer.* This type of buyer tends to play different suppliers off against each other. He or she will obtain several quotes and use these in the negotiation process to try to obtain a better price from the salesperson.
2. *The sales facilitator.* This buyer is the friendly buyer who is willing to do what is necessary to make the negotiations a success.
3. *The straight shooter.* This buyer is an honest person who behaves with integrity. Straight shooters will never use their position to obtain concessions, but will also ask direct and blunt questions to get to the crux of the matter. They keep the sellers informed and will not play one off against another.
4. *The socialiser.* This person enjoys personal interaction and will rather negotiate over lunch than in the office. There is often more social talk than business talk in these negotiations.
5. *The persuader.* This buyer strives to create a favourable impression with the seller and to encourage the seller to do business with the buying firm because of what they can offer in the long term (persuaders put effort into persuading the seller how good and important the buying firm is).
6. *The considerate buyer.* This buyer displays compassion and understanding for the salesperson and may even be willing to accept substitute products, different specifications or different prices to ensure that a deal is struck. The difference between this person and the sales facilitator is that with the considerate buyer the focus is on the salesperson, while the sales facilitator focuses on the sales negotiations.

It is essential that the successful salesperson understands and prepares for the different types of buyers he or she is likely to encounter when negotiating a deal.

BUYING ROLES
Six buying roles can be identified in the buying process, namely initiators, users, goalkeepers, influencers, deciders, purchasers/buyers and payers. Although these roles may be applicable

to both consumer and business markets, they are far more relevant in the business environment. Indeed, it is often the case that these individuals form part of a corporate 'buying centre', which can be described as an informal network of purchasing participants, including the individuals working for the purchasing or procurement department (the two terms are often used interchangeably, although it can be said that purchasing essentially involves 'buying' a product, while procurement is a more involved process involving the planning, implementation and evaluation of the purchase).

If one thinks about a typical business purchase (say of computers for use in the office), then it is easy to identify the various roles referred to above. For example, a department head (the initiator) may put in a request for the purchase of a new computer to be used by a staff member within the section (the user). This request may then go to the head of the IT section. The head then tasks someone in the IT section to gather information about alternate computers and specifications (the influencer). A committee (the deciders) may then decide on what computer to purchase, but not before the head of the IT section has put together the proposal, perhaps leaving out certain makes or models – here the head is acting as the gatekeeper. Once a computer has been decided on, someone in the purchasing department (the purchaser) is required to buy the computer, while someone in the finance department (the payer) will probably issue the cheque for the purchase .

It is essential that salespeople are aware of these various roles, as they may need to make contact with more than just the eventual purchaser. The good salesperson will develop a network of contacts within an organisation that includes all of the above persons.

SELLING ROLES

In business markets, there are essentially four different selling roles. Vitale and Giglierano have identified these as:[10]

- *The order taker.* This salesperson's role is quite low level and is focused on little more than taking orders and ensuring that the goods are delivered timeously and in order. The sales representatives of SA Breweries tend to fall into this category. Often the buyer has approached the seller for the products in question (e.g. Castle Lager) and no persuasion of the buyer is required. In this role, administrative skills are more important than selling skills.
- *The persuader/sustainer.* This is a slightly more involved role in which the salesperson strives to keep the buyer informed about and up to date with the latest products and prices. The salesperson will work towards convincing the buyer to buy his or her goods and will keep coming back for more orders. In this role, selling skills are very important.
- *The motivator/problem solver.* This is an even more complex role where the salesperson becomes involved in helping the buyer solve problems. The salesperson needs to more sensitive to the needs of the buyer, and the 'sales pitch' the salesperson will use is embodied in the selling of solutions rather than products. If the salesperson does his or her job well,

the buyer may even approach the salesperson for advice. In this role, human skills (listening, empathy, problem solving) are perhaps more important than just good hard-selling skills.

- *The relationship/value creator.* In this role, the salesperson strives to become the buyer's partner. This partnership is to everyone's benefit. The focus will not only be on developing solutions to problems, but the salesperson or team will work closely together with clients to identify their procurement needs, and the supplier may even work towards developing or adapting products to meet the customer's specific requirements. The salesperson may even work towards assisting in generating sales for clients. In this role, technical and management skills are more important.

TYPES OF SELLING

Newton identifies four different types of selling. These are as follows:[11]

- *Trade selling.* In this instance the main focus of the selling function is to increase sales throughput by providing merchandising and promotional support.
- *Missionary selling.* Missionary salespersons focus on facilitating sales through other channels. For example, the sales representative from Cadbury's may visit corner stores and encourage them to buy more Cadbury's chocolates from their local wholesaler; the representatives do not necessarily take orders themselves (but they help promote a product or group of products).
- *Technical selling.* The technical salesperson is the type of salesperson that is focused on convincing a buyer of the technical specifications and performance capability of the product they represent. Salespersons selling routers and data switches are examples of technical sales personnel.
- *New-business selling.* Here the main focus is on identifying new customers and generating sales from them.

Obviously each of these types of selling may involve different selling roles by different types of salespersons using different selling skills.

TYPES OF BUSINESS PURCHASES

It is also important to distinguish between the different types of purchases that are made in business markets, as the extent of personal selling that is involved in each of these types of purchases varies quite significantly. Kinney describes two types of business purchases, namely purchases of:[12]

- *Direct materials*, which are the raw materials inputs and component parts that organisations buy in order to convert them into finished goods. Kinney explains that if the buyer is an assembly-oriented manufacturer, direct materials consist of the parts and subassemblies that are incorporated into their own end product through their assembly operations, while in process industries like chemicals manufacture, direct materials are the feedstock, fuel and additives these firms convert into finished products.

- *Indirect materials*, which are described as all the other purchases that are necessary to run the business, but that do not become part of the manufacturer's end products. Indirect materials include things such as furniture, computers, lubricants, light bulbs and office supplies. Kinney argues that while manufacturers have a high proportion of spending for direct materials, other types of companies such as financial service firms predominantly buy materials that would be classified as 'indirect'.

Clearly, far greater personal selling effort is likely to be put into direct sales than into indirect sales. Also, direct sales are likely to be higher-value items than indirect sales. Usually what happens in most firms is that the salesperson or team will approach the organisation to negotiate a sale of certain products – be they raw materials or components. This initial negotiation may take quite some time and may involve considerable interaction between the salesperson (or team) and the buyer or buyers. These negotiations are usually undertaken at a strategic level and have major impact for both the buyer and seller.

However, once a contract has been negotiated, it may ultimately be in place for quite a long time and there may be many purchases that take place over time under the 'umbrella' of this primary contract. For example, an automotive manufacturer, such as Ford in Pretoria, may negotiate a contract with Silverton Engineering to supply it with radiators over the next three years (or up to a set value or number). Usually the contract will set out strict product specifications and manufacturing quality parameters that the supplier must meet. Then, over the next three years, Ford may regularly (perhaps weekly or monthly) order radiators from Silverton Engineering under this contract. Obviously the initial contract negotiation requires considerable personal selling input. However, subsequent purchases under the main contract will require little, if any, input from the salesperson who negotiated it.

Pride and Ferrell also refer to *new task purchases*, *straight rebuy purchases* and *modified rebuy purchases*.[13] These types of purchases are variants of the direct purchase referred to above:

- *New task purchase*. This occurs when an organisation purchases a product relating to a new job or project being undertaken by the buyer. In this instance, the salesperson will probably spend considerable time and effort on the contract negotiations.
- *The straight rebuy purchase.* This occurs when products are bought regularly, often under a blanket purchase order agreement, and is seen as casual order taking. In this case, the salesperson has little to do except, perhaps, take orders (although a clerk may be assigned to do this, or it may be done electronically).
- *The modified rebuy purchase.* Here the buyer wants a product similar to what he or she bought before, but with some modifications in the product specifications, the price or the delivery terms due to changing circumstances and needs. In this instance, the salesperson may again have some work to do in order to renegotiate the terms. Such negotiations are usually a little easier, as the salesperson is reasonably sure that the company intends buying from his or her organisation.

THE ROLE OF THE INTERNET

The Internet is having a dramatic impact on the procurement industry and also on the selling process in business markets. Using Internet-based technologies, it is now possible to source products and obtain quotes via the Internet. This has the effect of cutting out the role of the salesperson, and is referred to as 'disintermediation'.

The effect is particularly hard felt in cases where a sales intermediary performs a broking service by bringing buyers and sellers together in industrial markets. In such cases, the intermediary or broker will generally not make the source of the goods known to the buyer. Using the Internet, however, the buyer can now source the original manufacturer of the goods and thereby bypass the broker.

At the same time, using the Internet, it is possible to integrate the ordering and procurement activities of the purchasing firm with those of its many suppliers. These integrated systems enable the automated purchasing of goods based on trigger events such as low stock levels, increased sales, etc. Often such electronic purchasing (or e-procurement) happens without any human intervention. This does away with the role of the salesperson as order taker.

Some salespeople feel that this weakens the role of the salesperson, as the process of order taking was a means for the salesperson to keep in touch with the buyers and build up a relationship with them. Others argue that by doing away with the low-level process of order taking, the salesperson can now focus on more important strategic negotiations around new or modified contracts, and can focus greater effort on relationship building.

Whatever the view, there is little doubt that the Internet will radically change the selling process in the future.

MANAGING THE BUSINESS SALES FORCE[14]

It is important to realise that in discussing business markets we more often than not are referring to sales teams rather than individual salespersons. The task of managing the sales team and the selling process that the team uses becomes increasingly important in business markets.

The role of the sales manager varies from business to business. It is not unusual for sales managers to become involved in product innovation, research, strategic planning, budgeting, pricing, channel management, advertising, sales promotion, production and plant location decisions. Some sales managers may even be responsible for all the organisation's marketing activities. However, the more traditional functions of this position are organising, staffing, training, motivating, supporting and evaluating the sales team. The marketing strategy will provide the sales manager with some direction in attempting to define what marketing management wishes to accomplish with the sales force – who does what, when, and at what cost.

Competitive survival in the business market depends on an aggressive, well-trained and professional sales force. Today's marketplace requires salespersons who are keenly sensitive to customers' needs and equipped with the technical knowledge and necessary communication skills to operate efficiently and effectively to the mutual advantage of both the firm and its customers.

The function of sales management, then, is to ensure that the business sales force is managed so that it is responsive to market conditions and requirements in a way that generates maximum profits for the organisation.

It is also part of the sales management process to evaluate and control the sales force. Marketing management must ensure that sales goals and objectives are being met, or that proper progress is being made towards their accomplishment. Standards and objectives need to be developed as part of the sales strategy/plan that will make it possible to measure the salesperson's actual performance compared with planned performance.

Performance measures may be quantitative (e.g. rand or unit sales) or qualitative (e.g. the salesperson's attitude), as well as being based on inputs (e.g. the number of calls made) or outputs (e.g. the number of deals closed). The most common performance measure is the sales quota:

- *Sales quotas* provide the salesperson with a target at which to aim, and provide marketing managers with a source of control. Targets should be challenging, reflecting realistic market potential, but not unachievable. If targets are set too conservatively, they will not be a successful motivator and may lead to game playing by the salesperson. Quotas can be based on rand sales volume, unit sales, sales by type of account, gross margin or net profit.
- *Activity points* are given to salespeople for certain tasks such as number of calls made, new accounts generated, support service provided, and so on. Involving the sales representative in the quota-setting process is a good idea because this helps to provide timely feedback on possible reasons for falling short of the quota, and also to reward quota achievement meaningfully.
- *Performance evaluation* focuses not only on the salesperson, but also on territories, market segments, individual customers, products and average order size. Territories may need to be modified, customers may be dropped, or some segments may warrant heavier investment of sales resources.

OVERVIEW OF THE MODELS FOR BUSINESS SALES FORCE MANAGEMENT

This section deals with sales force deployment.[15] Traditionally, the task of sales management in business markets has been to improve sales effort effectiveness through administrative functions. This has led to a tendency to neglect efforts to improve sales force deployment strategy. Perhaps one reason for this neglect is the complex nature of sales deployment analysis.

Deployment refers to decisions about the size of the sales force, territorial design, and the organisation and allocation of the selling effort. As a chief executive officer once pointed out, sales managers should not be recruiters and cheerleaders but business managers of territories, districts and regions.

While many methods of deploying the sales force are available, such as workload analysis and return on time invested, over the last decade several sales force decision models have been developed that make the task of sales force deployment more manageable. However, there are several problems with these models.

These models require the collection and processing of large amounts of data, many are applicable to specific types of selling situations, and often management does not understand or trust the ability of computers to handle the mathematical formulae required for analyses. Typical approaches to sales force deployment analyses and decisions are shown in Table 14.1.

Table 14.1 *Approaches to sales force deployment analyses[16]*

Intuitive approaches	Systematic approaches	Decision model approaches
Experience	Potential	Empirical models
Judgement	Workload	Judgement-based models
Rules of thumb	Return on time invested (ROTI)	Combination models

Regardless of the method chosen, effective deployment of the industrial sales force involves:
- Estimating total market sales potential by geographic region and customer type
- Adjusting these estimates to reflect the organisation's sales potential
- Compiling these adjusted estimates into sales estimates for specific customers in geographical areas
- Evaluating trends that may affect potential sales
- Determining how many salespeople will be needed to bring about projected sales – this is referred to as workload analysis
- Assigning salespeople to territories and customers.

THE SELLING PROCESS IN BUSINESS MARKETS

In this book we have already covered the selling process in some detail. In this section we revisit the selling process discussed in previous chapters in the context of business markets.

1. *Prospecting.* In this first step the salesperson needs to identify and qualify potential business customers. The salesperson may identify potential customers from many sources including present customers, former customers, word of mouth, cold canvassing, directories, mailing lists obtained from specialist companies, personal contacts, response to advertising, and trade shows and exhibitions.

   Once a list of potential customers has been compiled, the salesperson must research these customers to determine whether the firm has a need for the product or service and the finance to purchase it. It may also mean targeting the right person in the client firm who can make a purchase decision within the firm.

2. *Pre-approach*. This may involve learning a bit more about the customer, and what the organisation's needs are and other relevant competitive information (the size of the company, its turnover, its position within the industry, etc.), as well as administrative information (e.g. where the company is located and who the key buyer is). It also involves planning a visit to the firm, perhaps by first phoning or e-mailing the prospect to see if he or she is willing to meet with the salesperson.

3. A*pproach*. The first contact with the buyer may be on an individual basis, involving only the salesperson or perhaps a colleague, together with the buyer. The main objective of this is to learn more about the customer and their needs in the context of the product being marketed. At this stage the salesperson may or may not make a presentation. In industrial selling it is more likely that the salesperson will thank the buyer for the information and request a second interview at which time a presentation will be made. This first contact is likely to lead to subsequent meetings and further presentations.

4. *Presentation(s)*. At the first presentation, the salesperson (or sales team) will strive to make a good first impression by being friendly, neat, on time and alert; and by shaking hands firmly and concentrating on the prospect. During the presentation, the salesperson will ask relevant questions, use referrals, identify benefits for the client, offer special services and generally try to make a favourable impression. The presentation may involve exhibits such as slides, charts, testimonials, case studies, examples and practical demonstrations. In addition, the salesperson will almost always provide a presentation 'pack' containing documentary information on all of the matters and issues discussed.

   The extent of subsequent presentations will depend on the complexity, importance and value of the purchase being negotiated. If it is a relatively small or low-level purchase, there may only be a single contact between buyer and seller. On the other hand, if the negotiations are about an expensive piece of factory equipment (an injection-moulding machine, for example), then there may be several 'rounds' of negotiations to discuss the exact needs of the client and the specifications required. It is also likely that in these subsequent negotiations the selling organisation will bring together a sales team to support the original salesperson who made the initial contact. The members of this team will each have different functions: some will be technical experts, some will be designers, and others may be workflow specialists or some other appropriate kind of service provider who adds value to the team effort.

5. *First trial close*. Depending on the complexity and nature of the sale, the salesperson or sales team may attempt to close the sale soon after the first presentation. The complex nature of business selling, however, will normally preclude such an early close. It is much more likely that there will be objections that need to be handled and several other issues that will need to be dealt with first.

6. *Handling objections.* It is common in business negotiations for buyers to lodge objections. Such objections may be based on the price, the lack of features of the product on offer, the timing (e.g. not being able to deliver the product on a given date) and what the competition has to offer. The salesperson should handle all objections directly, quickly and honestly. Also, since buyers often do not voice many objections, the salesperson should ask questions to ensure that no objections are overlooked. It should be remembered, however, that business negotiations are more about establishing a long-term relationship, so that it will not do the salesperson's efforts any good to just gloss over objections.
7. *Meeting objections.* In the case of business or industrial sales, it is unlikely that the objections mentioned by the buyers will be addressed merely by 'smooth talk' on the part of the salesperson. It is much more likely that these objections will require further discussion and planning that will translate into a revised offer on the part of the selling organisation. It is crucial that all objections are fully addressed and acceptable solutions found. Only if this is done will the buyer be prepared to enter into a long-term relationship with the seller.
8. *Final trial close.* In this step, the salesperson will use various techniques to elicit a signal from the buyer which will indicate how close he or she is to making a buying commitment.
9. *Closing the sale.* It is essential, in the sales process, to come to a point where a sale is made (this is referred to as closing a sale). The salesperson needs to know when and how to close the sale.
10. *Follow-up.* This is also a vital part of the selling process in business markets. It ensures that the product has arrived in good order and that the buyer was happy with the purchase. It also has to do with establishing a long-term relationship with the customer, which should ensure more sales at a later stage. Indeed, in business markets, particularly where high-value, essential goods are involved, this follow-up may be extremely important and may even involve specialists from the supplier working in the buyer's factory to ensure that the goods sold work properly and are fully integrated with the other machinery in the organisation.

What is important to appreciate from the above description is the effort involved in each of these steps. It is this effort (combined with complexity) that differentiates personal selling in consumer markets from personal selling in business markets.

SUMMARY
The role of the sales team in actuating the marketing concept makes it the primary consideration in the business marketer's promotional mix. The fact that the salesperson or team plays such a significant role in marketing communication represents a major difference between business marketing and consumer marketing, and mandates the necessity of understanding the business environment within which salespersons operate and the functions of sales management.

In this chapter we examined the task of personal selling in business markets and outlined the unique characteristics. We identified different selling roles and the different types of business purchases that can be made. We emphasised the impact that the Internet is likely to have on the personal selling process.

What is more, we acknowledged the need for salespeople to be effective, efficient and professional in the business selling environment, which would depend to a large extent on how well they are managed. Sales management, we pointed out, involves two primary areas, namely (1) planning a strategy for the effective deployment of the sales force; and (2) the administration of sales personnel. Strategy involves the management functions of planning, organising and controlling the selling effort, while sales force administration involves recruiting and training sales personnel.

In conclusion, personal selling involves persuasive and deliberate contact between the selling organisation and its business customers for the specific purpose of creating an exchange between them. Personal selling is the primary promotional tool utilised in business marketing and is generally supported by the other elements such as advertising, publicity and sales promotion. It is in this way that business selling differs greatly from consumer selling, which relies much more heavily on mass selling tools and advertising in particular.

CASE STUDY

Bubbles Plastics

Bubbles Plastics was established in Rustenburg in 1976 as a family business and has been run by the founder ever since trading commenced. The company is primarily concerned with the manufacture of plastic bags and has the capability of supplying large business organisations, small business ventures, as well as the private individual with a wide range of products.

The bag manufacturing process starts with the extrusion stage, where polythene granules are melted to form a 'tube' of continuous plastic that is wound onto a roll. The roll of plastic is then taken to printing where the client's logo, etc. is applied. Before being separated, the 'tube' of plastic is folded according to specification. In the final stage, cutting the plastic sheet separates the individual bags from each other. The completed bags are then packed into pre-determined quantities for distribution to customers based on specific orders they have placed, or are packed on the shelves of the firm's retail department for ad hoc sales. All off-cuts from the last stage are recycled, creating the polythene granules that are used at the start of the process. This saves money and helps the environment.

Not only does Bubbles Plastics manufacture its own plastic bags, but the company also stocks a comprehensive range of 'off-the-shelf' plastic bags for the casual customer. Additionally, the company is able to customise bags for business clients, both large and small. In 1985, the company diversified to include trade in other related products. It was at this time that it moved to new, much larger premises.

The firm's trading activities in other plastic products has grown over the years and Bubbles Plastics is now in a position to offer a formidable and diverse range of bagging. The company plans to revamp its current premises in the near future.

Source: Bubbles Plastics website: http://www.bubblesplastic.co.za

Questions

1. Would you consider Bubbles Plastics as representing a company active in the business-to-business market? Please justify your answer.
2. If you were a Bubbles Plastics salesperson tasked with selling plastic bags to Pick & Pay, how would you go about the sales process?
3. Would you consider plastic bags to be a direct or indirect material purchase for Pick n Pay? Please justify your answer.
4. If you were an injection-moulding company selling a new range of machines used for producing plastic bags, how would you go about selling these machines to Bubbles Plastics?

SELF-ASSESSMENT QUESTIONS

1. Explain the difference between personal selling in consumer markets and personal selling in business markets.

2. Explain the difference between consumer, industrial and business markets in the context of personal selling.

3. Describe the unique characteristics of personal selling in business markets.

4. Explain the link between the marketing concept and selling in business markets.

DISCUSSION QUESTIONS

1. Discuss the different roles of personal selling in business markets.

2. Discuss the impact of the Internet on personal selling in business markets.

3. Discuss how you would manage, evaluate and control your business sales team.

4. Discuss the selling process that a salesperson selling industrial lighting would go through.

NOTES

1. Dwyer, F.R. & Tanner, J.F. 2002. Business Marketing: Connecting Strategy, Relationships and Learning. (Second edition). New York: McGraw-Hill Irwin, pp. 303–304.

2. Vitale, R.P. & Giglierano, J.J. 2002. *Business-to-Business Marketing: Analysis and Practice in a Dynamic Environment.* Melbourne: Mason, South-Western, p. 357.

3. Ibid., p. 398.

4. Gibas, J.J. & O'Reilly, D. 2002. *The CIM Handbook of Selling and Sales Strategy.* London: Butterworth-Heinemann, pp. 291–292.

5. Futrell, C.M. 1999. Fundamentals of Selling. (Sixth edition). (International.) London: McGraw-Hill, p. 453.

6. Dibb, S., Simkin, L., Pride, B. & Ferrell, O.C. 2001. Marketing: Concepts and Strategies. (Fourth edition). (European.) Houghton Mifflin, p. 150.

7. School of Business Management, University of South Africa. 2004. *Industrial Marketing Management Study Guide.* Pretoria: UNISA, pp. 155–156.

8. Johnston, M.W. & Marshall, G.W. 2003. Sales Force Management. (Seventh edition). New York: McGraw-Hill Irwin, pp. 411–422.

9. Bingham, F.G., Gomes, R. & Knowles, P.A. 2005. Business Marketing. (Third edition). New York: McGraw-Hill, p. 176.

10. Vitale & Giglierano, op. cit.

11. Newton, D. 1973. *Sales Force Performance and Turnover.* Cambridge: Marketing Science Institute.

12. Kinney, S. 2000. *An Overview of B2B and Purchasing Technology.* Public Workshop: Competition Policy in the World of B2B Electronic Marketplaces. http://www.freemarkets.com

13. Pride, W.H. & Ferrell, O.C. *Marketing 2000.* Houghton Mifflin, p. 230.

14. *Study Guide,* School of Business Management, University of South Africa, op. cit., pp. 154–161.

15. Ibid., pp. 157–158.

16. Ibid., p. 158.

15

INFORMATION AND COMMUNICATION TECHNOLOGY

SPECIFIC OBJECTIVES TO BE ACHIEVED

This chapter introduces you to the application and role of information and communication technology in personal selling.

LEARNING OUTCOMES

After studying this chapter, you should be able to:

- Explain the influence of information and communication technology on the selling profession
- Identify the main components and uses of integrated software packages
- Identify the software packages that are likely to be found on the salesperson's notebook
- Explain the use of personal computers in personal selling
- Explain the use of cellphones
- Show how the guidelines for using email as a selling tool are applied
- Identify and explain the new technologies that are used in selling

INTRODUCTION

The information community has become a reality. Information and communication technology (ICT) has become part of our lives just like the telephone, radio and television. Technology has developed and integrated in such a manner that nearly all information is accessible at the touch of a few buttons. Employees currently focus their energy on the supply of an uncountable number of information services. The communication technology is developing at a great pace, and every year new or improved technology appears on the market. ICT does not have a long history, and most of the development in this field has taken place in the past decade. ICT is an instrument that salespeople and other business people can use to communicate more effectively in order to increase productivity and profits over the shortest possible time. The ICT that is available on the market provides many ways to help salespeople deliver a better service to customers. By using ICT salespeople empower themselves to deliver the required service to their customers on time.

THE IMPORTANCE OF ICT IN PERSONAL SELLING

Personal selling is shifting from a focus on influencing the client to managing the buyer-seller relationships. The traditional approach to selling has been replaced by the consultative approach, which is based on building relations with the client. Accurate communication is important in building relationships, and the new technology like email is fast, interactive and accurate. It can deliver the simplest message or the most complicated suggestion for speeding up the sales cycle. While the new developments in technology at the beginning of the 21st century often led to pessimistic speculations, the current wave of developments is generally viewed in a positive light. Sales representatives who do not keep in touch with their clients on a regular basis lose sales and income in the fast tempo of the modern world market.[1]

Selling-based technology applications will become an active part of the buyer-seller interaction in the future.[2] Technology must be viewed as a method of increasing productivity and as a solution to problems faced by sales managers. It is critically important that salespeople in business-to-business selling use the correct technology to build long-term relations with clients, because the technology influences the client-supplier relationship.[3] Organisations must make ICT part of their strategy to deliver a better service to their clients. They must make electronic catalogues available and carry out direct sales via the Internet.

The acceptance of technology-based systems by organisations can intimidate salespeople and these systems must not become the focal point in sales training. The focal point must be to train the salespeople to apply the advanced technology effectively in their profession.[4] The technology must be viewed as a range of instruments that can assist salespeople to concentrate on solving clients' problems; in other words, to deliver a service. The capacity and mobility of technology improves and changes continuously. More and more software is being developed to assist salespeople in managing their clients. The improvement in audiovisual technology has made presentations more interesting, and integrated telemarketing systems have enabled salespeople to do more business over the telephone.[5]

ICT must be available to salespeople to enable them to stay in contact with their clients. Salespeople must be trained to use the technology in order to solve clients' problems and to service them. Nobody can afford to be technologically uneducated. Managers must see to it that their sales force is up to date with new technologies. The sales managers must understand each salesperson's skills, fears and anxieties in order to be able to assist them to gain confidence that the technology will help them to do their job more effectively.[6]

In the 21st century the key to sales victories will be preparedness and access to answers, creativity, value and speed.[7] This implies that salespeople must have the following technology at their disposal, namely:

- High-speed online access at home and a good computer
- Their own email address and website
- The ability to contact clients and prospects by email
- Access to email wherever they are
- A cellphone (for calling, SMSs or voice mail)
- A pager
- A palmtop computer or a personal organiser
- A laptop computer
- CD-ROM

ICT affects the way salespeople do business today. Whatever technology salespeople use, they all benefit from the advances in the communication media. Developments in ICT have had the following major effects on the selling profession:

- Salespeople have access through their portable computers to the latest information on price, availability and order status.
- Salespeople use email to speed up communication and to store phone-in messages.
- Salespeople use word-processing and spreadsheet software to customise their sales letters, call reports, quotas and proposals.
- Salespeople use time management software to plan daily activities and schedule calls.
- Salespeople keep database files on prospects and customers for pre-calling and planning.
- Salespeople use telemarketing software to enhance call productivity.
- Salespeople make use of mobile phones to manage their time productively.

Salespeople will have to be supplied with the technology to be able to do their job. In the section that follows, the application of ICT in selling will be briefly discussed.

THE APPLICATION OF ICT IN PERSONAL SELLING
Introduction

An article on online shopping states the following:[8] 'If you're in the business of selling, you have no choice but to be in the business of electronic communications'. In the past the salesperson usually maintained customer contact through face-to-face meetings and phone calls. Now, the range of contact options has expended to include fax and email, the Internet and the World Wide Web, laptops, palmtops and sophisticated contact management software. There are a few points that should be noted concerning the use of technology in managing client relationships. Firstly, technology that is geared to increase the performance of professional salespeople is today readily accessible and affordable by many organisations. Secondly, cellphones and hands-free vehicle equipment assure mobility and comfort. With this go voicemail, faxing and notebook computers. Lastly, electronic communication technology opens doors for the way in which business will be conducted in the future.

With the introduction of the personal computer in the late 1980s, the way in which business was conducted began to change. In the future, sales techniques will have to improve as the salesperson adapts to the continually changing environment. Major changes have already taken place in the marketing of many products. Today's buying and selling processes involve many people at different levels of the organisation. Technology has increased productivity and has brought about client confidence. Retailers tend more and more to base sales, turnover and profits on computerised calculations, therefore the salesperson must have access to every piece of information about the retailer's purchasing needs, and so must be in possession of the necessary ICT.

Software for computers

It is the software packages (better known as computer programs) that drive the computer. Because salespeople have a wide range of needs, there are various software packages that apply to selling and marketing available on the market. These software packages are known as contact or relationship software. Such software is focused on giving salespeople support in building better relationships with their clients.[9] Because salespeople have a wide range of database management needs, a wide range of software packages is available for purchase. Another option is that businesses can have their programs tailor-made by appointing a programmer to write one that fits in with their specific needs.[10]

It is compulsory in selling to keep customer records. This is to ensure that sales representatives stay informed about their customers' needs. The customer record database must contain all the information the sales representatives have collected about their clients. It is especially important to keep a database in one-to-one marketing and in other circumstances where the salesperson must identify clients, differentiate clients, interact with clients and fit the product to the needs of the clients. Database management is important not only to personal selling but also to electronic marketing. It is necessary for organisations to have software packages that can generate leads, analyse clients, give credit information, support databases and process data.[11]

ICT offers the advantage of making great amounts of information available for decision making, and of automating processes that increase operational effectiveness. Before salespeople visit clients they must work through the database to put themselves in touch with the clients' needs. Many of the software packages available are especially developed for salespeople and most of them are compatible with IBM (International Business Machines) technology.

A modern sales office is likely to have a PC on every sales desk for personal productivity applications. These days, even laptop or notebook computers no bigger than an A4 pad can be very powerful. The latest addition to portable computers is the palmtop. The individual PC can be linked to a local area network or a wide area network (involving telecommunications over long distances) served by a central file server where company information is stored, or it can even be connected remotely to the Internet.[12] The software that is used with the hardware to drive the system provides a total integrated communications network.

The main components of integrated software packages and their uses are as follows:

- *Word-processing packages*. These handle text and are used for sales proposals, letters and reports.
- *Spreadsheets*. These handle numbers and are used to track sales revenues, for monthly sales reports, and to calculate commission and expenses.
- *Databases*. These store and manage information, and are used for customer records, product information and notes.
- *Communications packages*. If the computer has a suitable fax card, the salesperson can generate fax messages on the word processor and send them to fax addresses direct from the computer.
- *Presentation software*. This is used to generate professional presentations. These can be printed on acetate sheets for use with an overhead projector, or stored in a file for presentation directly from the laptop computer, which can be used with a projector that is capable of receiving a digital signal to project the slides onto a normal full-size projection screen.
- *Email.* This is used to communicate with clients via the Internet or with co-workers via the intranet by sending letters, proposals, etc. in electronic format.

Software packages are an integral part of computers (hardware). In the next section, the various forms of ICT that are available will be discussed.

Personal computers

Personal computers (PCs) are standard equipment for salespeople, who can use them in two ways. Firstly, the PC can be linked to a network that is served by a central file server that services all the representatives in the organisation. Alternatively, it can be used as a separate unit to which only the salesperson has access. The latter alternative is not effective and economical because the PC is not linked to the organisations' database. Most organisations use networks because these link all the PCs to one central database where all the information is available to the sales manager and to the sales representatives. This is done to ensure that all staff utilise the same source of information so that the organisation can function effectively.

The PC is used in selling to keep and update clients' and prospects' records on the database, to manage their stock levels and to monitor competitors. The PC enables sales representatives to save product information and specifications, plan routes, schedule appointments, write sales reports and keep a record of expenses. The PC also serves as support for the sales manager in managing the sales team.[13] Word processing is important because most sales representatives need to communicate with their customers in writing. The follow-up letter plays an important role in building customer relations. The writing of a letter is sometimes postponed because the sales representative must attend to other matters. The word processor enables the salesperson to write, print and post a letter within a few minutes. Sales representatives use PCs to perform the following tasks:[14]

- To access order forms and instructions
- To view and update critical sales information
- To contact management and perform other sales-related functions
- For inventory control
- For call reports
- For follow-up activities
- For order filling and shipping
- For service requests
- For data mining
- For credit approval

The PC is static and not mobile. The mobile ICT applications will be discussed next.

Portable computers

Portable computers are also referred to as mobile computers. They allow sales representatives to take their computers with them on sales calls. This means that they are available at all times and can be used as tools in selling. The mobile computers that are most frequently used by salespeople are as follows:

Handheld computers

The first application of computers in the selling field was to collect order entry data at retail level.[15] A wand or magnetic pen was used to read the product codes off shelf labels or order books. This model had only a one-way communication function, i.e. it transmitted information directly to headquarters by connecting the computer to a phone by means of an acoustic coupler. The orders placed with the salesperson were then transmitted from the client to the wholesaler to ensure that they would be delivered the next day. The advantages of the handheld computer were as follows:

■ It was faster than other systems where the orders have to be written out by hand, sent by post, or placed over the phone.
■ The magnetic pen eliminated mistakes that may occur when the product code had to be punched in by hand.
■ It reduced postage fees, telephone call costs and data-processing costs.
■ It enabled the representative to spend more time with clients.

Although the handheld computer made the representative's task easier, the fact that communication took place in only one direction – from the client to the organisation – was a disadvantage. This type of handheld computer has been replaced by modern technology such as palmtop and notebook computers.

Notebook computers

Mobile or portable computers are divided into two categories, namely notebook and palmtop computers. When notebook computers were first introduced, many organisations bought them to enable their representatives to function more productively and effectively in order to better satisfy the needs of their customers and build long-term relationships.

The PC of a few years ago has now become the notebook computer. Manufacturers have equipped the latest notebook computers with portholes and other accessories to enable salespeople to become even more mobile and to transfer information from the portable computer to their PC at the office.[16]

Notebook computers are used for the same purposes as PCs because the software is compatible. The notebook offers the same advantages as the PC, as well as a few additional ones:[17]

■ It gives salespeople mobility.
■ It ensures better communication between salespeople and office staff.
■ Salespeople can calculate financial options while busy with the client, and close the sale faster and more easily.
■ Reports can be completed faster while the salesperson is waiting for an appointment or during lunch hour.
■ It enables salespeople to spend less time at the office and more on the road.
■ It increases productivity because the salesperson has access to the client's database, diary and time schedules at any place and time.

- It reduces the need for salespeople to go to the office, and allows them to spend more time with the clients.
- It can be used effectively when integrated with PDAs (personal digital assistants), the Internet and cellphones. This is made possible by using the new technology known as WAP (wireless application protocol).

The purposes that portable computers are used for mean that the software for notebooks is not always the same as that used on the PC at the office. The following software modules can be found on the salesperson's notebook:[18]
- Leads management
- Contact management
- Diary and appointments
- Local marketing (promotion objectives)
- Fact searches
- Needs analysis
- Quotations and illustrations
- Sales aids
- Applicable forms

The latest technologies for portable computers that support the WAP technology are the electronic pen and the touch screen. These wireless selling-point technologies enable the salesperson to establish the availability of stock, organise the execution of the order, and complete the order forms and sales documents without any paperwork while busy with the client. The reliability, durability, service and support that laptop and notebook computers offer salespeople mean that these types of computers are becoming more and more popular, and explain why more and more organisations have started to use them in selling.

Palmtop computers

Palmtop computers are one of the latest additions to the range of portable computers. They have become a reality due to pharmaceutical sales representatives' need for mobility. Palmtops can be held in the pharmaceutical sales representative's palm, and fit into the inside pocket of a jacket. Although the palmtop computer is small, it is powerful. It has a colour screen and can capture data written onto the screen by handwriting recognition or typed in using the keyboard. Some models have a fold-up keyboard and others are equipped with ports and a battery charger station.[19]

The palmtop computer was originally designed to extend the application of personal and notebook computers. It allows sales representatives to carry the most important information that they may need along with them – such information includes details about the clients, contacts, calculation formulas, etc. The palmtop computer allows sales representatives to work away from office for a whole day, and at the end of the day they can synchronise any new information with their personal or notebook computer. The palmtop computer is not a personal organiser, because it has software that makes it possible to synchronise data with email and other software such as Outlook, Lotus Notes and Eudora Mail. It also integrates with Windows and NT. By using a Compact Flash Slot the memory of the palmtop computer can be expanded to 20 or 40 megabytes.

The palmtop computer also integrates with other electronic equipment such as computers, modems, printers and cellphones. It also makes use of WAP technology. If you look at functions of cellphones and palmtop computers then you will notice that cellphones are adapting to data-capturing functions while palmtop computers are adapting to communication functions.[20] Palmtops enable sales representatives to extract data so that they can be more productive, plan better, and even write their reports during sales calls. Using cellphones to download information is expensive, and the majority of representatives use landlines for this.

Every palmtop has different menus or screens. The menus work on a pick list, which is a list of potential clients that sales representatives can call on. Representatives can select the clients they want to talk to, and then the product they want to talk about. All this is done electronically. Palmtops also have calendar and personal planner functions which sales representatives can use to do their daily planning.

Electronic personal organisers

The electronic personal organiser has become a necessity for salespeople. Many salespeople replace their diaries and address books with personal organisers as the primary instrument for scheduling their activities and planning their time.[21] Names, addresses and phone numbers are stored in the organiser and are accessed by entering a code or the first three letters of a name. The personal organiser can also be used as a time monitor. It can warn the salesperson by emitting a signal, normally a beep, if he or she is spending more time with a client than planned. Thus electronic personal organisers are of great help when it comes to time management.

TELECOMMUNICATION TECHNOLOGY
Fax machines

Faxing is the process of transmitting text or graphic communications over telephone lines between two or more fax machines. These machines look like small photocopiers with a telephone attached. Faxing takes communication one step further because it enables salespeople to send and receive documents in seconds by using a standard telephone (analogue) or a cellphone (digital).[22]

The fax machine function is also available on computers in the form of a special built-in card and a fax modem, which can transmit information to other computers or fax machines via phone cables or WAP technology. Notebook computers equipped with a fax modem enable sales representatives to send faxes when on the road. When they are in their sales territory, they can use portable fax machines to send visit reports, orders, expense statements and other documents to the sales office or headquarters. Salespeople may even use a fax machine as a substitute for sales calls. The fax machine is still used to communicate with clients, especially in cases where the client requires a document. In such cases it is still cheaper to use a fax machine than to use the normal postal service.

The telephone

The telephone, through all the years of its existence, has played an important role in selling. Sales representatives still use the telephone when they are at the office to follow up on leads, make appointments, answer enquiries and service their clients. They can use the telephone for prospecting and qualifying, contacting inactive accounts, making appointments, reaching distant or small customers, making the sale and follow-up. The telephone allows clients to place orders themselves in cases where the salesperson is not needed to add value in the face-to-face contact sales situation.[23]

One of the most important ways in which telephone technology is currently used is in call centres.[24] Call centres are becoming a big business as consumers move into the telephone era. Any service-orientated company that offers a service with a toll-free 0800 number handles between one and 10 000 calls a day.[25] The information captured at the call centre is also available on the organisation's database for use by the sales representatives.

The telephone is also used to generate and qualify sales leads as prospects. The telemarketing staff carry out four functions in supporting the salespeople in the field: they supply support in general, they take orders, they deliver client services and they assist with the management of accounts. Because the new technology enables salespeople to be highly mobile, analogue telephones are not utilised much nowadays. Today's preference is for cellphones.

Cellphones

Since the introduction of the cellphone in South Africa in 1994 South African businesses have underrated the value of the digital telephone. Cellphones, audiovisual aids and other electronic technology can give organisations the competitive edge if they are utilised effectively and integrated with Internet technology.[26]

It is estimated that by the year 2005 there will be a billion cellphones in use worldwide, and a vast proportion of these will be equipped with multimedia functions.[27] WAP creates a direct link between cellphones and the Internet. WAP-based services are becoming an integral part of communications technology for one simple reason – freedom. This freedom includes freedom of time and place; freedom of choice; 'do on the move'; and 'know on the go'. WAP technology gives the salesperson the freedom to move, use time more efficiently and achieve more. It is changing the whole idea of mobility in the selling world. It is redefining the meaning of service and creating new and closer relationships between the salesperson and the clients. The cellphone has many applications:[28]

- It can be used for accessing information on the Internet.
- It can be used as a dictionary to help with spelling when typing messages, and to make the messages more understandable.
- It has improved memory capacity, allowing the storage of up to 500 messages.
- It has a calendar that enables the user to check appointments by day, week or month.

Most cellphones have built-in hardware modems that can connect to portable computers by infrared, thus eliminating all cables. The addition of these new applications makes the cellphone a powerful instrument. It assists sales representatives to access data much more quickly, and enables them to function more productively.

Voicemail

Voicemail is the term used to describe a variety of methods of sending or receiving voice messages from simple answering machines to complex computer mailboxes. Voicemail requires only a phone call to a computer that receives the message and stores it for further use. It integrates voice and digital technology, and allows a one-way communication where two-way communication is not needed.[29]

Voicemail enables sales representatives to stay in contact with the support staff at the office, to keep distributors informed about the availability of products and delivery times, and to carry out other telephonic communications that can be time consuming when it is necessary to talk to each individual. The system enables sales representatives to phone the office to find out if there are other messages that they must attend to. It increases the efficiency of sales representatives and offers them the following advantages:[30]

- All calls become productive because the other party will always be reached.
- Messages can be sent to different people at the same time.
- There is better communication between the sales manager and the sales representatives.

Voicemail is one of the greatest irritations for salespeople but the irritation can be overcome if they accept that voicemail is a response to their phone calls, that they only have to prepare a 30-second voicemail message before each phone call, that the message must influence the client, that it must identify a need, and it must be followed up with a fax or phone call. Voicemail offers the sales representatives the advantage of being able to communicate with staff members at the office and also with their clients. It gives them the opportunity to inform the clients beforehand.

Email

Email is the transmission of electronic messages via a modem between two or more computers that are linked to a network. In many organisations email has replaced the telephone as the primary method of communication. Organisations are using this method of communication more and more when sending short messages to their employees. Email allows the sales representatives to communicate with their clients by way of typing a message on the computer and sending it via a telephone, cable or satellite to an email address, which can be anywhere in the world.[31] It enables the sales representative to write messages at any time of day and to send them from the client's office or from a hotel room at night.

A brief email message can be used to update the manager. The following guidelines should be noted when using email as a selling tool:[32]

- Check the inbox regularly for new incoming emails.
- Email is a handy instrument for tracing leads but a poor one for closing the sale.
- Use email to create awareness by launching a direct email sales campaign.
- React immediately to leads received.
- Handle complaints received by using email rather than the telephone.
- If the prospect asks for a proposal, send it by email, even if it is complex.

Email is just as quick as a phone call and because the message is in writing it can be read again and again if necessary. Emailing also reduces the organisation's mailing costs. If used correctly, it can speed up the sales transaction.

The Internet

There is a direct relationship between clients' use of the Internet and the Internet knowledge of the sales force.[33] The Internet is a worldwide self-managed network that is linked to thousands of smaller networks and millions of computers and people to provide a mega-source of information. Legal questions regarding Internet transactions, however, have still not been fully worked out. Like the telephone system, the Internet reaches all the countries in the world. It provides sales representatives with access to research, data, people and mega-sources of information. Organisations spend a lot of money on hardware, software and training salespeople to use the Internet. If they are trained to use the Internet to its full capacity, it can be a powerful selling tool.

Salespeople should not regard the Internet as a threat to their job. They must avoid a commodity mentality (i.e. the notion that what you sell is no better or no worse than anyone else's product, and there is no inherent value in doing business with you[34]), get on the customer's side of the table and stay there, be known for what they know, and make sure that their company has a customer-friendly website. The Internet is an integral part of marketing and but must not be viewed as the only instrument of marketing. The focus must be on the clients – the Internet must be used to service the clients better. The Internet and e-commerce add new dimensions to the selling process. In some cases the salesperson is not required any more because even client services are fully automated. The Internet can be used as a competitive instrument in a changing environment.

Salespeople must be able to trace prospects and clients on the Internet. Purchasing information and data tracing form part of a good website. Salespeople and marketers must be aware that clients' behaviour changes when sales and marketing take place on the Internet. They must become familiar with the Internet as a means of advertising and promotion, tracing leads and selling directly. Interaction and contact with clients is important in Internet selling and e-commerce. The organisation must first change the salesperson's attitude toward the use and applications of technology by doing the following:[35]

- *Re-designing the sales process and introducing the software to clients* that open new accounts. It should not be an extra duty that the salesperson must perform.
- *Educating sales representatives about Web capabilities.* This is so that they can help their clients who ask about services on the Internet.
- *Presenting use of the Web as a win–win activity.* Salespeople may think that the Internet is a threat to them, but they should rather view it as a means of achieving a win–win situation for them and their clients. By referring their clients to the Internet for information and service requests, salespeople can concentrate on their income objectives.
- *Sharing the rewards.* Sales representatives will be much more likely to proactively recruit customers if they stand to gain financially from doing so. Costs can be reduced and both parties can benefit from this.

The sales force must not view the Internet and the website as threats to their job. They must know how to use them to search for data and information required, and use them as means of advertising and promotion, tracing leads and selling directly. The sales representatives must be aware that clients' behaviour changes when sales and marketing take place on the Internet. If the representatives are trained to use the Internet to its full capacity it can become a powerful selling tool.

Digital video discs

A digital video disc (DVD) is the same size as a CD-ROM (compact disc – read only memory) but has eight times more storage capacity. It enables the customer to see the product under different conditions and to actually interact with the program to see the benefits of the product first-hand.[36] All the information about the product that the representative must convey to the client is put on a DVD in a presentation format by the marketing people. They use sound, illustrations, pictures, animation and colour to inform the user about the product. The DVD can be run on a personal computer that is fitted with a DVD player. This technology enables the professional sales representative to give the client the whole presentation on DVD or only certain selected parts of it.

Marketing information systems

The marketing information system (MIS) forms an integral part of the management information system within an organisation. A marketing information system consists of people and equipment, and procedures for gathering, sorting, analysing and evaluating needed, timely and accurate information, and distributing it to marketing decision makers. The marketing information system is developed from internal company records, marketing intelligence activities, marketing research and marketing decision support analysis. Several of the electronic communication and information technologies that have been discussed so far can be linked to the management information system.[37]

An organisation needs information to learn about the environment. The information guides the management in its organisational decisions and actions even if the employees of the organisation change. It helps management to carry out their current functions better. On the other hand, the salespeople provide information that affects the management's strategic decision making. Because the sales representatives are in constant contact with the marketplace, they play an important role in information acquisition.

By analysing the internal reports on orders, sales, prices, costs, inventory levels and so on, management can spot opportunities and threats. All the information gathered is organised in databases such as consumer databases, product databases, salesperson databases and any other databases they require to make decisions. The discussion in this chapter has made it clear that sales representatives can be reached anywhere, no matter where they are, therefore ICT may have an influence on the sales representative's selling task.

NEW TECHNOLOGY DEVELOPMENTS IN SELLING

The integration of the various ICT applications that businesses use to conduct business into a management information system network has opened up a new field in selling, namely SFA (sales force automation).[38] *Sales force automation* is the term for those technologies that are used to improve communication in a sales organisation and to enhance customer responsiveness. These activities are used to improve the productivity of the sales force and the sales support personnel. Repwise and Wisdomware are software packages that interface with an organisation's management information system or enterprise resource planning (ERP) system. They are knowledge based and consist of an online collection of information that includes manuals, sales literature, pricelists and product information that can be divided into four categories, namely (1) key business issues facing the client; (2) how the company can meet the client's needs; (3) competitors' products; and (4) sales presentations that are effective for specific clients.[39] They can assist sales representatives to access information that is up to date via the technology that they use, at any place and at any time, as needed.

A further development is the mobile office. A mobile office is a vehicle equipped with the electronic communication and information technology that salespeople use to do their job. During the next five years, the four main components of e-commerce will be the personal computer, the cellphone, the television set and the car. The Ford Motor Company and other vehicle manufacturers have developed the concept of a mobile office built into their vehicles. In the year 2000 car manufacturers began converting their products into mobile electronic offices. In the new century they are going to make advanced communication technology available to millions of their customers by building it into their products. Vehicles will be equipped with Internet ports, an email facility that can read messages to passengers, and mobile communication and navigation systems. Everything will be voice controlled, even the dialling of phone numbers, with links to the laptop.[40]

TECHNOLOGY ETIQUETTE

The application of technology in selling also creates questions in the minds of salespeople who want to avoid violating the rules of good etiquette. Salespeople need to be aware of the etiquette that comes with the use of technologies to communicate in selling. When dealing with different cultures in selling it is important to apply proper etiquette, because people can view you as a person with bad manners.

Etiquette on the Internet is called 'netiquette' and it is based on the golden rule that you should do unto others as you would have them do unto you. There are certain things that salespeople should and should not do when they send email.[41]

Do the following:
- Respond as quickly as possible.
- Keep it short.
- Be polite and avoid flaming, i.e. sending an abusive email.
- Use the same principles as in writing business letters.

Do *not* do the following:
- Use email to convey sensitive information.
- Send repeat messages.
- Use capital letters: this is the equivalent of shouting.
- Send offensive content.
- Send the same message to a long distribution list.

When using a cellphone, salespeople should heed the following:
- Check your mailbox regularly for mail and voicemail.
- Switch off your cellphone (or the sound) when in meetings and seminars or with a customer, or switch to vibrate mode when in places where you can take a call but do not want to disturb others.

- Do not talk loudly on the phone when in a customer's reception area. Rather speak in a lower-than-normal voice.
- Be sensitive to other people's needs and comfort, and respect the personal space of other people.
- Make sure that there will be enough distance to keep the conversation private.
- Notify customers at the commencement of the meeting that an important call is expected and get their okay to take it.

Salespeople should avoid the following at any given time while with customers:
- Talking too loudly on the cellphone while outside customers' office
- Holding inappropriate conversations when with customers
- Rudely interrupting conversations with customers by answering the cellphone
- Checking for messages and missed calls while with customers
- Typing an SMS while talking to a customer
- Setting the cellphone on loud and/or annoying ring tones
- Talking where you may bother others or need confidentiality
- Holding conversations in public locations to discuss confidential business
- Taking an incoming call right in the middle of a transaction, proposal or meeting

Kate Zabriskie[42] refers to taking a call when in a meeting as follows:

> As the old saying goes, just because something can be done doesn't mean that it should be done. Whether you have called it yourself or are merely attending at someone's request, invitation, or order, a scheduled meeting is not the time for cell phone calls. The rings alone are intrusive; answering them is an even worse breach of etiquette. The message received by those at the meeting is that they are less important than the disembodied voice coming through the cell. Unless your intention is to make others feel insignificant (definitely not a cool move if your boss is waiting for you to get off the phone), then don't answer, turn it off, and get it out of sight.

When using voicemail, salespeople must heed the following:
- Update regularly and check for messages.
- If possible, inform your callers when you are on vacation or out of town.
- When leaving a message, state your full name, date and time of your call.
- Check your messages as often as possible and return all calls within two hours.

When using the fax machine always include a cover page with your fax number, your company's name, your name, the number of pages and your phone number on it. Apply the same principles as you would for any business letter when writing the fax, and check your grammar and use of language before sending it.

SUMMARY

ICT has become part of our lives, just like the telephone, radio and television. With the introduction of the personal computer in the late 1980s, the way in which business was conducted started to change. There are many ICT applications available on the market that can be applied to businesses. It is possible to buy software packages known as contact or relationship software which focus on assisting salespeople to build better relationships with their clients. However, many companies use tailor-made packages. The integrated software packages that are used most are word-processing packages, spreadsheets, databases, communications packages, presentation software and email.

Personal computers, portable computers such as handheld computers, palmtop computers, notebook computers, laptops and personal electronic organisers are widely used by business people to carry out various tasks. These electronic devices have different features that can be used in different situations. Salespeople will not all use the same technologies – the sales task will determine the type of technologies they use.

A variety of telecommunication technologies is used, such as fax machines, standard telephones and cellphones. Other electronic technology such as email, voicemail, the Internet and the intranet are widely used in selling. Salespeople must be aware of what types of technology are available to assist them to be more productive and to ease their workload.

ICT is developing so fast that it is becoming hard to keep track of. It is important that sales representatives keep up with the latest developments and trends when it comes to the applications of electronic technologies in selling. Sales force automation and the mobile office are a reality, and therefore salespeople must learn to use these new developments to their personal benefit and to that of their company and their customers.

Finally, the sales representative must be aware of communications etiquette and practise it when using ICT to communicate with customers.

CASE STUDY

Family Foods

Ivan Chauke, a senior sales representative working for Family Foods, is responsible for calling on clients in Mpumalanga and Limpopo province. His routes include several cities and towns (the number of clients is indicated in brackets after each city or town): these cities and towns are Bronkhorstspruit (2), Witbank (15), Middelburg (3), Belfast (1), Machadodorp (1), Kaapmuiden (1), Barberton (2), Nelspruit (10), Malelane (1), Komatipoort (1), White River (1), Hazyview (1), Sabie (2), Lydenburg (3), Hoedspruit (1), Phalaborwa (3), Tzaneen (3), Polokwane (6), Makhado (2), Musina (1), Potgietersrus (2), Naboomspruit (1), Nylstroom (2), and Bela Bela (2). The head office of Family Foods is situated in Ceres in the Western Cape, and every ⤴

Friday he must report to the regional office in Tshwane. The regional sales manager expects the representatives to make phone calls daily and report to him personally, but they still have to file weekly sales reports on Fridays. All the representatives have been issued with a laptop equipped with portholes and other accessories to enable them to become more mobile and to transfer information from the portable computer to their personal computers at the office. The laptops have a database that contains only the sales records of the representative's clients, and the product's price lists and discounts.

Ivan quickly learned that the technology is geared to increase his performance and that cellphones and hands-free vehicle equipment ensure mobility and comfort. He also realised that ICT could change the way in which business was conducted. Back at the office, he discussed the use of ICT with the other representatives, who agreed with him that they could integrate the laptops with other technologies to become more productive so that they could manage themselves and their clients better. During the sales meeting the matter was discussed, and a decision was taken to approach a consultant for advice and recommendations.

Question

You are a sales management consultant, and have been contracted to advise Family Foods on which technologies will suit them best and how these technologies can be integrated to increase productivity. Motivate your recommendations and give examples of how they can be implemented.

SELF-ASSESSMENT QUESTIONS

1. Why is ICT important to personal selling?

2. What forms of ICT must salespeople have at their disposal in order to be efficient?

3. What major influences does ICT have on the selling profession?

4. What are the main components of integrated software packages, and what are their uses?

5. What do sales representatives use personal computers for?

6. What are the advantages of portable computers?

7. What software can be found on a salesperson's notebook?

8. For what purposes can sales representatives use cellphones?

9. What is the purpose of a marketing information system?

10. What is a mobile office?

DISCUSSION QUESTIONS AND TOPICS

1. Discuss the use of voicemail by sales representatives.

2. 'It is critically important that salespeople in business-to-business selling should use the correct technology to build long-term relations with clients, because the technology influences the client–supplier relationship.' Discuss this statement.

3. Discuss the development of technology in selling.

4. Write a brief report on the application of technology in selling.

5. Discuss the use of the Internet in selling.

6. Discuss the use of email in selling.

7. Discuss the use of DVDs in selling.

NOTES

1. Lee, K. 2000. How your sales force can sell via email. *Denver Business Journal,* 7 April 2000, 51(i34):19B. Available at: http//web7.infotrac.lond.../purl=rc1_GBIM_0_A61760450&dyn=31!arfmt?sw_aep=tp_it (accessed on 10 April 2000).

2. Keillor, B.D., Bashaw, R.E. & Pettijohn, C.E. 1997. Sales force automation issues prior to implementation: The relationship between attitudes toward technology, experience and productivity *Journal of Business & Industrial Marketing,* 12(3–4): 209–220. Available at: http//web7.../purl=rc1_GBIM_0_A20057206&dyn=3!xrn_2_0_A20057206? swaep =tp_it (accessed on 10 April 2000).

3. Han, Sang-Lin. 1997. A conceptual framework of the impact of technology on customer-supplier relationships. *Journal of Business & Industrial Marketing,* 12(1): 22–32. Available at: http://clorinda.emerald-library.com/vl= 5689686/cl=26/nw=1/rpsv/cw/mcb/0885.../p22.html (accessed on 15 October 2001).

4. Haler, C. & Palmer, G. 1999. Putting technology to work in managing customer relationships. *The SA Journal of Marketing & Sales,* 5(4): 30–31.

5. Cooper, S. 1997. *Selling – Principles, Practice and Management.* Johannesburg: Pitman, p. 247.

6. Strout, E. 2000. Are your salespeople tech savvy? *Sales & Marketing Management,* July, 152(7): 109. Available at: http//web7.infotrac.lond.../purl=rc1_GBIM_0_A63668025&dyn=13!ar_fmt?sw_aep=tp it (accessed on 10 April 2000).

7. Gitomer, J. 2000. Salesman of tomorrow, or lost in yesterday? *Dallas Business Journal,* 18, 23 February, 26: 48. Available at: http://web3.infotrac.lo.../purl=rcl_GBIM_0_A65022828&dyn=4!arfmt?sw_aep=tp_it (accessed on 8 February 2001).

8. Palmer, P. 1998. On-line shopping: Will cybermalls reshape the retail industry? *The SA Journal of Marketing & Sales,* 4(5): 3–6.

9. Rix, P., Buss, J. & Herford, G. 1999. Selling: A Consultative Approach. (Second edition). Sydney: McGraw-Hill, p. 411.

10. Manning, G.L. & Reece, B.L. 1998. Selling Today: Building Quality Partnerships. (Seventh edition). New Jersey: Prentice Hall, p. 176.

11. Greenspan, R. 2000. Database marketing power. *E-Commerce Guide,* 1 August, pp. 1–3. Available at: http://ecommerce.internet.com/solutions/ectips/article/0,1467,6311_427591,00.html (accessed on 3 April 2000).

12. Allen, P. & Wootten, G. 1998. Selling. (Fifth edition). London: Pitman, pp. 260–261.

13. Quigg, B. & Wisner, B. 1998. *Selling the Right Way.* New Jersey: Prentice Hall, p. 14.

14. AvantGo Delivers Mobile Sales Application – Brief Article – Product Announcement. [Online]. Available at: http://www.findarticles.com/p/articles/mi_mOIGV/is_9_3/ai_78974912/print (accessed on 10 November 2004).

    Greene, C.L. 2003. *Selling Business 2000.* Melbourne: South-Western Thompson Learning, pp. 25–40.

    Pickering, C. 2003. *Sales Data in Motion.* [Online]. Available at: http://www.the manufacturer.com/content_print.html?header=article&contants_id=11 (accessed on 10 November 2004).

15. Soldow, G.F. & Thomas, G.P 1991. *Professional Selling – An Interpersonal Perspective.* New York: Macmillan, p. 408.

16. Baily, S. 1999. New generation notebooks – A mobile man's best friend! *Smart Office Computing,* September/October, pp. 14–23.

17. Haggard, B. 2000. The mobile office – notebooks, cellular phones and PDAs. *Business Technology,* 5(1): 8–14.

18. O'Connor, J. & Galvin, E. 1997. *Marketing and Information Technology – The Strategy, Application and Implementation of IT in Marketing.* London: Pitman, pp. 241–242.

19. *Business Technology.* 1999(a). An office in your hand. August, 4(7): 62–63.

20. Machenheimer, S. 1999. Colour palmtops stealing the limelight. *Smart Office Computing,* September/October, p. 37.

21. Rix et al., op. cit, pp. 404–410.

22. Manning & Reece, op. cit., pp. 347–348.

23. Coppet, J.I. & Staples, W.A. 1994. *Professional Selling: A Relationship Management Process.* Cincinnati: South-Western, p. 490.

24. Holgate, P. 1998. The business benefits of customers' interaction centres. *The SA Journal of Marketing & Sales,* 4(3):19.

25. Anon. 1999. *Finansies en Tegniek,* Bylae: Aftelling. 3(4) July: Bylae: Antwoordsentrums – die sleutel tot bestuur van kliëntediens, pp. 46–48.

26. *Sake-Rapport.* 1999. Met selfoon word alles geïntegreer. 10 October, p. 7.

27. Pekin, G. 2000. The mobile information society. *Business Technology,* March, 5(2): 36–38.

28. *Business Technology.* 1999d. Dual band and WAP hits South Africa. August, 4(7): 57.

29. Quigg & Wisner, op. cit., p. 15.

30. Manning & Reece, op. cit., p. 347.

31. Futrell, op. cit., pp. 171–172.

32. Lee, op. cit., p. 19B.

33. Keltner, B. 2000. How to move customers online. Sales & Marketing Management, 152(i3): 27. Available at: http//web7.infotrac.londo…/purl=rc1_GBM_0_A60116881&dyn=37!ar_fmt?sw_ aep=tp_it (accessed on 10 August 2000).

34. Graham, J.R. 2001. Making a winning presentation, or How to think like a listener. American Salesman, October. 46(10): 14. Available at: http://infotrac.london.g…/purl=rcl_GBIM_0_ A78738997&dyn=43!arfmt?sw_ aep=tp it (accessed on 27 November 2001).

35. Keltner, op. cit., p. 27.

36. Mondy R.W, Premeaux, S.R. & Young, J.R. 1998. Personal Selling – Function, Theory and Practice. (Fourth edition). Houston: Dame Publications Inc., pp. 286–287.

37. Kotler, P. 2003. Marketing Management. (Eleventh edition). New Jersey: Prentice Hall. pp. 123–124.

38. Stones, L. 2000. Sales force automation tools – the Holy Grail of customer service. Business Technology, 3 April, 5: 20–24.

39. Schmonsees, B. 1999. Has a tool for better sales. Wall Street Journal, 26 March, pp. A1, A5.

40. Van Rensburg, B. 2000. Jou voertuig – 'n mobiele kantoor. Beeld, 14 February, p. 15.

41. Alexander, A. 2003. Managing gadgets: a quick-hit guide – Workplace Technology – etiquette – Column. [Online] Available at: http//www.findarticles.com/p/articles/mi_ m5012/is1521/ai 99848538/print (accessed on 9 November 2004).

Chatfield-Taylor, C. 2001. Privacy, please – Ethics demand that access to attendees isn't abused. Corbin Ball Associates. [Online] Available at: http://www.corniball.com/articles_emarketing/index.cfm?fuseaction=cor_ArticleView&artID=413&sectionCode=art_email

EarthVision Cellulars. 2003. Cellular Phone Etiquette. [Online]. Available at: http://www.cellularphonenews.com/etiquette.htm (accessed on 9 November 2004).

E-mail Etiquette. 2001. [Online]. Available at: http://www.corniball.com/articles_emarketing/index.cfm?fuseaction=cor_ArticleView&artID=415&sectionCode=art_mail (accessed on 9 November 2004).

Gitomer, J. Cellphone ownership includes rules of etiquette. [Online]. Available at: http://louiseville/stories/2000/02/07/smallb4html (accessed on 9 November 2004).

Knowledge Base. 2004. [Online]. Available from: http://knowledgebase.laworks.org/etiquette/email.asp (accessed on 9 November 2004).

Martin, J.A. 2000. Test your e-mail etiquette. PC WORLD.COM. [Online] 28 September. Available from: http://archives.cnn.com/2000/TECH/computing?09/28/email.manners.idg/ (accessed on 9 November 2004).

Spring, T 1999. The ten commandments of e-mail. PC WORLD.COM. [Online] 31 March, Available from: http://www.cnn.com/TECH/computing/9903/31/commandments.idg/ (accessed on 9 November 2004).

Voice Mail Etiquette Guide. [Online]. Available at: http://www.rollins.edu/telecom/etiquette.html (accessed on 9 November 2004).

Voice Mail Etiquette. 2004. [Online]. Available at: http://www.customerfocusinc.com/voice-mail-etiquette.htm (accessed on 9 November 2004).

42. Kate Zabriskie. 2009.[Online]. Available at: http://www.sideroad.com/consultants/Business-Etiquette-Expert-Kate-Zabriskie.html (accessed on 25 September 2009).

FURTHER READING

Any of the following that deal with the topic: newspaper articles, journals, magazines, Internet articles.

Patcher, B. & Brody, M. 1995. *Complete Business Etiquette Handbook.* New York: Prentice Hall.

INDEX

Please note: Page numbers in *italics* refer to Tables and Figures.

compensation plan 42
competence 25
competition
    criticising 242
    law 245-6
Competition Act 245-6
competitors 103
    rearranging/damaging products 242
complaints
    and difficulties 14
    handling 232-3
completing a sale 217-8
complex products 286
complimentary approach 180
compliment method 222
computers
    handheld 309-9
    palmtop 310-1
    portable 308-11
    selling of 12
    word-processing packages 307
    see also software for computers
considerate buyer 291
consultative selling 37, 304
consumer
    choice process 67-9
    markets 286-6
    motivation 55-6
    products 12
    selling to 13
Consumer Affairs Committee 40
Consumer Protection Act 244-5
consumption pattern 58
contact details of customer 99
contracts 228
    of sale 243
conversion goals 114
cooking the books 240
coordinating the sales effort 19
co-workers, undermining 243
credit agreement 245
CRM systems 140
cultural differences 23
culture 63-5
    influences on *64*
    as segmentation tool 64
customer(s) 99, 228
    accounts classification, example *120*
    agreement 216-7
    analysis 61
    benefit or question approach 181
    and buyers 290-1
    buying amounts and sizes 100
    classification 119-20
    confidences 242
    contact details 99
    evolution of orientation 33-4
    information-accessing preference 78-9
    keeping over time *230*
    keeping through service 231-2
    knowing the 99-100
    losing of 231
    needs and wants 19, 53-4
    orientation 25
    past and future 100
    point of view 14
    prospective 19
    questions 216
    relationship process *36*
    requests 216
    retention 230-3
    satisfied 137

    stealing 243
customisation 268
    to meet user needs 286

D

databases 307, 316
data mining 140
deciders 58, 291-2
decision makers 159
demand 268-9, 286-7
dependability 25
derived demand 287
designing service channels, guidelines *271*
detail salesperson 13
digital video discs (DVDs) 315
direct mail 42, 139
direct marketing 32-3, 42, 101
direct materials 293
directories 140
direct request 220
direct response 42
direct seller 13
direct selling
    classical 41, 42
    definition 7-8
    history 3-5
    network 142
    no restrictions 42
    systems 42
Direct Selling Association (DSA) of South Africa 6, 39, 40
    Code of Conduct (Code of Ethics) 40, 44
    collective statistics from report sales 41-2
    full membership 44, 45
    member companies 45-9
    probationary membership 44
    Supplier Members' Ethical Responsibilities Code 45
    supplier membership 44, 45
Direct Selling Education Foundation (DSEF) 6
discounts 102-3
distance selling 42
Distell's Corrective Action Code 237, *237-9*
distraction, lack of 9
distribution of services 270

E

economy
    impact of selling profession 5-6
    and industry 103
electronic personal organisers 311
email 86, 304, 307, 314
endless-chain technique 137-8
enterprise resource planning (ERP) system 316
ethical behaviour
    individual's role 236-7
    organisation's role 237
ethical issues 10
ethics
    building relationships 236
    dealing with colleagues 242-3
    dealing with competitors 242
    dealing with customers 241-2
    dealing with employers 239-41
ethnicity 63
European countries 84
expense
    of personal selling 9-10
    unauthorised use of accounts 240
experiential choice process 68-9
expertise 101

F

FAB sequence 185